MW00825085

Christian Suter, Christ<
(Eds. for the World So<

Structures of the World Political Economy
and the Future Global Conflict and Cooperation

World Society Studies

A series edited by

the World Society Foundation
Zurich, Switzerland

www.worldsociety.ch

Volume 2014

LIT

Structures of the World Political Economy and the Future Global Conflict and Cooperation

Christian Suter, Christopher Chase-Dunn
(Eds. for the World Society Foundation)

LIT

Cover image: Gabriel Robert // www.gabrielrobert.ch.
Graphics: Walo von Büren, Zurich.

Bibliographic information published by the Deutsche Nationalbibliothek
The Deutsche Nationalbibliothek lists this publication in the Deutsche
Nationalbibliografie; detailed bibliographic data are available in the Internet at
http://dnb.d-nb.de.

ISBN 978-3-643-80184-5

A catalogue record for this book is available from the British Library

©LIT VERLAG GmbH & Co. KG Wien,
Zweigniederlassung Zürich 2014
Klosbachstr. 107
CH-8032 Zürich
Tel. +41 (0) 44-251 75 05
Fax +41 (0) 44-251 75 06
E-Mail: zuerich@lit-verlag.ch
http://www.lit-verlag.ch

LIT VERLAG Dr. W. Hopf
Berlin 2014
Fresnostr. 2
D-48159 Münster
Tel. +49 (0) 2 51-62 03 20
Fax +49 (0) 2 51-23 19 72
E-Mail: lit@lit-verlag.de
http://www.lit-verlag.de

Distribution:
In the UK: Global Book Marketing, e-mail: mo@centralbooks.com
In North America: International Specialized Book Services, e-mail: orders@isbs.com
In Germany: LIT Verlag Fresnostr. 2, D-48159 Münster
Tel. +49 (0) 2 51-620 32 22, Fax +49 (0) 2 51-922 60 99, E-mail: vertrieb@lit-verlag.de

In Austria: Medienlogistik Pichler-ÖBZ, e-mail: mlo@medien-logistik.at
e-books are available at www.litwebshop.de

Contents

About the World Society Foundation

The World Society Foundation (WSF) was established in 1982 by Peter Heintz with the aim of encouraging and supporting research on world society, that is, its emergence and historical evolution, its structure, its dynamics, and current transformation.

Until 2003, the main purpose of the Foundation's sponsoring activities was to finance entire research projects focusing on the various processes of social integration and disintegration within worldwide systems—world culture, world economy, world politics, and intergovernmental systems—and on how global processes affect the perceptions and actions of individual and collective actors worldwide. Its current sponsoring policy is to provide award programs for research papers and to support international conferences on world society topics. In accordance with this new policy, the Foundation has introduced its WSF Award Program for Research Papers on World Society and held a series of international conferences (2007, 2008, 2010, 2013) in order to maintain a network of excellent scholars interested in transnational and global research topics. The World Society Foundation Award honors outstanding research papers on world society that address a specific topic announced by the Foundation in its triannual Award Program. The World Society Foundation also publishes the book series "World Society Studies."

The World Society Foundation is domiciled in Zurich, Switzerland. The current members of the Board are: Volker Bornschier, Mark Herkenrath, Hans-Peter Meier and Christian Suter (President). Former members of the Board included: Peter Heintz, Karl W. Deutsch, Hans-Joachim Hoffmann-Nowotny, and Bruno Fritsch.

More detailed information on past research projects sponsored, the topics and recipients of the 2007–2013 WSF Awards, the WSF book series "World Society Studies," and the call for papers of the current WSF conference (2014–2015) can be found on the Foundation's website at www.worldsociety.ch.

Preface

In April 2013, the Institute for Research on World-Systems (IROWS) and the World Society Foundation (WSF) organized an international conference on "Structures of the World Political Economy and the Future Global Conflict and Cooperation" within the framework of the WSF Award Program for Research Papers on World Society. The conference was cosponsored by the Political Economy of the World-System (PEWS) Section of the American Sociological Association and took place at the University of California in Riverside (UCR). The conference brought together about eighty researchers and participants to investigate and debate the evolution of global economic and political structures and to discuss scenarios of future global conflict and cooperation—in three plenary and fourteen workshop sessions.

The aim of the conference was to contribute to a more comprehensive understanding of stability and change in global structures by analyzing and discussing key aspects of world societal order and transformation from historical, comparative and interdisciplinary perspectives. This volume contains a selection of fourteen contributions presented at the 2013 conference, including the eleven invited research papers, three of which were honored with the 2013 WSF Award.[1]

Many people have contributed to the realization of this volume and of the 2013 WSF-PEWS conference. First and foremost, the World Society Foundation and the editors would like to thank the authors for their stimulating contributions and their patience during the reviewing and copyediting process. A big thank-you is due to the staff and the students at the University of California-Riverside, notably to Nelda Thomas, Donita McCants-Carter, Mila Huston, Alexis Alvarez, Hiroko Inoue, Rebecca Alvarez, Gary Coyne, Tony Roberts, Alessandro Morosin, and Jason Struna, for helping to prepare and organize the 2013 conference. Our thanks also go to the other members of the organizing committee of the conference, to Matthew Mahutga (UCR), David A. Smith (UC-Irvine), and Immanuel Wallerstein (Yale), for their advice and their help with paper evaluation. For their excellent work on the editing we are indebted to Nora Linder and Diana Luna. We should also like

---

1   More details of the 2013 conference, the WSF Award Program for Research Papers, and the recipients of the 2013 WSF Award are available on the WSF website at http://www.worldsociety.ch.

to thank Rachel Matthey for the proofreading, Walo von Büren for the graphical representation of figures and tables and Gabriel Robert for the cover image and the conference poster. Finally, we are very grateful to the Faculté des Lettres et Sciences Humaines at the University of Neuchâtel for providing generous financial support for the publication of this volume.

Neuchâtel/Zurich and Riverside, June 2014
Christian Suter, President of the World Society Foundation
Christopher Chase-Dunn, Director of the Institute for Research on World-Systems

Stability and Change in the Structures of the World Political Economy

Christian Suter and Christopher Chase-Dunn

Recent transformations in the global political economy: Epochal shifts or long-term evolution?

The structures of the world political economy have been extensively analyzed and debated within world-systems analysis. The existence of strong systemic forces is one of the basic features common to world-systems, world society and world polity scholars. Immanuel Wallerstein (1974a; 1974b) in his seminal work on the emergence of the modern world-system and the capitalist world-economy during the "long" sixteenth century, but also other scholars (e.g., Heintz, 1982; Braudel, 1986 [1979]; Meyer, 1987; Modelski, 1987; Chase-Dunn, 1998; Bornschier, 2002), emphasized the high level of stability in the basic structures of the world political economy over the past decades and centuries.

Over recent years, however, the world has changed profoundly. The global financial crisis of 2008–2009 that spread from the United States to other core and semiperipheral countries, together with the subsequent European debt crisis and the protracted worldwide recession, deeply affected economic, political and social structures, both at national and local, as well as world-systemic levels. High unemployment, austerity measures and cutbacks in public spending, with the consequent increase in precariousness, vulnerability, and uncertainty of large parts of the population in the crisis-affected countries, have contributed to a rise in transnational anti-systemic social movements, popular protests, and resistance from below, but also to an increase in right-wing populist, xenophobic and racist mobilization. The high levels of persistent global inequalities, social polarization and exclusion that have evolved over the past twenty years have exacerbated the extent of the present crisis. Furthermore, the sudden demise of neoliberalism in the wake of the global financial and economic crisis has left behind an ideological vacuum and a crisis of legitimacy.[1]

---

1 The question of how global transformations impact on world societal structures has been also treated in earlier volumes of the WSF book series, see notably Herkenrath (2007a; 2007b), Suter (2010), and Suter and Herkenrath (2012).

Similarly, world political order has been increasingly characterized by conflicts over the past two decades. Western powers have been engaged in several wars in the Middle East. The "rogue" states of Iran and North Korea command a great deal of international attention. There is an increasing number of "failed" states with collapsing political institutions and state structures, notably in Africa and the Middle East, but also in Latin America. The recent Ukrainian civil war has escalated into a conflict between Russia and the European Union with the allied United States and the NATO countries. In South East Asia the smoldering conflict on regional supremacy between China and its neighbors is exacerbating. Finally, a handful of semiperipheral countries including China, South Korea, Brazil, India, and Russia continue to vie for a more central place on the world stage, and there appear to be significant factions on the UN Security Council that correspond to the divide between old and rising world powers. Thus, the world-system seems to be evolving toward an increasingly multipolar political structure in which the ability of the United States to generate hegemonic consensus and order has declined.

There is an additional feature which is unique to the current crisis: the far-reaching ecological degradation and exhaustion, the "end of cheap nature," as argued by Jason W. Moore in his contribution to this volume, which manifests itself in rising costs for energy, raw materials, food and labor. This ecological crisis undermines, according to many authors, the basic functioning of the existing, 500-year-old model of capital accumulation.

These recent developments in the global political economy, therefore, represent for some scholars a fundamental departure from the world-systemic structures of the past. As argued by William I. Robinson in his chapter for this volume, the current crisis is a deep structural, systemic crisis, not comparable to earlier episodes of crisis in the capitalist world-economy. The fundamental contradictions, inherent to the basic model of capitalism, are leading to an epochal, secular crisis, implying the end of the existing model of capital accumulation.

According to other authors the recent changes are, on the contrary, rather similar to those that have occurred in earlier centuries (like the crisis in the 1970s, the 1930s, or the 1870s). Capitalism, according to this view, is a long-lived structure, constantly evolving through periods of crisis, characterized by adaptation, transformation and restructuration. Major crises are essential to capitalism; they mark the beginning of a new cycle of capital accumulation, but not the end of capitalism. As emphasized by Fernand Braudel (1986 [1979], 626) in his analysis of the crisis of the 1970s, "capitalism as a system has every chance of surviving . . . it might even emerge strengthened from the trial."

Overview of the contributions

This volume debates the paradox of stability and change, i.e., the combination of strong systemic forces and the transformation of world economic and political order over the past decades in more detail. The fourteen contributions in this volume were originally presented at the joint conference of the World Society Foundation (WSF) and the Political Economy of the World-System (PEWS) Section of the American Sociological Association held at the University of California-Riverside, organized by the Institute for Research on World-Systems (IROWS) at the University of California-Riverside, the World Society Foundation and the Department of Sociology of the University of Neuchâtel, Switzerland. The volume is organized into three parts dealing with three core issues of the structures and dynamics of world societal order: the degree of stability and change in the world-economy, in the world polity, and in the "world-ecology."

The first of these three issues concerns the changing nature of global economic and social hierarchies, notably trends in income and wealth inequalites, as well as the transformation of the core-semiperiphery-periphery structure, but also the dynamics of ascriptive inequalities linked to gender, race, and location.[2] The second core topic refers to the degree of stability and change in world political structures, notably the transformation of global power structures, processes of political globalization and their impacts, the rise of social and political conflict and antisystemic movements, as well as the increase or decline in democratization. The third issue, finally, deals with the integration of ecological change into the theory of global economic and political transformation; this means theoretizing and conceptualizing "world-ecology" including its relationships with the world-economy and the world polity, as well as providing corresponding empirical evidence.

The first part of this volume addresses the world economic (re)structuring and contains six chapters. These contributions deal with the central dimensions of the global stratification system and its evolutionary dynamics, namely global income inequality and occupational stratification (the three chapters by Babones, Albrecht and Korzeniwicz, ElGindi), global wealth inequality (the chapter by Chesters), gender inequality (the chapter by Dunaway) and the complex relationships between racial, spatial and locational inequalities (the chapter by Reifer).

The chapter by *Salvatore J. Babones* investigates the degree of structuring and stability of relative income positions since the early nineteenth century. He demonstrates that there has been extraordinary stability of income inequality structures across eight world regions, with virtually no change in relative income positions between 1820 and 2008. Babones approaches the issue of structural persistence

---

2   A second forthcoming conference volume deals with additional aspects of global inequalities and the challenges involved from a world historical perspective (see Wallerstein et al., 2014).

in (regional) income positions in more detail by applying entropy-based conceptualizations and "Monte Carlo" modeling. His simulations for 104 countries over the period 1972–2010 point to the importance of two different types of structural forces: the structural equivalence model (structures remain relatively fixed) and the regular equivalence model (mobility within and changes in structures are possible). His simulation of regional income growth for the historical period 1820–2008 of the eight world regions further suggests that, despite the high degree of structuring, mobility is greater than would be expected by entropy models. The empirical evidence presented by Babones illustrates the potential of entropy-based methods for gaining a better understanding of the degree of stability and change in world-system structures.

Exploring patterns of urban wages across the different world regions, the chapter by *Scott Albrecht* and *Roberto Patricio Korzeniewicz* examines trends in income inequality between and within countries from 1982 to 2012, and investigates the impact of the global financial and economic crisis of 2008 on the global occupational stratification system. Based on unique data provided by the Union Bank of Switzerland, the authors reconstruct urban wages of twelve different occupational categories ranging from unskilled labor to engineers and managers for more than seventy cities all over the world. The empirical evidence demonstrates the extremely high level of inequality and polarization of contemporary world society and confirms the prime importance of (national) residence for explaining wage differences. The chapter shows that, despite considerable mobility of wages in the lower part of the global urban wage stratification system, there has also been high stability of structures in the sense that there are very few changes in relative income positions. The authors explain this paradox of high (relative) stability and substantial (absolute) mobility by the large salary gaps between cities. Notable exceptions, however, are the Chinese cities (as well as some other cities in fast-growing middle income countries) that experienced significant (relative) upward mobility and contributed to a certain convergence in the global occupational stratification system. This convergence, however, slowed down in the years following the global economic recession in 2008.

The chapter by *Tamer ElGindi* examines the trends in income inequality in fifteen African and Asian Muslim-majority countries between 1963 and 2002 and explores how economic globalization, notably foreign direct investment and foreign trade openness, has affected these trends. The empirical evidence presented by the author suggests rising income inequalities in most countries, with an average increase in the Gini coefficient from .41 in 1970 to .46 in 2000. Based on fixed-effects regression models, the chapter confirms that economic globalization (and foreign direct investment in particular) has the effect of increasing inequality in the Muslim world, as documented in previous research focusing on other world regions. Furthermore, ElGindi's analysis demonstrates that, in addition to these external factors, internal factors, notably secondary education enrollment and sectoral transitions—i.e., the classical argument of Kuznets on the inverted U-curve of economic inequality—are important predictors of increasing income inequality.

Comparing three core countries (the United States, the United Kingdom, Germany) with three semiperipheral nations (India, Russia, China), the chapter of *Jenny Chesters* tracks changes in the distribution of global wealth over the past twenty-five years utilizing Forbes data on global billionaires. The chapter demonstrates, on the one hand, the dramatic increase in global wealth held by billionaires, particularly during the 1990s and between 2003 and 2008. On the other hand, Chesters' analysis indicates a substantial decline in the share of global billionaires residing in the three core countries and a consequent increase in billionaires residing in the three semiperipheral countries—regarding both the amount of wealth held and the number of global billionaires. This changing pattern in the distribution of top wealth between core and semiperiphery took place particularly during the 2000s. The source of wealth of the semiperipheral global billionaires varies considerably: whereas Russian billionaires derived their fortunes principally from raw materials (mining, oil, gas), Chinese and Indian billionaires derived them mainly from manufacturing and technology. The chapter finally highlights the high geographical mobility of (semiperipheral) billionaires' wealth, documented notably for the United Kingdom, where more than half of the billionaries are immigrants. While this relocation of semiperipheral capital to the core may reinforce the stablity of the core-semiperiphery-periphery stratification system in the short and medium term, it illustrates at the same time the vulnerability of single states—including core states—and their dependence on global capital.

The chapter by *Wilma A. Dunaway* situates global social and economic inequalities within the context of gender hierachies which are examined from an entropy- and world-systems-theory-based perspective. As demonstrated by Dunaway, gender inequality and sexism are firmly embedded at every level and in the different spheres of contemporary world society—including knowledge production in general and world-systems theory in particular. Dunaway reminds us that the modern world-system has been based on gender hierarchies since its origins, transferred from feudalism and continuously adapted and modified in the course of capitalist accumulation over the past centuries. The economic and cultural devaluation, marginalization, and informalization of women's and household-based work (and the consequent expropriation of surplus) are central structural characteristics and systemic mechanisms of the modern world-system generating and accumulating gendered entropy. Dunaway points in her chapter to the friction between the increasingly individualistic approaches of Western feminism and the problems facing women in the global South; this friction inhibits the dismantling of the "arrow of women's time" and the emergence of new structures for a future egalitarian world.

The contribution of *Tom Reifer*, the last chapter of the first part, brings together recent theoretical and empirical studies on the evolutionary dynamic of the modern world-system with a focus on the various closely intertwined global stratification and polarization processes, notably the division into core, semiperipheral and peripheral zones, the racial-ethnic, national, gender, and class disparities, but also ecological degradation and polarization. The author emphasizes the centrality of the intersections between the different inequality structures and mechanisms and points to the growing awareness among anti-systemic and collective-action movements of the inseparability of questions like global justice, political democracy, equality, and sustainability.

The second part of this volume includes six chapters exploring the degree of stability and change in the world polity. These contributions address the issue of geopolitical power structures and hegemonic transition (notably the chapters by Bergesen, Hendler and Brussi, MacPherson), processes of political globalization and their impacts (the chapter by Roberts), waves of social and political conflict and of the mobilization of antisystemic movements (notably the chapters by MacPherson, Roberts, and Robinson), as well as processes of decreasing ("nominal") democratization and increasing authoritarianism (the chapters by Chung and Robinson).

Based on new historical research on World War II the chapter by *Albert J. Bergesen* reconsiders the process of hegemonic transition between 1914 and 1945 and explores scenarios of future great power conflicts. In reassessing the history of great power conflicts and hegemonic succession wars in the modern world-system, the author emphasizes the importance of two different logics: first, one underlying land power wars (like the Thirty Years' War of the seventeenth century or the World War II conflict between Germany and the Soviet Union from 1941–1945) and, second, one underlying sea power succession (like the Anglo-Dutch Wars of the seventeenth century or the World War II conflict between Imperial Japan and the United States from 1941–1945). According to Bergesen only wars among sea powers, and not those among land powers, are conflicts related to hegemonic succession within the capitalist world-system. Against the background of the different dynamics of land and sea power conflicts, the chapter concludes by exploring three possible scenarios of future global conflict: firstly, great power conflicts among land powers (i.e., China vs. Russia, Germany and Russia vs. China, Germany vs. Russia); secondly, hegemonic succession conflicts among sea powers (i.e., China vs. the United States), and thirdly, conflicts between sea and land powers.

The relationship between declining and rising hegemonic powers is explored in the chapter by *Bruno Hendler* and *Antonio José Escobar Brussi*. Based on Giovanni Arrighi's approach of systemic cycles of accumulation, the chapter conceptualizes the complex U.S.-Chinese relations that evolved over the past forty years as a relationship between a declining hegemon and an associated emerging power. The authors demonstrate that the U.S.-Chinese relationship became progressively less asymmetric and developed into a relation of "mutual dependence in balanced terms" characterized by deep economic vulnerabilities between the two countries. Comparing the current hegemonic transition to past transitional periods in the modern world-system—i.e., the hegemonic transition from the United Provinces to

Britain in the late seventeenth century and the transition from Britain to the United States in the early twentieth century—the authors find analogies (like processes of financialization and high military spending of the declining hegemonic power, as well as relative economic gains of the rising power) but also differences, notably, the high level of economic vulnerability of contemporary China (as the rising hegemonic power) to the United States.

Periods of hegemonic decline and transition are also used as a comparative framework by *Robert MacPherson*. In his chapter the author examines and compares syndicalist mobilization and the rise of antisystemic movements during the 1920s, at the end of British hegemony, with those during the 2000s, at the end of U.S. hegemony. The chapter describes the rise of syndicalist mobilization and the surge of social and political protest in the early 1900s in Europe and Latin America and demonstrates the subsequent institutionalization and cooptation of these movements in the wake of increasingly interventionist and reformist policies of the liberal state. The erosion of this "interventionist liberalism" and the related demise of institutionalized unionism that characterized the flexible and neoliberal model of capital accumulation during declining U.S. hegemony paved the way for the rise of a new, widely-coordinated, popular mass movement, particularly in the highly indebted, crisis-affected semiperiphery of Southern Europe. In addition to various "new social movements," global justice networks, anti-globalization and anti-austerity protest movements, syndicalist organizations, too, were involved and have often been at the forefront of this recent wave of popular mobilization.

The chapter by *Anthony Roberts* examines direct and indirect effects of economic and political globalization on corporatism and industrial conflict in the industrial relation systems of eighteen advanced capitalist countries over the past forty years. The chapter demonstrates that the level of industrial conflict and corporatism declined on average over the past decades, particularly since the 1980s. Variation in corporatism across the same countries, however, has steadily increased over the same period (whereas variation in industrial conflict has decreased). Based on panel data analysis applying fixed-effects and random-coefficient models, empirical evidence presented by the author suggests that economic globalization indirectly reduces corporatism and industrial conflict, notably through processes of deindustrialization and deunionization which have diminished the bargaining power of organized labor. As further demonstrated by the author, political globalization, too, significantly impacts on corporatism and industrial conflict: participation in intergovernmental organizations and ratifications of International Labour Organization conventions are associated with declining industrial conflict and corporatism. Economic and political globalization effects are, however, not homogenous across countries but vary considerably.

The chapter by *Rakkoo Chung* examines processes of democratization in the global South over the past decades by comparing the transition to democracy in South Korea and in Nigeria. Employing an elite conflict theory framework, the chapter conceptualizes this transition process as "nominal democratization" characterized by the paradox of an increase in formal democratic rules and institutions and a decrease in the quality of democracy. The chapter reveals the similarities and differences in the democratic transition of these two semiperipheral countries: while democratization in both countries eventually resulted in a low-level, "nominal" democracy, the South Korean transition process was driven from below by democratization movements (which, due to elite resistance, however, did not fully succeed), whereas the Nigerian democratization was largely elite-driven. The chapter emphasizes the responsibility of core countries, notably the United States (concerning South Korea) and the United Kingdom (regarding Nigeria) in this connection, as they installed and supported low-quality, nominal democracy in order to secure their own economic and geopolitical interests.

Exploring the mechanisms of, and the responses to, the global crisis of contemporary world capitalism, the chapter by *William I. Robinson* highlights the current shift towards increasingly authoritarian and repressive forms of global and national political order. Employing Poulantzas' notion of the "exceptional state" of the 1970s, Robinson conceptualizes the current state of world affairs as a "global police state" characterized by new forms of fascism, the militarization of society and "law and order" policy, including massive prison expansion (as a result of the "war on drugs," the "war on terrorism," and the criminalization of the poor and dispossessed), and the expansion of systems of panoptical surveillance, spatial and social control based on the new information technologies. Robinson reminds us that this shift towards social control and authoritarianism has to be placed in the context of the current deep crisis of hegemony at the world-systemic level and the consequent increasing mobilization of counter-hegemonic forces and transnational antisystemic movements.

The third part of this volume includes two chapters dealing, from a world-systems perspective, with conceptualization and measurement issues of global ecological transformation, including its impact on the structures of the world political economy.

The chapter by *Jason W. Moore* explores the implications of the end of cheap nature and proposes a concept for integrating environment and nature into the theory of capital accumulation. As emphasized by Moore, the appropriation of cheap nature represents a basic structural feature of the modern world-system since its origins, over all consecutive waves of capital accumulation and technical innovation. Frontier movements, i.e., territorial expansion and the extension of commodity relations to new spaces, have been essential in creating the four basic forms of cheap nature: cheap labor, cheap food, cheap energy and cheap raw materials. Moore points to the basic problem of capitalism which he describes as the exhaustion of these forms of cheap nature, resulting in a decline in the ecological surplus and consequent pressure to extend frontiers and to appropriate new uncommodified cheap natures. The chapter discusses the question of whether the current crisis of the capitalist world-ecology is just a "development crisis," i.e., a cyclical phenomenon which may be resolved, as in the past, through a new model of capital accumulation, or whether capitalism has entered into an epochal crisis, implying the end of cheap nature as an accumulation and civilizational strategy. The rising costs of energy, raw materials and food, but also of labor, in combination with fast closing frontiers, suggest, according to the author, a secular crisis of capitalism's cheap nature strategy.

Unequal access to the consumption of natural resources constitutes an important, but rarely treated, dimension of the stratification system of contemporary world society. The chapter by *Carl Nordlund* provides a conceptualization of ecological unequal exchange combining world-system and global commodity chain analysis with ecological economics. Employing the original notion of Arghiri Emmanuel, the chapter proposes a conceptualization of ecological unequal exchange that is based on factor cost differentials among nations, rather than on the typically used non- or under-compensated net transfers of biophysical resources. Furthermore, Nordlund based his operationalization of unequal exchange on direct indicators measuring actual trade flows, rather than on indirect indicators of resource usage and environmental burden. Using network-analytical procedures (blockmodeling), the analysis of bilateral trade flow data for 96 countries between 1990 and 2010 for three commodities representing the land production factor (coal, crude oil, and liquefied natural gas) reveals eight country clusters. The cluster mostly composed of high-income European countries (including Australia, Canada and Japan) and fast-growing middle-income Southeast Asian countries (e.g., China, Hong Kong, Korea, Singapore) enjoys a highly advantageous situation. Surprisingly, the position of the United States, though benefiting from unequal exchange, is less advantageous. The other countries, including most African, Latin American, East European, and Middle Eastern countries, suffer from disadvantages with regard to ecological unequal exchange. Furthermore, the commodity-specific analysis reveals considerable variation in the benefits and disadvantages across the eight country clusters.

References

Bornschier, Volker. 2002. *Weltgesellschaft. Grundlegende soziale Wandlungen.* Zurich: Loreto.

Braudel, Fernand. 1986 [1979]. *The Perspective of the World. Civilization and Capitalism, 15ᵗʰ–18ᵗʰ Century, Volume 3.* New York: Harper & Row.

Chase-Dunn, Christopher. 1998. *Global Formation: Structures of the World-Economy.* Lanham, MD: Rowman and Littlefield.

Heintz, Peter. 1982. A Sociological Code for the Description of World Society and Its Change. *International Social Science Journal,* 34(1): 11–21.

Herkenrath, Mark (ed.). 2007a. *Civil Society. Local and Regional Responses to Global Challenges.* World Society Studies Volume 2007/I. Berlin, Münster, Wien, and Zurich: LIT Verlag.

Herkenrath, Mark (ed.). 2007b. *The Regional and Local Shaping of World Society.* World Society Studies Volume 2007/II. Berlin, Münster, Wien, and Zurich: LIT Verlag.

Meyer, John W. 1987. "The World Polity and the Authority of the Nation-State." In George M. Thomas, John W. Meyer, Francisco O. Ramirez, and John Boli (eds.), *Institutional Structure: Constituting State, Society, and the Individual.* Beverly Hills: Sage.

Modelski, George. 1987. *Long Cycles in World Politics.* Seattle: University of Washington Press.

Suter, Christian (ed.). 2010. Inequality Beyond Globalization. Economic Changes, Social Transformations, and the Dynamics of Inequality. World Society Studies Volume 2010. Berlin, Münster, Wien, and Zurich: LIT Verlag.

Suter, Christian (ed.). 2012. *World Society in the Global Economic Crisis.* World Society Studies Volume 2011. Berlin, Münster, Wien, and Zurich: LIT Verlag.

Wallerstein, Immanuel. 1974a. *The Modern World-System I: Capitalist Agriculture and the Origins of the European World-Economy in the Sixteenth Century.* New York: Academic.

Wallerstein, Immanuel. 1974b. The Rise and Future Demise of the World Capitalist System: Concepts for Comparative Analysis. *Comparative Studies in Society and History,* 16: 387–415.

Wallerstein, Immanuel, Christopher Chase-Dunn, and Christian Suter (eds.). 2014. *Overcoming Global Inequalities.* Boulder, CO: Paradigm Publishers.

PART I

Stability and Change in the Core-Perihpery Hierachy and in World Inequality

1

Investigating the Degree of Structure in the World-Economy Using Concepts from Entropy Theory

Salvatore J. Babones

The social and geographical structure of rewards in the modern world-economy has been incredibly stable over time. According to data from Maddison (2010), the 188-year correlation of national income levels for the eight major world regions is a remarkable r = 0.956. There has been virtually no change in relative incomes for at least two centuries. This contradicts both standard neoclassical growth models and standard world-system models. The extraordinary stability of the structure of the world-economy cries out for more explicit modeling of structure. This contribution outlines a new approach to understanding the degree of structure in the world-economy based on entropy theory. Entropy models can be used to differentiate between regular equivalence and structural equivalence in hierarchical economic relationships as well as between random social change and indicators of purposeful social progress. Applied examples illustrate a variety of entropy-based models and provide a proof of concept for the approach.

Introduction

If the 1970s classics of dependency theory and world-systems analysis stand up well today, it is surely in part due to the fact that the structure of the world-economy is substantially the same today as it was in the 1970s. One might go out on a limb and make the same claim about Marx and the 1870s. In fact, if we are to believe Wallerstein (1974), the origins of the contemporary world-economy can be traced to the sixteenth century; if we are to believe Frank and Gills (1993), virtually to the beginning of time. Focusing for now on the knowable, it is clear that basic world-economic structures like "Europe dominates Africa" and "North America dominates Central America" have been with us for a long time, long enough to have become firmly embedded in our instinctive assumptions about the world. Such structures of domination have proved so stable that we essentially take them for granted.

Should we? The structure of the world-economy is clearly very stable, but how stable is it? How stable should it be under different models of economic change? Is the degree of stability of the structure of the world-economy itself stable, or is the degree of stability in the world-economy changing over time? Questions like these can only be answered if we can measure the degree to which the world-economy is structured at any one point in time within the context of well-defined statistical models. One way to approach this measurement challenge is through the application of concepts from entropy theory.

Entropy concepts have recently been applied in world-systems contexts by Grimes (2012) and Kick and McKinney (2012). Grimes (2012) is highly philosophical and is mainly concerned with the concept of entropic loss: the dissipation of energy (both metaphorically and literally) that occurs in the maintenance of social hierarchies. Kick and McKinney (2012) by contrast use entropy concepts mainly in their conventional scientific meanings, applying them to the understanding of environmental degradation and resource depletion. Hornborg (1998) and Lawrence (2009) similarly use entropy in the context of ecological unequal exchange. Frank (2006) uses entropy concepts extensively, but mainly as a broad synonym for "disorder." None of these sources uses entropy concepts to specify entropy-based statistical models.

Entropy-based modeling has however been used by Dezzani (2002) to study the degree of structure in global national income hierarchies. Dezzani's use of entropy is much more mathematically formal than that employed here. He studies countries' class-state transitions among core, semiperipheral, peripheral statuses in the world-economic hierarchy. While his use of entropy concepts is consistent with that presented here, it is much more narrowly focused on the technical analysis of status transition matrices. Dezzani has not broadened his approach to the study of social systems in general, though he does suggest that such a project might be productive.

Entropy conceptualizes the degree of disorder in a system. In thermodynamics, entropy is specifically defined as the amount of energy in a system that is unavailable for performing useful work. While this may at first seem to have little to do with the structure of the world-economy, the metaphoric reasoning linking physical systems and the economic system is actually very close. Consider a physical system that has high-pressure air on the left side separated by a valve from low-pressure air on the right side. A turbine can be rigged in the middle that would spin (and thus do useful work) when the valve is opened and air rushes from the left side to the right side. On the other hand, a similar physical system that has medium air pressure on both sides has the same amount of total energy in the system, but that energy is not configured in such a way that it could perform any useful work. The unbalanced system is more highly structured than the balanced system. By contrast, the balanced system is more entropic (has higher entropy) because its energy is not available for performing useful work.

Income levels in the world-economy are analogous to air pressure levels in the hypothetical physical system. A world-economy divided into high-income and low-income countries has more "potential to perform useful work" (in the entropic sense) than a world-economy in which all countries have the same medium income level, despite the fact that both systems may have the same overall level of income. The concept of "work" here is the generation of economic flows between countries. For example, in (economic) theory, capital is supposed to flow from rich countries

Figure 1: Relationships among entropy, inequality, and structure

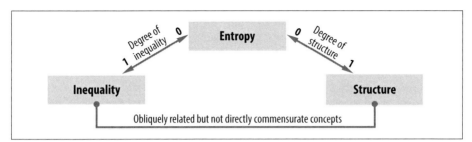

to poor countries, driving the metaphorical turbine and equalizing incomes across countries. This is the well-known theory of economic convergence. If all countries had the same medium income level, total global economic output might be the same, but the pressure for equalizing flows would be absent.

The connection between physical and economic concepts of entropy and equality is reflected in the fact that commonly-used indices of economic inequality, such as the Theil (1967) index, are formally derived from entropy theory. The concept of entropy, however, is much broader than the concept of inequality. Entropy is fundamentally a lack of structure, and income inequality between countries is only one among many ways that the world-economy can be structured. Other forms of structure that could be measured using entropy concepts include regional income structures (discussed below), networks of foreign direct investment (Dezzani and Johansen, 2012), structures of trade dependency (Babones et al., 2011), the macrosocial determinants of international migration flows (Sanderson, 2010), and the increasing international interlocking of boards of directors (Kentor and Jang, 2004), among many others. Low inequality is more entropic than high inequality, but high entropy does not necessarily imply high inequality. It may imply other forms of structure instead.

Figure 1 illustrates this point. On an inequality index (like the Theil index) high entropy would be associated with a low inequality score. At the same time, on some other kind of structural index, high entropy would be associated with a low structure score. A highly entropic state is one that has no inequality and no structure; when everyone in every country looks exactly the same, there can be neither inequality nor any other patterns in the economy. On the other hand, a high score on an inequality index may or may not be associated with a high score for some other measure of economic structure. It is impossible to have structure without generating at least some degree of inequality, but any given structural index may be only obliquely related to measures of income inequality.

In this chapter, entropy-based conceptualizations of world-system structure are explored using Monte Carlo simulation techniques in order to elucidate deep structures of the world-economy. First, simple correlations are used to study the long-term stability of the regional income structure of the world-economy over the period 1820–2008 using data from Maddison (2010). Second, ANOVA analyses are used to study the persistent salience of region for national income levels over the period 1972–2010 using data from the World Bank's World Development Indicators. Third, a Brownian motion model of national income change is used to describe the trajectory of regional average incomes over the period 1820–2008, again using data from Maddison (2010). The chapter concludes with suggestions of future directions for research based on entropy concepts and the implications of entropy-based research for the future of world society.

Long-term stasis in the macrostructure world-economy

The relative incomes of the world's major countries and regions have been very stable over time. Despite waves of colonization, world war, the rise of international communism, depression, more world war, decolonization, cold war, the fall of international communism, and the rise of neoliberalism, the geographical contours of the world's political economy are essentially the same today as they were in the nineteenth century. The richest areas then (western Europe and North America) are still rich today and the poorest areas then (Africa, indigenous Central America, South and Southeast Asia) are still poor today. Coastal China is still somewhere in the middle. Parts of East Asia have become very rich, but the richest part of all—Japan—was already middle-income by the late nineteenth century. Moreover, most of the richest places in East Asia today are cities that are descended from the European trading hubs of the precolonial (Shanghai, Taipei) and colonial (Hong Kong, Singapore) periods.

Until the recent incorporation of Portugal and Spain into the European Union (and consequent inrush of EU structural adjustment funds), the Europeanized areas of Latin America had national income levels that were roughly equal to those of their old rulers on the Iberian peninsula; with the switch to austerity politics in the European Union after 2008, national income levels on the Iberian peninsula seem to be converging back to Latin American levels. Russia today has almost exactly the same ratio of national income per capita to the core countries of western Europe as it did in 1913 (Babones, 2013). More than two hundred years after the American revolution, the twin financial centers of London and New York have remarkably similar income levels and economic structures (Sassen, 2001)—*plus ça change . . .*

In fact, according to data from Maddison (2010) the correlation of logged national income per capita in 1820 with logged national income per capita in 2008 for the eight major world regions is a remarkable $r = 0.956$. This relationship is depicted in Figure 2. Regions are used instead of countries to avoid sample selection problems (De Long, 1988): all regions of the world (but not all countries) are represented in Maddison (2010) for both 1820 and 2008. The correlation of 0.956 implies that over 90% of the variability in income levels across major world regions in 2008 can

Figure 2: Regional correlation of GDP per capita in 2008 with GDP per capita in 1820

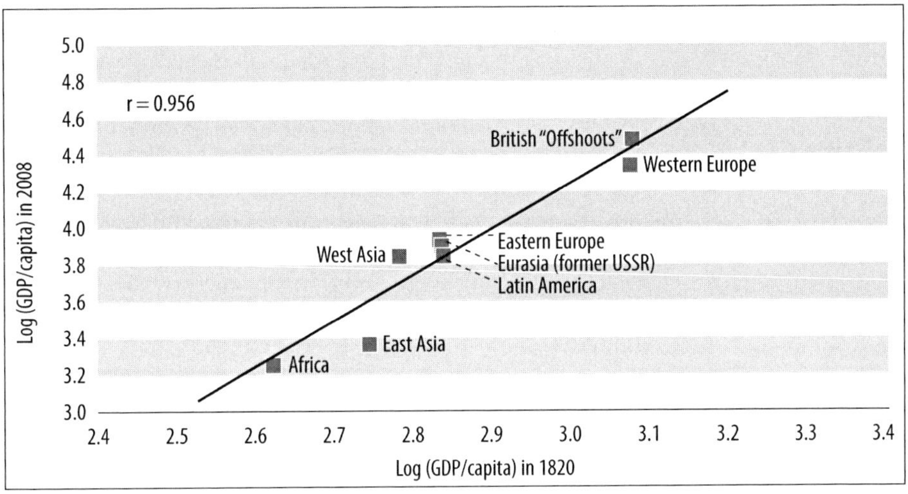

Notes: The British "Offshoots" are Australia, Canada, New Zealand, and the United States; note that Maddison includes India in "East Asia"; GDP per capita in real 2008 U.S. dollars.
Source: Based on data from Maddison (2010).

be explained by the differences already existing in 1820. There has been virtually no change in relative incomes after two centuries of otherwise massive social, political, and economic change.

Neoclassical economists have long predicted the gradual disappearance of such differences in income levels between countries and across regions of the world (Lucas, 1990). Two distinct approaches to studying convergence have been the subject of extensive research: sigma convergence and beta convergence. Sigma convergence is convergence in the overall variability of national income levels across countries. It is called "sigma" convergence because it is often operationalized by studying changes over time in the standard deviation (sigma) of the logged national incomes of the countries of the world. Beta convergence is the tendency of poorer countries to grow faster than richer countries over long time periods. It is called "beta" convergence because it is operationalized using the slope (beta) of a regression of long-term growth rates on initial national income per capita.

In principle, sigma and beta convergence are conceptually equivalent. In practice, however, the beta convergence approach makes it possible to control for factors other than initial national income per capita. This has led to the creation of "conditional convergence" models in which it is posited that beta convergence would have occurred had certain convergence conditions been met, among them appropriate social, political, and economic policies. Thus, a regression of long-term growth on initial income, controlling for policy variables, should reveal a significantly negative slope for income. The negative coefficient would indicate that, under ceteris paribus conditions in which all policy variables were held equal, rich countries would grow more slowly than poor countries.

It is now widely accepted that although there is little evidence of unconditional sigma or beta convergence among countries, conditional beta convergence occurs at a rate of roughly 2% per year (controlling for national social, political, and economic factors). This implies that a poor country with identical policies to a rich country would be expected to make up 90% of the income gap in approximately 114 years. Half the gap would be made up in 35 years. The cumulative effect of catch-up is nonlinear because 2% of the remaining gap is made up each year, not 2% of the total gap. Of course, this catch-up is only expected to occur under ceteris paribus conditions, and conditions are never ceteris paribus between rich and poor countries. For an up-to-date summary of the evidence on convergence, see Barro (2012).

The conditional convergence framework effectively blames poor countries for their failure to grow: if only they would pursue the same policies as rich countries (so the reasoning goes) they would become rich countries themselves (even if only after a century or more). The most famous argument of this type is that of Acemoglu et al. (2001), who purport to show that countries' colonial-era levels of respect for private property largely persist through today and are primarily responsible for their current levels of economic output. Alfaro et al. (2008) reinforces this conclusion for the contemporary era. It is now well-accepted in the economics literature that deficient social, political, and economic institutions in poor countries—primarily the lack of enforcement of contracts and the non-sanctity of private property rights—are responsible for their long-term failure to converge with rich countries.

The statistical results of studies like these seem convincing, but in their focus on the policy determinants of growth they seem to miss a major implication of the fact that no overall convergence has occurred in the nearly two centuries for which data are available. Moreover, the relative rankings of world regions have also been unchanged over this time period, as illustrated by Figure 2. In other words, not only has there been no convergence, but there has also been no shuffling of positions within the overall structure of the world-economy. This total stasis implies that poor countries collectively have for two centuries consistently maintained bad institutions that have been exactly bad enough to offset their respective expected convergence rates. No more, no less; exactly the same. One might legitimately ask: what is the probability of such a seemingly extraordinary occurrence?

Estimating the probability that the correlational structure of the regional incomes would persist at a level of r = 0.956 or higher is a simple entropy-type problem. The correlation of income in 2008 with income in 1820 is a measure of the degree of structure in the world-economy (one minus the correlation would be a measure of entropy). More sophisticated measures of structure exist, such as the Akaike (1974) Information Criterion (AIC) and the Bayesian Information Criterion

(BIC; Schwarz, 1978), but both of these are based on the regression residual sum of squares of a model, the numbers of predictive variables used in the model, and the numbers of cases used in estimating the model. Since the correlation of regional national income in 1820 with regional national income in 2008 has a fixed number of variables (one, initial national income) and a fixed number of cases (eight, the number of regions) both the AIC and the BIC are monotonically related to r. They thus add no relevant information to straightforward analysis conducted based solely on correlations.

One way to approach the problem of structural persistence is through the use of "Monte Carlo" modeling. As the name implies, Monte Carlo models involve the use of random chance in a modeling environment. If the institutional interpretation of the lack of sigma convergence is correct, the very high correlation between regional income in 1820 (the initial state) and regional income in 2008 (the final state) implies that all regions grew at near-identical average rates over the 188-year period (or had growth rates that varied in a strictly linear fashion). To the degree that where any region had slightly "better" or "worse" institutions than required to keep its growth rate exactly aligned with that necessary to offset conditional convergence, the correlation between the initial state and the final state would be reduced. Monte Carlo modeling can be used to estimate the impact that such incidental variability in institutions would have had on the correlation between the initial state and the final state.

Figure 3 reports the results of four Monte Carlo models of post-1820 regional economic growth. All four model scenarios start from an initial state in which regions have 1820 levels of national income per capita as given by Maddison (2010), logged base 10. In the first (left-most) model, each region was assigned a random growth rate drawn from a normal distribution with mean 0 and standard deviation equivalent to 1% compound annual growth (0.004321 on the log scale). This implies that approximately 95.4% of the time a region is assigned a random growth rate between –2% and +2% per year. The overall mean growth rate is irrelevant for modeling convergence or divergence. The annual growth rate randomly assigned to each region is compounded for 188 years to produce a simulated national income level for 2008, the final state. The correlation between actual national income in 1820 and simulated national income in 2008 is calculated and then a new simulation based on a new set of randomly-generated regional growth rates is begun. A total of 10,000 simulations were conducted for each model scenario.

The curves plotted in Figure 3 are the cumulative distributions of the simulated correlations under four different random growth scenarios. The simulated correlations appear on the horizontal axis; in theory they can fall anywhere from –1 to +1. The cumulative distribution of simulated correlations appears on the vertical axis. The point on each curve corresponding to a given correlation represents the proportion of the 10,000 simulations that resulted in correlations equal to or less than the given correlation. Under the first scenario in which each region grows at

Figure 3: Simulated regional correlations of GDP per capita in 1820 (initial state) with GDP per capita in 2008 (final state) under four different scenarios for growth rates after 1820

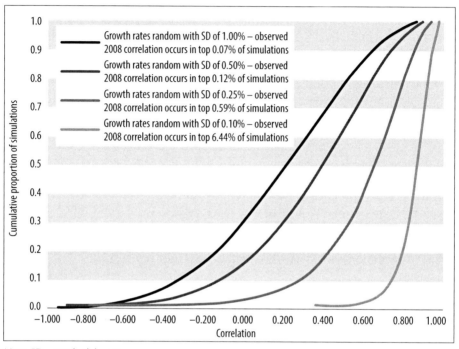

Notes: SD = standard deviation.
Source: Based on data from Maddison (2010).

a random growth rate drawn from a normal distribution with a standard deviation equivalent to a 1% growth rate, the correlation between initial and final regional incomes was less than or equal to the observed correlation of r = 0.956 in 99.93% of the simulations run. It was greater than or equal to r = 0.956 in just 0.07% of simulations. In the context of the conditional convergence model, this implies that if regional institutions varied enough from perfect convergence-preventing calibration to produce growth rates 2% above or below the global mean, it is very unlikely that the actual configuration of regional incomes observed in 2008 could have resulted.

The 1% standard deviation random growth scenario is a bit of a straw man, since actual long-term growth rates vary by much less than plus or minus two percentage points. Three other, more realistic, models were run with random growth standard deviations of 0.50%, 0.25%, and 0.10%. Only in the final 0.10% scenario is the actual observed correlation of r = 0.956 realistically within the realm of probability. Even in this relatively conservative scenario, final income levels that correlate r = 0.956 or better with initial income levels occur in only 6.44% of simulations.

No one knows for certain how much randomness there is in the quality of political-economic institutions or their translation into annual rates of economic growth. Actual estimates of compound annual growth rates from Maddison (2010) range from a low of 0.8% in Africa and East Asia to highs of 1.7% in the British offshoots and 1.6% in western Europe (contrary to convergence theories, initially rich countries grew slightly faster). The actual regional standard deviation of growth rates is 0.32%. These figures say nothing about how much random variation we should be observing in institutions and their impacts on growth rates, but if the random variation has a standard deviation of as much as 0.10%—and if we trust Maddison's data—the observed correlation between regional income in 1820 and regional income in 2008 is too high.

Conditional convergence theory requires that the random component of regional growth rates resulting from random deviations in institutional quality have a standard deviation of 0.10% or less. Given the endless variety of world cultures, this seems impossibly low. Entropy analyses thus suggest that the standard economic theory of conditional convergence is too much a just-so story, too perfect to be true. The real world should have more entropy—more disorder—than conditional convergence theory would allow. The observed persistence of a high level of structure in the world-economy over long time periods is likely due to something other than a coincidentally perfect storm of pathological institutional heritages.

Monte Carlo models of the continuing salience of region

So why is the world-economy so highly ordered? The explanation that the legacy of colonial-era institutions determined countries' growth rates for the ensuing two centuries falls apart because it (implicitly) assumes that these institutions were praeternaturally perfectly calibrated to produce just the right relative growth rates to ensure a stable long-term structure in the world-economy. An alternative approach would be to link the continuing persistence of regional income differentials to persisting world-systemic forces of hegemony and exploitation.

An open secret behind the instrumental variable models that dominate the economics literature on conditional convergence is that these models don't actually measure the effects of nineteenth-century institutions per se. Technically, they merely infer the effects of a latent variable that is correlated with today's distribution of national institutions in countries around the world. For all we know, that latent variable might just as well be labeled "world-system position" as "protection of private property." That is to say, world-system position may be the common cause of nineteenth-century income levels, twenty-first-century income levels, and twenty-first-century institutional frameworks for private property rights.

Social scientists arguing from dependency (Frank, 1969), neocolonial (Galtung, 1971), and world-systems (Wallerstein, 1974) perspectives have long recognized the existence of strong systemic forces that generate and maintain the existence of income hierarchies within and across countries. The characteristics of the structure of the world-economy have been studied extensively. An important open question is whether individual country mobility is possible within that structure despite the fact that the overall structure is relatively fixed or individual countries instead occupy relatively fixed specific positions within the larger structure. Wallerstein (1974, 349; 1994, 8) is unambiguously of the view that the structure is fixed but mobility within the structure is possible. Babones (2005; 2011), on the other hand, considers the particular structural positions of particular countries in the larger world-system to be relatively fixed.

This debate is a manifestation of the familiar social network differentiation between regular equivalence and structural equivalence in hierarchical relationships (Mahutga, 2006). Regular equivalence is the phenomenon that all members of a class share the same hierarchical relationship to all members of a different class: all parents have class interests that are sharply differentiated from the class interests of all children. Structural equivalence is the phenomenon that particular members of one class have particular hierarchical relationships to particular members of another class: parents come into direct personal conflict with their own children. Babones (2013) presents evidence of structural equivalence for semiperipheral countries (Russia and the countries of east central Europe remain structurally tied to western Europe despite the seventy-year communist interlude), while Babones et al. (2011) present evidence of regular equivalence for peripheral countries (China has displaced European countries in the export dependence structures of peripheral countries while leaving the overall structure of export dependence unchanged).

Entropy models can be applied in many different ways to shed additional light on the debate between regular and structural equivalence as models of world-system structure. One way to think about structure is to ask: do countries grow at essentially random rates (with respect to their current structural positions), leading to many opportunities for world-system mobility, or do countries grow at structurally determined rates, biasing them toward maintaining their initial positions indefinitely? This question relates to the ultimate systemic drivers of growth, not intermediate factors like levels of education, economic openness, industrial policy, etc. The question is whether or not all these factors, and thus ultimately countries' growth rates, are determined with (structural equivalence) or without (regular equivalence) respect to countries' structural positions in the world-economy. At first glance this may seem like a stacked deck against the regular equivalence argument, but in fact the best evidence is that countries of all income levels grow at roughly the same average growth rate, regardless of initial income level (Rodrik, 2011).

Two Monte Carlo simulations have been constructed to implement regular and structural equivalence models of economic growth based on regional structures in the world-economy. Regional structures are used instead of the more familiar world-system categories (core, semiperiphery, periphery) to help avoid endogeneity in the construction of the categories themselves. National income per capita data are taken from the "Atlas" current dollar series (based on 3-year smoothed exchange rates) of the World Bank's World Development Indicators database. All figures have been deflated to 2005 U.S. dollars using a U.S. Bureau of Economic Analysis GNP deflator. Data substantially covering the period 1972–2010 are available for 105 countries constituting 84% of the world's population. In six scattered cases in which data were missing for a single year a loglinearly interpolated or extrapolated estimate was substituted for that year. Only one country was available for the World Bank's "Europe & Central Asia" region (Hungary), so it was excluded from the

Table 1: Countries included in 1972–2010 regional trend analyses

East Asia & the Pacific	Latin America & the Caribbean	Sub-Saharan Africa	Western Europe & the Anglosphere
China	Argentina	Benin	Australia
Fiji	Bahamas	Botswana	Austria
Indonesia	Barbados	Burkina Faso	Belgium
Japan	Belize	Burundi	Canada
Korea, Republic	Bolivia	Cameroon	Denmark
Malaysia	Brazil	Central African Republic	Finland
Papua New Guinea	Chile	Chad	France
Philippines	Colombia	Congo, Democratic Republic	Germany
Singapore	Costa Rica	Congo, Republic	Greece
Thailand	Dominican Republic	Côte d'Ivoire	Greenland
	Ecuador	Gabon	Iceland
Middle East & North Africa	El Salvador	Gambia	Italy
Algeria	Guatemala	Ghana	Liechtenstein
Egypt, Arab Republic	Guyana	Guinea-Bissau	Luxembourg
Israel	Honduras	Kenya	Malta
Morocco	Jamaica	Lesotho	Monaco
Oman	Mexico	Madagascar	Netherlands
Saudi Arabia	Nicaragua	Malawi	Norway
Syrian Arab Republic	Panama	Mali	Portugal
Tunisia	Paraguay	Mauritania	Spain
	Peru	Niger	Sweden
South Asia	Puerto Rico	Nigeria	Turkey
Bangladesh	St. Vincent and the Grenadines	Rwanda	United Kingdom
India	Trinidad and Tobago	Senegal	United States
Nepal	Uruguay	Seychelles	
Pakistan	Venezuela	Sierra Leone	
Sri Lanka		South Africa	
		Sudan	
		Togo	
		Zambia	
		Zimbabwe	

analyses to yield a final sample of 104 countries. These are summarized, by region, in Table 1. The regions are based on the World Bank's official regions, but with rich countries reassigned from the World Bank "developed" category to their respective geographical regions.

The first simulation (Figure 4) is intended to replicate one interpretation of the regular equivalence argument. The results presented in Figure 4 are meant to shed light on the argument, not to serve as a definitive test; other perfectly reasonable interpretations of regular equivalence are possible. In the simulation underlying Figure 4, each of the 104 countries listed in Table 1 is assigned an initial state equal to its actual national income per capita (log base 10) in 1972. A random growth rate is then sampled from a normal distribution with mean and standard deviation equal to the mean and standard deviation of the compound annual growth rates of all 104 countries over the period 1972–2010. These are reported at the bottom of Table 2. Each country's assigned growth rate is then applied to its initial income level and compounded for 38 years to yield a simulated 2010 level of national income (final state). This process is repeated independently for each of the 104 countries in the database. A total of 1000 simulations were run.

The entropy concept used in Figure 4 is the R^2 of an ANOVA regression of simulated national income on region. As with the correlations used in Figure 3, this is actually a structure concept, not an entropy concept; a corresponding entropy measure would be $1 - R^2$. The actual degree of structure (R^2) for the observed national income levels for each year is plotted as the dotted line in Figure 4. It turns out that the actual degree of regional structure in the world-economy rose slightly from $R^2 = 0.71$ in 1972 to $R^2 = 0.74$ in 2010, though it is possible that this increase is simply due to improved data quality in the later period.

Table 2: Parameters used in 1972–2010 regional trend analyses

Region code	Log units		Equivalent percentages		Number of countries
	Mean growth	Standard deviation growth	Mean growth	Standard deviation growth	
EAP	0.01613	0.00909	3.78%	2.12%	10
LAC	0.00894	0.00469	2.08%	1.08%	26
MNA	0.01201	0.00759	2.80%	1.76%	8
SAS	0.00758	0.00329	1.76%	0.76%	5
SSA	0.00173	0.00875	0.40%	2.04%	31
WES	0.01387	0.00359	3.25%	0.83%	24
Global (all countries)	**0.00879**	**0.00832**	**2.04%**	**1.93%**	**104**

Notes: Log units: growth is expressed as an annual increment in log (GDP/capita). Equivalent percentages: growth is expressed as an annual compound growth rate. EAP = East Asia & the Pacific, LAC = Latin America & the Caribbean, MNA = Middle East & North Africa, SAS = South Asia, SSA = Sub-Saharan Africa, WES = Western Europe & the Anglosphere.

The grey lines in Figure 4 represent the median and 95% confidence interval for the degree of structure present in the simulated country data for each year 1973–2008. Annual point estimates are derived by pooling data from all 1000 simulations, ranking them from lowest to highest R^2 score, and fining the 2.5th, 50th, and 97.5th percentiles of R^2 for each year. Over time the degree of structure is expected to decline (as countries go their random ways) and the range of likely degrees of structure widens. The actually existing degree of structure in 2010, an R^2 of 0.74, is not within the 95% confidence interval of this (highly stylized) regular equivalence model.

Figure 5 implements the equivalent structural equivalence model. Again, it represents just one interpretation of structural equivalence, and cannot be considered a definitive test. In the simulations underlying Figure 5 each country is assigned growth level drawn from a normal distribution with a mean and standard deviation based on the mean and standard deviation of the 38-year compound annual growth rates of the countries in its region (reported in Table 2). The idea is that in a structural equivalence framework countries are constrained to behave in ways that are typical of their regions rather than being free to grow (or shrink) according to the range of global experiences. Note that the fact that the regional growth standard deviations are in general lower than the global growth standard deviation may implicitly favor the structural equivalence model over the regular equivalence model, though this additional randomness should be counterbalanced by the fact that the structural equivalence model starts from six widely different regional mean growth

Figure 4: Monte Carlo model for regional salience, regular (global) parameterization, 1972–2010

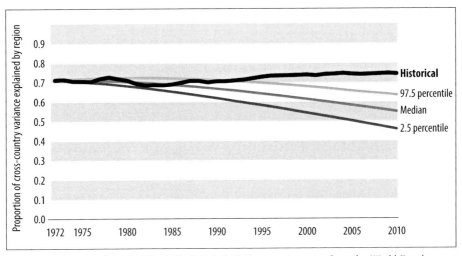

Source: Based on data from the World Bank "Atlas" GNP per capita series from the World Development Indicators database.

Figure 5: Monte Carlo model for regional salience, structural (regional) parameterization, 1972–2010

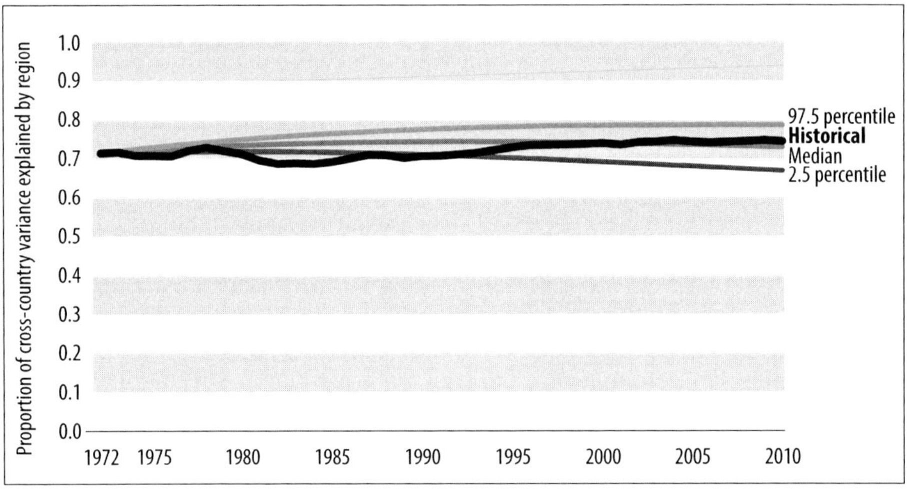

Source: Based on data from the World Bank "Atlas" GNP per capita series from the World Development Indicators database.

rates. In any case it turns out that the median and 95% confidence intervals for the structural equivalence model depicted in Figure 5 are much more consistent with the actual trajectory of the regional structure (black line) than the equivalent results from Figure 4.

The results of the simulations depicted in Figures 4 and 5 certainly do not resolve the debate over the regular versus structural equivalence of countries' positions in the world-economy. These two simulations are highly stylized, simplistically speci-fied, and possibly biased in favor of the structural equivalence argument. In any case it might be that both models are right for different zones of the world-economy. The models depicted in Figures 4 and 5 do, however, open the door to a new set of techniques for studying the degree and types of structure in the world-economy.

Early disadvantage, continuing repression, or just random chance?

Both economic conditional convergence theory and world-systems approaches to understanding the income structure of the contemporary world-economy proceed from an assumption that the forces that determine a country's national income levels are relatively stable over time. In the conditional convergence literature the stable force is the country's institutional heritage, while in the world-systems litera-ture the stable force is the operation of the larger capitalist world-economy. Both perspectives implicitly assume that change is difficult. This is perhaps inevitable, given that there has been so little change: perspectives that led to predictions of rapid and widespread national income mobility wouldn't have attracted many adherents, given the near-universal long-term income stability suggested by the data collected by Maddison (2010). One way or another, it would seem that empirical models of national income growth must posit the existence of some dampening force that prevents runaway mobility.

Is this true? Seeing the structure of the world-economy through the lens of entropy theory suggests an alternative model of stability: what if every country simply grew every year at a random rate? In other words, what if countries actually behaved like the gas molecules for which the concept of entropy was originally developed? Gas molecules bump off each other in a random process called Brownian motion. Brownian motion is a Markovian stochastic process, meaning that the change in any time period is independent of the change in all previous time periods. In a Brownian motion model of national income growth, each country's national income would grow at random each year without regard to its growth in previous years. This random growth should be sampled anew each year from a normal distribution with mean zero and standard deviation based on reasonable assumptions about the degree of randomness embedded in national growth rates.

The Brownian motion model corresponds to the proposition that today's dramatic inequalities between world regions arose through the creation of the modern world and the crystallization of the modern world-economy in the sixteenth century. After that point, incomes simply drifted at random. If the inequalities generated early in the history of the modern world-system were great enough, they could in theory persist to this day. The 188 years of data represented in Maddison (2010) may, in fact, be too short a time period over which to observe any meaningful deterioration in the structure of the world-economy. After all, who is to say how long is the longue durée? On the other hand, if continuous repressive processes of hegemony and exploitation are largely responsible for the persistence of structures of inequality in the world-economy, the world-economy might be more highly structured today than would be possible under a Brownian motion growth model.

Figure 6 depicts the results of a Brownian motion model of regional income growth for the period 1820–2008 based on a normal standard deviation equal to the actual standard deviation of the 188-year compound annual growth rates of the eight world regions from Maddison (2010): 0.001460 on the log scale, equivalent to 0.32%. The entropy concept is once again operationalized in structural terms by the correlation coefficient (as in Figure 3) though results are reported on a year-by-year basis (as in Figures 4 and 5). The simulation median and confidence interval are calculated as per Figures 4 and 5. Clearly, the observed correlation of regional income levels in 2008 with initial regional income levels in 1820 are not consistent with the Brownian motion model depicted in Figure 6. The early disadvantage model can safely be rejected. Strangely, however, the observed degree of structure is actually

Figure 6: Simulation of regional correlations of GDP per capita from 1820
           (initial state) to 2008

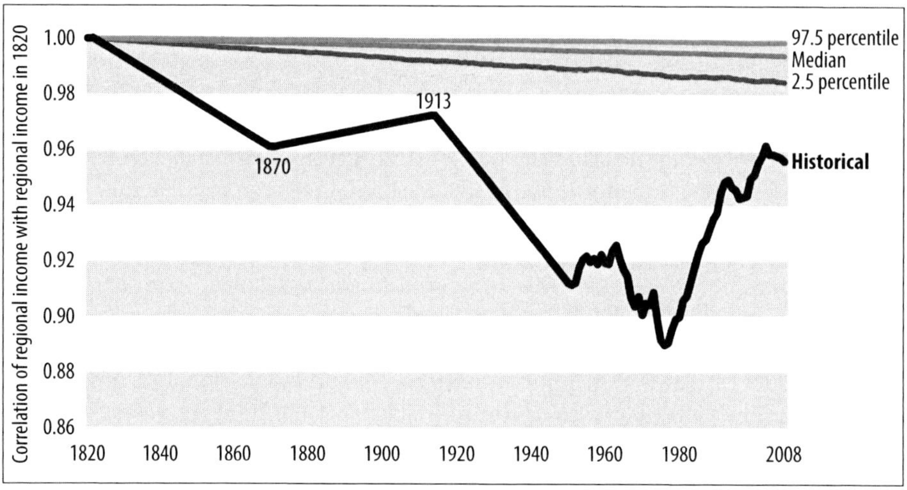

Notes: Simulation based on a Brownian motion growth model with a random standard deviation equivalent
to 0.32%.
Source: Based on data from Maddison (2010).

much lower than what would be predicted by the simple Brownian motion model
for all years throughout the study period. How is that possible?

The fact that actual levels of structure are much lower than would be expected
under random annual growth rates is theoretically, but not numerically, surprising.
Random variations in annual growth rates can produce only minor shifts in relative
incomes over "just" 180 years. To understand this, consider that in 1820 Africa had
one-third the income per capita of western Europe. It would take 41 years of consistent 1% excess African growth every year just to get from there to half of Europe's
level, and with a standard deviation of 0.32% excess growth of 1% would only occur about once in every 1000 years. Thus, the fact that actual levels of structure
are much lower than would be implied by the Brownian motion model suggests
that real structural mobility does exist in the world-economy. The rise of the OPEC
countries and the Asian tigers, or much more modestly (in per capita terms) the rise
of China, all indicate the existence of more mobility than would be possible through
annual random chance alone.

The greatest mobility, however, has been shown by the already-rich countries
of western Europe and the British offshoots. Over 188 years they went from being
three times as rich as Africa to being 12 times as rich as Africa. So much for convergence.

Future directions and implications for world society

Concepts from entropy theory can be used to generate meaningful insights about the structure of the world-economy. Entropy-based techniques are particularly useful because they open up potentially productive directions for future research that lie outside of the standard cross-national regression modeling framework. Cross-national regression modeling is not going to be displaced anytime soon as the workhorse method of quantitative macro-comparative research, but the available data have now been very extensively studied. So much has been discovered already that it is now difficult to discover anything substantively new. As a result, frontier research in the cross-national regression tradition is now focused mainly on estimation issues. Entropy-based techniques have the potential to break this stalemate, at least so far as our understanding of world-system structure and mobility are concerned. We have only taken the first steps toward this new way of understanding the structure of the world-economy.

The techniques developed here are only an illustration of the ways that entropy concepts can be applied to understanding the world-economy and world society more broadly. Any social science relationship involving structure, ordering, or hierarchies can in principle be studied using concepts derived from entropy theory. Entropy concepts can also be used to differentiate between (random) social change and (purposeful) social progress. For example, for any given level of inequality in a society, the degree to which incomes are structured by occupation should naturally decline over time due to random change. The economy-wide structuring of individual incomes by occupational category, however, is considered by UNCTAD (2010, 93–94) to be an important mechanism for promoting high levels of productivity and employment. Whether or not this theory is correct, entropy techniques would be ideally suited to its evaluation.

Entropy models are especially well-suited to the study of economic crises. Exploratory analyses of entropy trajectories using data based on annual exchange rates (not reported here) suggest that economic crises are associated with temporary disorganizations of the structures of the world-economy. This makes sense: crises are periods of rapid change. This is certainly a potentially productive area for policy-relevant research.

The illustrative findings that are presented here confirm that the overall structure of the world-economy is highly persistent over time. This may be due to dysfunctional institutions in poor countries, but is seems more likely that it is due to the operation of world-systemic forces of one kind or another (or both kinds). Whatever the cause, the cure is not obvious. No matter how it is measured (beta convergence or sigma convergence) the gap between rich and poor countries has hardly changed in nearly two centuries. Entropy-based analyses, however, additionally tell us that the structure of the gap between rich and poor has remained remarkably stable over two centuries. China's dramatic economic transformation does nothing to contradict this view; in recent years China has merely returned to its 1870 income level *vis-à-vis* the West (Babones, 2011). What was, is.

Prior scholarship on the application of entropy concepts to social science has generally followed Frank (2006) in using the law of increasing entropy as a metaphor for the decline and fall of resource-exploitative contemporary capitalism. This metaphorical usage is not incorrect, but it is perhaps not very productive. Meaningful global social integration and the creation of an inclusive world society depend on a realistic understanding of the forces that shape our world. Important among these are structural forces of order and disorder. While structure can be studied obliquely using regression methods (e.g., beta convergence) and inequality measures (e.g., sigma convergence), it can be studied directly using entropy concepts. Monte Carlo simulation provides an additional boost, making it possible to model latent systemic structures that cannot be directly observed. Entropy concepts applied within a Monte Carlo modeling framework can potentially go a long way toward improving our understanding of global-scale social structural change.

References

Acemoglu, Daron, Simon Johnson, and James A. Robinson. 2001. The Colonial Origins of Comparative Development: An Empirical Investigation. *American Economic Review*, 91: 1369–1401.

Akaike, Hirotugu. 1974. A New Look at the Statistical Model Identification. *IEEE Transactions on Automatic Control*, 19: 716–723.

Alfaro, Laura, Sebnem Kalemli-Ozcan, and Vadym Volosovych. 2008. Why Doesn't Capital Flow from Rich to Poor Countries: An Empirical Investigation. *Review of Economics and Statistics*, 90: 347–368.

Babones, Salvatore J. 2005. The Country-Level Income Structure of the World-Economy. *Journal of World-Systems Research*, 11: 29–55.

Babones, Salvatore J. 2011. The Middling Kingdom: The Hype and the Reality of China's Rise. *Foreign Affairs*, 90(5): 79–88.

Babones, Salvatore J. 2013. A Structuralist Approach to the Economic Trajectories of Russia and the Countries of East-Central Europe since 1900. *Geopolitics*, 18(3): 514–535.

Babones, Salvatore J., Robin M. Farabee-Siers, and Francisco J. Morales. 2011. Dependency Trends in the Globalization Era: Evidence from Export Partner Concentration. *Population Review*, 50: 134–149.

Barro, Robert J. 2012. Convergence and Modernization Revisited. NBER Working Paper, 18295, National Bureau of Economic Research, Cambridge.

De Long, Bradford. 1988. Productivity Growth, Convergence, and Welfare: Comment. *American Economic Review*, 78: 1138–1154.

Dezzani, Raymond J. 2002. Measuring Transition and Mobility in the Hierarchical World-Economy. *Journal of Regional Science*, 42: 595–625.

Dezzani, Raymond J., and Harley Johansen. 2012. The Role of Foreign Direct Investment as a Structural Development Indicator of the Hierarchical World Economy. *Environment and Planning A*, 44: 580–604.

Frank, Andre Gunder. 1969. The Development of Underdevelopment. *Monthly Review,* 18(4): 17–31.

Frank, Andre Gunder. 2006. "Entropy Generation and Displacement: The Nineteenth-Century Multilateral Network of World Trade." In Alf Hornborg and Carole Crumley (eds.), *The World System and the Earth System: Global Socioenvironmental Change and Sustainability since the Neolithic.* Walnut Creek: Left Coast Press.

Frank, Andre Gunder, and Barry Gills. 1993. "The 5,000-Year World System: An Interdisciplinary Introduction." In Andre Gunder Frank and Barry Gills (eds.), *The World System: Five Hundred Years or Five Thousand?* Oxford: Routledge.

Galtung, Johann. 1971. A Structural Theory of Imperialism. *Journal of Peace Research,* 8: 81–117.

Grimes, Peter E. 2012. "World-Systems as Dissipative Structures: A New Research Agenda." In Salvatore J. Babones and Christopher Chase-Dunn (eds.), *Routledge Handbook of World-Systems Analysis.* Oxford: Routledge.

Hornborg, Alf. 1998. Towards an Ecological Theory of Unequal Exchange: Articulating World-System Theory and Ecological Economics. *Ecological Economics,* 25: 127–136.

Kentor, Jeffrey, and Yong Suk Jang. 2004. Yes, There Is a (Growing) Transnational Business Community: A Study of Global Interlocking Directorates 1983–98. *International Sociology,* 19: 355–368.

Kick, Edward, and Laura McKinney. 2012. "World-System Structure, Natural Capital and Environmental Entropy." In Salvatore J. Babones and Christopher Chase-Dunn (eds.), *Routledge Handbook of World-Systems Analysis.* Oxford: Routledge.

Lawrence, Kirk S. 2009. The Thermodynamics of Unequal Exchange Energy Use, CO_2 Emissions, and GDP in the World-System, 1975–2005. *International Journal of Comparative Sociology,* 40: 335–359.

Lucas, Robert E. 1990. Why Doesn't Capital Flow from Rich to Poor Countries? *American Economic Review,* 80: 92–96.

Maddison, Angus. 2010. *Statistics on World Population, GDP and Per Capita GDP, 1-2008 AD.* Groningen: Groningen Growth and Development Centre, University of Groningen.

Mahutga, Matthew C. 2006. The Persistence of Structural Inequality? A Network Analysis of International Trade, 1965–2000. *Social Forces,* 84: 1863–1889.

Rodrik, Dani. 2011. The Future of Economic Convergence. NBER Working Paper, 17400, National Bureau of Economic Research, Cambridge.

Sanderson, Matthew R. 2010. Reconsidering the Study of International Migration: A Way Forward for Macrostructural Migration Research. *International Migration,* 48: 179–193.

Sassen, Saskia. 2001. *The Global City: New York, London, Tokyo.* Second editon. Princeton: Princeton University Press.

Schwarz, Gideon E. 1978. Estimating the Dimension of a Model. *Annals of Statistics,* 6: 461–464.

Theil, Henri. 1967. *Economics and Information Theory.* Chicago: Rand McNally.

UNCTAD (United Nations Conference on Trade and Development). 2010. *Trade and Development Report 2011: Employment, Globalization and Development.* Geneva: UNCTAD.

Wallerstein, Immanuel M. 1974. *The Modern World-System, Vol. I: Capitalist Agriculture and the Origins of the European World-Economy in the Sixteenth Century.* New York: Academic Press.

Wallerstein, Immanuel M. 1994. "Development: Lodestar or Illusion?" In Leslie Sklair (ed.), *Capitalism and Development.* Oxford: Routledge.

2

Global Wages and World Inequality: The Impact of the Great Recession

Scott Albrecht and Roberto Patricio Korzeniewicz

This chapter presents and analyzes a new dataset on urban wages across the world that allows us to (1) explore patterns and trends in inequality between- and within-countries, focusing specifically on (2) the impact of the 2008 crisis and the ensuing Great Recession on wages across the world. We construct the dataset from surveys of prices and earnings by UBS. These data allow us to reconstruct average wages and benefits for over a dozen occupational categories (ranging from construction laborers and unskilled female factory workers, to bus drivers, managers and engineers) for more than 70 cities across the world (in high-, middle-, and low-income nations). We find that global recession slowed convergent trends, especially wage growth for low-wage tradable goods producers. We posit that the constructed perceptions of skill justify these wage gaps, and that changing perceptions are an important correlate of mobility.

Introduction

The Union Bank of Switzerland (now UBS) began collecting data on average wages across a sample of occupations in cities around the world in the 1970s. Returning every three years, UBS expanded its coverage to more than a dozen occupations in more than 70 cities in 2012. The data alone are an important contribution to the literature, as most studies on social stratification and mobility are generally limited to a small number of high-income nations or based on methodologically inconsistent data sources. Using the UBS data we are able to reconstruct comparable wage trends across countries and skill levels.

Our data provide compelling evidence that national residence has been a significant and stable force shaping the relative distribution of wages. City of residence alone explains more than three-quarters of wage variance. But the data also indicate that in the last twenty years, some sectors of the world labor force experienced significant upward mobility, led by producers of tradable goods in low-wage regions. These producers have gained ground relative to both (a) workers in nontradable activities (such as services) within those same cities, and (b) tradable goods producers in high-wage cities. In general, the wide gap that characterized wages in the core and the periphery prior to the 1990s had been shrinking for much of the last two decades, driven primarily by the growth of China and a few other peripheral and semiperipheral countries. Finally, our analysis indicates that the Great Recession that started in 2008 did little or nothing to upset the established global wage hierarchy, but instead effectively slowed down global tendencies towards convergence.

Our interpretation of these events can depend on our initial perspective. If we were to emphasize the convergence of the 1990s and 2000s, we could argue that critical paradigms on world inequality and stratification tend to underestimate the extent to which poor or "peripheral" areas, once having such a status, might undergo transformations that generate upward mobility. On the other hand, focusing on the impact of the 2008 financial crisis and subsequent recession, we are reminded that global economic interdependence can generate vulnerabilities that might reinforce deeply entrenched patterns of inequality. A world-systems perspective can be most productive when showing an ability to capture these two essential features—change and continuity—in the making of the contemporary world-economy.

Data and methodology

We assess change and continuity by focusing on wage stratification and patterns of mobility. Efforts to construct a world-economic perspective on trends in mobility and stratification have been constrained by the self-reinforcing tendencies (a) to collect data on a national level; and (b) to theorize stratification and mobility as taking place primarily—if not wholly—within national boundaries. Most data on inequality, for example, have been drawn from national surveys of individuals and/ or households, collected primarily by national statistical agencies for the purpose of shaping policies at a national level. Consequently, the available data on social stratification and mobility (e.g., returns to skill and education) are generally limited to a small number of high-income nations or methodologically inconsistent across countries. Our research represents an initial, modest step towards overcoming these constraints by developing a disaggregated, global wage dataset that, while modest, moves us toward a more global mapping of mobility and stratification.

Our dataset draws on the wage estimates periodically published by UBS. Since 1970, UBS has conducted a survey of prices and salaries every three years, designed to provide clients of the bank with accurate international price and wage comparisons. The number of cities included in the survey changed over time, growing from 31 in 1970 to 73 in 2009 (29 of the 31 cities surveyed in 1970 were included in 2012). While Japan, Australia, Canada, the United States, and Western Europe accounted for three-quarters of the sample in 1970, their share diminished to less than half (32 of 73) in 2009, giving way to greater representation of cities in Eastern Europe (12), Asia (13), the Middle East (6), Africa (2) and Latin America (8). By 2003, the cities in our sample are located in countries that together account for 76.4% of the world's population, up from around 66%–70% in the 1980s.

The most significant deficiency in global coverage is China; Shanghai and Beijing do not show up in the sample until 1997 and 2006, respectively. Where necessary, to compensate for this deficiency, we draw on a modified sample in which we impute Chinese wages using other data sources to estimate past wages for these cities (Yang et al., 2010).

The original 1970 survey included only five occupations (automobile mechanics, bank tellers, bus drivers, primary school teachers and secretaries). Departments heads were added in 1973, building laborers, female factory workers, and skilled industrial workers in 1976, and cooks, engineers, and saleswomen in 1979. These 12 occupations are tracked consistently to the present. Recently, product managers were added to the list in 2003, call center agents in 2006, and financial analysts in 2012. In each case, occupations are explicitly, extensively, and consistently defined to allow for reliable comparisons over time and across regions, and it is this quality—the combination of longitudinal as well as global coverage—that most sets these data apart.

UBS does not directly report hourly wages. Instead, we estimate gross hourly wages by converting pay per year into pay per week and dividing that value by the average number of working hours. On their methodology, UBS (2012, 6) reports that "the survey was conducted locally by mutually independent observers" and that "more than 50,000 data points were collected and included in the survey evaluation." The goals, conceptual definitions and standards guiding data collection are much more precise and homogenous than what can be found across national surveys. Using these precise definitions, the UBS sample allows us to cover a wide range of occupations across nations, and to compare returns to precisely defined measures of human capital across those nations. The function of this survey is to provide a consistent and reliable picture of wage costs across a range of occupations, cities and over time, and it is this quality that makes the data ideal for our purposes.

Because wages are reported as occupational averages we cannot estimate the sampling error for significance testing, and our interpretation of the results reflect this limitation. Along those lines, the same occupation-specific sampling that makes wages comparable across regions also means that not all occupations are represented in the sample (e.g., the data does not include any wage estimates for computer programmers) and that the sample does not capture composition effects (e.g., we do not know the ratio of building laborers to department heads in each city). This means we cannot definitively compare average wage levels for entire cities across cities or overtime. Instead, when we refer to a city as high or low wage, or to wages in a city rising or falling over time, we mean that wage returns to labor in those specific occupations (which, presumably, reflect a broader range of occupations as well) are high or low, rising or falling. Finally, UBS samples only urban areas, so our results reflect wage dynamics for urban workers only.

UBS collects data on gross and net wages; in this chapter we look only at gross wages, or wages before taxes and government transfers. We do this for two reasons. First, gross wages are consistent with our goal, to assess longitudinal changes in wage costs, not the impact of government redistribution (Lindert, 2000). Second, a proper consideration of net wages would require us to resolve complicated questions—e.g., the value of social security or health services. We hope to address these issues in other iterations of this research. Unless explicitly stated, wages in this chapter reflect constant U.S. dollars, that is, wages are converted to U.S. dollars based on the current exchange rate and then adjusted for inflation.

We do not use PPP-adjusted wages. Principally, this is because we our interested in comparing wage costs and trends across countries and industries, not consumption. Also, existing measures of purchasing power do not deserve the confidence they are granted by many social scientists, who ignore the complexities in comparing consumption costs across countries and over time (Korzeniewicz et al., 2004). We hope to address some of these issues using price data collected by UBS in future research. For our purposes here, we are confident that we are using the most correct indicator.

Results from these data are consistent with other global measures of production and inequality. For example, the correlation between within-city Gini inequality using the wage data and within-country inequality as reported by the World Bank (2011) for 2009 is .609, and that increases to .836 when we exclude countries that are more than 25% rural (Korzeniewicz and Albrecht, 2012). The correlation between the average wage for cities and Gross National Income per capita exceeds .9 for that same year.

We use this unique dataset to analyze trends and patterns in global wages. For these calculations, we refer to the intersection of a city and occupation (e.g., a Chicago Primary School Teacher) as a city/occupation combination (COC). Our calculations begin by reconstructing the global hierarchy of COCs and tracking their mobility over time. Then, to assess whether patterns vary in more specific ways among workers, we explore these trends by differentiating regional wage and skill levels, whether workers are involved in tradables or nontradables, and the intersections of these attributes. Next, we take a closer look at the last decade and assess the impact of the 2008 Great Recession on global wage trends. Finally, we explore alternative models of national and global wage inequality that help us discuss our findings as they relate to contending theories of wage convergence and divergence.

Findings

Unsurprisingly, reflecting a long-standing feature of the world-economy since the nineteenth century, wages vary widely between cities located in high- and low-income nations. For example, the average hourly wage in New York based on the 12 surveyed occupations has been more than 10 times higher than in Mumbai in every sampled year between 1982 and 2012. In fact, even though the average rate of growth of wages has been higher in Mumbai than New York, the absolute real wage gap between the two cities is larger in 2012 than in any other sampled year.[1] Further, the absolute wage gap between the lowest and highest paid occupations in Mumbai in 2012, female factory workers ($0.56/hour in 2012 dollars) and product managers ($9.02), is smaller than the gap between Mumbai product managers and female factory workers in New York (who earned $18.05/hour). Given three strategies for pursuing higher wages—enjoy national economic growth, upgrade skills, or look for higher returns to existing skills elsewhere—the latter clearly offers large potential gains for Mumbai workers.

Mumbai is not the only city to have its wages dwarfed by those in New York. The lowest wage surveyed in New York City in 1982 was higher than the highest wage in five cities (Mexico City, Istanbul, Manila, Jakarta, and Mumbai). New York City's lowest wage in 2012 was higher than the highest wage in 19 of 72 cities, and in cities on every continent but Australia.

Figure 1 illustrates the interaction between location and occupation. This figure combines the average hourly wage in 2012 dollars for the same set of occupations in four cities (Mumbai, Buenos Aires, Madrid and New York City). As illustrated by the figure, in 1982 all twelve occupations in Mumbai had average hourly wages below the lowest paid occupations in Madrid and New York City. On the other hand, in Buenos Aires the lowest wages in 1982 overlapped with the top of the distribution in Mumbai, while the highest wages were comparable with their counterparts in Madrid and overlapped with the lowest wages in New York City.

Thirty years later, wage gains in Mumbai and Madrid are most apparent. Workers in these two cities experienced real wage gains exceeding 50% on average. Workers in Buenos Aires and New York, on the other hand, saw wages increase by just over 10%. The wages of top earners in Buenos Aires and Madrid were comparable in 1982, but this was not the case in 2012; the average wage of the three highest paid occupations in Madrid in 1982 were less than 50% higher than that same group in Buenos Aires, but are 2.6 times greater in 2012. The reverse is true of Mumbai and Buenos Aires. Top wage earners in Mumbai substantially closed the gap between 1982 and 2012. In all, though, the wage hierarchy is largely unaltered. Wages are highest in New York, then Madrid, Buenos Aires, and Mumbai.

These results contradict the common sense expectation that those employed in high-wage occupations in poor countries earn more than those employed in low-wage occupations in rich countries. This common sense expectation reflects an orthodox model of social stratification in the global economy; focusing on global patterns of wage inequality, as illustrated in Figure 1, offers an alternative standpoint from which to think about social stratification. We now proceed to provide a more detailed account of changing patterns of stratification from a global perspective.

---

1   In 2012 dollars, the average wage in Mumbai increased 70% versus 12% in New York, but 70% of $1.83 is less than 12% of $29.41, so the absolute gap increased from $27.57 to $29.89.

Figure 1: Real wages in selected cities, 1982 and 2012

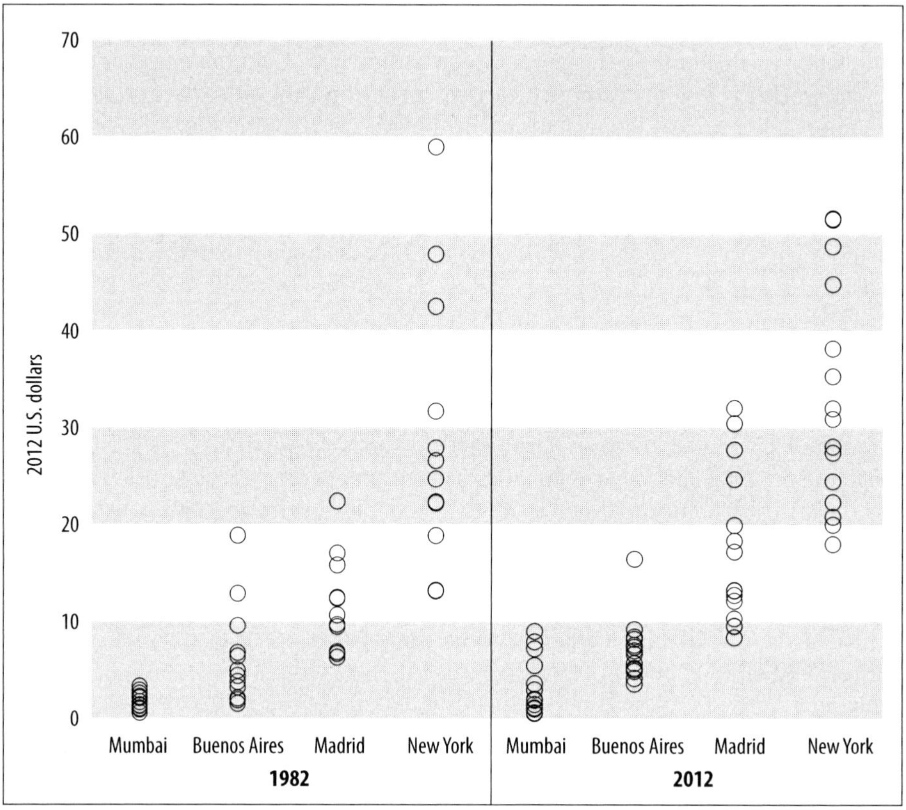

Sources: Own calculations based on Union Bank of Switzerland (1982) and UBS (2012).

Mapping wages and tracking global mobility

What has been the extent of continuity and change in global wage inequality? Following the criteria discussed in our previous examples, Figure 2 contains a more exhaustive mapping of how the city/occupation combinations (COC) stood relative to one another in 1985–1988 and 2009–2012. Each COC is identified by the city symbol (see Appendix for an explanation of the COC abbreviations used henceforth) and a number signifying its rank order within that city. We divided the observed range of hourly wages into ten equal intervals, ranging from zero to the global maximum based on two year averages, and located each COC within its corresponding interval. For example, "mub(1–11)" in row 1 and column 1 of Figure 2 means that eleven of the twelve lowest wage occupations in Mumbai were below 10% of the global maximum in 1985–1988 *and* in 2009–2012; "lis(12)" in row 2, column 4 reflects the movement of the highest wage occupation in Lisbon from the 2nd interval in 1985–1988 to the 4th in 2009–2012. Figure 2, then, captures the continuities and changes in the relative position of COCs between the mid-1980s and the early 2010s.

The first observation is that wages at both endpoints are approximately log-normally distributed, with more workers clustered in the first few intervals and few workers populating the highest. In 1985–1988, 215 of 550 COCs, just ten short of half, are in the first interval with wages at or below 10% of the global maximum. The top five intervals (50% or more of the global maximum) contain only 21 COCs. The distribution in 2009–2012 is less skewed; that value fell from 1.44 in 1985–1988 to .83 in 2009–2012. There are only 239 COCs in the bottom two intervals (versus 350 in 1985–1988) and 52 COCs in the top five intervals.

This "de-skewing" reflects broad upward mobility of COCs versus the global maximum (COCs in cells above the diagonal—the shaded boxes—experienced upward mobility relative to the global maximum during this period, and *vice versa*); 306 of 550 COCs are in a higher interval in 2009–2012 and only 19 fell to a lower interval. The most upward movement came from the 2nd and 3rd intervals in 1985–1988 (10%–30% of the global maximum). More than three-quarters of these COCs were in a higher interval in the subsequent year.

The data in Figure 2 suggest that the story of global wages between the mid-1980s and now is as much about continuing stratification as it is about mobility. Logged wages in 1985–1988 explain 85.4% of the variation in logged wages in 2009–2012, leaving only 14.6% to be explained by economic trends and measurement error. Despite broad mobility relative to the global maximum, the global rank of COCs, the global wage hierarchy, looks today much like it did 25 years ago. The rank order correlation between the two periods is $r=.928$; about one-third of COCs moved fewer than 20 spots or 3.5 percentage points, and two-thirds moved fewer than 55 spots or 10 percentage points. One explanation for this apparent paradox of mobility in a stable hierarchy is that the wage gaps between workers in different cities (as illustrated in Figure 1) are so large that higher growth rates over 25 years were not enough, *yet*, to move some lower wage workers ahead of higher wage workers.

Analysis of variance

The next figure formally charts the large wage gaps between workers in different cities (as illustrated in Figure 1) and responsible for the stable wage hierarchy. Applying ANOVA, we have estimated COC log wages using city of residence and occupation for each of the ten most recent sample years, again using two-year

Figure 2: Mobility table 1985/1988 to 2009/2012

2009/2012

<table>
<tr><td></td><td></td><td>1</td><td>2</td><td>3</td></tr>
<tr>
<td rowspan="10">1985/1988</td>
<td>1</td>
<td>mub(1-11) cai(1-10) nrb(1-10)
man(1-12) rio(1-8) jka(1-12) bgk(1-9)
mex(1-10) sao(1-6) ibl(1-7) hgk(1)
bog(1-9) klp(1-9) sng(1-5) bsa(1-9)
sol(1-4) car(1-6) tel(1) mna(1-4) joh(1-5)</td>
<td>cai(11) mub(12) mna(6) mex(11-12)
lis(1-7) car(9) sao(7-10) bog(10)
rio(9-10) bgk(10-11) ibl(8-10) ath(1-7)
hgk(2-7) bsa(10-11) sol(5-6) nic(1-4)
mad(1-4) tel(2-5) sng(6-8)</td>
<td>cai(12) sol(7) lis(8-11) dbl(1)
par(1-2) mad(6)</td>
</tr>
<tr>
<td>2</td>
<td>mna(5) car(7-8) nrb(11)</td>
<td>nic(5) ath(8) mad(5) klp(10-11)
hgk(8-9) tel(6-8) vna(1) sng(9-10)
nrb(12) bog(11-12) bsa(12) joh(6-9)
car(10-11) tor(1) mna(7-10) bgk(12)</td>
<td>tel(9) nic(6-7) ibl(11) ath(9-11) lux(1-4)
par(3-6) dbl(2-4) mad(7-8) chi(1-2)
rio(11) sol(8) mil(1-6) vna(2-4) sao(11)
ldn(1-5) brs(1-4) hel(1-4) joh(10) tor(2)
syd(1-5) ams(1-4) stk(1-5) tok(1-2)
mon(1-2) fnk(1) sng(11) klp(12)</td>
</tr>
<tr>
<td>3</td>
<td></td>
<td>car(12)</td>
<td>par(7) brs(5) mna(11) stk(6) ibl(12)
las(1) ams(5) fnk(2-3) tok(3-4)
chi(3) mon(3-5) tor(3-7)</td>
</tr>
<tr>
<td>4</td>
<td></td>
<td></td>
<td>fnk(4) hgk(10) nyc(1)</td>
</tr>
<tr><td>5</td><td></td><td></td><td></td></tr>
<tr><td>6</td><td></td><td></td><td></td></tr>
<tr><td>7</td><td></td><td></td><td></td></tr>
<tr><td>8</td><td></td><td></td><td></td></tr>
<tr><td>9</td><td></td><td></td><td></td></tr>
<tr><td>10</td><td></td><td></td><td></td></tr>
</table>

Sources: Own calculations based on Union Bank of Switzerland (1971–1997) and UBS (2000–2012).

Figure 2 (continued)

2009/2012

4	5	6	7	8	9	10		
							1	
lis(12) dbl(5-8) sol(9-11) nic(8-9) ath(12) las(2) tel(10) nyc(2-3) mad(9-10) ams(6) mon(6) syd(6-7) vna(5) hel(5-7) zur(1) stk(7) ldn(6)	mad(12) sao(12) sol(12) osl(4)						**2**	
cop(1) zur(2) mad(11) hel(8-9) syd(8) dbl(9) tel(11) joh(11) lux(5-6) ldn(7-9) las(3-4) brs(6-7) tok(5-6) par(8-9) vna(6-9) ams(7-8) gva(1) hgk(11-12) rio(12) mil(7-10) stk(8-10) osl(1-3) nic(10) nyc(4) mon(7-8) sng(12) tor(8-9) chi(4)	syd(10) ams(9-10) vna(10) gva(2) nic(11-12) cop(2-5) osl(5-9) joh(12) nyc(6-7) zur(3-4)	lux(8) dbl(11) mil(12) cop(6-7)		par(12)			**3**	
syd(9) tok(7-8) brs(8-9) mna(12) lux(7) fnk(5-8) mon(9-10) nyc(5) chi(5-8) las(5-6)	ldn(10-11) dbl(10) brs(10) mil(11) gva(3-5) osl(10) zur(5-6) hel(10-11) las(7-8) stk(11) ams(11) chi(10) fnk(9) tor(10) tok(9-10) nyc(8)	syd(11) cop(8-10) ldn(12) gva(7) zur(7)	lux(10) osl(11) par(11)	osl(12) syd(12)			**4**	**1985/1988**
chi(9) mon(11)	gva(6) las(9-10) vna(11) tor(11)	brs(11) nyc(9-10) lux(9) stk(12) par(10) zur(8)	dbl(12) zur(9) ams(12) chi(12) hel(12) cop(11)	gva(10)	vna(12)	lux(12)	**5**	
	tok(11)	tor(12) fnk(11)	las(12) nyc(11) gva(8)	brs(12) zur(11)	lux(11)		**6**	
	mon(12) fnk(10)	chi(11) las(11)		gva(11) cop(12)			**7**	
		tok(12)	zur(10)	nyc(12)	zur(12)		**8**	
			gva(9)				**9**	
			fnk(12)				**10**	

Sources: Own calculations based on Union Bank of Switzerland (1971–1997) and UBS (2000–2012).

Figure 3: Analysis of wage variance by city and occupation

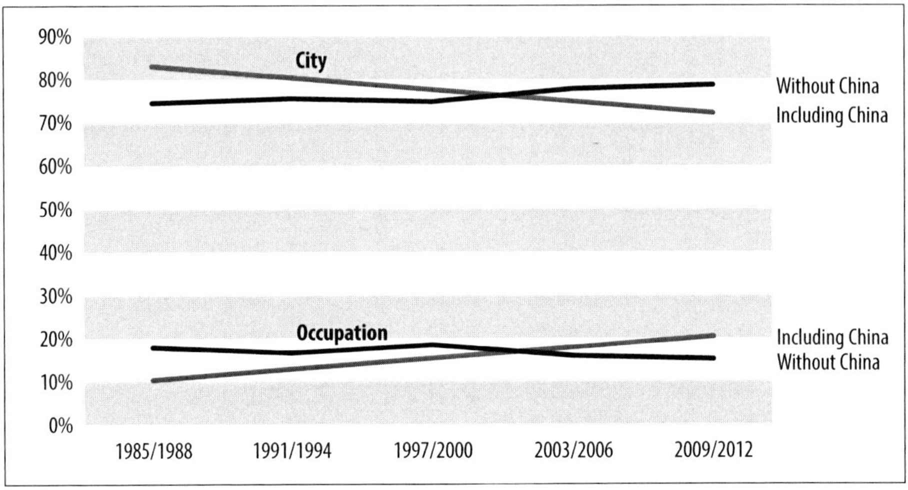

Sources: Own calculations based on Union Bank of Switzerland (1971–1997) and UBS (2000–2012).

averages.[2] Because mainland China is excluded from the first set of estimates—we do not have wage data for Beijing and Shanghai until the late 1990s—we added a second set of estimates in which we estimated wages in these cities back to 1985–1988 and weighted COCs by the number of large cities (1,000,000+ residents) in each country; wages are estimated using wage data by region and industry from Yang at al. (2010). We do not replicate the analysis for the intervening years.

The unweighted estimates indicate that occupation explains less than 20% of wage variance, while city of residence explains between 75% and 80%; this is consistent with other estimates that between-country inequality is responsible for three-quarters or more of global inequality (Korzeniewicz et al., 1997). These patterns have been fairly stable over time; the importance of city of residence has been increasing gradually over time while occupation has become less important. Comparing the first set to the second set of estimates, the impact of China (and India to a lesser extent) is clear: the role of location is greater at the beginning of the period when we add China's relatively low wages and large population, and *vice versa* for occupation, but location is significantly less important today (though still many times more important than occupation). As China, and India, slowly move into a global "middle

---

2   This analysis was first executed using all available data for each year. Second, a subsample was created using only COCs with data available for all ten sample years. Finally, COCs were weighted to represent the distribution of population between regions (North America/Oceania, Latin America/Caribbean, Western Europe, Eastern Europe, Africa, Middle East, Asia). While the results vary slightly by the sample and weighting used, these differences are not substantial.

class," and wages within these countries diverge, occupation becomes increasingly important and location less important on a global scale.

In summary, when comparing wages globally, roughly 20% of an individual's wages can be explained by their level of education, type of employment, sex, marital status, experience, etc. Another 70% is explained by where they live. These estimates are consistent with other decompositions of world inequality that suggest that between-nation disparities account for two-thirds to three-quarters of global inequality, and that global convergence disappears when China is removed from the sample (see Korzeniewicz et al., 1997; Milanovic, 2005). If wages in China continued to grow at this rate—wages tripled between 1997 and 2007 according to Yang et al. (2010)—such increases could revolutionize the global wage structure in the next couple of decades, but wage growth there has slowed, so long-term prospects for such global wage convergence still is uncertain.

Modeling global wages

In addition to allowing us to compare wages for similarly credentialed workers in cities around the world, we can use the detailed definitions of sampled workers to map global wage trends based on other individual-level characteristics. We focus here on skill, operationalized by using the education and experience of each COC, and distinguishing the trajectory of workers engaged in the production of tradable goods.

The relationship between skill and wages is self-evident. More skilled workers can either 1) produce the same good more efficiently or 2) produce a good that less skilled workers cannot replicate, and therefore demand higher pay. The relationship between the production of tradable goods and wages is more complex. The key quality of tradable goods (and services) is that their production and consumption are not geographically linked. Because location explains between 70% and 80% of wages globally, producers of tradable goods are competing in a fundamentally different labor market than producers of nontradable goods.

The Heckscher-Ohlin trade model is a formal representation of this relationship. According to the Heckscher-Ohlin model, prices should converge between regions as they export those products that use their abundant factors of production. Regions rich in capital and skill will export goods that require high levels of capital and skill, while low wage regions will export labor-intensive goods. Consequently, wages for less skilled workers in low-wage regions producing tradable goods should converge with similar workers in high-wage regions, and the returns to skill across regions should also converge.

In an earlier paper (Korzeniewicz and Albrecht, 2012), to test the relationship between location, skill and tradable good production on wages over time, we modeled wages for 1982, 1991, 2000 and 2009. Then, using the single year coefficients, we estimated hypothetical wage trends for ideal-type high- and low-skill workers of tradable and nontradable goods in high- and low-wage cities.

Per capita GDP was the single most important variable shaping wage levels. Alone, national location explained between 67.9% of the cross-sectional variation in 1982 and 78.7% in 2009.[3] These results are generally consistent with the ANOVA results in Figure 3.

Skill also had a positive and significant association with wage, but the returns to skill were significantly lower in high-income countries in 1982 and 1991: the highest more-skilled-to-less-skilled wage ratios are found in lower-income regions.[4] Rising wages or less-skilled workers in poor cities reduced returns to skill in low-income countries in 2000 and 2009.

We used these results to estimate wage trends for eight counterfactual workers-high/low-income x skilled/unskilled x tradable/nontradable. Throughout the period, the gap between workers in high-income and low-income countries was inviolate; unskilled workers in high-income countries consistently earned more than skilled workers in low-income countries. Most workers enjoyed some wage growth over the period, but one group, unskilled, low-wage workers, experienced strong, consistent wage growth throughout the period.[5]

Wage disparities after the Great Recession

Between 2004 and 2007, global gross domestic product per capita grew at an average 2.62% per annum. That figure dipped to 0.15% in 2008, and global production per capita fell 3.37% in 2009. The global economy rebounded in 2010, and it continued to grow, but at a slower clip, in 2011 (see Figure 4, World Bank, 2012).

Reduced production was the result of a financial crisis centered in the rich world, but the impact of the crisis was truly global. Among the 224 countries in the World Bank database with the relevant data, 87% experienced slower average growth in per capita GDP in 2008 and 2009 than in the previous three years. Technically speaking, though, it was not a global recession but a mostly-global recession. Of the 224 countries, 49% experienced increased production per capita in 2009 while 36% experienced a contraction that exceeded 3% of per capita GDP. More to the point, high income countries, as classified by the World Bank, saw their production con-

---

3   Variance explained is estimated by regressing location (log of national GDP per capita) on the residual after controlling for skill and employment in the production of tradable goods.

4   Also, the effect of location is larger in Model 2, because the larger wage ratios in low-income cities are masking the wage differentials between cities.

5   These results did not change when China was added to the sample and observations were weighted by city population.

Figure 4: Percent change in gross domestic capital per capita, 2000–2011

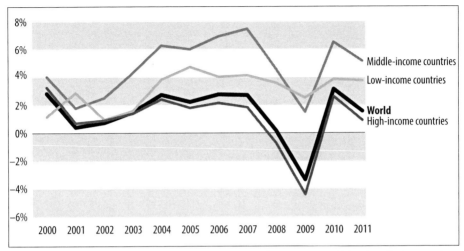

Notes: High, middle and low income are based on World Bank designation and the plotted values are those reported by the World Bank for high, middle and low-income countries.
Source: World Bank (2012).

tract by 4.44%. Middle- and low-income economies continued to grow on average through 2009 but at a much slower rate (World Bank, 2012).

The impact on wages was less dramatic. The International Labor Organization reported that "the global growth in real average wages was reduced by half in 2008 and 2009, compared to earlier years," and unemployment peaked at 210 million (ILO, 2010). The results from our sample are consistent with the ILO estimate. Real average wage growth from 2000 to 2006 hovered around 1.8% per year before falling by half in 2009 to 0.9%. Wages, like production, also rebounded nicely after 2009. Real wages grew by 4.2% per annum after 2009 to 2012, so that wages in 2012 actually exceeded projected values based on growth between 2000 and 2006. Consistent with the fall in production, average hours worked per week also fell slightly in 2009, from 41.4 hours in 2003 and 41.3 in 2006 to 41.0 in 2009. Hours worked climbed back to 41.4 in 2012, an increase equal to about half a work week over the course of a year.

Figure 5 charts average annual wage growth rates around the recession (2006–2009 and 2009–2012) and the decade before (1997–2006) by the wage level for that COC in the first year (1997, 2006 or 2009). Wage growth rates are fitted using locally weighted scatterplot smoothing (lowess) using a narrow bandwidth (.4) against the wage in the first year; in other words, the growth rate between 2006 and 2009, for example, is estimated using the wage in 2006. The line reflects typical growth rates from that point in the wage distribution; higher values reflect higher growth rates.

Figure 5: Lowess growth rates by wages

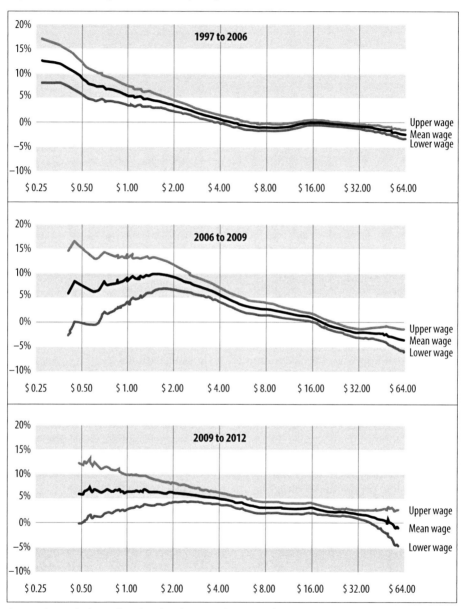

Sources: Own calculations based on data from UBS (1997–2012).

Consequently, a negative slope indicates (beta-)convergence in wages as lower-wage workers experience higher average wage growth rates than high-wage workers. Confidence intervals are estimated using m=n resampling and re-estimation.

The rate of convergence for the first two periods was similar—the correlation between the log wage and growth rate for 1997–2006 was –.322 versus –.324 for 2006–2009—but the nature of that convergence was very different. In the first period, convergence largely reflected very low-wage workers catching up with those in the upper half of the distribution. But from 2006 to 2009, wage growth was strongest in the 3rd quartile while wages of the richest workers fell substantially. Then, from 2009 to 2012 wage growth slowed for lower-wage workers while rich workers saw their wages rebound (except for workers at the very top of the distribution subject to statistical regression).

These patterns reflect, or were driven by, wage trends in China. In 1997, all mainland China COCs were in the bottom 20% of the wage distribution and wages for these workers grew by 9.0% per year on average to 2006. As a product of this growth, COCs in Beijing and Shanghai in 2006 ranged from the bottom of the distribution to just above the median, and more than a third of COCs were above the 25th percentile. Wages for Chinese workers grew at an astonishing 14.3% year on year and wages for Chinese workers in that 3rd quartile grew at 19.6%. Between 2009 and 2012 wage growth for Chinese workers slowed to a still healthy 8.4%.

Global trade contracted faster and further than global production during the crisis. For the first half of 2009, exports from advanced economies, by volume, were more than 10% lower than they had been in 2006 and about 17% lower than 12 months earlier. And unlike production, the impact on trade was even greater for emerging economies. Exports from these countries fell more than 20% by volume from mid-2008 to mid-2009, below the level of exports in 2006 (CPB Netherlands Bureau for Economic Policy Research, 2013).

Workers employed in the production of tradable goods in low-wage cities had enjoyed the most rapid wage growth (Korzeniewicz and Albrecht, 2012). This is captured in Figure 6 for 2006–2009 as wage growth for these workers kept pace with nontradable workers in their same cities and outpaced tradable good workers in high-wage cities. But collapsing global trade caught up with these workers between 2009 and 2012 as their wages fell relative to nontradable goods producers in those same cities, relative to tradable good producers in high-wage cities, and in absolute terms on average.

High-wage earners saw their wages contract in 2009, but then rebound strongly in the next three years. Wages for low-wage earners continued to grow through the crisis and after, but at a slower rate absolutely and relative to high-wage earners between 2009 and 2012. Tradable good producers in low-wage cities, the big winners of global wage convergence for more than a decade, took a big hit as global exports collapsed in 2009, and their wages contracted to 2012. All in all, due to the combined effect of these outcomes, the 2008 financial crisis and the subsequent

Figure 6: Lowess growth rates by wage and tradable good production

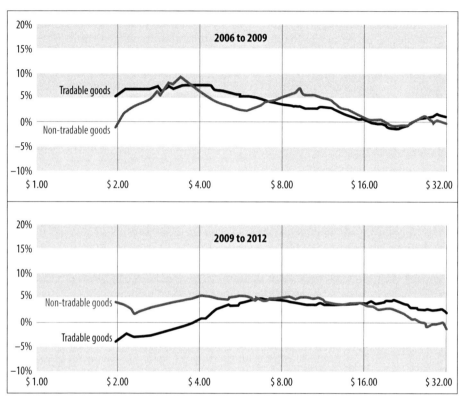

Sources: Own calculations based on data from UBS (2006–2012).

Great Recession slowed overall global wage convergence, erasing some of the relative gains made by low-wage earners between 2006 and 2009. Thus, drawing on the
sample of 727 COCs with wage data in 2006 and 2012, city of residence explained
77.0% of the variance in log wages and occupation explained another 14.6% in 2006;
in 2012, city of residence explained 78.0% of log wages and occupation explained
13.9%. If anything, rather than a blurring of national boundaries, location has become of slightly greater importance in explaining global wage differentials.

Our findings provide compelling evidence that the city/national location of
workers has been, and continues to be, the single major attribute shaping the distribution of wages worldwide. Moreover, we showed that over the past thirty years
there has been considerable stability in the global distribution of wages, and that
transcendent mobility has been rare across the COCs in our data. On the other
hand, our findings also indicate that more recently in China, as well as in some
wealthier countries, the COCs included in our data did experience some significant

relative movement within the global distribution of wages. In particular, producers of tradable goods in poorer cities appear to have gained ground relative to both workers in nontradable activities within those same cities, and tradable good producers in high-wage cities. The data suggest that this convergence became more pronounced immediately after the 2008 crisis, but has slowed down over the Great Recession.

Discussion

The world is a highly unequal place. Similarly credentialed workers with similar employment living in different cities can earn wages measured at different orders of magnitude. This holds true after controlling for the most pertinent work-related achieved characteristics—occupation, education, experience—and individual-level demographics, such as sex, age, marital status, etc. The approach we did not pursue is to seek to explain wage gaps by accounting for macro-level variables—education quality, physical capital and infrastructure, etc. (e.g., Krueger, 1968; Summers and Heston, 1988)—because that would miss the larger point. If we assume workers in Mumbai are inherently as capable as workers in New York, these wage differences fundamentally reduce to a single ascribed characteristic: location. One could argue that no other single system for categorizing people outside of chattel slavery has so effectively structured one's economic opportunities.

At a macro level, our findings help us understand why the interpretation of patterns and trends in global inequality remains a field riddled by contention. The critical perspective sees that polarization and inequality persist in the distribution of wages across countries. Decades of strong wage growth for those at the bottom of the distribution had little impact on global inequality, and a global recession that originated in the rich world unwound some of the progress that low-wage workers had won.

The modernizing paradigm, on the other hand, focuses on convergence and mobility in world inequality. From this perspective, wage gaps reflect internal characteristics of countries that make low-wage workers less capable or efficient; for example, a McKinsey Global Institute report concluded that 75% of Indian engineers and 90% of Chinese engineers are not suitable for employment in a multinational corporation (Farrell et al., 2005). But global integration drove up wages for less-skilled, low-wage exporters for decades, and middle-income country workers continued to enjoy strong wage growth through the recession.

Often, those working in the critical paradigm underestimate the potential for upward mobility in poor areas of the world, though some authors have explored ways in which global hierarchies can be transformed (e.g., Arrighi and Drangel, 1986; Arrighi, 1994; Wallerstein, 1996 [1983]). Wage growth for less-skilled, low-wage exporters is not yet transformative, but only because the gaps were so large. Booming wages in China, whose workers have already moved up in the global hierarchy, will soon force a reassessment; while wages stalled at the bottom of the distribution in recent years, wage growth in China picked up speed. Researchers adopting a critical perspective must make greater efforts to understand how underprivileged populations, in China and elsewhere, gained significant ground on workers in core countries.

On the other hand, the modernist paradigm should recognize that it was those workers furthest from the epicenter of the global financial crisis, less-skilled low-wage workers, that the ensuing recession hit hardest in terms of wage growth. To further complicate matters, wages in high-income countries rebounded nicely and were higher in 2012 than in 2006 even as unemployment rolls got longer. We know that national institutions manipulate competition within countries—economists focus on how such intervention mars the efficient allocation of resources. These same institutions also protect certain workers and employers from global competition while intensifying it among others.

The logic is similar to that employed by Adam Smith. For Smith (1976 [1776], Book I, 133), in regards to the craft system of his era: "[t]he intention [of such] regulations is to restrain the competition to a much smaller number that might otherwise be disposed to enter into the trade. The limitation of the number of apprentices restrains it directly. A long term of apprenticeship restrains it more indirectly, but as effectually, by increasing the expence of education." Skill was more than a technical capacity that made a worker more productive, and thus more competitive. It was a mechanism for regulating competition, disavowing categorically the "unskilled."

Fundamentally at issue are global definitions of "skill." It is at this juncture that ascription of workers in low-wage regions are naturalized. State efforts in rich countries to manage global economic forces—e.g., trade and immigration restrictions—are often explicitly motivated by the need to protect domestic workers from "cheap" foreign labor. These labor supplies are said to be inferior and/or undesirable specifically when engaged in the same activities that can be performed at home.

These perceptions can become self-reinforcing because they prevent workers from competing on equal footing. When Robert Lucas' (1990) explored reasons capital fails to flow from rich to poor countries, his third offering is that capital markets are imperfect. Relative ignorance about international political risk and real human capital, as well as regulations on trade and capital flows, can discourage investment in underprivileged areas. Investors, and social scientists, are reduced to using the subjective assessment of a few human resource professionals to estimate how technical capacity is distributed across 1.5 million workers (in the case of Chinese engineers as portrayed in the McKinsey report).

We cannot directly assess technical capacity, because there are inadequate global institutions for credentialing skill (which are imperfect efforts even on a national scale). Skill, hence, emerges not as the specific technical capacities associated with performing certain tasks, but as a socially constructed, ascribed category that entails a distinction between workers facing lesser or greater competition among their ranks. There is no doubt that technical capacity might vary across countries, however, the common sense perception and institutional arrangements that shape its global allocation are not based on objective measures of skill, but on the socially managed representations of it.

Acknowledgements

This research benefited from feedback we received at the 2013 WSF-PEWS conference at UC Riverside. We would like to thank those responsible for organizing the conference.

References

Arrighi, Giovanni. 1994. *The Long Twentieth Century: Money, Power, and the Origins of Our Times.* London: Verso.

Arrighi, Giovanni, and Jessica Drangel. 1986. The Stratification of the World-Economy: An Exploration of the Semiperipheral Zone. *Review,* X(1): 9–74.

CPB Netherlands Bureau for Economic Policy Research. 2013. World Trade Monitor. URL: http://www.cpb.nl/en/number/cpb-world-trade-monitor-including-march-2013 (accessed May 23, 2013).

Farrell, Diana, Martha Laboissiere, Jaeson Rosenfeld, Sascha Sturze, and Fusayo Umezawa. 2005. *The Emerging Global Labor Market. Part II: The Supply of Offshore Talent in Services.* San Francisco, CA: McKinsey Global Institute.

ILO (International Labour Office). 2010. *Global Wage Report 2010/11: Wage Policies in Times of Crisis.* Geneva: ILO.

Korzeniewicz, Roberto Patricio, and Scott Albrecht. 2012. Thinking Globally about Inequality and Stratification: Wages across the World, 1982 to 2009. *International Journal of Comparative Sociology,* 53: 419–443.

Korzeniewicz, Roberto Patricio, and Timothy Patrick Moran. 1997. World-Economic Trends in the Distribution of Income, 1965–1992. *American Journal of Sociology,* 102: 1000–1039.

Korzeniewicz, Roberto Patricio, Angela Stach, Vrushali Patil, and Timothy Patrick Moran. 2004. Measuring National Income: A Critical Assessment. *Comparative Studies in Society and History,* 46(3): 535–586.

Krueger, Anne 0. 1968. Factor Endowments and Per Capita Income Differences among Countries. *Economic Journal,* 78: 641–659.

Lindert, Peter H. 2000. "Three Centuries of Inequality in Britain and America." In Anthony Barnes Atkinson and Francois Bourguignon (eds.), *Handbook of Income Distribution.* Amsterdam: Elsevier.

Lucas, Robert. 1990. Why Doesn't Capital Flow from Rich to Poor Countries? *The American Economic Review,* 80(2): 92–96.

Milanovic, Branko. 2005. *Worlds Apart: Measuring International and Global Inequality.* Princeton: Princeton University Press.

Smith, Adam. 1976 [1776]. *An Inquiry into the Nature and Causes of the Wealth of Nations.* Chicago: the University of Chicago Press.

Summers, Robert, and Alan Heston. 1988. A New Set of International Comparisons of Real Product and Price Levels: Estimates for 130 Countries, 1950–1985. *Review of Income and Wealth,* 34: 1–25.

UBS. 2000–2012. *Prices and Earnings around the Globe.* Zurich: UBS.

Union Bank of Switzerland. 1971–1997. *Prices and Earnings around the Globe.* Zurich: Union Bank of Switzerland.

Wallerstein, Immanuel. 1996 [1983]. *Historical Capitalism with Capitalist Civilization.* London: Verso.

World Bank. 2011. *World Development Indicators.* URL: http://data.worldbank.org/data-catalog/world-development-indicators (accessed December 27, 2011).

World Bank. 2012. *World Development Indicators.* URL: http://data.worldbank.org/data-catalog/world-development-indicators (accessed September 26, 2012).

Yang, Dennis Tao, Vivian Weijia Chen, and Ryan Monarch. 2010. Rising Wages: Has China Lost its Global Labor Advantage? Discussion Paper, 5008, Institute for the Study of Labor, Bonn, Germany.

Appendix: City/occupation combinations (COC) abbreviations

City	Abbr.	City	Abbr.	City	Abbr.	City	Abbr.
Abu Dhabi	abu	Dubai	dbi	Luxembourg	lux	San Francisco	sfc
Amsterdam	ams	Dublin	dbl	Lyon	lyn	Santiago	san
Athens	ath	Düsseldorf	dus	Madrid	mad	Sao Paulo	sao
Auckland	auk	Frankfurt	fnk	Manama	mna	Seoul	sol
Bangkok	bgk	Geneva	gva	Manila	man	Shanghai	shg
Barcelona	bar	Helsinki	hel	Mexico City	mex	Singapore	sng
Basel	bas	Hong Kong	hgk	Miami	mia	Sofia	sof
Beijing	bjn	Houston	hou	Milan	mil	Stockholm	stk
Beirut	bei	Istanbul	ibl	Montreal	mon	Sydney	syd
Berlin	brl	Jakarta	jka	Moscow	mos	Taipei	tap
Bogota	bog	Jeddah	jed	Mumbai	mub	Tallinn	tal
Bratislav	blv	Johannesburg	joh	Munich	mun	Tehran	ten
Brussels	brs	Karachi	kar	Nairobi	nrb	Tel Aviv	tel
Bucharest	buc	Kiev	kev	New York	nyc	Tokyo	tok
Budapest	bud	Kuala Lumpur	klp	Nicosia	nic	Toronto	tor
Buenos Aires	bsa	Lagos	lag	Oslo	osl	Vienna	vna
Cairo	cai	Lima	lma	Panama	pan	Vilnius	vil
Caracas	car	Lisbon	lis	Paris	par	Warsaw	war
Chicago	chi	Ljubljana	lub	Prague	prg	Zurich	zur
Copenhagen	cop	London	ldn	Riga	rig		
Delhi	dli	Los Angeles	las	Rio de Janeiro	rio		
Doha	dha	Lugano	lug	Rome	rom		

3

Income Inequality and Economic Globalization: A Longitudinal Study of 15 Muslim-Majority Countries (1963–2002)

Tamer ElGindi

Evidence from recent revolutions in the Middle East and their consequences indicates that income inequality—along with other factors—could well affect the stability of nations. Arab countries in specific, and the broader Muslim countries in general, have been under dictatorial regimes for decades, preceded by foreign colonization that greatly helped to shape these countries' futures. Western powers were (and still are) consistently keen to stretch their influence to extract these countries' vast natural resources—either directly or indirectly—in a certain way that resembles a standard core-periphery relationship as explained by world-systems scholars. What are the trends in income inequality in these countries? And how has economic globalization, manifested in trade openness and increased foreign direct investment, affected income inequality? This research utilizes a world-systems approach to unravel some of the underlying complexities of this phenomenon by exploring potential causes for increasing income inequality in 15 Muslim-majority countries during 1963–2002. I estimated different models using fixed-effects regression models on an internal development model and world-systems indicators. Results showed that both trade openness and foreign direct investment have robust positive effects on income inequality, while other economic/social/political variables did not show the same robust effects. These findings add to previous literature on globalization's effects on income inequality and warrant policymakers to fully integrate income inequality as a major factor in their development plans.

Introduction

The worldwide debate over income inequality generates controversial results: Neoclassical economists argue that income inequality between nations is converging, and world-systems theorists argue that it is diverging. However, both groups agree that *within-nation* income inequality has increased in the last two decades. Although research on both between- and within-nation income inequality consistently produces vast amounts of literature, this research focuses only on *within-nation* income inequality. Specifically, this chapter aims to unravel some of the complexities underlying the increasing within-nation income inequality by exploring some potential causes in 15 Muslim-majority countries during 1963–2002. Using a world-systems perspective, which emphasizes the importance of the world as the unit of analysis, this chapter analyzes both internal as well as external factors contributing to income inequality, and presents the first longitudinal cross-national analysis of possible factors leading to income inequalities for the designated countries and time frame.

Various recent indicators show a disturbing concentration of wealth in a small percentage of the world's population. Dicken (2011) indicated that 20 percent of the world's population residing in the highly developed countries possesses about 80 percent of world income, trade, investment, and communication technology, while 20 percent of the world's population living in poor countries owns only around one percent. Moreover, McMichael (2012) noted that this increasing gap has left over one billion people in chronic hunger. Within developing countries, income inequality is the highest in Latin American countries, more equitable in East Asian countries (Korzeniewicz and Moran, 2009), and somewhere in between in the Middle East and North African countries. However, generally speaking, income inequality is more common today and more countries have higher Gini coefficients than in the 1980s, according to the United Nations Human Development Reports (UNDP Human Development Report Office, 2010).

Among the approximately 49 Muslim-majority countries in Africa and Asia, most have plentiful natural resources, particularly oil and natural gas, along with other minerals as seen in the Gulf countries, North African countries, and other Asian countries. Although a study on this whole set of countries would be interesting, there are several limitations. First, Gulf countries with huge oil revenues and relatively small populations act as outliers that could bias the results. Second, data are limited because income inequality indicators are largely unavailable or unreliable for most of these countries. Therefore, I chose those countries that represent various levels of development, have some common background, and for which income inequality data were available.[1]

The 15 countries investigated are resource-rich, predominantly Muslim countries with similar colonial histories. Using the United Nations Human Development Index (HDI)[2] for 2011, four of them are located within high HDI (Iran, Malaysia, Tunisia, and Turkey), seven are located within medium HDI (Algeria, Egypt, Indonesia, Iraq, Jordan, Morocco, and Syria), and four are located within low HDI (Bangladesh, Eritrea, Nigeria, and Pakistan). With the exception of Iran and Turkey, all other countries have been victims of foreign colonization starting in the nineteenth century (or before) and extending almost until the mid-twentieth century.

---

1   The 15 countries chosen here represent almost 75 percent of the total population of all 49 Muslim-majority countries.

2   The Human Development Index was developed to countervail the prominent dogma at that time which suppressed development mainly in economic advances while neglecting other important development indicators. The HDI focuses more on human well-being along with economic advances. Thus, it consists of three basic components: (1) life expectancy, (2) an education index, and (3) Gross National Income (GNI) per capita.

However, all gained their independence through worldwide nationalist movements in the 1950s and the 1960s. The significance of this research lies in its focus on countries that have not received much attention in quantitative studies within cross-national research. In fact, according to Korzeniewicz and Moran (2009), most of the cross-national research has focused on wealthy countries such as the European Union (EU) and those among the Organization for Economic Cooperation and Development (OECD), which represent a small percentage of the world's population. Further, Muslim-majority countries comprise approximately one-quarter of the world's population, a significant proportion globally.

A closer look at these countries reveals, on average, increasing income inequality throughout the mid-1960s through the early 2000s, as shown in the Gini coefficients depicted in Figure 1. The average Gini in 1970 was 41, increasing to 46 in 2000. Most of these countries gained independence during the 1950s and 1960s, when their nationalist policies were geared towards socialism, which helped to reduce income inequalities to some extent, or at least prevent them from increasing.[3] But at the end of this stage, income inequality began to rise as oil prices collapsed in the early 1980s[4] and globalization increased along with the aggressive adoption of neoliberal policies throughout the world. Although in some cases East Asian countries were able to mitigate income inequality through investments in human capital, thereby improving education along with land and asset reforms in the 1950s and 1960s (Korzeniewicz and Moran, 2009), Arab countries that were heavily dependent on fossil fuels tended to underinvest in their human capital, given the plunder of revenues they received from high oil prices in the early 1970s.[5] Those countries' relatively vast natural resources also made them a target for foreign colonization that most likely reinforced increasing income inequalities, as will be discussed later.

The major concerns with rising income inequality lie in the potential consequences, which Nel (2008) summarized in the following points. First, as economic research describes, high levels of income inequality depress economic growth. Second, increased polarization breaks social cohesion between the different classes of a society. Third, poorer classes have highly restricted access to financial and other resources. Fourth, and most important, violence and civil conflicts could result, as seen in the recent instability and revolutions in the Middle East.

Income inequality, a popular topic for some time, has attracted more attention, manifested in greater trade openness and foreign direct investment, especially as

---

3   Nationalization, land reforms, free public education along with other measures helped reduce income inequality as some evidence suggests.

4   More than half of these countries depend tremendously on fossil fuels for their energy consumption such that their fossil fuel dependence as a percentage of GDP was as high as 99 percent compared with a world average of 80 percent in 2002.

5   Underinvestment here refers to the *quality* of services offered to their populations rather than increases in *aggregate* numbers, as explained later.

Figure 1: Gini coefficients for the 15 countries, 1963–2002

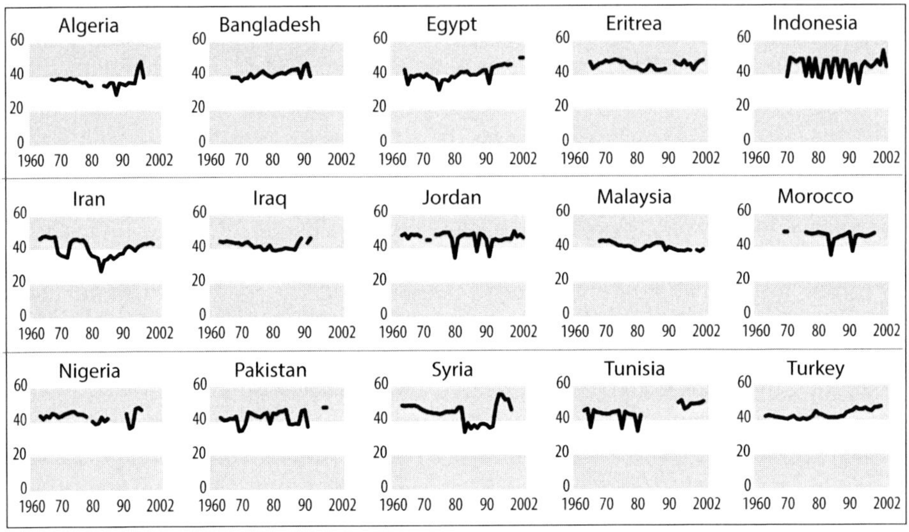

Sources: See Appendix A.

the pace of economic globalization has quickened since the early 1980s. The results of economic globalization and broader economic development on income inequality have been quite controversial, generating mixed results depending on the countries and operational variables under investigation. This research adds to the world-systems literature through the investigation of a new set of countries. Finally, this research examines various internal and external factors to offer a fresh explanation on the topic of within-nation income inequality in the context of Muslim-majority countries.

Literature review

The complex relationship between income inequality and its various potential causes forces researchers to study it "as a world-historical, highly complex phenomenon rather than as a universal and inevitable transition" (Korzeniewicz and Moran, 2009, 113). Income inequality can be defined as the uneven income distribution within a society present in the concentration of wealth and income within the hands of a small percentage of the whole population.[6] The most widely used measures are

---

6   It is also worth mentioning here that wealth would show even higher inequalities than income alone, but researchers typically measure income inequality because data are more readily available for income than for wealth. However, as Firebaugh (2003) indicated, using income inequality as a proxy for wealth inequality in cross-country regressions should not be a problem

the Theil and Gini indices, which have values ranging from 0 to 100, with lower values implying more equal income distribution.

A strand of research in sociology based on both dependency and world-systems theories that appeared in the late 1960s and early 1970s tried to assess the effects of economic globalization and transnational corporations (TNCs) on income inequality and economic growth. Bornschier et al. (1978) examined the effect of foreign investment and aid on economic growth and income inequality and found that foreign direct investment aggravated income inequality within countries. Firebaugh (1992) challenged their theory, arguing that foreign investment spurs economic growth and that both variables co-vary in a positive manner. However, Firebaugh's discussion was confined mainly to economic growth and did not include the implications of foreign investment on income inequality.

In research linking dependency to inequality, Evans and Timberlake (1980) acknowledged that high levels of income inequality in Third World countries could be attributed to the penetration of TNCs in local markets. They concluded that foreign investment causes higher income inequality and further disrupts the structure of the labor market. Considering Firebaugh's critique, Dixon and Boswell (1996) demonstrated that foreign capital *penetration*—as opposed to foreign investment only— tends to increase income inequality and diminish economic growth.

In their study of 88 countries from 1967 to 1994, Alderson and Nielsen (1999) showed that the stock of foreign direct investment (FDI) had a positive effect on income inequality. In another study of 16 OECD countries, Alderson and Nielsen (2002) concluded that the outflow of direct investment had a positive effect on income inequality. They also argued that southern imports to OECD countries had a similar positive effect on income inequality, which can be explained by the reduction of demand for low-skilled labor in OECD countries. Finally, in a study of central and east European states during 1990–2000, Bandelj and Mahutga (2010) attributed some of the variation in income inequalities to neoliberal practices, such as privatization and foreign investment that fluctuated in these countries after the fall of the Soviet Union.

Most of sociological research regresses a measure of income inequality on economic growth along with other development indicators, typically known as the internal development model. To assess external influences, other factors such as the stock of foreign investment and a proxy for trade openness are added.[7] Finally, some research also includes a measure for political structure, either using a dummy vari-

---

since "both measures of distribution generally vary together in cross-sections" (Aghion et al. 1999, 1617–1618).

7   Babones and Vonada (2009) used three different measures to assess trade openness: (1) imports as a percent of GDP, (2) exports as a percent of GDP, and (3) trade as a percent of GDP.

able or some scale to indicate the degree to which a nation is geared towards democratic or autocratic regimes.

This research builds on previous sociological research and integrates other variables pertinent to world-systems theory that might explain income inequality in the specific countries studied. Thus, the model first incorporates the internal development model, and then examines several other independent variables that I refer to as world-systems indicators, a term used by Beer and Boswell (2002). These indicators are (1) economic globalization as manifested in trade openness and foreign direct investment, (2) natural resource dependency, and (3) political structure. In addition, this study incorporates two additional control variables—colonization and a regional dummy.[8]

The baseline internal development model

In addition to the *external* factors that influence income inequality, *internal* factors also play a role. Economist Simon Kuznets (1955) explained the inverted U-curve describing the relationship between economic growth and income inequality as follows: At earlier stages of development, income inequality increases as labor moves from agriculture (typically low-paid) to the manufacturing (higher-paid) sector. This wage disparity between the agricultural and nonagricultural sectors produces sector dualism. As industrialization spreads, more people move to urban areas and join the labor force, thereby balancing the wage level in the industrial sector and decreasing income inequalities.

Nielsen (1994), influenced by Kuznets' (1955) earlier explanation, outlined four core variables to describe the relationship between economic growth and income inequality: (1) sector dualism, (2) percentage of the labor force in agriculture and agriculture as a percent of Gross Domestic Product (GDP), (3) secondary school enrollment, and (4) natural rate of population growth. Sector dualism is calculated as $| p - L |$, where p is the percentage of labor force in agriculture and L is the agriculture's share of GDP.[9] The spread of education plays a vital role in explaining the internal development model. The more access people have to education, the higher their skills, and in turn, the higher their wages. Consequently, income inequalities are reduced when more people receive education. Further, population growth may create a surplus of young labor, which tends to drive down wages, widening income disparities. A variable indicating population growth rates was included in the model

---

8   Both control variables are dummy variables. Colonization is a dummy variable indicating whether the country has been a former colony or not, whereas the regional dummy is a dummy variable indicating the geographical location of the country (Africa or Asia).

9   Due to lack of data regarding sector dualism variables for these countries, this variable has not been included; rather, agriculture's share of GDP has been included, which should offer a fair explanation of the shift from the agricultural to the manufacturing sector.

to capture this effect. In sum, higher increases in population can be expected to lead to widening income disparities.

World-systems indicators

Economic globalization

Economic globalization is probably the most widely debated factor in income inequality because of the changes arising since the early 1980s with the neoliberal agenda. Two major contributing factors to economic globalization are trade openness and foreign direct investment. Though globalization can be defined in various ways, I prefer Wallerstein's (2004, 86) definition: "the opening of all frontiers to the free flow of goods and capital (but not of labor)." But globalization's link to income inequality is not as straightforward as some people would like to believe, and measuring its effect on inequality is quite difficult. Amin (2004, 218) explained this phenomenon by saying:

> Establishing a link between globalization and inequality is fraught with difficulty, not only because of how globalization is defined and how inequality is measured, but also because the entanglements between globalization forces and "domestic" trends are not that easy to separate out . . . However, there is sufficient evidence to conclude that contemporary processes of globalization have been accompanied by a rise in global inequality and vulnerability.

Two contending views emerge when discussing globalization. The first view, held mainly among world-systems scholars and pioneered by Wallerstein, Arrighi, and others, argues that global capitalism has been ongoing for centuries, and therefore, is not really a *new* phenomenon. In fact, Wallerstein (1974) dated global capitalism back to the rise of the modern world economy in Europe, referred to as the long sixteenth century (1450–1640). The second view is held by proponents of globalization who view it as a recent phenomenon stretching back almost three decades with the adoption of neoliberal policies in both the United States and the United Kingdom and then most of the world. Although I agree with world-systems scholars, there are nonetheless *qualitative* changes that occurred in the contemporary world economy that tend to differ from earlier times as Dicken (2011) indicated. He stated that both the "*nature* and the *degree* of interconnection in the [current] world economy" has varied dramatically from earlier times especially with advances in information technology and the compression of time and space (Dicken, 2011, 6).

Although tempting in some cases, drawing causal inferences between globalization and income inequality might not be straightforward, as Babones and Vonada (2009) explained. They argued that this unidirectional argument might draw strong support within the realm of public policy, but within the academic field results are far from settled. Previous research tended to focus on one of the two major aspects of economic globalization; however, this research assesses the effects of both aspects—trade openness and foreign direct investment—on income inequality using separate models, as explained in the next section.

Trade openness

Trade has been a controversial issue since the inception of the General Agreement on Tariffs and Trade (GATT), and later the World Trade Organization (WTO), among developed and developing countries.[10] As with the two contending views on globalization, two views emerge regarding the merits of free trade. Pro-globalizers argue that countries should specialize in products for which they possess an abundant factor of production (Heckscher-Ohlin-Samuelson Theory), thereby developing a comparative advantage in certain products, as British political economist David Ricardo advised. Further, they argue that the processes of the world factory, global commodity chains, and the new international division of labor (NIDL) confirm the fact that different tasks are assigned to different countries based on their specialties and comparative advantages. Those espousing the other view of globalization see this relationship as a hierarchical and ordered stratification that exemplifies power relationships between core and peripheral countries, which in turn generates different levels of economic growth and development (Mahutga and Smith, 2011). Core countries tend to specialize in more capital-intensive goods while peripheral countries specialize in labor-intensive ones.

In theory, the most direct effect of trade liberalization on income inequality is the revenue loss accruing to governments because of tariff reductions. Governments are obliged to cut their expenditures for various items, which in many cases leads to reductions in budget allocations for education, health, housing, and other essential services. As Chang (2008) indicated, tariffs are an easier method to generate revenues than taxes because most poor countries lack efficient tax collection capabilities. Empirically, results have been controversial. For example, a report by the International Monetary Fund (IMF) argued that trade globalization has had an "equalizing impact" (IMF, 2007, 154). Yet, there is no general consensus regarding this fact and it remains debatable within the academic field. Milanovic (2005) and Ravallion (2001) concluded that openness has been associated with higher inequality in poor countries and lower inequality in rich countries. Savvides (1998) also reported similar results for less developed countries. His analysis showed that less developed countries with more open economies have experienced higher income inequalities during the late 1980s. Further, in their study of 65 developing countries

---

10   The GATT was initially signed in 1943 as an agreement to regulate international trade and was superseded by the WTO in 1995.

during the period 1980–1999, Meschi and Vivarelli (2009) reported that developing countries that traded with high-income countries experienced a worsened internal income distribution.

However, Babones and Vonada (2009) found no robustly significant relationship between trade openness and income inequality in their study of a wide panel of countries for the years 1975, 1985, and 1995. Further, Dollar and Kraay (2002) argued that openness had no significant effect on inequality levels. In their study of 69 countries during 1960–1996, Reuveny and Li (2003) concluded that trade in fact reduces income inequality. Clearly, results are controversial and are context-dependent on both the countries and the time under investigation.

For this investigation, the majority of the countries were not developed industrially when globalization was expanding in the early 1980s; therefore, I argue that, on average, their domestic industries were not able to withstand international competition and have been negatively affected. Further, these countries' national budgets have been burdened by the decrease in their governments' tariffs. Therefore, a positive relationship between trade openness and income inequality can be expected.

Foreign direct investment

Neoliberals argue that foreign capital is good for economies because it brings money, skills, and technology among other benefits to host countries, which helps these economies to grow and develop their productive capacities. However, as Chang (2008) indicated, foreign investment also has limitations and problems. He argued that, although these investments bring foreign currency to host countries, they also might generate burdensome demand for foreign currency.[11] Further, he added that FDI might lead to a destruction of domestic industries by eliminating them from competition. In addition to harming the domestic economy, Kentor (2001) explained how increasing FDI could lead to income disparities. First, foreign investment helps to establish (or restore) a new small upper class that typically earns higher salaries than their counterparts in the public sector. Second, much of the revenues accruing to companies is repatriated abroad rather than reinvested in the domestic economy. Third, national governments establish a business climate suitable to foreign investors that might act to impede domestic labor's attaining more benefits.

During the last three decades, many studies using data for a wide range of countries demonstrated that foreign investment is associated with higher income inequalities. For example, earlier studies such as Bornschier et al. (1978) showed that foreign investment increases income inequalities within countries. Further, Portes

---

11   Additional demand could be in the sort of importing capital equipment or contracting for foreign loans (Chang, 2008).

(1976) and Chase-Dunn (1998) demonstrated that TNCs have led to increasing income disparities within developing countries. Evans and Timberlake (1980) revealed that increasing income inequality is linked to foreign capital dependence in poor countries, while Dixon and Boswell (1996) emphasized that it is foreign capital *penetration* that fosters income inequality. Recently, in their study of central and eastern European states, Mahutga and Bandelj (2008) and Bandelj and Mahutga (2010) explained that increasing foreign investment is associated with increasing income inequality.

The larger portion of FDI in all these countries is concentrated in extractive industries, mainly oil, natural gas, and mining. In extractive industries, governments possess stronger negotiation power with TNCs because, as Dicken (2011) indicated, the bargaining balance tilts more towards the states after TNCs make huge initial investments. Therefore, states should be able to accomplish better agreements, which could translate into more revenues for other services. This bargaining power is seen less often in fast moving technologies in which TNCs can easily shift their operations from one country to another. Among the states in this study, a positive association between foreign investment and income inequality can be expected because of corruption in some of them, along with their weak presence in the face of huge TNCs.[12]

Natural resource dependency

The plethora of natural resources in many countries can act as a double-edged sword, both a blessing and a curse.[13] Resource-rich countries tend to depend more on their *physical* resources while underinvesting in their *human* resources, and resource-poor countries do just the opposite. For example, Japan and South Korea have paid more attention to their education systems and enhancement of human capital in compensation for their scarce physical resources. Possible corruption arises from natural resources, when government officials take sides with TNCs, and thus, income inequality might be associated with more resource-rich countries. In their study of Latin American countries, Leamer et al. (1999) found relatively high inequality levels associated with resource-rich countries especially during the initial stages in their development path. Further, Gylfason and Zoega (2002) showed theoretically, as well as empirically, that increased dependence on natural resourc-

---

12   In addition, corruption among some (or maybe many) government officials in these "sensitive" industries (oil, gas, and mining) further exacerbates loss of revenues that could accrue to the public if correctly utilized and redistributed in an efficient manner.

13   There is a huge literature on "resource curse" and how abundance of natural resources could lead to slower economic growth rates as well as increased political corruption and violent conflicts.

es tends to be associated with less economic growth and greater inequality across countries.

Although most of the literature on natural resource dependency seems geared more towards the effect on economic growth, political structures, and internal conflicts, an interesting link also might be found between natural resource dependency and income inequality, because most of the countries in this study have huge ratios of natural resource dependency as a percent of GDP. According to the World Bank Development Indicators in 2002, the average value for natural resource dependency for the 15 countries was 16 percent compared with two percent for the whole world.[14] More importantly, resource-rich countries are usually potential targets for foreign colonization, as explained later. The argument here is that countries that are highly dependent on natural resources are prone to higher income disparities.

Political structure

The political structure, rather than the political regime *per se*, is considered a determinant of income inequality. Rather than examining this structure in a rather simplistic way by dividing political regimes into either democratic or autocratic regimes, this study utilized a scale index consisting of various indicators, including, but not limited to, political participation, political competition, and civil liberties. Nel (2008) adopted a similar approach in his study of developing countries when assessing the relationship between income inequality and political factors.

The basic and well-known theory about the relation between political structure and income inequality goes as follows: In countries with large income inequalities, people typically vote for more redistribution policies such as transfer payments or higher taxes on the rich. However, in the absence of a democracy, this voting process is not applicable, and even if it exists *theoretically*, voting might be obstructed by local elites (through lobbying or the buying of votes of legislators) who hold the power and are able to formulate policies that benefit them at the expense of the majority (Barro, 2000). Although some research indicated a positive relationship between equality and democratic societies (Persson and Tabellini, 1994; Reuveny and Li, 2003), other studies such as Nel (2008) found that regime change *per se* is not a significant predictor for subsequent inequality.

One important aspect of political structure that needs further investigation, and is not explicitly addressed in this research, is the interaction between local elites and transnational capitalist classes. Thus, in addition to the internal factors, the relation between economic class elites in periphery countries with their counterparts in core countries shapes development policies within the peripheral countries and the re-

---

14   Natural resource dependency is measured as the sum of all rents from oil, natural gas, coal (hard and soft), minerals, and forest rents as a percent of GDP.

sulting income (in)equalities. As Chase-Dunn and Rubinson (1977) explained when discussing power-block formation in peripheral countries, economic elites within these countries could act as suppressors, or at least try to limit nationalist development policies that favor domestic manufacturing production. Similarly, Acemoglu and Robinson (2006, 115) stated: "Political elites will block beneficial economic and institutional change when they are afraid that these changes will destabilize the existing system and make it more likely that they will lose political power and future rents."

Additional controls: Colonization and a regional dummy

With the exception of Iran and Turkey, the remaining 13 countries in this study were British, French, Italian, or Dutch colonies until they gained independence beginning in the early 1950s. Previously colonized countries are more prone to suffer from larger income inequalities, according to Korzeniewicz and Moran (2009). They explained that European colonizers institutionalized certain arrangements in their colonized countries that enabled them to concentrate wealth and power within the elite class and exclude large amounts of the population. Moreover, as Nel (2008) indicated, colonizers keen on securing the factor endowments and natural resources in these countries established power within a small circle from within, along with local networks comprised of local elites. Finally, in his study of 139 countries during 1947–1998, Angeles (2006) concluded that colonialism explains a major part of the variation in income inequality across countries. Further, considering the discrepancy between policies adopted in Asian countries and those in African countries to deal with income inequality, this study included a regional dummy to address whether location has a significant impact on subsequent inequality.

Data and methods

Sample

The dataset included in this research comprises 15 countries—Algeria, Bangladesh, Egypt, Eritrea, Indonesia, Iran, Iraq, Jordan, Malaysia, Morocco, Nigeria, Pakistan, Syria, Tunisia, and Turkey—for the period 1963 to 2002. Despite the fact that these countries differ in level of development, they share some common characteristics, such as Muslim-majority populations and similar government-adopted development paths since gaining their independence. Further, most of these countries are quite rich in natural resources, which might have made them desirable targets for foreign colonization. The time frame also includes various developmental modes, such as more socialist regimes in the 1950s and 1960s to more liberal and open economies from the 1970s onward.

More importantly, these countries also represent major geopolitical interests for Western countries because of their locations and their rich natural resources. Further, the recent revolutions in the Middle East, specifically in some of these countries (Tunisia, Egypt, Libya, and the continuous struggle in Syria), and the instability accruing from this unrest augment these countries' importance. Moreover, many in the West fear that the Islamist movements in these countries could threaten their economic and geopolitical interests in this region of the world.

Similar to previous inequality studies (Alderson and Nielsen, 1999; 2002; Mahutga and Bandelj, 2008; Bandelj and Mahutga, 2010), this research utilized an unbalanced panel structure, implying that countries contribute with different numbers of observations over time.[15] Panel data are commonly used to deal with unobservables that plague causal inferences, as Halaby (2004) indicated.[16]

Pooled cross-section time series analysis

With data being more available in recent years in the field of inequality, panel data have been tested to estimate the effects of various determinants of income inequality. As opposed to cross-section data (previously more prevalent), panel data have various benefits. Wooldridge (2009) indicated that panel data allow control for unobserved characteristics relevant to the specific group under study. Further, since panel data are longitudinal, dynamic processes can be studied, which in turn enables more *solid* causal inferences to be drawn, considering that the model is correctly specified and the three criteria for causality are satisfied.[17] Issues that are typically hidden in cross-sectional data can be revealed. Finally, as Wooldridge (2009) emphasized, panel data allow scholars to study the effects of lags in behavior that might result from various policy decisions.

To overcome the threat of heterogeneity bias and to control for unobserved time-invariant factors, researchers have utilized either fixed-effects models (FEM) or random-effects models (REM).[18] As Wooldridge (2009) discussed, the key issue in determining which model to use has to do with whether we can assume that unobserved time-invariant factors are uncorrelated with *all* explanatory variables. As a result, I chose to use FEM for a couple of reasons: First, results of the Hausman test were favorable to FEM; second, one could assume that various time-invariant

---

15 See Appendix A for a list of countries/observations.

16 As Halaby (2004) indicated, there are two types of unobservables that could be problematic: (a) time-invariant unit-specific unobservables and (b) time-varying unit-specific unobservables.

17 In order to draw causal inferences, three main criteria must be satisfied: (1) association, (2) time order, and (3) elimination of alternative explanation (non-spuriousness).

18 Alderson and Nielsen (1995; 1997; 1999; 2002), and Bandelj and Mahutga (2010) used REM while Mahutga and Bandelj (2008) used FEM.

factors (geographical location, historical background, and so on) could well be correlated with some of the explanatory variables, biasing results for REM; third, FEM is a much more conservative and convincing tool for policy analysis, as Wooldridge (2009) indicated; finally, this research focuses on *within-nation* inequality, which is better described by FEM. However, since FEM wipes out dummy variables from the regression, I also estimated Prais-Winsten coefficients with Panel Corrected Standard Errors (PCSE) to incorporate the colonization and regional dummies, as Beck and Katz (1995) advised.

Additionally, the idiosyncratic error should be uncorrelated with the explanatory variables across all time periods, as Wooldridge (2009) explained. Therefore, the models estimated here were adjusted for first-order autoregressive (AR1) processes. I analyzed the data using Stata 12.1. Various diagnostic tests were conducted to assess the correct specification of the model along with the possible existence of any outliers or influential observations. Both tests showed that the full model (including all independent variables) was correctly specified and that there were no significant outliers to bias the results.

Dependent variable

The dependent variable used in this analysis was the Gini coefficient. According to Korzeniewicz and Moran (2009), both Theil and Gini indices satisfy the five most highly desired characteristics for inequality indicators.[19] Babones and Alvarez-Rivadulla (2007) outlined the various attempts to compile good quality income inequality data since the first well-known compilation by Deininger and Squire (1996), followed by the Luxemburg Income Study (LIS), the United Nations University's World Institute for Development Economics Research (UNU-WIDER), and other more recent data. However, as Galbraith and Kum (2005, in Babones and Alvarez-Rivadulla, 2007, 6) described, the problem is that the data are "so spotty and inconsistent" that Galbraith and Kum called for using differences in wages as a proxy for nationally measured income inequality. This research used the Estimated Household Income Inequality Dataset (EHII) published by the University of Texas Inequality Project (UTIP), a dataset of 154 counties with nearly 3200 observations during 1963–2002.[20] Compared with all other sources of income inequality data,

---

19   As Korzeniewicz and Moran (2009, 123) indicated, these five highly desired properties for an inequality indicator are: "(1) it is symmetrical; (2) it is income scale-invariant; (3) it is invariant to absolute population levels; (4) it is defined by upper and lower bounds; and (5) it satisfies the Pigou-Dalton principle of transfers (any redistribution from richer to poorer reduces the inequality measure, and vice versa)."

20   The income inequality indicators in the EHII dataset is "based on the relationship between inequality of household incomes, inequality of industrial pay, and other variables" (Galbraith and Kum, 2005, 117).

this dataset is the most complete for the countries under study in the designated time frame.

Independent variables

The independent variables included two sets of indicators: the baseline internal development model and the world-systems indicators. The internal development model includes variables for the agriculture share in GDP, secondary enrollment, and population growth. World-systems indicators include two measures of FDI, three measures of trade openness, a measure of natural resource dependency, and a measure for political structure. In addition, two other control variables discussed earlier were included. Several variables were logged to correct for skew: FDI stock as a percentage of GDP, FDI flow as a percentage of GDP, trade as a percentage of GDP,

Table 1: Variables used in the analysis of income inequality in 15 countries for the period 1963–2002

Variable	Mean	Standard deviation
Dependent variable		
Gini index	42.981	(4.425)
Internal development model		
Agriculture as a % of GDP	19.724	(9.994)
Secondary education	45.715	(21.464)
Population growth	2.455	(0.875)
Economic growth	6.848	(0.845)
World-systems indicators		
Foreign direct investment: stock	2.490	(1.149)
Foreign direct investment: flow	−0.686	(2.239)
Trade openness: trade	3.915	(0.584)
Trade openness: exports	3.086	(0.682)
Trade openness: imports	3.303	(0.568)
Natural resources as a % of GDP	1.744	(1.671)
Polity (from strongly democratic (+10) to strongly autocratic (−10))	−3.344	(5.992)
Colony (1 = country has been a former colony, 0 = country has not been a former colony)	–	–
Africa (1 = country located in Africa, 0 = country outside Africa)	–	–

Notes: Dashes = dummy variable.
Sources: See Appendix A.

exports as a percentage of GDP, imports as a percentage of GDP, and finally, natural resources as a ratio of GDP.

To present a more solid case for causal inference, lagged independent variables were included in the models so that the dependent variable was measured at time *t* and the independent variables were measured at time *t − 1*. This one-year lag was adopted because there was no *a priori* reasoning for a certain time lag, following Bandelj and Mahutga's (2010, 2142) logic. Although using a wider time window would strengthen the causal inference and better capture dynamic processes, the number of observations would decrease tremendously, leading to inaccurate results.

In sum, the models presented here are for lagged independent variables and corrected for first-order autoregressive processes (AR1). Table 1 lists all independent variables and statistical summaries. Appendix A lists their descriptions and their sources and Appendix B presents correlation coefficients. Finally, I estimated Prais-Winsten coefficients with PCSE (Table 3) to incorporate dummy variables not included in the fixed-effects models.

Results

Results for the fixed-effects regression models are presented in Table 2 while results from the panel-corrected standard errors are presented in Table 3.[21] As shown, nine models examined the various hypotheses. Models (1) and (2) assessed the relationship between economic growth and income inequality along with the inverted U-curve, and Model (3) the internal development model. The remainder—Model (4) through Model (9)—tested the world-systems indicators.

The inverted U-curve

Model (1) addresses the relationship between economic growth and income inequality. The coefficient for GDP per capita was positive and highly significant, indicating how higher economic growth rates are associated with higher income inequalities. This positive sign reinforced the conditions seen in countries experiencing revolutions—relatively high economic growth rates could be accompanied by increasing income inequality levels. Model (2) explains income inequality through the inclusion of real GDP per capita and its squared term to examine the inverted U-curve of income inequality that Kuznets (1955) described. The coefficient for GDP per capita was positive and highly significant, whereas the coefficient for its squared term was negative and highly significant affirming Kuznets inverted U-curve hypothesis.

---

21   Since the focus of this research is on fixed-effects models, I will only emphasize results from panel corrected standard errors when I include dummy variables, namely the colonization and Africa dummies.

Table 2: Unstandardized coefficients from fixed-effects regression models of income inequality on world-systems indicators and internal development model in 15 countries, 1963–2002

Dependent variable: Gini	1	2	3	4	5	6	7	8	9
GDP/capita (log)	14.78***	28.57***							
	(12.91)	(7.45)							
GDP/capita (log)^2		−3.856***							
		(−3.77)							
Agriculture (% of GDP)			−2.615**	−1.743	−1.856	−2.017	1.086	1.036	1.07
			(−3.09)	(−1.20)	(−1.27)	(−1.32)	(1.36)	(1.29)	(1.32)
Secondary education			3.064***	4.56***	4.06**	4.158**	2.389***	2.405***	2.328**
			(3.85)	(3.47)	(2.96)	(2.93)	(3.62)	(3.52)	(3.24)
Population growth			1.303*	0.487	0.479	0.478	0.312	0.258	0.273
			(2.49)	(1.03)	(1.00)	(0.99)	(0.69)	(0.57)	(0.59)
FDI Stock (% of GDP)				20.77***	20.97***	20.97***			
				(7.94)	(7.80)	(7.73)			
Nat. resources (% of GDP)					−1.032	−1.019		0.023	0.012
					(−0.57)	(−0.56)		(0.02)	(0.01)
Polity						−0.063			0.039
						(−0.36)			(0.35)
Trade (% of GDP)							21.64***	21.14***	21.13***
							(10.01)	(9.60)	(9.58)
Constant	−1.21	−7.778***	41.67***	21.89***	22.28***	22.05***	4.798*	5.831*	5.953*
	(−0.66)	(−3.85)	(50.62)	(15.09)	(15.01)	(14.80)	(2.08)	(2.53)	(2.57)
n	396	396	247	149	147	147	244	242	242
R^2	0.304	0.329	0.091	0.408	0.401	0.402	0.373	0.370	0.371

Notes: t-statistics in parentheses, * p<0.05, ** p<0.01, *** p<0.001.
Sources: See Appendix A.

Internal development model

In the internal development model [Model (3)], three variables were significant.[22] First, agriculture as a percent of GDP had a negative sign, indicating that as the agricultural sector increases—a sector with more equal pay—income inequality decreases, a result that aligns with Kuznets' hypothesis. However, subsequent models showed a change in sign when trade instead of FDI was introduced, and the coefficient for agriculture also became insignificant, which might be due to relatively high collinearity between trade and agriculture coefficients. Secondary education

---

22   Since agriculture as a percent of GDP and secondary enrollment are highly correlated, both variables were orthogonalized, following Draper and Smith (1981).

Table 3: Unstandardized coefficients form panel corrected standard errors of income inequality on world-systems indicators and internal development model in 15 countries, 1963–2002

Dependent variable: Gini	1	2	3	4	5	6	7	8	9	10	11
GDP/capita (log)	−0.549	9.418									
	(−0.53)	(0.59)									
GDP/capita (log)^2		−1.716									
		(−0.64)									
Agriculture (% of GDP)			−0.056	0.696	1.328*	1.370*	1.619**	0.305	0.659	0.709	0.665
			(−0.13)	(1.14)	(2.21)	(2.33)	(2.65)	(0.63)	(1.46)	(1.59)	(1.20)
Secondary education			0.600	0.226	0.506	0.581	0.866	0.589	0.399	0.468	0.416
			(1.38)	(0.40)	(0.96)	(1.10)	(1.44)	(1.38)	(1.05)	(1.17)	(0.97)
Population growth			−0.259	−0.034	−0.299	−0.413	−0.183	−0.309	−0.525	−0.608	−0.689
			(−0.60)	(−0.08)	(−0.75)	(−1.04)	(−0.41)	(−0.69)	(−1.18)	(−1.36)	(−1.39)
FDI stock (% of GDP)				3.569***	3.181**	3.312***	2.920*				
				(3.42)	(3.20)	(3.40)	(2.39)				
Nat. resources (% of GDP)					−2.528***	−2.608***	−2.906***		−1.837**	−1.950**	−1.964**
					(−3.92)	(−4.14)	(−4.15)		(−3.00)	(−3.11)	(−3.15)
Polity						−0.097	−0.049			−0.059	−0.07
						(−1.26)	(−0.48)			(−0.90)	(−0.94)
Trade (% of GDP)								2.096	3.12*	3.17*	3.132
								(1.27)	(2.00)	(2.06)	(1.60)
Colony							−0.875				0.115
							(−0.78)				(0.10)
Africa							1.942				−0.433
							(1.54)				(−0.35)
Constant	44.68***	30.43	43.92***	40.08***	42.53***	42.38***	42.46***	40.33***	40.18***	40.14***	40.42***
	(14.42)	(1.32)	(35.79)	(25.86)	(26.97)	(27.46)	(28.70)	(13.99)	(15.13)	(15.25)	(−12.66)
n	410	410	260	161	159	159	159	257	255	255	255
R^2	0.618	0.618	0.682	0.767	0.755	0.747	0.749	0.685	0.671	0.663	0.655

Notes: t-statistics in parentheses, * p<0.05, ** p<0.01, *** p<0.001.
Sources: See Appendix A.

enrollment was positive and highly significant in all the different models. Although contrary to the expectation that more access to education would decrease inequality, this positive association might have an explanation: Despite increased enrollment in all countries during the last four decades, the *quality* of the service offered remains an issue. Finally, the coefficient for population growth is positive and significant, confirming that a higher population leads to excess in labor supply and, in turn, suppresses wages and increases income inequality. However, this correlation does not remain significant across all models, though the sign is consistent.

World-systems indicators

Model (4) introduced FDI, including FDI stock as a percentage of GDP. As expected, FDI had a positive and highly significant effect on income inequality, confirming previous studies.[23]

Model (5) added natural resources as a ratio of GDP, and the coefficient had a negative and insignificant effect on income inequality, quite contrary to expectations. The negative sign implies that countries' dependence on natural resources might not be associated with increasing inequality. However, the negative sign was not consistent throughout the models and, in fact, was positive when trade was introduced. Therefore, a clear direction for this specific variable cannot be identified.

Model (6) added political structure to the model. The coefficient was negative and insignificant, implying no clear effects of the political structure on income inequality.

Model (7) introduced trade as a ratio of GDP instead of FDI stock, and Models (8) and (9) added variables of natural resources as a ratio of GDP and political structure, along with the trade variable. Trade as a ratio of GDP was positive and highly significant in all models, implying a strong association between economic openness and higher income inequalities.[24] The coefficient for natural resources as a percent of GDP was positive and insignificant, whereas political structure was now positive but still insignificant. Finally, models that included FDI stock as a ratio of GDP explained a slightly higher variation in income inequality than their counterpart with trade as a ratio of GDP, seen in the higher R-squared in the earlier model. Prais-Winsten coefficients were estimated with PCSE to incorporate both dummy variables. However, both coefficients revealed insignificant outcomes (See Table 3).

Discussion and conclusion

Generally, within-nation income inequality has been increasing, but the factors causing, or at least influencing, this increase are far from settled. Economic globalization, manifested mainly in increased FDI and trade openness, is considered to have aggravated income inequality in the last two to three decades, and these results confirm this belief. In this study, the positive and highly significant coefficients for both the FDI measures and the trade measures imply a positive association between

---

23   I also ran models using FDI flows as a ratio of GDP (rather than stock), and the coefficient was always positive and significant.

24   Besides trade as a ratio of GDP, I also conducted models using both exports and imports separately as a ratio of GDP, and both ratios also showed some positive and significant results. However, when coefficients for trade and agriculture as a percent of GDP are orthogonalized due to possible high collinearity, the coefficient for trade is no longer significant despite remaining positive.

these variables and deepening income inequalities. Therefore, developing countries should aim for a mixture of domestic and foreign investment while combating the negative consequences accruing from foreign capital penetration, as Dixon and Boswell (1996) noted. Further, as Chang (2008) indicated, governments in developing countries need to be selectively strategic about the industries in which they allow foreign investment, while at the same time *possibly* banning it in other industries.[25]

Although trade definitely benefits developing countries, it also increases their reliance on imports while decreasing governments' revenues through reduction in tariffs. Therefore, it is fair to say that governments have incurred the bigger portion of these losses, while private businesses (TNCs specifically) have been able to capitalize on different trade agreements and tariff reductions to increase their revenues. In sum, although both FDI and trade openness tend to explain a huge part of the variation seen in income inequality, FDI tends to explain a bigger portion.

The internal development model along with real GDP per capita and its square term are quite significant in some of these models, implying that both *external* as well as *internal* factors have shaped income inequality in recent decades.[26] The positive association between education enrollment rates and income inequality can be explained by the continuous deterioration of education services in these countries, resulting in increases in enrollment rates but simultaneously higher income disparities. Returns on investments in free public education initiated in the early times after independence have not been good for most of these countries. A major focus for policymakers should be on improvements in the *nature* of education (critical and creative thinking) rather than only on increased enrollment rates *per se*.

The variable for political structure did not reveal any significant results throughout the different models. Perhaps a better operational variable that would reflect the interconnectedness between local elites in these countries with their transnational counterparts would reveal more significant and interesting results. In general, colonization and the regional dummy showed insignificant results; however, some significance was seen when the lagged independent variables were not used. Colonization had a positive and significant coefficient in some of the models, indicating that countries that were former colonies are prone to higher income inequality in subsequent times. However, the regional dummy—though insignificant—had an unpredicted negative sign, implying that countries located in Africa tend to have less inequality than their counterparts in Asia, which does not fit the empirical evidence that Asian countries, on average, have reduced income inequality during the

---

25   In fact, Chang (2008) explained that all currently developed countries, with few exceptions, have at some time either strictly regulated or even banned FDI in some industries, including Britain, the United States, Japan, South Korea, and Finland, among several others.

26   Further, results are strengthened even more when models are conducted *without* the lagged independent variables showing consistently significant coefficients.

1950s and 1960s through investments in education and other reforms. Future research could be improved with additional controls, such as government expenditures, unemployment rates, and others that were omitted in this analysis because of lack of data for this set of countries.

Results from this research are generally consistent with world-systems theory and research conducted on FDI and trade; that is, economic globalization negatively affects developing countries' economies, specifically, increasing income inequality. This research adds to the literature of globalization by focusing on a new set of countries and adopting a wider time frame than previous studies and also presents a more solid case for drawing causal inferences regarding income inequality. Specifically, when states rely on extractive industries, they are in a relatively stronger bargaining position to negotiate better deals with TNCs and increase their revenues, which could be allocated to essential services. Even more important, despite not *yet* being highly integrated within the global system, most of these countries were negatively affected in some ways from economic globalization, according to these results. These results are an early alert for those countries if they are keen on developing in a way that benefits not only some of their people but the masses.

In addition, future research could focus on shorter time frames for which more data sets are available. Other studies could utilize more dynamic models that capture dynamic processes and deal with violations for strict exogeneity in dynamic panel models such as the Generalized Method of Moments (GMM). Finally, scholars investigating income inequality might find it useful to conduct case studies to delve deeper into specific variables that seem to be country-specific to achieve more reliable and deeper perspectives.

Acknowledgments

I thank my advisor, Professor Luis Suarez-Villa, for his support and input throughout the development of this whole project. Special thanks to Professor David Smith for his insightful comments on earlier drafts and Professor Nina Bandelj for her extensive assistance, and in particular in the quantitative section. Finally, I would like to thank all my colleagues from the global reading group for their generous comments on earlier drafts.

References

Acemoglu, Daron, and James A. Robinson. 2006. Economic Backwardness in Political Perspective. *American Political Science Review,* 100(1): 115–131.

Aghion, Phillipe, Eve Caroli, and Cecilia Garcia-Penalosa. 1999. Inequality and Economic Growth: The Perspective of the New Growth Theories. *Journal of Economic Literature,* 37: 1615–1660.

Alderson, Arthur, and François Nielsen. 1995. Income Inequality, Development, and Dualism: Results from an Unbalanced Cross-National Panel. *American Sociological Association,* 60(5): 674–701.

Alderson, Arthur, and François Nielsen. 1997. The Kuznets Curve and the Great U-Turn: Income Inequality in U.S. Counties, 1970 to 1990. *American Sociological Review,* 62(1): 12–33.

Alderson, Arthur, and François Nielsen. 1999. Inequality, Development and Dependence: A Reconsideration. *American Sociological Review,* 64(4): 606–631.

Alderson, Arthur, and François Nielsen. 2002. Globalization and the Great U-Turn: The Growth of Direct Investment in 16 OECD Countries. *American Journal of Sociology,* 107(5): 1244–1299.

Amin, Ash. 2004. Regulating Economic Globalization. *Transactions of the Institute of British Geographers,* 29: 217–233.

Angeles, Luis. 2006. Income Inequality and Colonialism. *European Economic Review,* 51(5): 1155–1176.

Babones, Salvatore, and Maria Jose Alvarez-Rivadulla. 2007. Standardized Income Inequality Data for Use in Cross-National Research. *Sociological Inquiry,* 77: 3–22.

Babones, Salvatore, and Dorian C. Vonada. 2009. Trade Globalization and National Income Inequality – Are They Related? *Journal of Sociology,* 45(1): 5–30.

Bandelj, Nina, and Matthew C. Mahutga. 2010. How Socio-Economic Change Shapes Income Inequality in Post-Socialist Europe. *Social Forces,* 88(5): 2133–2162.

Barro, Robert J. 2000. Inequality and Growth in a Panel of Countries. *Journal of Economic Growth,* 32: 5–32.

Beck, Nathaniel, and Jonathan N. Katz. 1995. What to Do (and Not to Do) with Time-Series Cross-Section Data. *The American Political Review,* 89(3): 634–647.

Beer, Linda, and Terry Boswell. 2002. The Resilience of Dependency Effects in Explaining Income Inequality in the Global Economy: A Cross-National Analysis, 1975–1995. *Journal of World-Systems Research,* 8(1): 30–59.

Bornschier, Volker, Christopher Chase-Dunn, and Richard Rubinson. 1978. Cross-National Evidence of the Effects of Foreign Investment and Aid on Economic Growth and Inequality: A Survey of Findings and a Reanalysis. *American Journal of Sociology,* 84(3): 651–683.

Chang, Ha-Joon. 2008. *Bad Samaritans: The Myth of Free Trade and the Secret History of Global Capitalism.* New York: Bloomsbury Press.

Chase-Dunn, Christopher. 1998. *Global Formation: Structures of the World Economy.* Lanham, MD: Rowman & Littlefield Publishers, Inc.

Chase-Dunn, Christopher, and Richard Rubinson. 1977. Toward a Structural Perspective on the World-System. *Politics and Society,* 7(4): 453–476.

Deininger, Klaus, and Lyn Squire. 1996. A New Data Set Measuring Income Inequality. *The World Bank Economic Review,* 10(3): 565–591.

Dicken, Peter. 2011. *Global Shift: Reshaping the Global Economic Map in the 21ˢᵗ Century.* New York: The Guilford Press.

Dixon, William J., and Terry Boswell. 1996. Dependency, Disarticulation, and Denominator Effects: Another Look at Foreign Capital Penetration. *American Journal of Sociology*, 102(2): 543–562.

Dollar, David, and Aart Kraay. 2002. Growth is Good for the Poor. *Journal of Economic Growth*, 7(3): 195–225.

Draper, Norman R., and Harry Smith. 1981. *Applied Regression Analysis*. Hoboken, NJ: Wiley and Sons, Inc.

Evans, Peter, and Michael Timberlake. 1980. Dependence, Inequality, and the Growth of the Tertiary: A Comparative Analysis of Less Developed Countries. *American Sociological Review*, 45(4): 531–552.

Firebaugh, Glenn. 1992. Growth Effects of Foreign and Domestic Investment. *The American Journal of Sociology*, 98(1): 105–130.

Firebaugh, Glenn. 2003. *The New Geography of Global Income Inequality*. Cambridge, MA: Harvard University Press.

Galbraith, James K., and Hyunsub Kum. 2005. Estimating the Inequality of Household Incomes: A Statistical Approach to the Creation of a Dense and Consistent Global Data Set. *Review of Income and Wealth*, 51(1): 115–143.

Gylfason, Thorvaldur, and Gylfi Zoega. 2002. Inequality and Economic Growth: Do Natural Resources Matter? Working Paper 712(5). Center for Economic Studies & IFO Institute for Economic Research, Munich, Germany.

Halaby, Charles. 2004. Panel Models in Sociological Research: Theory into Practice. *Annual Review of Sociology*, 30(1): 507–544.

IMF (International Monetary Fund). 2007. *World Economic Outlook, October 2007: Globalization and Inequality*. Washington, DC: IMF. URL: http://www.imf.org/external/pubs/ft/weo/2007/02/pdf/text.pdf (accessed April 17, 2011).

Kentor, Jeffrey. 2001. The Long Term Effects of Globalization on Income Inequality, Population Growth, and Economic Development. *Social Problems*, 48(4): 435–455.

Korzeniewicz, Roberto, and Timothy Moran. 2009. *Unveiling Inequality: A World Historical Perspective*. New York: Russell Sage Foundation.

Kuznets, Simon. 1955. Economic Growth and Income Inequality. *The American Economic Review*, 45(1): 1–28.

Leamer, Edward, Hugo Maul, Sergio Rodriguez, and Peter K. Schott. 1999. Does Natural Resource Abundance Increase Latin American Income Inequality? *Journal of Development Economics*, 59(1): 3–42.

Mahutga, Matthew C., and Nina Bandelj. 2008. Foreign Investment and Income Inequality: The Natural Experiment of Central and Eastern Europe. *International Journal of Comparative Sociology*, 49(6): 429–454.

Mahutga, Matthew C., and David A. Smith. 2011. Globalization, the Structure of the World Economy and Economic Development. *Social Science Research*, 40(1): 257–272.

McMichael, Philip. 2012. *Development and Social Change: A Global Perspective*. Thousand Oaks, CA: SAGE.

Meschi, Elena, and Marco Vivarelli. 2009. Trade and Income Inequality in Developing Countries. *World Development,* 37(2): 287–302.

Milanovic, Branko. 2005. *Worlds Apart: Measuring International and Global Inequality.* Princeton, NJ: Princeton University Press.

Nel, Philip. 2008. *The Politics of Economic Inequality in Developing Countries.* New York: Palgrave Macmillan.

Nielsen, François. 1994. Income Inequality and Development: Dualism Revisited. *American Sociological Review,* 59(5): 654–677.

Persson, Torsten, and Guido Tabellini. 1994. Is Inequality Harmful for Growth? *The American Economic Review,* 84(3): 600–621.

Portes, Alejandro. 1976. On the Sociology of National Development: Theories and Issues. *American Journal of Sociology,* 82(1): 55–85.

Ravallion, Martin. 2001. Growth, Inequality and Poverty: Looking beyond Averages. *World Development,* 29(11): 1803–1815.

Reuveny, Rafael, and Quan Li. 2003. Economic Openness, Democracy, and Income Inequality: An Empirical Analysis. *Comparative Political Studies,* 36(5): 575–601.

Savvides, Andreas. 1998. Trade Policy and Income Inequality. *Economic Letters,* 61(3): 365–372.

UNDP Human Development Report Office. 2010. *Human Development Report 2010. The Real Wealth of Nations: Pathways to Human Development.* New York: United Nations Development Programme. URL: http://hdr.undp.org/sites/default/files/reports/270/hdr_2010_en_complete_reprint.pdf (accessed May 28, 2011).

Wallerstein, Immanuel. 1974. The Rise and Future Demise of the World Capitalist System: Concepts for Comparative Analysis. *Comparative Studies in Society and History,* 16(4): 387–415.

Wallerstein, Immanuel. 2004. *World-Systems Analysis: An Introduction.* Durham and London: Duke University Press.

Wooldridge, Jeffrey M. 2009. *Introductory Econometrics: A Modern Approach.* Mason, OH: South-Western Cengage Learning.

Appendix A: Sample, variables, and data sources

Countries included and country/year observations

Algeria (1967–1997), Bangladesh (1967–1997), Egypt (1964–2002), Eritrea (1965–2001), Indonesia (1970–2002), Iran (1963–2000), Iraq (1963–1992), Jordan (1963–2002), Malaysia (1968–2001), Morocco (1967–2000), Nigeria (1963–1996), Pakistan (1963–1996), Syria (1963–1998), Tunisia (1963–2001), Turkey (1963–2000).

The data used for the analyses was estimated in 2008.

Gini index (dependent variable)

Gini coefficients are the most commonly used measure of inequality. They are expressed in percentage terms with values ranging from 0 to 100 with the value 0 indicating perfect equality and the value 1 indicating perfect inequality. The estimated household income inequality (EHII) is based on pay inequality and manufacturing share along with dummies for data type. The data used here is for the compilation that was done in 2008. *Source:* The Estimated Household Income Inequality (EHII) data set provided by the University of Texas Inequality Project (UTIP). URL: http://utip.gov.utexas.edu/data.html, see also Galbraith and Kum (2005).

Internal development model

Agriculture as a percent of GDP: It is calculated as the value added of agriculutre to GDP. Value added is the net output of a sector after adding up all outputs and subtracting intermediate inputs. *Source:* World Bank Development Indicators online database. URL: http://data.worldbank.org/data-catalog/world-development-indicators.

Secondary school enrollment: This is the gross enrollment ratio for secondary education in all programs. Total is the total enrollment in secondary education, regardless of age, expressed as a percentage of the population of official secondary education age. *Source:* World Bank Development Indicators online database. URL: http://data.worldbank.org/data-catalog/world-development-indicators.

Population growth: Population growth (annual %) is the exponential rate of growth of midyear population from year t – 1 to t, expressed as a percentage. *Source:* World Bank Development Indicators online database. URL: http://data.worldbank.org/data-catalog/world-development-indicators.

GDP per capita (in constant 2000 U.S. dollars): Gross domestic product per capita is gross domestic product divided by midyear population. Data are in constant 2000 U.S. dollars, logged for skew with a base 10 log transformation. *Source:* World Bank Development Indicators online database. URL: http://data.worldbank.org/data-catalog/world-development-indicators.

World-systems indicators

Foreign capital stock/GDP (log): The stock of FDI a country accumulates over time through foreign investments. Measured as a ratio of inward foreign direct investment stock to GDP, logged for skew with a base 10 log transformation. *Source:* United Nations Conference on Trade and Development (UNCTAD). URL: http://unctadstat.unctad.org.

Foreign capital flow/GDP (log): The annual amount of inward foreign direct investment into the host country. Measured as a ratio of FDI inflows to GDP, logged for skew with a base 10 log transformation. *Source:* United Nations Conference on Trade and Development (UNCTAD). URL: http://unctadstat.unctad.org.

Trade/GDP (log): Trade is the sum of exports and imports of goods and services measured as a share of GDP, logged for skew with a base 10 log transformation. *Source:* World Bank Development Indicators online database. URL: http://data.worldbank.org/data-catalog/world-development-indicators.

Exports/GDP (log): Exports of goods and services represent the value of all goods and other market services provided to the rest of the world. Measured as a ratio of exports to GDP, logged for skew with a base 10 log transformation. *Source:* World Bank Development Indicators online database. URL: http://data.worldbank.org/data-catalog/world-development-indicators.

Imports/GDP (log): Imports of goods and services represent the value of all goods and other market services received from the rest of the world. Measured as a ratio of imports to GDP, logged for skew with a base 10 log transformation. *Source:* World Bank Development Indicators online database. URL: http://data.worldbank.org/data-catalog/world-development-indicators.

Natural resources/GDP (log): Total natural resources rents are the sum of oil rents, natural gas rents, coal rents (hard and soft), mineral rents, and forest rents. Measured as a percentage of GDP, logged for skew with a base 10 log transformation. *Source:* World Bank Development Indicators online database. URL: http://data.worldbank.org/data-catalog/world-development-indicators.

Polity Scale: The polity score is computed by subtracting the autocratic score from the democracy score. It consists of various elements: (1) competitiveness of political participation, (2) openness and competitiveness of executive recruitment, and (3) constraints on the chief executive. The resulting polity scale ranges from +10 (strongly democratic) to –10 (strongly autocratic). *Source:* Polity IV Project. Political Regime Characteristics and Transitions, 1800–2010, Center for Systemic Peace. URL: http://www.systemicpeace.org/inscr/inscr.htm.

Colony (dummy variable)

A dummy variable indicating whether a country has been a former colony or not. It is equal to one if country was a former colony, zero otherwise. *Source:* CIA the World Factbook. URL: https://www.cia.gov/library/publications/the-world-factbook.

Africa (dummy variable)

A regional dummy indicating the location of the country. It is equal to one if located in Africa, zero otherwise. *Source:* CIA the World Factbook. URL: https://www.cia.gov/library/publications/the-world-factbook.

Appendix B: Correlation coefficients for variables included in analyses

	1	2	3	4	5	6	7	8	9	10	11	12	13
1 Gini													
2 GDP per capita	−0.037												
3 Agriculture (% of GDP)	0.005	−0.581											
4 Secondary education	0.030	0.413	−0.115										
5 Population growth	−0.240	−0.246	0.037	0.021									
6 FDI stock	0.309	0.383	−0.540	0.082	−0.205								
7 FDI flow	0.269	0.175	−0.126	0.223	−0.069	0.607							
8 Trade	0.099	0.372	−0.543	0.254	0.172	0.641	0.628						
9 Exports	0.047	0.563	−0.563	0.326	−0.010	0.595	0.544	0.935					
10 Imports	0.133	0.217	−0.487	0.188	0.303	0.627	0.646	0.964	0.816				
11 Nat. resources (% of GDP)	−0.362	−0.106	0.358	0.183	−0.083	−0.222	0.050	0.020	0.106	−0.063			
12 Polity	−0.075	0.419	−0.054	0.025	−0.261	0.166	0.203	0.044	0.156	−0.050	−0.052		
13 Colony	−0.014	−0.392	0.000	−0.044	0.357	0.175	0.201	0.426	0.288	0.515	0.177	−0.508	
14 Africa	0.068	−0.098	−0.264	−0.269	−0.403	0.328	0.028	0.040	0.036	0.041	0.134	−0.405	0.355

Sources: See Appendix A.

4

The Effect of Neoliberalism on the Distribution of Wealth in the World Economy

Jenny Chesters

The adoption of neoliberal economic policies in the advanced economies located in the core led to the relocation of manufacturing from core nations to semiperipheral nations. Semiperipheral nations were well placed to take advantage of the new opportunities opened up by neoliberal policies becoming exporters rather than importers of manufactured goods, boosting the value of their economic output and raising the living standards of their residents. This chapter tracks changes in the distribution of wealth between 1987 and 2011 focusing on the proportion of global billionaires residing in three core nations: the United States, United Kingdom and Germany and three semiperipheral nations: India, Russia and China. The results suggest that the distribution of wealth on a global level changed over the past 25 years moving from the core to the semiperiphery.

Introduction

For much of the past few centuries, global wealth has been concentrated in a handful of core nations within the world economy. Core nations imported raw materials from peripheral and semiperipheral nations and exported manufactured goods to these nations exploiting the global market to ensure the prices of commodities remained low and the prices of manufactured goods remained high. When the advanced economies in the core embraced neoliberalism during the 1980s and 1990s, governments lost control over the flow of capital into and out of their national economies. Manufacturing in core nations relocated to peripheral and semiperipheral nations with cheaper labor and lower environmental standards. Peripheral and semiperipheral nations were well placed to take advantage of the new opportunities which opened up when nations in the core adopted neoliberal policies and became importers rather than exporters of manufactured goods. Consequently, there has been a "dramatic reconfiguration of the geography of production and location of politico-economic power" (Harvey, 2010, 31).

This chapter examines the redistribution of wealth on a global level from a world-systems theory perspective using data published in annual lists of the wealthiest people by *Forbes Magazine*.

Global capitalism and world systems theory

World-systems theory is a hierarchical classification of nations based on an axial division of labor that divides the world into three interdependent zones: the core, the periphery and the semiperiphery (Wallerstein, 2004). The core consists of the wealthiest, most powerful nations in which a relatively large percentage of economic activities generate high returns. The periphery consists of the poorest, least powerful nations in which a relatively high proportion of economic activities generate low returns (Chase-Dunn, 1989). The semiperiphery is located between these two extremes.

Core nations are able to dominate global production due to their domestic and international strength. Domestically, they promote the accumulation of capital through "tax policy, government purchasing, sponsorship of research and development, financing of infrastructure development" (Wallerstein, 1988, 156). Internationally, they are able to deploy their political, military and economic power to enforce unequal rates of exchange thereby acquiring raw materials at cheaper prices. The capital-intensive production of highly profitable goods is concentrated in the core whilst the production of goods requiring lower levels of capital investment but high levels of labor power are dispersed throughout the semiperiphery and periphery (Chase-Dunn, 1989). Competition between semiperipheral and peripheral nations ensures that labor costs remain low. Gross Domestic Product (GDP) per capita is relatively high in core nations. For example, in 2011, GDP per capita was US$48,112 in the United States, US$38,974 in the United Kingdom and US$44,021 in Germany (World Bank, 2013).

The periphery includes the least developed countries with less stable political regimes and little military power such as those in sub-Saharan Africa. The economic structure of peripheral countries lacks the diversification necessary for self-perpetuating growth (Peacock et al., 1988). Their reliance on the production of a narrow range of agricultural products leaves them vulnerable to the manipulation of global markets. For example, cash crops grown for export monopolize resources such as good agricultural land and labor without any guarantee that the global market price for the products will provide an income high enough to sustain the workers employed in their production. Furthermore, peripheral countries need to attract capital and import products from nations in the other zones to maintain their agricultural production. GDP per capita is exceptionally low in peripheral nations. For example, in 2011, GDP per capita was just US$231 in the Democratic Republic of Congo and US$357 in Ethiopia and US$496 in Sierra Leone (World Bank, 2013).

Semiperipheral nations display various combinations of core-like and peripheral-like characteristics. For example, Australia is a postindustrial economy that relies heavily on its exports of natural resources such as coal and iron-ore to maintain a high standard of living, whereas China exploits its comparative advantage in labor power to provide cheap manufactured goods for the global market which are far too expensive for the majority of the workers producing them, and their unemployed peers, to be able to purchase. GDP per capita varies widely in semiperipheral nations. For example in 2011, GDP per capita was US$1509 in India, US$5445 in China, US$12,995 in Russia and US$61,789 in Australia (World Bank, 2013).

Movement between the zones is possible with nations moving up or down the hierarchy in accordance with their relative wealth and power (Anderson and Chase-Dunn, 2005). The United States is the most notable example of upward mobility, moving from being a peripheral colony of Great Britain to being the preeminent world power within the core. The fortunes of two nations, China and India, are of particular interest in this chapter and research suggests that both have experienced upward mobility. Between 1975 and 2000, both nations were located in the periphery (Babones, 2005) and experienced upward mobility due to rapid economic growth in the last two decades of the twentieth century (Clark, 2010). According to Clark (2010, 1150), between 1980 and 2000, China experienced a higher than average mobility score of 0.144 (compared to 0.096) suggesting that China moved upwards in the hierarchy at a faster than average rate. On this measure, India also experienced upward mobility with a score of 0.071. World Bank (2013) GDP per capita figures confirm that both India and China experienced rapid economic growth between 1975 and 2010 with India's GDP per capita increasing from US$160 in 1975 to US$450 in 2000 and to US$1509 in 2011 and China's GDP per capita increasing from US$175 in 1975 to US$949 in 2000 and to US$5445 in 2011. These findings suggest that both India and China moved from the periphery to the semiperiphery between 2000 and 2010 and support Anderson and Chase-Dunn's (2005) classification of India and China as semiperipheral nations.

Wallerstein (2004) argues that each nation is part of the global economy, therefore, as capitalism expands, levels of exploitation increase as wealth becomes increasingly concentrated within the core. Capitalist economies prioritize the endless accumulation of capital over the development of more equal distributions of wealth. On a national level, the owners of capital exploit wage laborers and, on a global level, wealthy core nations exploit poorer semiperipheral and peripheral nations. Initially, wealth from Asia, South America and Africa was transferred to the European core via colonization. Using their political and military power, European nations were able to "plunder the wealth of non-capitalist nations" (Harvey, 2010, 109). In many cases, although the colonies gained political independence, economic exploitation continued via the unequal exchange of raw materials for processed goods (vertical trade) and the repatriation of profits from foreign investment (Chase-Dunn and Grimes, 1995; Lee et al., 2007; Clark, 2010).

Core nations are also transferring the environmental costs of production and transportation to the periphery (Rice, 2007; Frey, 2011). For example, the environmental costs of scrapping the container ships that transport around 80 percent of manufactured goods and raw materials around the world has been transferred to India, Bangladesh, China, Pakistan, Vietnam and the Philippines (Frey, 2011). As

Frey's (2011) research documented, the scrap metal is sold returning a profit to the transnational corporations who control shipping, at the expense of the health and well-being of the poor rural immigrants who dismantle container ships without any training or safety equipment. The workers are exposed to toxic gases and chemicals and are oblivious to the dangers of asbestos. The transference of "anti-wealth" to the periphery illustrates how capital accumulation in the core is dependent upon environmental contamination in the periphery (Frey, 2011).

The transition to market economies in the former Soviet Union states and in China led to a rapid expansion of the global economy opening up new markets for manufactured goods and providing new, and very cheap, sources of labor for exploitation. When China opened its economy to the world in 1979 (Harvey, 2010), capital was about to become increasingly mobile due the adoption of neoliberal economic policies in core nations. China's current position as the preeminent manufacturer of cheap goods for world markets resulted from the combination of its vast reserves of low-cost labor; innovations in transportation which lowered the cost of shipping raw materials and manufactured goods; the mobility of capital which allowed companies to relocate their factories close to sources of cheap labor; reductions in trade barriers; and the relentless pursuit of the accumulation of capital which underpins the capitalist world economy.

Neoliberalism

Neoliberalism is based on classical economic theory which posits that markets operate efficiently, are "self-correcting and self-stabilizing" (Quiggin, 1999, 250), therefore, the role of the state is to "create and preserve an institutional framework characterized by strong private property rights, free markets and free trade" (Harvey, 2005, 2). Within the market, individuals "act in a rational manner in order to maximize their material benefits" (Woodward, 2005, 41). Markets operate efficiently when self-interested buyers and self-interested sellers have "perfect knowledge" and utilize that knowledge to make rational decisions (Woodward, 2005, 42). In other words, the buyers and sellers have all of the information they need to assess the value of, the demand for and the supply of any particular product and of any alternative products. Thus buyers can know the minimum price that sellers will sell for and sellers can know the maximum price that buyers will buy at. Intervention by governments is seen as undermining market efficiency, providing opportunities for uncompetitive businesses to remain in operation. However, despite regarding government intervention as unnecessary, markets rely on government regulations to "prevent fraud, enforce contractual obligations and ensure the integrity of the currency" (Woodward, 2005, 44).

Although corporations began off-shoring production in the late 1960s, it was not until the wholesale deregulation of financial markets and the removal of trade barriers during the 1980s and 1990s that commodity chains became fully developed and the manufacturing of final products for sale in core nations was moved to low-cost countries (Harvey, 2010). In the 1960s, some manufacturers set up factories in peripheral nations to manufacture particular parts which were then shipped to core nations to be assembled (Harvey, 2010). Innovations in transportation, such as the containerization of shipping, and in communications, such as the internet, together with the removal of constraints on the movement of capital facilitated the transference of manufacturing and therefore jobs from the core to the periphery and the semiperiphery. Countries in the periphery and semiperiphery were well placed to take advantage of these opportunities having reserve armies of displaced rural workers desperate for jobs.

In core nations, from the late 1970s onwards, governments began deregulating financial sectors allowing for closer integration of markets. Investments in production were replaced by investment in stocks, shares, property and other assets resulting in the decline of economic power related to production and an increase in the economic power related to finance (Harvey, 2005). In the banking sector, interest rate ceilings on deposits and loans were removed and controls over bank lending and liquidity levels were lifted (Woodward, 2005). Financial deregulation increased competition in the lending market which in turn led to an easing of lending standards, a lowering of lending margins and the creation of new investment products, such as credit default obligations (Bloxham and Kent, 2009; Harper and Thomas, 2009).

After the deregulation of the financial sectors in core nations, banks became "increasingly interconnected by an intricate web of financing, investment and hedging operations" (Carmassi et al., 2009, 980), therefore, when asset prices fell, initially in the United States but eventually in Europe, the complex interconnections between financial institutions around the world began to unravel creating the Global Financial Crisis of 2008–2009 (Carmassi et al., 2009). Banks became suspicious of each other no longer believing that they had adequate knowledge of the risks involved in lending to each other, the wholesale finance market froze (Harper and Thomas, 2009) and the myth that markets were capable of "self-correcting and self-stabilizing" (Quiggin, 1999, 250) was dispelled. It was only due to the actions of central banks intervening in the market by generously supplying liquidity that a calamitous crash in stock prices and a surge of bankruptcies in highly leveraged economies around the world was prevented (Rotheli, 2010). For example, the U.S. Treasury took on five trillion dollars' worth of mortgage liabilities from Fannie Mae and Freddie Mac, spent over US$85 billion bailing out American International Group, the banks' insurance company, and set aside a further US$700 billion to purchase or insure the troubled assets held by banks (Pomfret, 2010, 33). The Global Financial Crisis provided a potent reminder of the dangers of allowing the market a free hand exposing the truth that without some form of state intervention, capitalism tends to self-implode. The logic of capitalism depends upon the generation of new profit-making opportunities so that capital accumulation can occur at an ever increasing rate (Harvey, 2010). The shift from profit derived from production to profit derived from investment deprived workers in core nations of their jobs, inflated asset prices making home ownership increasingly unaffordable and pushed levels of personal debt to unsustainable levels.

During the neoliberal reform era, governments of all political persuasions became convinced that the sale of state assets and the privatization of state corporations were necessary to maintain economic growth. In the core nations, large corporations were the major beneficiaries taking control of state infrastructure at less than replacement costs, however, in some semiperipheral nations privatization made a few individuals exceedingly wealthy and powerful. For example, in Mexico, Carlos Slim Helu took control of the telecommunications system in the early 1990s and was worth an estimated US$74 billion in 2011 (Forbes, 2011).

As the core adopted neoliberal economic policies, the communist states transitioned from centrally-planned economies into marketized economies, adopting many of the neoliberal reforms and privatizing state assets. In Russia, the privatization of state assets including steel mills and oil fields in the early 1990s resulted in the creation of a small group of oligarchs, businessmen who controlled sufficient resources to influence national politics, regulations and judiciary (Guriev and Rachinsky, 2005). Although shares in state assets were initially given to tens of millions of workers, ownership quickly consolidated as workers sold their shares (Guriev and Rachinsky, 2006). In 2003, 22 Russian oligarchs controlled 39 percent of sales and 42 percent of employment in Russia (Guriev and Rachinsky, 2005). In 2011, each of the 25 wealthiest Russians, collectively worth an estimated US$290 billion, had initially made their fortunes from their control over former state assets (Forbes, 2011).

The development of the capitalist class in China is also linked to the rapid privatization of state assets, particularly land. Since the 1980s, almost 180 million Chinese have been removed from their land to allow for the development of mega cities and manufacturing hubs (Harvey, 2010). Consequently, property developers have amassed great fortunes by acquiring land from farmers at very little cost and very little effort due to the inability of farmers to resist their demands. Local officials have the power to evict farmers with little compensation and then sell the land to developers at a considerable profit. For example, land in the village of Dawu purchased by the Loudi city government in 2007 for 38,000 yuan per mu (equivalent to one sixth of an acre) was sold to developers for 600,000 yuan per mu in 2008 who subsequently sold it for 1.2 million yuan per mu in 2011 (SMH, 2011). With property prices increasing by 140 percent, on average, since 1998, it is unlikely that these displaced farmers will have any chance of buying into any of the new housing developments that are replacing their farms (SMH, 2011). After losing their homes and their livelihoods, the farmers were forced to migrate to urban areas in search of employment, thus creating a vast army of cheap labor which is currently being exploited to produce manufactured goods for export around the world providing a relatively small group of entrepreneurs with the opportunity to become exceptionally wealthy in a very short period of time.

India transitioned from a centrally planned economy after the severe economic crisis it encountered in 1991. After gaining independence from the United Kingdom in 1947, successive democratically elected governments held a tight grip on economic development through their control over private economic activity (Krueger, 2002). Government-owned monopolies controlled the finance sector, including insurance and all banks (after they were nationalized in 1969), telecommunications, the import of certain goods, such as petroleum, and the export of some commodities, such as sugar (Krueger and Chinoy, 2002). The importation and export of goods was highly regulated by a licensing system and tariffs and import quotas ensured that local manufacturers were shielded from competition. After 1991, the government adopted a range of modified neoliberal policies to liberalize trade: reducing tariffs, easing restrictions on Foreign Direct Investment, devaluing the currency and removing controls over exports (except for agricultural products). Between 1999 and 2001, the telecommunications sector was opened to competition and new investors were encouraged to apply for licenses; trade barriers were further relaxed lifting the controls over the importation of consumer goods; and the insurance industry was also opened up to competition (Krueger and Chinoy, 2002). Government-owned technology parks were set up with special arrangements designed to boost foreign investment and generate income from information-technology-related services. The software industry was nurtured by supportive labor and tax laws, such as having to pay no tax for the first five to eight years. By 2005, seven percent of India's exports were due to computer programming services, software exports and other information-technology-related services such as call centers (OECD, 2007).

Global billionaires

Although the wealthiest individuals in the world were largely concentrated in the core nations during the 1980s, 1990s and early 2000s, growth in the number of new billionaires has been strongest in the semiperiphery (Chesters, 2013). Between 2003 and 2011, the number of billionaires located in three semiperipheral nations, India, Russia and China, increased by almost 1200 percent from 23 to 268. These three nations benefited from opportunities created by the off-shoring of production from the core to the semiperiphery and their vast reserves of natural resources which they have been able to develop, initially with funding from the core.

Capitalists invest where they expect to realize the greatest returns, therefore, billionaire wealth generally trends along the same path as new technology. For example, in the United States, as Harvey (2010) points out, the Robber Barons of post-civil war America made their fortunes from the railroads. In the early decades of the twentieth century, a new generation made their fortunes from innovations in manufacturing, like Henry T. Ford. In the latter part of the twentieth century, innovations in computer technology made the likes of Bill Gates exceptionally wealthy. More recently, financialization has created a new crop of billionaires, such as Charles Stanford.

According to Harvey (2010, 40) capitalists can be categorized into six groups: finance capitalists, those who make their money from the interest they charge on loans; merchant capitalists, those who buy cheap goods and sell them at higher prices, such as Sam Walton who founded the Wal-Mart chain; property capitalists, those who collect rents; rentiers, those make their money from royalties, such as Gina Rinehart; asset traders, those who trade in stock and shares, debts and contracts, such as Warren Buffet; and industrial capitalists, those who buy labor power and the means of production to manufacture goods, such as Lakshmi Mittal.

Having the freedom to decide where they may invest allows the owners of capital to select investments which will generate the highest returns. Currently, in many nations, investment in assets is generating a higher rate of return than investment in the production of goods and services. Not constrained by national governments or national obligations, billionaires are free to invest anywhere in the global economy. Moving capital from nations providing low rates of return, such as those in the core, to those providing high rates of return, such as those in the periphery and semiperiphery, increases the rate of capital accumulation redistributing global wealth and spawning new billionaires.

The effect of neoliberalism on the distribution of wealth

In order to examine the effect of neoliberalism on the distribution of wealth in the global economy, I focus on the billionaires located in three core nations and three semiperipheral nations to show how the shift to neoliberal economic policies in the core provided opportunities for these three semiperipheral nations to marketize and become fully integrated into the global economy. The former communist states, Russia and China, have transitioned from complete state control to almost open-market economies and India, although a democracy since achieving self-governance in 1947, transitioned from a planned economy to a market economy (Subramanian and Jayaraj, 2009). The United States, the United Kingdom and Germany have been selected to represent the core due their having the highest proportions of billionaires located in core countries in 2011. The United States and the United Kingdom were the vanguards of neoliberalism, deregulating and privatizing state assets during the Reagan/Thatcher regimes in the 1980s. Germany has maintained a stricter regulatory regime in regards to employment conditions and wages but, like the United States and the United Kingdom, is as well-integrated into the financial markets of the global economy.

The graph in Figure 1, derived from figures published by the World Bank (2013), tracks the trends over time in the ratio of each country's GDP per capita to world GDP per capita from 1987 to 2011. In two of the core nations, the United States and

Figure 1: Ratio of country's GDP per capita to world GDP per capita

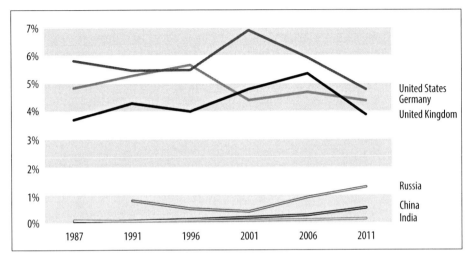

Source: World Bank (2013).

Germany, the ratio declined and in the United Kingdom the ratio increased slightly. The ratio of U.S. GDP per capita to world GDP per capita declined from 5.8 to 4.8 between 1987 and 2011. Between 1987 and 2011, the ratio of German GDP per capita to world GDP per capita declined from 4.8 to 4.4 whereas the ratio of UK GDP per capita to world GDP per capita increased from 3.7 to 3.9. The ratio increased for each of the semiperipheral nations, only marginally in India from 0.10 to 0.15, but substantially in China from 0.07 to 0.5. The World Bank did not publish GDP per capita for Russia in 1987, however between 1991 and 2011, the ratio of GDP per capita in Russia to world GDP per capita increased from 0.8 to 1.3.

These trends were not monotonic with the ratio for each of the core nations fluctuating during this 25-year period. For the United States, the ratio peaked at 6.9 in 2001 before declining dramatically; for the United Kingdom, the ratio peaked at 5.4 in 2006 before dropping back to almost the same level as in 1987; and in Germany, the ratio peaked at 5.7 in 1996, declining sharply until 2001 and then plateaued. The ratio for Russia initially declined between 1991 and 2001 from 0.8 to 0.4 before increasing between 2001 and 2011. The ratios for China and India steadily increased between 1991 and 2011.

A comparison of figures collated by Davies et al. (2009) for 2000 and Keating et al. (2011; 2012) for 2011 show that increasing GDP per capita was accompanied by increasing wealth/capita. Between 2000 and 2011, wealth per capita increased from US\$2973 to US\$15,075 in China and from US\$1146 to US\$3331 in India. Between 2000 and 2012, wealth per capita increased from US\$2530 to US\$9353 in Russia. Davies et al. (2009) also provide the 2000 wealth Gini coefficients, one measure of within-nation inequality, for the six nations of interest in this chapter: 0.801 in the United States; 0.697 in the United Kingdom; 0.667 in Germany; 0.669 in India; 0.699 in Russia and 0.550 in China. Research in trends over time in wealth inequality within nations is scarce, however, Li and Zhao (2009, 106) provide evidence of increasing wealth inequality in China with percentage of total wealth held by the wealthiest 10 percent increasing from 31 to 41 percent between 1995 and 2002 and the percentage share of total wealth held by the poorest 20 percent declining from 5.8 to 2.8 percent. According to Wolff (2010), wealth inequality in the United States increased between 1983 and 2009 with the share of total household wealth held by the wealthiest one percent increasing from 33.8 to 37.1 percent and the share held by the poorest 40 percent declining from 0.9 to –0.8 percent.

Another indication of the distribution of wealth within a nation is the comparison of median wealth per adult to mean wealth per adult. The closer the ratio is to one, the less skewed the distribution. Data collated by Keating et al. (2011; 2012) shows that in 2011, the mean wealth/adult in the United Kingdom was US$257,881 and the median wealth/adult was US$121,852. The ratio of median wealth/adult to mean wealth/adult was 0.47. In the United States, the mean wealth/adult was US$248,395 and the median wealth/adult was US$52,752 resulting in a ratio of 0.21 indicating that wealth inequality in the United States is much higher than it is in the United Kingdom. In 2011, the ratio of median wealth/adult to mean wealth/adult was 0.36 in China and 0.23 in India. In 2012, the ratio of median wealth/adult to mean wealth/adult was 0.10 in Russia indicating that wealth is highly concentrated in each of these nations, but particularly so in Russia.

Global billionaires and their wealth

Although it is possible to track trends over time in the global distribution of wealth on a country-by-country basis, for simplicity I restrict my analyses to six countries: the United States, the United Kingdom, Germany, India, Russia and China. Data on the wealth holdings of the billionaires in these six nations, as well as the total wealth holdings of all billionaires, are derived from lists published annually by *Forbes Magazine*. These lists are compiled by journalists therefore their validity is linked to the extent that the wealth holdings are public knowledge (Atkinson, 2006, 6). Due to the reluctance of national governments to routinely collect data on the wealth holdings of individuals, these lists provide the only comparable data on the wealth holdings of individuals. Wealth is defined as the current value of all marketable assets less the current value of debts. The values are converted to U.S. dollars using the exchange rate current at the time each list is compiled. Consequently, the wealth of individuals residing outside of the United States is determined to some extent by the exchange rate between the U.S. dollar and the currency of the country in which they reside at the time each list is compiled.

Figure 2: Trends over time in the number of global billionaires

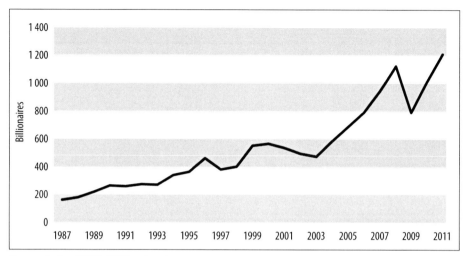

Sources: Forbes (1987–2011) various issues.

In this chapter, I use data on net worth, country of residence and source of wealth. The total net worth variable is a continuous measure ranging from US$1 billion. The values are adjusted to account for inflation using the annual Consumer Price Index (CPI) published by the U.S. Bureau of Labor Statistics (2012). I convert the values for each year into 2011 U.S. dollars by multiplying the value by the CPI for 2011 and then dividing that figure by the CPI for the relevant year. For example, to convert the 1987 value into 2011 dollars, I multiply the 1987 value by 224.9 (the CPI for 2011) and then divide that figure by 113.6 (the CPI for 1987). Between 1998 and 2001, *Forbes* includes information on country but does not specify whether this pertains to country of residence or country of citizenship and in 2002 only country of citizenship is listed. I used the information from either preceding years or later years where possible to code country of residence in these years. If the individual was only listed in these years, I used the country/country of citizenship information for country of residence.

According to the annual lists published by *Forbes*, the number of global billionaires increased sevenfold from 162 in 1987 to 1210 in 2011. Although the general trend was upward, the number of billionaires declined in 1991 largely due to the recession in the United States, in 1997 due to the Asian Financial Crisis, in 2002 due to the Dot.Com crash and in 2009, due to the Global Financial Crisis. In the five years between 2003 and 2008, the number of billionaires more than doubled from 476 to 1125. After this brief period of rapid growth, the number of billionaires declined to 793 in 2010 but recovered to 1210 in 2011. The graph presented in Figure 2 charts the fluctuations in the number of global billionaires between 1987 and 2011.

Figure 3: Trends over time in the total wealth of global billionaires

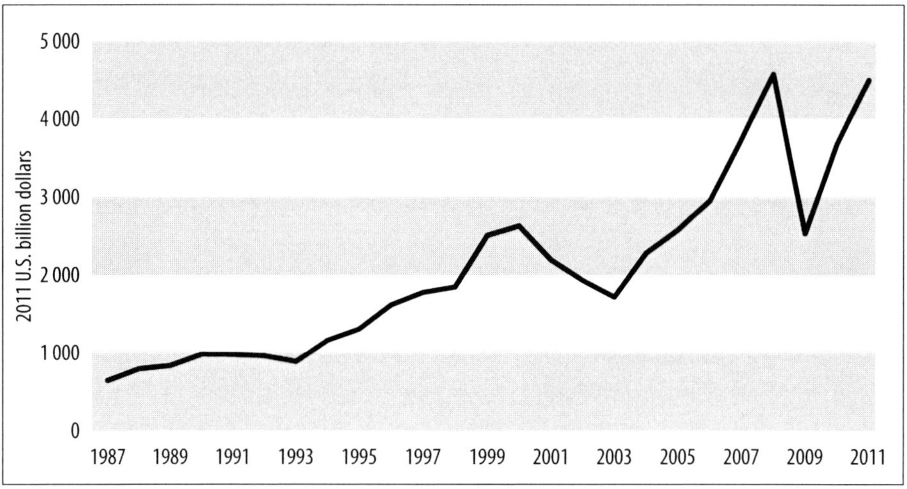

Sources: Forbes (1987–2011) various issues.

There has also been a dramatic increase in the total wealth held by the global billionaires. In 1987, the 162 billionaires were collectively worth US$642 billion (in 2011
dollars) and by 2011, the 1210 billionaires were collectively worth US$4497 billion.
Total billionaire wealth increased gradually from US$642 billion to US$981 billion
between 1987 and 1990 before declining during the U.S. recession from US$978
billion in 1991 to US$887 billion in 1993. Total billionaire wealth then increased to
US$2629 billion in 2000 before declining to US$1715 billion in 2003. Between 2003
and 2008, total billionaire wealth more than doubled to US$4576 billion, before
plummeting to US$2532 billion in 2009 due to the effects of the Global Financial
Crisis and then recovering to US$3679 billion in 2010. The graph presented in
Figure 3 charts the fluctuations in the collective wealth of the global billionaires
between 1987 and 2011.

National comparisons

In 1987, the 162 global billionaires were located in 24 nations and in 2011, the 1210
global billionaires were spread across 55 nations suggesting that the wealthiest individuals in the world were less likely to be concentrated within core nations in
2011. Appendix A lists the percentage of global billionaires residing in each nation
in 1987, 1991, 1996, 2001, 2006 and 2011. Rather than discuss changes in each of the
nations, in this section, I focus on three core nations: the United States, the United
Kingdom and Germany and three semiperipheral nations: India, Russia and China.
Figure 4 charts trends overtime in the share of global billionaires residing in these

Figure 4: Trends over time in percentage of global billionaires in each nation

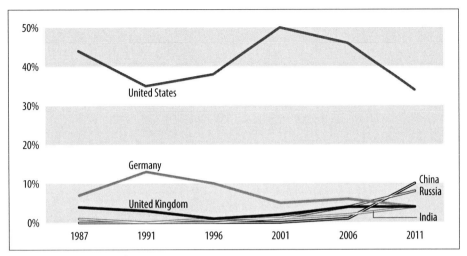

Sources: Forbes (1987–2011) various issues.

six nations. Overall, the percentage of global billionaires residing in the three core nations declined from 55 percent in 1987 to 41 percent in 2011, whereas the percentage of global billionaires residing in the three semiperipheral nations increased from one percent in 1987 to 22 percent in 2011. In 1987, the remaining 44 percent of global billionaires were spread across 20 other nations and in 2011, the remaining 37 percent of global billionaires were spread across 49 other nations.

Looking at the trends within each of the six selected nations, the data show that these trends are not monotonic for the core nations with the share of global billionaires residing in the United States declining from 44 percent in 1987 to 35 percent in 1991 before increasing to 50 percent in 2001 and then declining to 34 percent in 2011. The share of global billionaires residing in the United Kingdom declined from four percent in 1987 to one percent in 1996 before increasing to four percent in 2006 and then plateauing. The share of global billionaires residing in Germany initially increased from seven percent in 1987 to 13 percent in 1991 before declining to five percent in 2001 and then increasing to six percent in 2006 before declining again to four percent in 2011. On the other hand, for each of the semiperipheral nations the percentage share of global billionaires increased monotonically over time. China experienced the most rapid growth, increasing its share of global billionaires from one percent in 2006 to 10 percent in 2011.

As the number of billionaires increased and the number of nations with billionaire residents increased, global billionaire wealth was redistributed. Appendix B lists the percentage of global billionaire wealth held by billionaires residing in each nation in 1987, 1991, 1996, 2001, 2006 and 2011. The graph in Figure 5 shows trends

Figure 5:   Trends over time in percentage of billionaire wealth held by billionaires in each nation

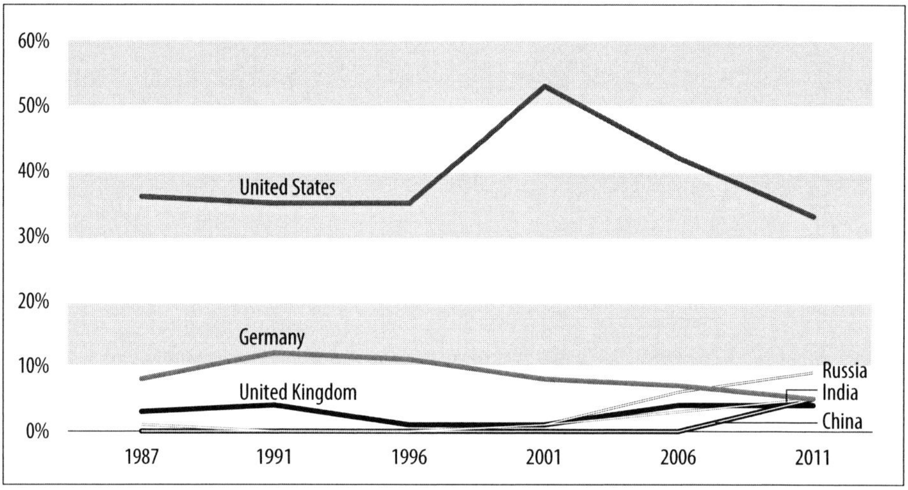

Sources: Forbes (1987–2011), various issues.

over time in the share of billionaire wealth held in the six nations of interest. In 1987, the three semiperipheral nations accounted for just one percent of global billionaire wealth whereas the three core nations accounted for 46 percent of global billionaire wealth. In 2011, billionaires residing in India, Russia and China held 19 percent of global billionaire wealth and billionaires residing in the United States, the United Kingdom and Germany held 42 percent of global billionaire wealth. In 1987, the remaining 53 percent of global billionaire wealth was spread across 20 other nations and in 2011, the remaining 39 percent of global billionaire wealth was spread across 49 other nations.

The share of global billionaire wealth held by billionaires residing in the United States declined marginally from 36 percent in 1987 to 35 percent in 1991 before increasing to 53 percent between 1996 and 2001 and then declining to 33 percent in 2011. The share of global billionaire wealth held by billionaires residing in the United Kingdom declined from three percent in 1987 to one percent in 1996, was steady between 1996 and 2001, increased to four percent in 2006 and then plateaued. The share of global billionaire wealth held by billionaires residing in Germany initially increased from eight percent in 1987 to 12 percent in 1991 before steadily declining to five percent in 2011. On the other hand, for each of the semiperipheral nations the percentage share of global billionaire wealth held by billionaires increased monotonically over time. China experienced the most rapid growth, increasing its share of global billionaire wealth from 0.4 percent in 2006 to five percent in 2011.

In 1996, the United Kingdom was home to one percent of global billionaires who between them held just one percent of global billionaire wealth. Fifteen years later, four percent of global billionaires, holding four percent of billionaire wealth, resided in the United Kingdom. The key explanation for the United Kingdom's increased share of global billionaires and billionaire wealth is the migration of established billionaires to the United Kingdom. Of the 50 billionaires residing in the United Kingdom in 2011, only 22 were born in Britain. Immigrants accounted for six of the ten wealthiest people living in Britain in 2011: Lakshmi Mittal was born in India and made his fortune from manufacturing steel in India; John Frederiksen was born in Cyprus and made his fortune from transporting oil and now owns oil rigs throughout the world; Leonard Blavarik was born in Russia, initially immigrated to the UnitedStates and made his fortune from Russian oil before relocating to the United Kingdom; Hans Rausing was born in Sweden and inherited his fortune from his father; Charlene de Carvalho-Heineken was born in the Netherlands and inherited her fortune from her father; and Anil Agarwal was born in India and made his fortune from natural resources in India. The migration of billionaires to the United Kingdom highlights the transportability of capital. Some billionaires, typically the Russians, regard the United Kingdom as a safe haven and have relocated themselves and their capital away from potential threats of renationalization of their assets and imprisonment after the arrest and imprisonment of Khordorkovsky in 2003 (Guriev and Rachinsky, 2006).

Source of wealth

The annual *Forbes* lists include information on the source of wealth allowing for some comparisons between nations and over time. In 1987, 12 percent of the 72 billionaires residing in the United States had derived their fortunes principally from the finance/banking sector and through their investment activities whereas 17 percent had derived their fortunes from manufacturing. In 2011, 27 percent of the 406 billionaires residing in the United States had derived their fortunes principally from finance/banking/investments and nine percent had derived their fortunes principally from manufacturing. There were only six billionaires residing in the United Kingdom in 1987, all of whom were born in the United Kingdom and had derived their fortune from a different source. Of the 22 nonimmigrant billionaires residing in the United Kingdom in 2011, 23 percent had derived their fortunes from real estate, 23 percent had derived their fortunes from retail and 18 percent had derived their fortunes from banking/finance/investments. Of the 13 billionaires residing in Germany in 1987, three had derived their fortunes from banking/finance and the remaining 10 had derived their fortunes from a variety of sources including manufacturing and retail. In 2011, 21 percent of the 43 billionaires residing in Germany had derived their fortunes from manufacturing and 19 percent had derived their fortunes from retail.

In 2011, 26 percent of the 97 billionaires residing in Russia had derived their fortunes from mining/oil/gas whereas 17 percent had derived their fortunes from banking/insurance and investments. In 2011, 33 percent of the 120 billionaires residing in China had derived their fortunes from manufacturing, 14 percent had derived their fortunes from real estate and just five percent had derived their fortunes from finance/investments. In 2011, 25 percent of the 51 billionaires residing in India had derived their fortunes from manufacturing and 24 percent had derived their fortunes from technology, such as software companies and telecommunications. Banking and investments were the main sources of wealth for just two billionaires in India.

Discussion and conclusion

This chapter set out to examine the effect of neoliberalism on the distribution of wealth in the world economy. The results presented here suggest that global wealth has been redistributed from the core to the semiperiphery. During the latter half of the twentieth century, core nations adopted neoliberal economic policies which resulted in the transference of manufacturing and manufacturing jobs from the core to the periphery and facilitated the upward mobility of three peripheral nations, India, Russia and China into the semiperiphery. Local entrepreneurs in these three nations were well-placed to take advantage of the opportunities provided by the neoliberal economic policies adopted in the core. With vast reserves of relatively cheap labor, industrial expansion in both India and China fuelled both increasing GDP per capita and wealth inequality. As China became the preeminent exporter of manufactured goods, its GDP per capita increased from US$249 to US$5445 between 1987 and 2011 and wealth per capita increased from US$2973 in 2000 to US$15,075 in 2011 (Davies et al., 2009; Keating et al., 2011; World Bank, 2013). In India, the relaxation of barriers to trade and Foreign Direct Investment, and the availability of a relatively well-educated, low-paid workforce facilitated the expansion of Information and Technology industries, pushing GDP per capita from US$346 in 1987 to US$1509 in 2011. Wealth per capita increased from US$1146 in 2000 to US$3331 in 2011 (Davies et al., 2009; Keating et al., 2011; World Bank, 2013). Exploiting its vast reserves of natural resources in a buoyant commodities market, Russia improved its GDP per capita from US$3429 in 1989 to US$12,995 in 2011. Wealth per capita increased from US$2530 in 2000 to US$9353 in 2011 (Davies et al., 2009; Keating et al., 2012; World Bank, 2013).

By examining the redistribution of global billionaires and the redistribution of billionaire wealth, I was able to show that as jobs were transferred from nations in the core to nations in the periphery and semiperiphery, wealth followed the jobs. Capital investment in production creates jobs; therefore as capital moved to peripheral and semiperipheral nations with cheaper costs of production, jobs were relocated to the periphery and semiperiphery. In core nations, capital investment in assets and innovative financial products did little to generate new jobs to replace those lost from the manufacturing sector. The percentage of global billionaire wealth held by billionaires residing in the United States, the United Kingdom and Germany declined from 46 percent to 42 percent between 1987 and 2011, whereas the proportion of billionaire wealth held by billionaires residing in India, Russia and China increased from one percent to 19 percent between 1987 and 2011. During this same period the ratio of GDP per capita in the United States to world GDP per capita declined from 5.8 to 4.8 and the ratio of GDP per capita in China to world GDP per capita increased from 0.07 to 0.5.

Having the freedom to move their capital around the globe now that restrictions to trade and investment have been largely removed, billionaires, particularly those from semiperipheral nations, have become mobile, relocating to core nations with higher standards of living and more capital-friendly laws. This may facilitate a return of global billionaire wealth to the current core. On the other hand, if a large proportion of the billionaires currently residing in India, Russia and China do not relocate to the core, these three nations may become incorporated into an expanded core. Given that capitalist economies prioritize the accumulation of capital and therefore require a high level of inequality in the distribution of wealth so that the wealthy are able to exploit the poor and extract profit, it is unlikely that a multi-core economy will eventuate. A multi-core world economy would be inherently unstable as capitalists in each core would need to compete with each other for opportunities to exploit the periphery.

Acknowledgements

The data used for this chapter come from the Global Inequality dataset compiled by Jenny Chesters, University of Canberra, Jesper Roine, Stockholm School of Economics and Daniel Waldenstrom, Uppsala University.

References

Anderson, E.N., and Christopher Chase-Dunn. 2005. "The Rise and Fall of Great Powers." In E.N. Anderson and Christopher Chase-Dunn (eds.), *The Historical Evolution of World-Systems.* Palgrave: New York.

Atkinson, Anthony B. 2006. Concentration among the Rich. WIDER Research Paper, 2006/151, United Nations University World Institute for Development Economics Research, Helsinki, Finland.

Babones, Salvatore. 2005. The Country-Level Income Structure of the World Economy. *Journal of World Systems Research,* 11(1): 29–55.

Bloxham, Paul, and Christopher Kent. 2009. Household Indebtedness. *The Australian Economic Review,* 42(3): 327–339.

Bureau of Labor Statistics. 2012. CPI Indexes. URL: http://www.bls.gov/cpi/#tables (accessed November 30, 2012).

Carmassi, Jacopo, Daniel Gros, and Stefano Micossi. 2009. The Global Financial Crisis: Causes and Cures. *Journal of Common Market Studies,* 47(5): 977–996.

Chase-Dunn, Christopher. 1989. *Global Formation: Structures of the World-Economy.* Cambridge, MA: Basil Blackwell.

Chase-Dunn, Christopher, and Peter Grimes. 1995. World-Systems Analysis. *Annual Review of Sociology,* 21: 387–417.

Chesters, Jenny. 2013. Wealth Inequality and Stratification in the World Capitalist Economy. *Perspectives in Global Development and Technology,* 12: 248–267.

Clark, Rob. 2010. World System Mobility and Economic Growth, 1980–2000. *Social Forces,* 88(3): 1123–1152.

Davies, James B., Susanna Sandstrom, Anthony Shorrocks, and Edward N. Wolff. 2009. The Level and Distribution of Global Household Wealth. Working paper, 15508, National Bureau of Economic Research, Cambridge. URL: www.nber.org/papers/w15508 (accessed March 29, 2011).

Forbes Magazine. 1987–2011. Various issues. URL: http://www.forbes.com/wealth/billionaires (accessed August 29, 2011).

Frey, R. Scott. 2011. Breaking Ships in the World-System: An Analysis of Two Ship Breaking Capitals, Alang, India and Chittagong, Bangladesh. Paper presented at the Global Capitalism and Transnational Class Formation Conference. Prague, Czech Republic, September 16th–18th, 2011.

Guriev, Sergei, and Andrei Rachinsky. 2005. The Role of the Oligarchs in Russian Capitalism. *Journal of Economic Perspectives,* 19(1): 131–150.

Guriev, Sergei, and Andrei Rachinsky. 2006. The Evolution of Personal Wealth in the Former Soviet Union and Central Eastern Europe. WIDER Research Paper, 2006/120, United Nations University World Institute for Development Economics Research, Helsinki, Finland.

Harper, Ian, and Mike Thomas. 2009. Making Sense of the GFC: Where Did It Come from and What Do We Do Now. *Economic Papers,* 28(3): 196–205.

Harvey, David. 2005. *A Brief History of Neoliberalism.* Oxford: Oxford University Press.

Harvey, David. 2010. *The Enigma of Capital and the Crisis of Capitalism.* London: Profile Books.

Keating, Giles, Michael O'Sullivan, Anthony Shorrocks, James B. Davies, Rodrigo Lluberas, and Antonios Koutsoukis. 2011. *Global Wealth Report 2011.* Zurich: Credit Suisse AG Research Institute.

Keating, Giles, Michael O'Sullivan, Anthony Shorrocks, James B. Davies, Rodrigo Lluberas, and Antonios Koutsoukis. 2012. *Global Wealth Report 2012.* Zurich: Credit Suisse AG Research Institute.

Krueger, Anne O. 2002. "Introduction." In Anne O. Krueger (ed.), *Economic Policy Reforms and the Indian Economy.* Chicago: Chicago University Press.

Krueger, Anne O., and Sajjid Chinoy. 2002. The Indian Economy in a Global Context. In Anne O. Krueger (ed.), *Economic Policy Reforms and the Indian Economy.* Chicago: Chicago University Press.

Lee, Cheol-Sung, François Nielsen, and Arthur S. Alderson. 2007. Income Inequality, Global Economy and the State. *Social Forces,* 86(1): 77–112.

Li, Shi, and Renwei Zhao. 2009. Changes in the Distribution of Wealth in China 1995–2002. In James B. Davies (ed.), *Personal Wealth from a Global Perspective.* Oxford Scholarship Online. URL: www.oxfordscholarship.com (accessed October 3, 2011).

OECD (Organization for Economic Cooperation and Development). 2007. *Economic Survey of India.* Paris: OECD.

Peacock, Walter Gillis, Greg A. Hoover, and Charles D. Killian. 1988. Divergence and Convergence in International Development: A Decomposition Analysis of Inequality in the World System. *American Sociological Review,* 53(6): 838–852.

Pomfret, Richard. 2010. The Financial Sector and the Future of Capitalism. *Economic Systems,* 34: 22–37.

Quiggin, John. 1999. Globalisation, Neoliberalism and Inequality in Australia. *The Economic and Labour Relations Review,* 10(2): 240–259.

Rice, James. 2007. Ecological Unequal Exchange: International Trade and Uneven Utilization of Environmental Space in the World System. *Social Forces,* 85(3): 1369–1392.

Rotheli, Tobias F. 2010. Causes of the Financial Crisis: Risk Misperception, Policy Mistakes, and Banks' Bounded Rationality. *The Journal of Socio-Economics,* 39(2): 119–126.

SMH (Sydney Morning Herald). 2011. 50 million Chinese left homeless by developers. Sydney Morning Herald, October 24, 2011. URL: http://www.smh.com.au/business/50-million-chinese-left-homeless-by-developers-20111024-1mg0p.html (accessed October 25, 2011).

Subramanian, S., and D. Jayaraj. 2009. The Distribution of Household Wealth in India. In James B. Davies (ed.), *Personal Wealth from a Global Perspective.* Oxford Scholarship Online. URL: www.oxfordscholarship.com (accessed October 3, 2011).

Wallerstein, Immanuel. 1988. The Great Expansion: The Incorporation of Vast New Zones into the Capitalist World Economy (c. 1750–1850). *Studies in History,* 4: 85–156.

Wallerstein, Immanuel. 2004. *World-Systems Analysis: An Introduction.* Durham and London: Duke University Press.

Wolff, Edward N. 2010. Recent Trends in Household Wealth in the United States: Rising Debt and the Middle Class Squeeze—an Update on 2007. Working Paper, 589, Levy Institute. URL: http://www.levyinstitute.org/pubs/wp_589.pdf (accessed October 3, 2011).

Woodward, Dennis. 2005. *Australia Unsettled: The Legacy of "Neo-liberalism."* French's Forest: Pearson.

World Bank. 2013. Indicators: GDP/capita. URL: http://data.worldbank.org/indicator/ (accessed May 19, 2013).

Appendix A: Percentage of global billionaires

	1987 %	1991 %	1996 %	2001 %	2006 %	2011 %
Argentina			0.65	0.74	0.13	0.17
Australia	1.23	0.38	0.22	0.56	0.76	1.4
Austria		0.77			0.5	0.33
Bahamas					0.13	
Bahrain			0.22			
Belgium				0.19	0.13	0.08
Bermuda				0.19	0.25	
Brazil	1.85	1.15	2.16	1.12	2.02	2.23
Canada	2.47	1.92	1.08	2.97	2.4	1.82
Cayman Islands					0.13	0.08
Chile			1.08	0.37	0.25	0.33
China				**0.19**	**1.01**	**9.92**
Colombia	1.23	0.77	0.65	0.19	0.25	0.17
Costa Rica				0.13		
Cyprus						0.08
Czech Republic					0.13	0.25
Denmark		0.38	0.43	0.37	0.25	0.25
Ecuador			0.22			
Egypt				0.19	0.25	0.66
Finland						0.08
France	1.85	3.46	3.23	2.79	1.89	1.07
Germany	**6.79**	**12.69**	**10.13**	**5.2**	**5.67**	**3.55**
Gibraltar					0.38	
Greece		0.77	0.86	0.56		0.08
Hong Kong	3.7	2.69	3.88	2.6	2.65	3.22
India	**0.62**	**0.38**	**0.65**	**0.74**	**2.4**	**4.21**
Indonesia	0.62	1.15	2.16	0.37	0.25	0.91
Ireland			0.22	0.37	0.5	0.33
Israel		0.38	0.65	0.93	0.76	1.07
Italy	3.09	1.92	1.29	3.16	1.51	0.99
Japan	14.81	15.77	8.62	5.39	3.4	2.23
Kazakhstan					0.5	0.58
Kuwait	0.62		0.22	0.19	0.38	0.25
Lebanon	1.23	0.38	0.43	0.19	0.13	0.25
Liechtenstein			0.22	0.19		
Malaysia		0.38	2.37	0.74	0.88	0.66
Mexico	0.62	0.77	3.23	2.42	1.26	0.91

Appendix A (continued)

	1987 %	1991 %	1996 %	2001 %	2006 %	2011 %
Monaco					0.76	0.41
Netherlands	1.23	1.15	0.65	0.37	0.38	0.33
New Zealand				0.19	0.25	0.25
Nigeria						0.17
Norway				0.37	0.5	0.33
Peru			0.22			
Philippines		0.38	1.94	0.56	0.38	0.33
Poland					0.38	0.33
Portugal				0.37	0.13	0.25
Romania						0.08
Russia				**1.49**	**4.04**	**8.02**
Saudi Arabia	3.09	2.31	1.51	1.49	1.39	0.74
Singapore	0.62	0.77	0.86	1.12	0.63	0.74
South Africa			0.43	0.37	0.25	0.33
South Korea	1.23	1.54	1.51	0.37	0.5	1.24
Spain	0.62	1.15	0.65	1.49	1.26	1.16
Sweden	0.62		0.43	0.93	0.63	0.5
Switzerland	1.85	4.62	3.02	2.97	2.65	2.07
Taiwan	1.85	1.92	1.51	0.93	0.63	2.07
Thailand		0.77	2.16	0.37	0.38	0.33
Turkey		1.15	0.65	0.93	2.65	3.14
Ukraine					0.38	0.74
United Arab Emirates				0.19	0.5	0.41
United Kingdom	**3.7**	**2.69**	**1.08**	**2.23**	**4.16**	**4.13**
United States	**44.44**	**35**	**38.15**	**50**	**45.65**	**33.55**
Venezuela		0.38	0.43	0.37	0.25	0.17

Notes: Percentage of global billionaires refers to billionaires residing in each nation.
Sources: Forbes (1987–2011) various issues.

Appendix B: Percentage of global billionaire wealth

	1987 %	1991 %	1996 %	2001 %	2006 %	2011 %
Argentina	0	0	0.59	0.31	0.06	0.14
Australia	0.62	0.25	0.16	0.35	0.56	1.19
Austria	0	0.66	0	0	0.56	0.34
Bahamas	0	0	0	0	0.06	0
Bahrain	0	0	0.09	0	0	0
Belgium	0	0	0	0.06	0.11	0.07
Bermuda	0	0	0	0.12	0.11	0
Brazil	1.54	0.61	1.63	0.82	1.27	2.75
Canada	4.13	4.09	1.40	2.70	2.68	1.78
Cayman Islands	0	0	0	0	0.09	0.05
Chile	0	0	0.78	0.15	0.29	0.95
China	**0**	**0**	**0**	**0.08**	**0.43**	**5.39**
Colombia	1.23	0.68	0.37	0.09	0.34	0.42
Costa Rica	0	0	0	0	0.04	0
Cyprus	0	0	0	0	0	0.02
Czech Republic	0	0	0	0	0.11	0.27
Denmark	0	0.22	0.43	0.24	0.35	0.22
Ecuador	0	0	0.11	0	0	0
Egypt	0	0	0	0.06	0.28	0.45
Finland	0	0	0	0	0	0.04
France	1.23	2.46	3.26	3.81	3.26	2.58
Germany	**7.65**	**11.73**	**11.50**	**8.10**	**6.76**	**4.52**
Gibraltar	0	0	0	0	0.26	0
Greece	0	0.39	0.95	0.42	0	0.06
Hong Kong	2.99	1.99	6.56	2.93	3.42	3.90
India	**0.62**	**0.20**	**0.42**	**0.82**	**2.56**	**4.69**
Indonesia	0.62	1.10	2.64	0.17	0.14	0.57
Ireland	0	0	0.15	0.19	0.28	0.22
Israel	0	0.41	0.35	0.57	0.61	0.69
Italy	2.10	1.76	1.44	2.66	1.73	0.96
Japan	26.17	20.66	7.99	5.17	2.53	1.73
Kazakhstan	0	0	0	0	0.33	0.43
Kuwait	0.31	0	0.27	0.35	0.57	0.29
Lebanon	0.93	0.42	0.38	0.18	0.05	0.17
Liechtenstein	0	0	0.13	0.08	0	0
Malaysia	0	0.25	2.31	0.42	0.56	0.70
Mexico	0.40	0.62	2.27	1.97	1.92	2.78

Appendix B (continued)

	1987 %	1991 %	1996 %	2001 %	2006 %	2011 %
Monaco	0	0	0	0	0.96	0.79
Netherlands	2.00	1.35	0.79	0.31	0.25	0.20
New Zealand	0	0	0	0.06	0.14	0.24
Nigeria	0	0	0	0	0	0.35
Norway	0	0	0	0.15	0.41	0.27
Peru	0	0	0.09	0	0	0
Philippines	0	0.20	2.11	0.21	0.17	0.25
Poland	0	0	0	0	0.15	0.20
Portugal	0	0	0	0.17	0.08	0.20
Romania	0	0	0	0	0	0.05
Russia	**0**	**0**	**0**	**0.72**	**5.75**	**9.38**
Saudi Arabia	1.85	1.67	1.46	2.36	2.56	1.25
Singapore	0.39	0.46	1.06	0.65	0.53	0.47
South Africa	0	0	0.36	0.34	0.30	0.37
South Korea	0.62	1.84	2.09	0.15	0.60	0.84
Spain	0.31	0.69	0.36	0.91	1.47	1.37
Sweden	1.85	0	0.92	2.08	0.82	0.95
Switzerland	1.73	3.66	3.74	2.86	4.28	2.56
Taiwan	2.16	1.13	2.21	0.65	0.63	1.39
Thailand	0	0.34	1.87	0.14	0.31	0.40
Turkey	0	0.93	0.79	0.77	1.03	1.42
Ukraine	0	0	0	0	0.15	0.73
United Arab Emirates	0	0	0	0.11	0.44	0.22
United Kingdom	**2.93**	**4.22**	**1.08**	**1.47**	**4.35**	**4.18**
United States	**35.63**	**34.72**	**34.66**	**52.50**	**41.93**	**33.36**
Venezuela	0	0.29	0.21	0.57	0.37	0.17

Notes: Percentage of global wealth refers to wealth held by the billionaires residing in each nation.
Sources: Forbes (1987–2011) various issues.

5

Sexism after Bifurcation? The Arrow of Women's Time and Utopistics for a New World Order

Wilma A. Dunaway

The arrow of women's time is driven by the gendered entropy accumulated from these systemic operations across five centuries. The modern world-system had three significant initial sexist conditions: the transfer of gender inequalities from feudalism, the capitalist devaluation of women's work, and the structuring of semiproletarianized households. Consequently, sexism is embedded at every level from the macroscopic to the fractals of gender inequality that are embedded in households, workplaces and culture. Sexism is a systemic survival mechanism through which capitalists extract hidden and visible surpluses from households and women and externalize systemic costs to them. The arrow of women's time has sustained gender inequalities, and it insures that sexism will be a systemic survival mechanism into the future. As a result, the arrow of women's time confronts us with formidable barriers to a future egalitarian world.

We are living in the creative turmoil of a humane civilization struggling to be born.
Dr. Martin Luther King, Jr., 1964 Nobel Peace Prize acceptance speech

Disorder in the world-system

Since the early 1980s, Immanuel Wallerstein (1995, 155–156) has warned that the modern world-system is in terminal crisis and that it has bifurcated twice since the late 1960s. Wallerstein developed his notion of bifurcation from Prigogine (1980) who startled the scientific world when he posited that new forms of order emerge from systemic crises. While he insisted that a system is more than the sum of its parts, he contended that subsectors can operate independently to push the system far from equilibrium, causing systemic chaos (Schieve and Allen, 1982, 31–38). Periodically, these disorderly fluctuations lead to a bifurcation where the system is thrust into an uncertain period, as it attempts to achieve a new form of order (Nicolis and Prigogine, 1989; Prigogine, 1996).

Prigogine (1996, 157–162) identifies an irreversible *arrow of time* as the source of the tendency of a complex system to move toward bifurcation. Prigogine points to three elements of *entropy* accumulation that drive this arrow of time. At an ever-increasing pace, the system generates entropy by shifting resources inequitably across its subsystems and by consuming and transforming energy into degraded forms. Then the system becomes more disorganized, as it tries to manage and to externalize that entropy. As the system struggles to overcome the negative impacts of entropy, it generates new entropy that exacerbates its chaos (Nicolis and Prigogine, 1989).

As disorder worsens, a dissipative system vacillates chaotically and reaches a bifurcation point (Prigogine, 2003, 19–27). One of the worst uncertainties of such dissipative systems is that there is not a single bifurcation point at which they "become" new structures (Prigogine, 1980). A post-bifurcated age, like our current historical period, can be disheartening because it takes so long for a new order to emerge. There are several cascading bifurcations, each leading to long periods of resource depletion and entropy transfer. As a result, the new dissipative system will "seem to prolong indefinitely" the emergence of new structures (Stengers, 1997, 70). Thus, complexity science helps us comprehend that there will not be a singular, one-time, "big bang" *demise* of the modern world-system (cf. Wallerstein, 2000, 71–105). To paraphrase T. S. Eliot's *The Waste Land*, this post-bifurcated age is not likely to end with a "bang", but a "whimper."

Wallerstein (1995, 156) predicts that we are "in the midst of a process of cascading bifurcations" that may last fifty years or longer. Since the struggle for change will be long, Wallerstein (1987, 206) cautions that "it is most useful to think of this end not as some sharp line but as a band of time, a 'transition' during which the oscillations . . . become greater and more erratic." Our post-bifurcated period will exhibit "wild fluctuations in everything" and "fierce political battles" globally over the trajectory of the new order system (Wallerstein in Samalavicius, 2013, 2). Given the sexist history of the modern world-system (Wallerstein, 1995), it is certain that males and females will be impacted differently by these cascading bifurcations and their chaos. We should not be surprised that our post-bifurcated world-system is not moving in the direction of dismantling sexism. In complexity science terms, a post-bifurcated system is usually more polarized and inequitable than its predecessor (Prigogine, 1996). Thus, the period between 2000 and 2050 will be characterized by widening inequality and misery (Wallerstein, 1995; 1999; 2004a). In this context, there is little rationale to hope that sexism and gender inequalities will disappear. Nor are there any current indicators that we can expect a decline in the polarization between the minority of economically and politically privileged women and the rest of the world's females who struggle against legally and socially discriminatory and/ or politically repressive contexts (United Nations, 2003; 2006; 2010; UNWOMEN, 2011).

No vision for a future more egalitarian world is realistic unless it conceptualizes through the lens of the everyday lives of the majority of the world's women (Masini, 1983; Milojevic, 2012). Therefore, I will argue from the vantage point of the majority of the world's females who are at the most severe risk in this post-bifurcated world-system, i.e., females of Asia, Africa, Latin America, post-socialist countries, and the most economically disadvantaged females of the Global North.[1] Since 1998, the United Nations has defined poverty as

> a denial of choices and opportunities, a violation of human dignity. It means lack of basic capacity to participate effectively in society. It means not having enough to feed and cloth a family, not having a school or clinic to go to, not having the land on which to grow one's food or a job to earn one's living, not having access to credit. It means insecurity, powerlessness and exclusion of individuals, households and communities. It means susceptibility to violence, and it often implies living on marginal or fragile environments, without access to clean water or sanitation (UNESCO, 1998).

By these indicators, a majority of the females of Asia, Africa and Latin America, half or more of the females of post-Socialist European countries, a high proportion of female immigrants to rich countries, a majority of peoples of color and of indigenous origin in rich countries, and the poorest fifth of the females of rich countries are trapped in conditions that meet the UN definition of impoverishment (UNWOMEN, 2011). Moreover, 80 percent of the world's women and households are impoverished when evaluated against a realistic poverty measure that reflects contemporary realities.[2]

The irreversible "arrow of women's time" and systemic change

In order to analyze the gendered manifestations of bifurcation and systemic emergence, I offer the conceptual metaphor of an irreversible *arrow of women's time* that emerged and has endured in the modern world-system. Sexism is "a quintessential product of capitalist civilization" (Wallerstein, 1995, 79) which persists like incurable malignancies that pervade every capitalist space (von Werlhof, 2007). On the one hand, the dissipative modern world-system routinely transfers entropy, resources and knowledge, leading to *polarization* in which it dominates and exploits many to insure that a few thrive (Prigogine, 1996). On the other hand, the modern world-system manages crises through a *hierarchy of survival mechanisms* that

---

1   Throughout the rest of the essay, I will refer to this majority disadvantaged category as "Global South" females.

2   Former World Bank economist, Lant Pritchett, (now at Harvard University) and the mainstream Center for Global Development contend that the global poverty guidepost of US$1.25 a day is kept for political reasons to allow core-controlled development organizations to exhibit fictitious indicators of progress toward eradication of poverty. They contend that the poverty indicator should be elevated to US$10 to US$15 daily globally (Kenny, 2013). Indeed, the World Bank (2008) estimates that 80 percent of the world's population is impoverished when US$10 is set as the indicator of poverty.

further exacerbate inequality (Schieve and Allen, 1982, 127–129). In the modern world-system, these systemic survival mechanisms are gendered. On the one hand, capitalists appropriate the means of social reproduction and household provisioning to support market production (von Werlhof, 1984). On the other hand, capitalists employ sexist practices to keep production costs low, institutionalizing gender inequalities (Schieve and Allen, 1982, 127–128). Furthermore, patriarchal ideologies are employed to legitimate and to rationalize gendered hierarchies of domination and oppression (Milojevic, 2012). These forms of entropy drive the arrow of women's time, increasing the probability that sexism will be transferred into the future.

Emergence of the irreversible "arrow of women's time"

This arrow of women's time is likely to persist into the future because post-bifurcated systems are not cleansed of their histories. A system cannot forget its historic starting points (Prew, 2003) or its survival mechanisms (Schieve and Allen, 1982, 127–129) since it transfers such *initial conditions* at bifurcation (Nicolis and Prigogine, 1989, 170–182; Stengers and Prigogine in Stengers, 1997, 44). As it evolves after bifurcation, the system feeds off entropy and information transfers from its past (Nicolis and Prigogine, 1989, 217–238; Prigogine, 1996, 61–64). One of the initial conditions of the modern world-system was the *transfer of patriarchy and sexism from feudalism*. While capitalism modified these gender hierarchies, it did not eliminate them (Eisenstein, 1979; von Werlhof, 2007). The second initial condition was the *economic and cultural devaluation of women's work*. Through its "ideological framework of oppressive humiliation," capitalism marginalizes most of women's unpaid and paid labors outside the formal economy and devalues them in comparison to paid work in formal sectors (Wallerstein, 1995, 102, 25). In this way, the modern world-system expropriates hidden surpluses and "dark value" from households and women (Clelland, 2012; Dunaway, 2012).

The third initial sexist condition was the *semiproletarianization* of households. Historically, the vast majority of the world's workers—especially women—have never been employed in formal economic sectors (Wallerstein, 1995; ILO, 2012). In reality, new processes of nonwaged and informal sector labor have been created far more rapidly and consistently than workers have been integrated into waged jobs (Tabak and Crichlow, 2000). As a result, household-based work—not wage labor—has been predominant in the modern world-system (Smith et al., 1984, 141). Capitalists have always promoted the continued existence of semiproletarian households because they make possible "the lowest possible wage" (Wallerstein, 1995, 91) and the exploitation of producers who work without wages (von Werlhof, 1984). Moreover, wages covered only part of the cost of reproducing the labor force, requiring workers to depend upon nonwaged resources (Smith and Wallerstein, 1992, 254, 262). Even though women's household-based labors are a structural systemic necessity, capitalists obscure their economic value. Even when women's nonwaged work supports formal commodity production, capitalism lays a "veil of invisibility" over those female labors (von Werlhof, 1984).

Gendered entropy transfers into post-bifurcated capitalism

The arrow of women's time has relentlessly sustained sexism, and it has transferred significant gendered entropy into this post-bifurcated age. For the first time in recorded history, women represent only 49 percent of the world's population. Campaigns to stem population growth, abortion of girl fetuses, and high mortality of pregnant women and young girls account for this historical decline in the early twenty-first century. Worldwide, women control very little wealth, 70 percent of the illiterate adults are females, and there is an increasing trend toward feminization of poverty (United Nations, 2010). Twentieth century gains against sexism were highly polarized, the small advances concentrated in a few rich countries. Thus, there is a wide quality-of-life gap between core females and the rest of the world's women (Romero, 2000, 1016). In sharp contrast, a majority of Global South females are poor and situated in patriarchal societies. Most of them manage vulnerable semiproletarianized households for which they undertake a diverse portfolio of paid and unpaid labors inside and outside their households (Dunaway, 2012). Furthermore, occupational gender segregation is increasing. Global South men are nearly twice as likely as women to enter formal sector jobs. Women primarily earn income from precarious informal sector activities, and their home-based piecework accounts for half the industrial labor force in the Global South. More than half of Global South females reside in peasant and indigenous households that disproportionately experience landlessness, absolute poverty, debt bondage and malnutrition (ILO, 2012).

In their communities, households and workplaces, females are more frequently the victims of multiple forms of physical violence than males. Moreover, new forms of public gendered violence have emerged in the face of women's activism, educational gains and integration into waged workplaces. In addition, females are targeted for rape and a disproportionate share of violence during warfare and in refugee camps (United Nations, 2006; Muñoz Cabrera, 2010). In short, gendered entropy accounts for most of the worst inequalities of this post-bifurcated world-system.

The arrow of women's time and systemic externalities

The modern world-system is characterized by "excess entropy production" (Nicolis and Prigogine, 1989, 71) which must be externalized. The arrow of women's time is grounded in these systemic *externalities*. At the macroscopic level, the core externalizes social and ecological entropy and "exports disorder" to periphery and semiperiphery (Biel, 2006). At microscopic levels, capitalists externalize most of the costs of commodity production to households and to ecosystems, and these processes are highly gendered (Dunaway, 2012). First, capitalism externalizes to mothers the costs associated with the bearing and raising of successive generations of laborers. Complexity scientist Richard Adams observes that the two most basic survival mechanisms of capitalist society are "the organic womb of the mother" and the household in which this woman reproduces and sustains human laborers (Schieve and Allen, 1982, 127–128). Second, capitalists externalize chronic scarcities to households. The modern world-system concentrates wealth and ecological assets into very few hands, limiting resources for Global South women to sustain household provisioning. Ecological degradation and income shortfalls are disproportionately externalized to females, and women are the household members who must contribute the labor needed to care for those made ill by environmental risks or resource depletion (Dunaway, 2012). Since agriculture and fishing have been increasingly integrated into world commodity chains, women's subsistence food production has declined sharply. As a result, per capita food intake has steadily declined in most Global South households (Patnaik, 2008), and females bear the brunt of that malnutrition (Food and Agriculture Organization, 2012).

Third, capitalist crises and structural changes force households to restructure their internal dynamics. Since early eras of colonialism, Global South households have repeatedly reshaped themselves to confront resource shortfalls associated with structural crises of the modern world-system. Fourth, work to consume capitalist commodities is externalized to households and to women. Finally, capitalists disrupt households in order to meet systemic demands for cheap laborers. In every century of the modern world-system, capitalists have destabilized households to remove members for labor migrations (Dunaway, 2012).

The systemic fractals of sexism in households

In addition, the arrow of women's time is externalized as *fractals of systemic sexism* in everyday life. In complexity science, a fractal is a microcosm of a never-ending pattern that replicates itself across different levels of a system (Briggs, 1992). Thus, structural sexism assumes a fractal nature throughout the modern world-system, thrusting miniature replicas everywhere. For that reason, households exhibit systemic fractals of the class, race and gender hierarchies that are embedded in the arrow of women's time. Let me provide three examples. One sexist fractal is *inequitable allocation of work*. Worldwide, women work more total paid and unpaid hours than men, and the inequalities are most severe in Global South households. Compared to boys, Global South girls do more of the unpaid household labor, and they are more often kept out of school to work. Even when wives provide significant income to their households, their contributions do not afford them enough power to shift to males a fairer division of labor. A second sexist fractal is *inequitable distribution of resources.* Access to resources is determined by hierarchical power struggles in which male income earners most often dominate. Even when they contribute more labor power to household survival than males, most Global South females receive lower levels of food, income, education and health care (Dunaway, 2012). A third sexist fractal is the targeting of females for domestic violence (United Nations, 2006; Muñoz Cabrera, 2010).

Crisis in structures of knowledge about sexism and Global South women

The current crisis in our structures of knowledge makes us ill equipped to see the many tentacles of sexism that constrain the everyday lives and labors of Global South women.[3] The first pattern in our gendered knowledge crisis is the gender bifurcation in knowledge production. Because "there has been political, economic and scholarly resistance to incorporating gender into the structures of knowledge" (Wallerstein, 2013a), capitalist science "has ignored women as subjects" and has "utilized a priori assumptions about gender differences that are not based on realistic research" (Wallerstein, 1999, 38). Feminist scientists warn that Western science is a "masculinist project" in which "cultural ideals of gender" shape the production of scientific theory (Keller, 1984, 3–5, 80, 178). However, the myth of intellectual objectivity "insulates the scientist from social responsibility" for dismissing women (Keller, 1983, 16). Through their "patriarchal logic of exclusion," Western scientists discard women's questions from their research agendas, and they reject female knowledge constructions (especially from the Global South) as invalid (Shiva, 1993, 26).

There is empirical evidence that these feminist scientists are correct. Bluntly put, men simply do not study women in either the hard sciences or the social sciences (Woolston, 2001). In fact, they fail to incorporate females into their research questions, even when both genders are impacted by the phenomenon being investigated (Wilson, 2012). Because of this gender clustering, research about women is overwhelmingly conducted by females whose projects face gender discrimination in scholarly prestige and funding allocations (Ferree, 2005; Ritchie, 2009). The world-systems perspective offers an example of gender-bifurcated knowledge production. In the 1970s and 1980s, Wallerstein (1995, 102–104) emphasized that the modern-world system is grounded in "oppressive humiliation" through the ideological frameworks of sexism and racism. Moreover, foundational thinkers pointed to the centrality of sexism and households to capitalism.[4] Despite those intellectual roots,

---

3   This gendered knowledge crisis derives from the larger crisis in the structures of knowledge that Wallerstein (1991) has been warning about for two decades.

4   For early conceptual background developed by Binghamton University's Fernand Braudel Center Research Working Group on Households, Labor Force Formation and the World-Economy, see *Review* 3(2), 5(3), 7(2) and 10(1), now available on JSTOR. For other sources, see Smith et al. (1984), Smith and Wallerstein (1992), Dunaway (2012).

women, sexism and households are severely under-represented in the knowledge production of world-systems analysts (Dunaway, 2001). Judging from my interactions over the last 25 years, many of my world-systems colleagues (male and female) operate out of the mindset that "women's issues" are irrelevant to the questions they investigate, thereby practicing the "patriarchal logic of exclusion" that Shiva (1993, 34) condemns.

Absence of women from future and utopian studies

The second pattern in our gendered knowledge crisis is the absence of women from future and utopian studies (Haug, 2000).[5] Whether radical or mainstream, the vast majority of futurist thinkers have excluded women from their new world scenarios (Daly, 1978; Sardar, 1993; Gunnarsson-Ostling, 2011; Milojevic and Inayatullah, 2011).[6] As a result, the fields of future and utopian studies are "pre-feminist" (Milojevic, 2008, 332).[7] On the one hand, "most practicing futurists are still men, and most of them still marginalize gender as an issue" (Jarva, 1999, 393). On the other hand, "the questions asked, the statistics collected, the larger frameworks of knowledge remain technocratic, oblivious to feminist epistemologies and to issues central to women" (Milojevic and Inayatullah, 2011, 3). Radical visionaries, such as Bloch (2000), Harvey (2000), and Wright (2010), neglect women. Furthermore, future imaginings have been "colonized" in the sense that the Global South is almost completely absent (Sardar, 1993; Gunnarsson-Ostling, 2011).

To complicate matters, Western feminists have rejected future world thinking in the postmodern era (Sargisson, 1996; Schor, 1997; Barr, 2000; Felski, 2000; Kitch, 2000; Laslett and Brenner, 2000; McKenna, 2001; DeKoven, 2004; Milojevic et al.,

---

5   Historically, it is quite ironic that the futures field has such a gender-biased track record. Italian sociologist Eleonora Masini is considered to be "the mother of future studies" because she played such a significant role as secretary general of the World Future Studies Federation. Over her long tenure with that organization, she advocated for the inclusion of women and of gendered research, including focus on the Third World (Dator, 2005).

6   In addition to reliance on the studies of others, I conducted my own assessment. A search of *Sociological Abstracts* drew 66 future world articles since 1995, none of them with discussion of women or sexism. The *Future Studies Research Journal* has published no articles with a focus on women or sexism. Gunnarsson-Ostling (2011) found 78 articles in the journal *Futures* that integrate women, but those represent a tiny percentage of the journal's total article output. Moreover, more than half of these articles are critiques of gender biases rather than gendered futurist scenarios.

7   For example, centrist/critical books by McRae (1995), DeSantis (1996), Dyson (1997), Jacoby (2005) and Hayden and El-Ojeili (2009) ignore women. The goal of the WORLD 2000 Project was "to define the emerging global system," but it directed no attention to women or sexism (Slaughter, 1993). No attention to gender or women is summarized in overviews of futurist models and schools of thought (Samet, 2011).

2008; Eisenstein, 2009; Salleh, 2009).[8] Like their male counterparts, however, the few feminist futurists overlook Global South societies and women. Furthermore, most non-Western feminists focus on strategies for activism around contemporary problems, failing to articulate future world goals for women (e.g., Bhavnani et al., 2003; Wilson et al., 2005).

Twenty-first century crisis of Western feminism

The third pattern in our gendered knowledge crisis is the troubled state of Western feminism. The divisions and debates have grown so sharp that many scholars question whether feminism has a future (Elam and Wiegman, 1995; Hirsch and Keller, 1997; Laslett and Brenner, 2000; Redfern and Aune, 2010; McRobbie, 2008; McRobie, 2012). Feminism has been judged harshly for embracing postmodernism and post-structuralism in ways that exacerbate the divisions among women (Benhabib, 1991; Felski, 2000; Joeres, 2000; Bal, 2001; Gamble, 2001; Gibson-Graham, 2006; Fraser, 2009; Salleh, 2009). In the face of postmodernism, the gulf between academic and activist feminists has widened (Neville-Sington and Sington, 1993; Joeres, 2000; Messer-Davidow, 2002).[9] Since 2000, several scholars have raised concerns that feminist theory has been co-opted by neoliberalism (Hawkesworth, 2000; Romero, 2000; Messer-Davidow, 2002; Gibson-Graham, 2006; Eisenstein, 2009; Fraser, 2009; Gupta, 2012), as women's studies programs have shift toward "gender mainstreaming" and away from the kinds of critiques that typified earlier generations (Eisenstein, 2009; Fraser, 2009; McRobie, 2012). Marxist, socialist and ecological feminists contend that their perspectives have been marginalized by postmodern feminism, vastly diminishing structural analyses of capitalist impacts on women (von Werlhof, 2007; Salleh, 2009).

Feminism is highly fragmented across a broad spectrum of female identities and geographies (Walker, 1995; Looser and Kaplan, 1997; Marchand and Runyan, 2000; Henry, 2004; Tasker and Negra, 2007).While some Western feminists celebrate those differences as their greatest strength (Eisenstein and Jardine, 1990; Waller and Marcos, 2005; Walby, 2011), critics argue that feminist theorists celebrate diversity as a strategy to avoid bringing dissident standpoints into the dominant conceptual core. Since the 1970s, Western women of color and immigrant females have chal-

---

8   In my search of nine feminist journals and three databases, I found no articles with a focus on future world visions. Feminist utopian thinking has been concentrated in analyses of fiction and science fiction (Kessler, 1990; Milojevic, 2008), and there has been some concentration of feminist thinking around a matriarchal superiority in the future (Eller, 2001). For assessments of twenty-first century feminist futurist directions, see Sargisson (2012), McKenna (2001), Eichler et al. (2002), Bhavnani et al. (2003), Bird et al. (2003).

9   Conflicts between Western academic feminists and non-Western feminist activists even play out in global organizations such as the World Social Forum (Alvarez et al., 2003).

lenged feminism for overlooking them (Hooks, 1984; Wallace, 1997; Radford-Hill, 2000; Romero, 2000; Springer, 2002). Conservative women have entered the fray to attack feminism for its exclusion of religious females (Schneiders, 2000; Hunt, 2004) and for destructive impacts on Western families (Sommers, 1995; Graglia, 1998; O'Beirne, 2006).

To exacerbate these Western critiques, Global South scholars have accused feminists of ignoring non-Western women, of misrepresenting them through reductionist and essentialist stereotypes, and of engaging in intellectual and activist colonialism toward them (Mani, 1992; Shiva, 1993; Wilkinson and Kitzinger, 1996; Flew, 1999; Mindry, 2001; Bhavnani et al., 2003; Wilson et al., 2005; Waller and Marcos, 2005; Green, 2007). On the one hand, non-Western scholars challenge the ethnocentric feminist presumption that all women follow the same evolutionary path of progress (Romero, 2000, 1013). On the other hand, they reject the feminist notion that all women suffer similar inequality because of their shared gender (Amos and Parmar, 1984; Mohanty, 1988; Aguilar, 2000). Non-Western women activists also reject the notion of "global feminism" because they see it as a euphemism for Western feminist advocacy around universal sisterhood and neoliberal development agendas (Hassim, 2005, 179). In short, feminism is not the catalyst for future change that some scholars have hoped (Huckle, 1983; Masini, 1993). With an eye toward shaping our utopistics, we cannot leave the future to Western feminists who spend far more time debating one another than they do listening to Global South women or to potential male allies.

In addition to those dilemmas of feminism, I am concerned about four conceptual blinders. First, I agree with feminists Nancy Fraser (2009) and Claudia von Werlhof (2007) that the postmodern and neoliberal turns of feminism have led the field away from structural critiques of capitalism. Second, core Western feminist theories define *men* as the enemy that is holding women back from equality. Absent from such theories is assessment of the ways in which sexism and patriarchy are systemic mechanisms of capitalism (von Werlhof, 2007). Third, Western feminist theories do not conceptualize the *nonwaged* labors that typify the lives of Global South females. On the one hand, Western feminist theory points to unpaid work as the female labor that is exploited in households, thereby excluding a large scope of household-based paid labors (Dunaway, 2012). On the other hand, Western feminists place waged/salaried workers at the heart of their theories (e.g., Weeks, 2011; Jones, 2012), and many of them naively view entry of women into the paid labor force as evidence of progress toward gender equality (Romero, 2000; Eisenstein, 2009). While they worry disproportionately about the "glass ceiling" faced by a tiny percentage of affluent Western females, they fail to recognize that a majority of the world's women (historically and now) are trapped precariously in the informal sector (Tabak and Crichlow, 2000; United Nations, 2003).

The fourth conceptual weakness is that Western feminism has been grounded in political hostility toward housewives and households since its origins (Johnson and Lloyd, 2004). Core feminist theories define the individual woman as the unit of analysis, conceptualizing the household as the primary structural source of gendered oppression. This approach does not help us analyze the lives of Global South women who engage in multiple forms of labor inside and outside their households that force them to confront many types of oppression simultaneously (United Nations, 2006; Muñoz Cabrera, 2010). Nor does a focus on individual females reveal the structural mechanisms through which capitalists drain hidden surpluses from households and women (Clelland, 2013). Turning the theoretical lens upon individuals leads us away from the analysis of capitalism as the source of gendered oppression. Consequently, this individualistic approach leads to the formulation of political agendas that prioritize rebellion against husbands rather than activism against the many forms of systemic sexism that confront females, especially in the Global South.

Given the disconnections between the problems facing Global South females and the theoretical and political preoccupations of Western feminists, it is naive to assume that feminism provides fertile ground to guide us toward a more egalitarian future. In complexity science terms, we need to be skeptical about the forms of Western feminism that are transferred at future bifurcations, primarily because of the class, racial, ethnocentric and pro-capitalist biases that are embedded in that knowledge.

Bringing gendered "creative turmoil" into our utopistics

For two decades, Wallerstein (1998) has advocated *rational utopistics* through which we can influence the transition to a postcapitalist system. As part of our utopistics, he reminds us to "show that gender is a structuring variable that intrudes everywhere, even into zones that seem incredibly remote" (Wallerstein, 1999, 243, 86, 238). I argue that we need new structures of gender knowledge that move away from the class, race, and core biases that distort our knowledge production. In this final section of the essay, I will offer recommendations about how we can bring Global South women into our utopistics. In this intellectual endeavor, I engage ideas from Wallerstein, Prigogine, complexity scientist Isabelle Stengers, mathematical biophysicist Evelyn Fox Keller, and theoretical physicist Vandana Shiva.

Question research agenda exclusions

The first recommendation that these thinkers offer is that scholars should be self-questioning about why they exclude certain topics from their research agendas. Stengers (1997) is concerned that scientists construct knowledge through a process that authorizes and rewards *exclusion* of many worthwhile questions. What gets produced as knowledge depends on the consensus reached in scientific communities (Keller and Longino, 1996, 274), whose rankings are determined by funding and publishing marketplaces in which a few research priorities and dominant paradigms have the greatest value (Stengers, 1997, 128). As the creators of universal laws of economic efficiency, scientists form a fraternal order that protects the interests of the world's accumulators of capital. Thus, pro-capitalist scholars determine "what scientific questions are asked" and "what scientific risks are worth taking." In short, the practice of science is grounded in criteria of "value added" to economic interests (Wallerstein, 1995, 130).

Keller (1982) and Stengers (1997) point to the centrality of the selection process to knowledge production. Wallerstein (2004b, 120–121) agrees, contending that mythical claims of objectivity are used to "hide the intrusion of values" into decision-making about research choices. Selection of theoretical model and research methodology is politically motivated by the training of scientists "to devalue and to scorn" research about questions that are not rewarded by the scientific community. In their choices to ignore, scientists purposefully or unwittingly exercise the power to silence less-valued questions and research topics (Stengers, 2010, 20). Moreover, they mythologize science to be "the only legitimate mode of knowledge" (Wallerstein, 2004b, 13), and they disdain knowledge that is developed outside dominant paradigms (Stengers, 2011, 27). Consequently, capitalist science is "imagination in the service of power" (Stengers, 1997, 74, 116), and its "mode of certifying truth" is intended to constrain anticapitalist dissension (Wallerstein, 2004b, 35).

Keller (1996, 32) argues that "hierarchical and positivist orderings of what can count as knowledge" provide the justifications for scientists to grant themselves permission to ignore women's topics. By doing so, they engage in ideological "polarization of gender" which circumvents new knowledge construction about women (Keller, 1983, 16–18). While choices to ignore questions about women are cloaked in claims of objective criteria, selections are actually grounded in a gendered hierarchy of hidden rules that "authorize the exclusion" of groups and topics that either have less value or that challenge conventional wisdom (Stengers, 2010, 172). By exercising their powers of disqualification and exclusion, scientists "silently assume the ability to judge on behalf of what is not questioned." Thus, they adhere to ideological and economic criteria that guide them away from the closed box of gender investigations. Consequently, Stengers (2011, 285, 398) argues, capitalist science is "haunted by the ghosts of those who have [been] reduced to silence or ridicule" by such biased scientific reasoning.

What can we do to avoid these traps? Stengers (1997, 113) advises scholars to stop granting themselves the "right to ignore" problems that are less valued by the scientific community. In this regard, Keller (1982, 594) warns that "background assumptions can be and most frequently are invisible." Thus, "unreflective acceptance of such assumptions" causes investigators to construct barriers against research questions that challenge those precepts. Marxist utopian Daniel Singer (1999, 221–222) contends that radical scholars need to engage in collective and personal introspection in order to overcome the gender omissions of the Left. "We men in particular," he advises, "must proceed with a deep self-examination to discover the prejudices inherited for generations, their unsuspected weight, the extent to which they condition our behavior."

What rules of thumb for self-introspection do feminist scientists offer? Prigogine and Stengers (in Stengers, 1997, 51–52) observe that "scientists are not doomed to behave like Kuhnian sleepwalkers; they can, without having to give up being scientists, take the initiative, seeking to integrate new perspectives and questions." Keller (1987, 80, 90) warns that researchers should continuously reevaluate their criteria for "good" science. They should begin by questioning the degree to which they can be "objective" since "the force of beliefs, interests, and cultural norms enters into the process by which effective knowledge is generated." She also challenges scholars to admit that "equations between science and power, between objective and masculine, and between power and domination shape our conceptions of both science and gender." When defining target of study and research questions, Stengers (2011, 229) advises scholars to ask themselves: "Who/what are the 'excluded others' whose relevance and significance I am denying?" In simpler terms, I would add that researchers (both male and female) need to ask themselves this question: "If I look out at my subject matter and never see women, why is that?" The answer is very rarely going to be that there are no women there.

There are always rationalizations against change, so how do we get past them? The excuse I have heard most often from colleagues is that gendered analyses are just too difficult. Since all investigations are involved and time-consuming, Stengers (2011, 180) contends scholarly evaluation of difficulty is determined by the value they assign to the subject or question. A second excuse I have heard frequently is that males consider gender to be the sphere of women. Ignorance, or the act of ignoring, is a dangerous form of knowledge entropy, Prigogine (1996, 24) warns. Wallerstein (1999, 246) adds that clinging to self-perceived turf boundaries leads to "new ignorances." That, he insists, "is the worst of scholarly sins, and the greatest possible deterrence to clarity." In that vein, I would add that the gendered crisis in our structures of knowledge has been caused by intellectual silencing of women in the same ways that females are subordinated and devalued by capitalism. When researchers ignore sexism, they help capitalists to construct and to maintain their veil of invisibility over the exploitation of women's work and gender inequalities. "Our mind set is so stunted that we cannot dream up alternatives," Peterson (2011, 195) argues. "Rather than reflect critically on how we got here and its costs, we . . . deny any need to rethink how we think." To put it bluntly, research that excludes sexism is a pro-capitalist activity. Even among scholar-activists seeking to change the world for the better, research choices to ignore sexism and women sustain gender exploitation in this post-bifurcated age and work against attaining a more humane postcapitalist system.

Practice science of the hidden and the forgotten

The second recommendation that these thinkers offer is that researchers should practice science of the hidden and the forgotten. Stengers (2010, 71) complains that scientists routinely overlook "what is concealed," creating a closed box of questions and topics that are excluded from knowledge construction. Consequently, Prigogine and Stengers (in Stengers, 1997, 51–52) argue that investigators need to prioritize "the more hidden" patterns. They should begin every research project, they insist, by asking themselves two questions: "What lines of inquiry have been hidden?" and "Why have those ideas been devalued and forgotten?" Similarly, Wallerstein (1995, 84) points out that scientism "creates veils that hinder perception of the underlying operations of historical capitalism." Vandana Shiva (1993; 2007) adds that a "mono-culture of the mind" derives from this connection between capitalism and Western science. Since the modern world-system seeks to conceal who and what it exploits and damages, capitalist science deters research that opens up those silenced realms. For that reason, feminist Spike Peterson (2011, 196) insists that the central research objectives are "to become aware of 'hidden' obstacles" and "to rethink assumptions" that prevent recognition of directions that challenge capitalism. "The heavy hand of scientism is part of what needs to be removed," Wallerstein (2004b, 5, 115) adds, including the "deceptive, self-serving mythologies" of scientists that encourage the silencing of certain knowledge. He argues that we should be compelled by the opposite goal, i.e., "to uncover in whose interests and in what ways realities are hidden, and then justified as normal, as inevitable, indeed as rational" (Wallerstein, 2013a).

"If the doors of perception were cleansed," poet William Blake wrote, "everything would appear as it is. But we see all things through narrow chinks." To overcome this myopic distortion of the world, Stengers (2011, 416) admonishes researchers to "dream the dark," i.e., to be preoccupied with the questions that scientific experts "blacklist." If we dream the dark, as Stengers counsels, what knowledge might we acquire to battle the arrow of women's time? We might come to understand that researchers do not see or choose to explore sexism because capitalists conceal it and mystify its effects as benign or nonexistent. Indeed, sexism resists visibility because it is most profitable for capitalists when it is hidden (Peterson, 2011, 197). We might comprehend that all macrostructural problems, like hegemonic rivalry and global warming, have gendered manifestations that need to be analyzed. We might construct new knowledge about the hydralike reaches of gender inequalities, including the roles of women in sustaining patriarchy and sexism. We might address critical attention to the obscured and undisclosed ways in which Global South women's labors subsidize capitalism and keep commodity prices low for affluent consumers (Clelland, 2012; 2013).[10] We might clarify the ways in which capitalist profits are maximized because semiproletarianized households absorb so much of the externalized entropy of the modern world-system (Dunaway, 2012). We might see the ways in which patriarchy and sexism are being reconsolidated to steal Global South women's work for twenty-first century capitalist agriculture and industry (von Werlhof, 2007; Dedeoglu, 2013). We might more clearly conceptualize the linkages between the many forms of gendered violence and the "normal" operations of the capitalist world-system (Muñoz Cabrera, 2010). Even though it is embedded everywhere, sexism is hard to see, as it silently orders everything. As feminist Spike Peterson (2011, 197, 195) cautions, however, "we cannot . . . come to terms with, or effectively move beyond what we refuse to see." *Seeing* what is hidden will not by itself be enough to end sexism, but it is the first necessary "dream-the-dark" step that most scholars have not yet taken.

Practice science as poetic listeners

Stengers and Prigogine provide us with a third recommendation. They exhort investigators to "be poetic listeners" (Stengers, 1997, 58) in order to see and to focus on the "small and insignificant" that they typically think is too unimportant to study. A poetic stanza will help readers to grasp Stengers and Prigogine's complex meaning. Emily Dickinson wrote the powerful line: "I heard a fly buzz when I died." Stengers and Prigogine (in Stengers, 1997, 48–49) are challenging us to be just as focused as this dying person in our attention to small phenomena that may have unexpected systemic impacts. Disturbances by "the small and unnoticed" can "cause new systems to be born," they insist. In this post-bifurcated age, the distinctions we have been accustomed to making between macroscopic and microscopic are no longer valid. During chaos, microscopic inputs can "reverberate their effects throughout the system" (Stengers, 1997, 69). Consequently, we cannot afford to continue to follow outdated prejudices about what research should be ignored. Far from equilibrium, minor fluctuations may "play a role in changing the macroscopic regime of a system." In other words, what was once too small to make the research agenda can now have great significance because "the system has become sensitive" in ways that it was not in the past. In this sense, the small and the unimportant "take on meaning" that the researcher did not previously accord them (Stengers, 1997, 9).

    What happens to women has been routinely assigned to the realm of the *ignored microscopic*, on the assumption that sexism is "unrelated noise" (Stengers, 1997,

---

10   For example, Clelland (2012; 2013) has introduced the gendered notion of *dark value* to explore the economic value of women's invisible work, contending that their labors provide most of the energy that drives capitalist commodity chains. "Almost all labor–paid or unpaid–contributes to chains of value," he argues, "but these are invisible 'gifts' to commodity chains that increase household misery in the periphery" (Clelland, 2013, 81).

9) that will not determine the direction of systemic change. However, complexity scientists contend that small "collective phenomena" (Stengers and Prigogine in Stengers, 1997, 48–49) can have macroscopic impacts at or near bifurcations. If they are correct in their predictions, the cumulative "small" miseries of Global South females and households and the thousands of women's resistance efforts around the world are likely to have an unexpected impact on structural outcomes in coming decades.

In this post-bifurcated age, that which has been considered too "small" to attract research attention may become more noisy than Dickinson's buzzing fly in a death chamber. I have previously called your attention to a number of overlooked "buzzing flies" with respect to women, but there is another buzzing fly in the *arrow of women's time* that Western scholars ignore. Evelyn Fox Keller (1983, 15) points out that Western science devalues analysis of everyday life. Thus, capitalism has structured a science that treats the problems, needs and resistance of ordinary people as distractions that are irrelevant to systemic outcomes.

One of the fractals of everyday life that is overwhelmingly ignored by Western social scientists is the centrality of *dignity* to perceptions of a better life, especially among non-Western peoples. When I was a young girl, the Ku Klux Klan beat my Cherokee father and left him dying in a field in the racially-segregated U.S. South. After a recovery that required months, Dad organized his Indian, Black and poor white sharecropping neighbors into a perilous resistance plan. My father had never heard of Karl Marx, but he understood that capitalist economics lay at the heart of their suffering. So they burned the barn of the affluent Klan leader and left a letter in his mailbox that warned: "For each of us you hurt or cheat, we will hurt your pocketbook." When I read in college about the lynchings that were the fate of such rebellious people of color, I asked my father how he and my mother could risk everything in the face of such ruthless power. He responded "Life without Dignity is worse than physical death." Many contemporary resistance movements embrace this philosophy. At its 2013 meeting, for instance, the World Social Forum added the rallying cry "DIGNITY" to its previous slogan "Another World Is Possible" (Wallerstein, 2013b).

Yearning for dignity shields oppressed people from being paralyzed by the sense that the modern world-system is too strong for them to confront. When people are ready to risk everything for dignity, they rebel against the fairytale of progress in ways that can push capitalism toward crisis. Strikingly, however, dignity is not a variable in Western theories because social scientists claim they cannot measure it.

Conclusion

The arrow of women's time is driven by five centuries of accumulated gendered entropy and externalized costs. The modern world-system had three significant initial sexist conditions: the transfer of gender inequalities from feudalism, the capitalist devaluation of women's work, and the structuring of semiproletarianized households. The arrow of women's time is driven by the gendered entropy accumulated from the systemic operations of these three historical starting points. Moreover, sexism is a systemic survival mechanism through which capitalists extract hidden and visible surpluses from households and women and externalize systemic costs to them. All these sexist processes subsidize global capital accumulation and help the system manage crises. Thus, the modern world-system cannot rid itself of gender inequalities without threatening capitalist profits. Finally, sexism is embedded at every level from the macroscopic to the fractals of gender inequality that are embedded in households, workplaces and culture. Consequently, the arrow of women's time has relentlessly sustained gender inequalities, and it insures that sexism will be a systemic survival mechanism into the future. As a result, the arrow of women's time confronts us with formidable barriers to a future egalitarian world. Unless current conditions change drastically, most of the world's women will still be far from reaching gender parity with males in the twenty-fourth century (United Nations, 2010).

I am sure you have heard this dialectical rhyme by Hughes Mearns: "Last night I saw upon the stair a little man who wasn't there. He wasn't there again today. Oh, how I wish he'd go away." But I doubt you have ever heard the moral in his final stanza. "As I was sitting in my chair, I knew the bottom wasn't there, nor legs, nor back. But I just sat, ignoring little things like that." Each of us makes political and moral proclamations about the future world order when we ignore women and sexism. "We must put at the forefront of our consciousness and our action," Wallerstein (2009, 11) cautions, "the three fundamental inequalities of the world—gender, class, and race." Unless we become more proficient at *seeing* and more committed to *including* women—especially the majority of the world's females concentrated in the Global South—we cannot hope to dismantle the arrow of women's time that will carry sexist entropy into the future. As physicist utopian John Polkinghorne cautions, "the future is not up there waiting for us to arrive; we make it as we go along" (Holte, 1993, 101).

References

Aguilar, Delia. 2000. Questionable Claims: Colonialism Redux, Feminist Style. *Race and Class,* 41(3): 1–12.

Alvarez, Sonia, Nalu Faria, and Miriam Nolbre. 2003. "Another (Also Feminist) World Is Possible." *Revista Estudos Feministas,* 11(2): 199–220.

Amos, Valerie, and Pratibha Parmar. 1984. Challenging Imperial Feminism. *Feminist Review,* 17: 3–19.

Bal, Nieke. 2001. "Enfolding Feminism." In Elisabeth Bronfen and Misha Kavka, (eds.), *Feminist Consequences: Theory for the New Century.* New York: Columbia University

Press.Barr, Marlene (ed.). 2000. *Future Females, The Next Generation: New Voices and Velocities in Feminist Science Fiction.* Lanham, MD: Rowman and Littlefield.

Benhabib, Sayla. 1991. Feminism and Postmodernism: An Uneasy Alliance. *Praxis International,* 11(2): 137–150.

Bhavnani, Kum-Kum, John Foran, and Priya Kurian. 2003. *Feminist Futures: Re-Imagining Women, Culture and Development.* London: Zed.

Biel, Robert. 2006. The Interplay between Social and Environmental Degradation in the Development of the International Political Economy. *Journal of World-Systems Research,* 12(1): 109–147.

Bird, Delya, Wedney Were, and Terri White (eds.). 2003. *Future Imaginings: Sexualities and Gender in the New Millennium.* Crawley: University of Western Australia Press.

Bloch, Ernest. 2000. *The Spirit of Utopia.* Palo Alto, CA: Stanford University Press.

Briggs, John. 1992. *Fractals: The Patterns of Chaos.* New York: Touchstone.

Clelland, Donald. 2012. "Surplus Drain and Dark Value in the Modern World-System." In Salvatore Balbones and Christopher Chase-Dunn (eds.), *Routledge Handbook of World-Systems Analysis.* London: Routledge.

Clelland, Donald. 2013. "Unpaid Labor as Dark Value in Global Commodity Chains." In Wilma Dunaway (ed.), *Gendered Commodity Chains: Seeing Women's Work and Households in 21st Century Global Production.* Palo Alto, CA: Stanford University Press.

Daly, Mary. 1978. *Gyn/Ecology: The Metaethics of Radical Feminism.* Boston: Beacon Press.

Dator, James. 2005. The WFSF and I. *Futures,* 37(5): 361–385.

Dedeoglu, Saniye. 2013. "Patriarchy Reconsolidated: Women's Work in Three Global Commodity Chains of Turkey's Garment Industry." In Wilma Dunaway (ed.), *Gendered Commodity Chains: Seeing Women's Work and Households in 21st Century Global Production.* Palo Alto, CA: Stanford University Press.

DeKoven, Marianne. 2004. *Utopia Limited: The Sixties and the Emergence of the Postmodern.* Durham: Duke University Press.

DeSantis, Hugh. 1996. *Beyond Progress: An Interpretive Odyssey to the Future.* Chicago: University of Chicago Press.

Dunaway, Wilma. 2001. The Double Register of History: Situating the Forgotten Woman and Her Household in Capitalist Commodity Chains. *Journal of World-Systems Research,* 7(1): 2–31.

Dunaway, Wilma. 2012. "The Semiproletarian Household over the *Longue Duree* of the World-System." In Richard Lee (ed.), *The Longue Duree of the Modern World-System.* Albany, NY: SUNY Press.

Dyson, Freeman. 1997. *Imagined Worlds.* Cambridge: Harvard University Press.

Eichler, Margrit, June Larkin, and Shelia Neysmith. 2002. *Feminist Utopias: Revisioning Our Futures.* New York: Inanna.

Eisenstein, Hester. 2009. *Feminism Seduced: How Global Elites Use Women's Labor and Ideas to Exploit the World.* Boulder: Paradigm.

Eisenstein, Hester, and Alice Jardine (eds.). 1990. *The Future of Difference*. New Brunswick: Rutgers University Press.

Eisenstein, Zillah. 1979. *Capitalist Patriarchy and the Case for Socialist Feminism*. New York: Monthly Review Press.

Elam, Diam, and Robyn Wiegman (eds.). 1995. *Feminism beside Itself*. London: Routledge.

Eller, Cynthia. 2001. *The Myth of Matriarchal Prehistory: Why an Invented Past Won't Give Women a Future*. New York: Beacon Press.

Felski, Rita. 2000. *Doing Time: Feminist Theory and Postmodern Culture*. New York: New York University Press.

Ferree, Myra. 2005. It's Time to Mainstream Research on Gender. *Chronicle of Higher Education*, August 12: 33.

Flew, Fiona. 1999. Local Feminisms, Global Futures. *Women's Studies International Forum*, 22(4): 393–403.

Food and Agriculture Organization. 2012. *The State of Food Insecurity in the World*. Rome: Food and Agriculture Organization.

Fraser, Nancy. 2009. Feminism, Capitalism and the Cunning of History. *New Left Review*, 56: 97–117.

Gamble, Sarah (ed.). 2001. *Routledge Companion to Feminism and Postfeminism*. London: Routledge.

Gibson-Graham, J. K. 2006. *The End of Capitalism (As We Knew It): A Feminist Critique of Political Economy*. Minneapolis: University of Minnesota Press.

Graglia, F. Carolyn. 1998. *Domestic Tranquility: A Brief against Feminism*. Dallas, TX: Spence.

Green, Joyce (ed.). 2007. *Making Space for Indigenous Feminism*. Black Point, NS: Fernwood.

Gunnarsson-Ostling, Ulrika. 2011. Gender in Futures: A Study of Gender and Feminist Papers Published in *Futures*, 1969–2009. *Futures*, 43: 1029–1039.

Gupta, Rahila. 2012. Has Neoliberalism Knocked Feminism Sideways? *Centrestage*, January 4: 13–15.

Harvey, David. 2000. *Spaces of Hope*. Los Angeles: University of California Press.

Hassim, Shireen. 2005. Voices, Hierarchies and Spaces: Reconfiguring the Women's Movement. *Politikon: South African Journal of Political Studies*, 32: 175–193.

Haug, Frigga. 2000. On the Necessity of Conceiving the Utopian in a Feminist Fashion. *Socialist Register*, 36: 53–66.

Hawkesworth, Mary. 2000. "Confounding Gender." In Carolyn Allen and Judith Howard (eds.), *Provoking Feminisms*. Chicago: University of Chicago Press.

Hayden, Patrick, and Chamsy El-Ojeili (eds.). 2009. *Globalization and Utopia: Critical Essays*. New York: Palgrave Macmillan.

Henry, Astrid. 2004. *Not My Mother's Sister: Generational Conflict and Third Wave Feminism*. Bloomington: University of Indiana Press.

Hirsch, Marianne, and Evelyn Keller (eds.). 1997. *Conflicts in Feminism*. London: Routledge.

Holte, John (ed.). 1993. *Chaos: The New Science*. Lanham, MD: University Press of America.

Hooks, Bell. 1984. *Feminist Theory: From Margin to Center*. Boston: South End Press.

Huckle, Patricia. 1983. "Feminism: A Catalyst for the Future." In Jan Zimmerman (ed.), *The Technological Woman*. Westport, CT: Praeger.

Hunt, Helen. 2004. *Faith and Feminism: A Holy Alliance*. New York: Atria Books.

ILO (International Labour Organization). 2012. *Global Employment Trends for Women*. Geneva: International Labour Organization.

Jacoby, Russell. 2005. *Picture Imperfect: Utopian Thought for an anti-Utopian Age*. New York: Columbia University Press.

Jarva, Vuokko. 1999. Dissenting Identities: Karelian Strong Women's Futures Voices. *Futures*, 31(2): 235–244.

Joeres, Ruth-Ellen B. 2000. Feminism and the Word Wars. *Signs*, 25(4): 1153–1156.

Johnson, Lesley, and Justin Lloyd. 2004. *Sentenced to Everyday Life: Feminism and the Housewife*. New York: Berg.

Jones, Bernie. 2012. *Women Who Opt Out: The Debate over Working Mothers and Working Family Balance*. New York: New York University Press.

Keller, Evelyn. 1982. Feminism and Science. *Signs*, 7(3): 589–602.

Keller, Evelyn. 1983. Feminism as an Analytic Tool for the Study of Science. *Academe*, 69(5): 15–21.

Keller, Evelyn. 1984. *Reflections on Gender and Science*. New Haven: Yale University Press.

Keller, Evelyn. 1987. Women Scientists and Feminist Critics of Science. *Daedalus*, 116(4): 77–91.

Keller, Evelyn. 1996. "Feminism and Science." In Evelyn Keller and Helen Longino (eds.), *Feminism and Science*. New York: Oxford University Press.

Keller, Evelyn, and Helen Longino (eds.). 1996. *Feminism and Science*. New York: Oxford University Press.

Kenny, Charles. 2013. Why Ending Extreme Poverty Isn't Good Enough. *Bloomsburg Business Week*, April 28.

Kessler, Carol. 1990. Bibliography of Utopian Fiction by US Women, 1836–1988. *Utopian Studies*, 1(1): 1–58.

Kitch, Sally. 2000. *Higher Ground: From Utopianism to Realism in American Feminist Thought and Theory*. Chicago: University of Chicago Press.

Laslett, Barbara, and Johanna Brenner. 2000. 21st Century Academic Feminism in the US: Utopian Visions and Practical Actions. *Signs*, 25(4): 1231–1235.

Looser, Devoney, and Ann Kaplan (eds.). 1997. *Generations: Academic Feminists in Dialogue*. Minneapolis: University of Minnesota Press.

Mani, Lata. 1992. "Multiple Mediations: Feminist Scholarship in the Age of Multinational Reception." In Helen Crowley and Susan Himmelweit (eds.), *Knowing Women*. Milton Keynes, UK: Open University Press.

Marchand, Marianne, and Anne Runyan. 2000. *Gender and Global Restructuring: Sightings, Sites and Resistances*. London: Routledge.

Masini, Eleonora. 1983. *Visions of Desirable Societies*. New York: Pergamon.

Masini, Eleonora. 1993. *Women as Builders of Alternative Futures*. Report 11. Trier: Centre for European Studies, University of Trier.

McKenna, Erin. 2001. *The Task of Utopia: A Pragmatist and Feminist Perspective*. Lanham, MD: Rowman and Littlefield.

McRae, Hamish. 1995. *The World in 2020, Power, Culture and Prosperity: A Vision of the Future*. London: Harper Collins.

McRobbie, Angela. 2008. *The Aftermath of Feminism: Gender, Culture and Social Change*. Thousand Oaks, CA: Sage.

McRobie, Heather. 2012. Gender Mainstreaming: The Future of Feminism? Or Feminism's Disappearing Act? *Centrestage*, January 22: 12–14.

Messer-Davidow, Ellen. 2002. *Disciplining Feminisms: From Social Activism to Academic Discourse*. Durham, NC: Duke University Press.

Milojevic, Ivana. 2008. Timing Feminism, Feminising Time. *Futures*, 40: 329–345.

Milojevic, Ivana. 2012. Why the Creation of a Better World Is Premised on Achieving Gender Equity. *Journal of Futures Studies*, 16(4): 51–66.

Milojevic, Ivana, Karen Hurley, and Anne Jenkins. 2008. Futures of Feminism. *Futures*, 40(4): 313–318.

Milojevic, Ivana, and Sohail Inayatullah. 2011. Feminist Critiques and Visions of the Future. *Metafuture*. URL: www.metafuture.org/articles-by-sohail-inayatullah/feminist-critiques-and-visions-of-the-future/ (accessed February 14, 2014).

Mindry, Deborah. 2001. Nongovernmental Organizations, "Grassroots," and the Politics of Virtue. *Signs*, 26: 1187–1211.

Mohanty, Chandra. 1988. Under Western Eyes: Feminist Scholarship and Colonial Discourses. *Feminist Review*, 30: 61–88.

Muñoz Cabrera, Patricia. 2010. Intersecting Violences: A Review of Feminist Theories and Debates on Violence against Women in Latin America. London: Central American Women's Network. URL: http://www.cawn.org/assets/Intersecting%20Violences%20FINAL.pdf (accessed June 1, 2013).

Neville-Sington, Pamela, and David Sington. 1993. *Paradise Dreamed: How Utopian Thinkers Have Changed the Modern World*. London: Bloomsbury.

Nicolis, Gregoire, and Ilya Prigogine. 1989. *Exploring Complexity: An Introduction*. New York: W. H. Freeman.

O'Beirne, Kate. 2006. *Women Who Make the World Worse and How Their Radical Feminist Assault Is Ruining Our Families*. New York: Penguin.

Patnaik, Prabhat. 2008. The Accumulation Process in the Period of Globalisation. *Economic and Political Weekly*, June 28: 108–113.

Peterson, V. Spike. 2011. "A Long View of Globalization and Crisis." In Barry Gills (ed.), *Globalization in Crisis*. London: Routledge.

Prew, Paul, 2003. "The 21st Century World-Ecosystem: Systemic Collapse or Transition to a New Dissipative Structure?" In Wilma Dunaway (Ed.), *New Theoretical Directions for the 21st Century World-System*. Westport, CT: Praeger.

Prigogine, Ilya. 1980. *From Being to Becoming*. San Francisco: W. H. Freeman.

Prigogine, Ilya. 1996. *The End of Certainty: Time Chaos, and the Laws of Nature*. New York: Free Press.

Prigogine, Ilya. 2003. *Is Future Given?* London: World Scientific.

Radford-Hill, Sheila. 2000. *Further to Fly: Black Women and the Politics of Empowerment*. Minneapolis: University of Minnesota Press.

Redfern, Catherine, and Kristin Aune. 2010. *Reclaiming the f Word: The New Feminist Movement*. London: Zed.

Ritchie, Timothy. 2009. "Gender Biases in Research." In Jodie O'Brien (ed.), *Encyclopedia of Gender and Society*. Thousand Oaks, CA: Sage.

Romero, Mary. 2000. Marking Time and Progress. *Signs*, 25(4): 1013–1016.

Salleh, Ariel. 2009. The Dystopia of Technoscience: An Ecofeminist Critique of Postmodern Reason. *Futures*, 41(4): 201–209.

Samalavicius, Almantas. 2013. A New World System: Interview of Immanuel Wallerstein. *Eurozine*, February 8: 18–19.

Samet, Robert. 2011. Exploring the Future with Complexity Science: The Emerging Models. *Futures*, 43: 831–839.

Sardar, Ziauddin. 1993. Colonizing the Future: The "Other" Dimension of Futures Studies. *Futures*, 25(2): 179–187.

Sargisson, Lucy. 1996. *Contemporary Feminist Utopianism*. London: Routledge.

Sargisson, Lucy. 2012. *Fool's Gold: Utopianism in the 21st Century*. London: Palgrave Macmillan.

Schieve, William, and Peter Allen (eds.). 1982. *Self-Organization and Dissipative Structures: Applications in the Physical and Social Sciences*. Austin: University of Texas Press.

Schneiders, Sandra. 2000. *With Oil in Their Lamps: Faith, Feminism, and the Future*. New York: Paulist Press.

Schor, Juliet. 1997. "Utopias of Women's Time." In A. Lenning, M. Bakker, and I. Vanwesenbech (eds.), *Feminist Utopias in a Postmodern Era*. Tilburg: Tilburg University Press.

Shiva, Vandana. 1993. *Monocultures of the Mind: Biodiversity, Biotechnology and Agriculture*. London: Zed.

Shiva, Vandana. 2007. *Democratizing Biology: Reinventing Biology from a Feminist, Ecological and Third World Perspective*. Boulder: Paradigm.

Singer, Daniel. 1999. *Whose Millennium? Theirs or Ours?* New York: Monthly Review Press.

Slaughter, William. 1993. WORLD 2000: An International Planning Dialogue to Help Shape the New Global System. *Futures,* 25(1): 5–21.

Smith, Joan, and Immanuel Wallerstein (eds.). 1992. *Creating and Transforming Households: The Constraints of the World-Economy.* Cambridge: Cambridge University Press.

Smith, Joan, Immanuel Wallerstein, and Hans-Dieter Evers (eds.). 1984. *Households and the World-Economy.* Thousand Oaks, CA: Sage.

Sommers, Christina. 1995. *Who Stole Feminism? How Women Have Destroyed Women.* New York: Touchstone.

Springer, Kimberly. 2002. Third Wave Black Feminism? *Signs,* 27(4): 1059–1082.

Stengers, Isabelle. 1997. *Power and Invention: Situating Science.* Minneapolis: University of Minnesota Press.

Stengers, Isabelle. 2010. *Cosmopolitics I.* Minneapolis: University of Minnesota Press.

Stengers, Isabelle. 2011. *Cosmopolitics II.* Minneapolis: University of Minnesota Press.

Tabak, Faruk, and Michaeline Crichlow (eds.). 2000. *Informalization: Process and Structure.* Baltimore: Johns Hopkins University Press.

Tasker, Yvonne, and Diane Negra (eds.). 2007. *Interrogating Postfeminism: Gender and the Politics of Popular Culture.* Durham: Duke University Press.

UNESCO. 1998. Statement of Commitment to Eradicate Poverty. URL: www.unesco. org/most/acc4pov.htm (accessed June 1, 2013).

United Nations. 2003. *The World's Women 2000: Trends and Statistics.* New York: Oxford University Press.

United Nations. 2006. "In-Depth Report on All Forms of Violence against Women." URL: http://daccess-dds-ny.un.org/doc/UNDOC/GEN/N06/419/74/PDF/N0641974. pdf?OpenElement (accessed February 14, 2014).

United Nations. 2010. *Human Development Report.* New York: United Nations.

UNWOMEN. 2011. *Progress of the World's Women: In Pursuit of Justice.* URL: http:// progress.unwomen.org/pdfs/EN-Report-Progress.pdf (accessed June 1, 2013).

von Werlhof, Claudia. 1984. "The Proletarian Is Dead: Long Live the Housewife?" In Joan Smith, Immanuel Wallerstein, and Hans Evers (eds.), *Households and the World-Economy.* Thousand Oaks, CA: Sage.

von Werlhof, Claudia. 2007. No Critique of Capitalism without a Critique of Patriarchy! Why the Left Is No Alternative. *Capitalism Nature Socialism,* 18(1): 13–27.

Walby, Sylvia. 2011. *The Future of Feminism.* London: Polity.

Walker, Rebecca. 1995. *To Be Real: Telling the Truth and Changing the Face of Feminism.* New York: Anchor Books.

Wallace, Michele. 1997. *To Hell and Back: On the Road with Black Feminism.* Pamphlet. New York: Olympia X.

Waller, Marguerite, and Sylvia Marcos (eds.). 2005. *Dialogue and Difference: Feminisms Challenge Globalization.* New York: Palgrave Macmillan.

Wallerstein, Immanuel. 1987. Historical Systems as Complex Systems. *European Journal of Operational Research,* 30: 203–207.

Wallerstein, Immanuel. 1991. *Unthinking Social Science: The Limits of 19th Century Paradigms*. London: Basil Blackwell.

Wallerstein, Immanuel. 1995. *Historical Capitalism with Capitalist Civilization*. London: Verso.

Wallerstein, Immanuel. 1998. *Utopistics or Historical Choices for the 21st Century*. New York: New Press.

Wallerstein, Immanuel. 1999. *The End of the World As We Know It: Social Science for the 21st Century*. Minneapolis: University of Minnesota Press.

Wallerstein, Immanuel. 2000. *The Essential Wallerstein*. New York: New Press.

Wallerstein, Immanuel. 2004a. *Alternatives: The United States Confronts the World*. Boulder: Paradigm.

Wallerstein, Immanuel. 2004b. *The Uncertainties of Knowledge*. Philadelphia: Temple University Press.

Wallerstein, Immanuel. 2009. Crisis of the Capitalist System: Where Do We Go from Here? Harold Wolpe Lecture, University of KwaZulu-Natal, South Africa. *Monthly Review Magazine*, December 12, 2009. URL: http://mrzine.monthlyreview.org/2009/wallerstein121109.html.

Wallerstein, Immanuel. 2013a. "Foreword." In Wilma Dunaway (ed.), *Gendered Commodity Chains: Seeing Women's Work and Households in 21st Century Global Production*. Palo Alto, CA: Stanford University Press.

Wallerstein, Immanuel. 2013b. The World Social Forum: Still Meeting Its Challenge. Commentary No. 350, Fernand Braudel Center, Binghamton University. URL: http://www2.binghamton.edu/fbc/commentaries/archive-2013/350en.htm (accessed February 14, 2014).

Weeks, Kathi. 2011. *The Problem with Work: Feminism, Marxism, Antiwork Politics and Postwork Imaginaries*. Durham, NC: Duke University Press.

Wilkinson, Sue, and Celia Kitzinger (eds.). 1996. *Representing the Other: A Feminism and Psychology Reader*. Thousand Oaks, CA: Sage.

Wilson, Robin. 2012. Scholarly Publishing's Gender Gap. *Chronicle of Higher Education*, October 22: 21–22.

Wilson, Shamillah, Anasuya Sengupta, and Kristy Evans (eds.). 2005. *Defending Our Dreams: Global Feminist Voices for a New Generation*. London: Zed.

Woolston, Chris. 2001. The Gender Gap in Science. *Chronicle of Higher Education*, October 22: 23–24.

World Bank. 2008. Development Indicators. URL: www.data.worldbank.org/indicators (accessed June 1, 2013).

Wright, Erik Olin. 2010. *Envisioning Real Utopias*. London: Verso.

6

The Battle for the Future Has Already Begun: The Reassertion of Race, Space and Place in World-Systems Geographies and Anti-Systemic Cartographies

Tom Reifer

In the last few decades, leading world-systems analysts, notably Immanuel Wallerstein and Giovanni Arrighi, have argued that after some 500 to 700 years of evolution, the capitalist world-system is undergoing fundamental transformation. Indeed, a host of other authors argue that, given current trajectories and instabilities accompanying today's discontinuous changes, either a new system or systems will emerge, or at the very least that future trajectories of geo-economic regions and the global system will differ in fundamental, albeit unknown ways, from past cycles and secular trends as the latter reach their asymptotes. How to map such changes though? As Wallerstein (1974, 9) noted in *The Modern World-System*, ". . . the proper understanding of the social dynamics of the present requires a theoretical comprehension that can only be based on the study of the widest possible range of phenomena, including through all of historical time and space," calling for a unidisciplinary approach to the study of social change (emphasis added). In this same volume, Wallerstein wrote of two major watersheds in world history, the Neolithic Revolution and the creation of the modern world-system. And yet, Arrighi and Wallerstein themselves have for the most part not heeded this call to analyze planetary and human evolution over this broader time period, focusing instead largely on the capitalist world-system and earlier geo-economic regions, primarily Western Europe and East Asia. Longer periods of human evolution, from the Paleolithic to the present, have instead been analyzed by a host of other scholars. This chapter brings together recent, theoretically informed empirical studies on human evolution over the *longue durée*. The focus is on the reassertion of race, space and place in world-system geographies and anti-systemic cartographies, as well as on examining political projects for more democratic, egalitarian, peaceful and ecologically sustainable futures, on new and enlarged social foundations, in our most recent geological era, the Anthropocene.

Introduction

World-systems analysis, as pioneered most especially by Immanuel Wallerstein and Giovanni Arrighi, can be seen as both a continuation and original reworking of the analysis of geo-economic regions early on adumbrated by the *Annales* school. Here, there is a laser-like focus on the geohistory of different world regions in terms of their precolonial heritage, the impact of colonialism, the Atlantic slave trade and the "postcolonial" period. In the last few decades, many leading world-systems analysts, perhaps most prominently Wallerstein and Arrighi, have argued that after some 500 to 700 years of evolution, the capitalist world-system is undergoing fundamental transformations. These and a host of other contemporary authors argue that, given current trajectories and instabilities accompanying today's discontinuous changes, either a new system or systems will emerge or at the very least that future trajectories of geo-economic regions, the global system and anti-systemic movements will differ in fundamental ways from past developments. How to map such changes though?

In *The Modern World-System*, Wallerstein (1974, 9) argued that ". . . the proper understanding of the social dynamics of the present requires a theoretical comprehension that can only be based on the study of the widest possible range of phenomena, including through all of historical time and space," calling for a unidisciplinary approach to the study of social change (emphasis added). In the introduction to his landmark work, Wallerstein wrote of two major watersheds in world history, the Neolithic Revolution and the creation of the modern world-system. And yet, Wallerstein and Arrighi have for the most part not heeded this call to analyze planetary and human evolution over this broader time period, focusing instead largely on the capitalist world-system, and to a lesser, but increasing, extent (for Arrighi at least) on earlier geo-economic regions, primarily Western Europe and East Asia. Longer periods of human evolution, from the Paleolithic to the present, have instead been analyzed by a host of other scholars. This chapter brings together recent, theoretically informed empirical studies on human evolution over the *longue durée*. The focus is on the reassertion of race, space and place in world-system geographies and anti-systemic cartographies, as well as on examining political projects for more democratic, egalitarian, peaceful and ecologically sustainable futures, on new and enlarged social foundations, in our most recent geological era, the Anthropocene.

The new social scientific discourse on the origins of global inequalities and world-systems geographies

To understand the present and future, we must first understand the past. Some 250 years ago Rousseau wrote his famous *Discourse on the Origins of Inequalities.* Today, with the tremendous advances in the social and natural sciences on these questions, it is necessary to revisit key concepts in world-systems analysis, in order to understand the origins of contemporary inequalities and possible future trajectories. Here Giovanni Arrighi's (1973) work on labor reserves offers a fruitful start, intersecting as it does with much of the most important classical and contemporary work comparing world regions, central to understanding both the Neolithic revolution and capitalist development and underdevelopment, as well as the prospects for a more egalitarian and democratic world over the *longue durée.* Of particular importance in complementing Arrighi's vision is the important work of the last forty years on epidemiology, demography, biogeography and the Neolithic Revolution. To varying degrees, authors in these areas, perhaps most notably Alfred Crosby (2003; 2008) and Jared Diamond (2005 [1997]), have demonstrated the sustained advantage of many particular regions of the world that came to productive agriculture, rising populations, complex stratified social systems and state formation associated with the early onset of the Neolithic Revolution, notably Eurasia, relative to counterparts such as, in the Americas, Oceania and Sub-Equatorial Africa.

In recent decades, simultaneous with the reemergence of Chinese-led East Asia, there has been a great renewal of interest in what is today referred to as the "great divergence" between Europe, its white settler offshoots and East Asia. Today, it is increasingly recognized that the divergence in wealth and power between these two regions really dates much later than previously believed, specifically to the period after 1800. Equally as important, however, is the growing recognition of what James Belich (2009; 2010) refers to as the second great divergence, between the white-settler states of the Anglo world, those countries that Alfred Crosby (2003) calls the "neo-Europes," and those of its Spanish-Portuguese counterparts (see also Magubane, 1996). This growing awareness also has crucial implications for the world historical comparison of continents and related geo-economic regions, particularly Sub-Saharan Africa and Eurasia, something rarely done, given the more traditional macrohistorical comparison of Western Europe and East Asia.

This brings us to a crucial open question as to what are the processes that have facilitated the division of the modern world-system into core, semiperipheral and peripheral zones, albeit with pronounced racial-ethnic, national and gender disparities across the time and space of the global system, including within all these zones. For attention to the tripartite zonal division of the capitalist world-economy should not distract our attention from equally important racial-ethnic, national and gender divisions within core, semiperipheral and peripheral zones (Du Bois, 1969 [1935]; Sen, 2000; Magubane, 1996; Balibar and Wallerstein, 2011 [1991]). Moreover, in the making of the modern world-system, categorical inequalities—as Charles Tilly (1999) called them—of race, ethnicity, gender, and nation have been seamlessly intertwined, including to intimately related questions of class.

First and foremost among those analyzing these processes have been African diaspora intellectuals such as W.E.B. Du Bois and C.L.R. James, who along with others such as Oliver Cox, Aimé Césaire, Franz Fanon and Walter Rodney, initially adumbrated what later came to be called world-systems analysis. More recently of course there have been the fundamental contributions of Immanuel Wallerstein, as well as Anibal Quijano, Walter Mignolo and Ramon Grosfoguel. These authors implicitly or explicitly sharply critiqued common place understandings of the process of development and underdevelopment, specifically underscoring the limits of the traditional focus on the concept of "unequal exchange," as did Giovanni Arrighi, inspired in part by these very authors. As Arrighi (1990a, 11–13) powerfully argued:

Equally important have been two other mechanisms, which we may designate as unilateral transfers of labor, on the one hand, and of capital, on the other . . . Historically, unilateral transfers of labor and capital have been both forcible and voluntary . . . voluntary transfers are far more efficacious than forcible transfers wherever and whenever differentials between and among locales in the level and security of rewards have become large enough to create a widespread and strong incentive for owners of labor and capital resources to transfer such resources to sites in which the returns are highest and most secure.

Unilateral transfers of this kind have been far more important than unequal exchange in the expansion of the core to include most of the so-called lands of new settlement, the United States in the first place, in the late nineteenth and early twentieth centuries. The effects of these transfers on the "sending" countries were not at all uniform. Overall, however, the effect was an unprecedented polarization in the hierarchies of wealth, power, and welfare of the capitalist world-economy.[1]

What Arrighi (2007; 2010 [1994]) is referring to here, at least in part, is what has come to be called comparative settler colonialisms from Africa to the Americas. Here, as noted above, it is important to highlight both the division of the world-system into core, semiperipheral and peripheral locales, while also underscoring racial-ethnic, national, class, and gender divisions within these very zones (Balibar and Wallerstein, 2011 [1991]). Thus, though of course significant to large income gaps between nations and regions go back to the earliest centuries of the European-centered world-economy, as the nineteenth century progressed, class position became increasingly determined by location, reflecting as it did the growth of inequalities between nations, a widening divergence of development trajectories still very much with us in the present (M. Davis, 2001b; Maddison, 2007; Williamson, 2011).

Recently, James Belich (2009; 2010, 53) in books such as *Replenishing the Earth: The Settler Revolution and the Rise of the Anglo-World, 1783–1939* has added greatly to our knowledge of the two great divergences. And while it is crucial to point out that from 1500 to 1820 some 80% of all the persons who came to the Americas were enslaved black Africans, this forcible transfer of labor laid the foundations of prosperity for the voluntary migrants, that massive influx of persons who came to be considered on the white side of the color line and their related vast demographic growth—eventually in the hundreds of millions—characterizing white colonial settlement in what Alfred Crosby (2008) in his *Ecological Imperialism: The Biological Expansion of Europe, 900–1900* called the "neo-Europes." As Belich (2010, 53) notes:

In 1790, the trans-Appalachian West contained 109,000 American settlers. In 1920, this figure has risen to 62 million. These millions were not impoverished backwoodsmen,

1   On this, see also Hoerder (2002).

but among the richest people on the planet, with giant cities such as Chicago, which had grown from 100 people in 1830 to 2.7 million ninety years later. This was probably the most explosive form of growth in human history . . . The American West has a forgotten twin, however, born at much the same time, to much the same parents, and growing at much the same remarkable rate. This was the British "West," later known as the "white dominions" of Canada, Australia, New Zealand, and South Africa. In 1790, this fragmented West contained about 200,000 European settlers, mostly French. By 1920, it had 24 million people, mostly British and Irish . . .

Moreover, from the 1780s to 1920 the weight of numbers of the Spanish and Anglo-American worlds reversed, with the latter going from a fifth of the size of Spain to twice the size, at 152 million persons and then to 200 million by 1930, not to mention the 400 million subjects of the British Empire (Belich, 2009, 4). During this period the world witnessed the entwined remaking of race, space and place in the global system, as poignantly underscored to varying degrees by Arrighi, Bernard Magubane (1996), David Brion Davis (2006), Robin Blackburn (2011a; 2011b) and a host of others (Kakel, 2011; Sampson, 2012). Indeed, as Arrighi was fond of noting, to a substantial extent, the capitalist world-economy was built on African labor, (Latin) American resources and Asian markets. Here, white-settler colonialisms, with the pronounced use of black African and other forced slave labor, stitched together an expanding world-system. In the lands that became the United States too of course, the areas of "new settlement" involved the extermination and forced removal of much of the indigenous population, while simultaneously becoming, over time, a virtual "black hole" attracting labor and capital from around the world in the nineteenth and twentieth centuries that would provide for the remaking of the global system on the new and enlarged social foundations of U.S. hegemony (Calloway, 2003; Reifer, 2009; 2010a; 2010b; Arrighi, 2010 [1994], 60; Kakel, 2011).

Moreover, as Arrighi (1990b), M. Davis (2002) and Milanovic (2005; 2010; 2012) have argued in different albeit complementary ways, at the time of the penning of "The Communist Manifesto," namely on the eve of the world revolution of 1848, class position was determined to a significant degree by one's class position within the nation-state. Yet, around this very period, class position began to be increasingly determined by location within the world-system, as the global polarization of wealth took an exponential leap forward. As Bourguignon and Morrison (2002, 733–734) demonstrated:

> within-country inequality . . . represented 80 percent or more of total inequality in the first half of the 19th century . . . [but] by 1950, within-country inequality accounted for only 40 percent of total world inequality—half its share in 1820 . . . To summarize . . . world income inequality worsened dramatically over the past two centuries.

Milanovic (2012, 127, 129) subsequently clarified the key points in his "Global Inequality: From Class to Location, From Proletarians to Migrants," the title here underscoring the centrality of what Seyla Benhabib (2004) calls *The Rights of Others* in a global system in which what Ayelet Shachar (2009) calls *The Birthright Lottery*, where national citizenship, and its intersection with race, space and place, determines one's life chances to a great degree:

> the global Gini in 1850 amounting to 53.2 points, can be broken down into 25.9 Gini points (49 percent) due to location, and 27.3 Gini points (51 percent) due to class. Thus, around mid-19th century, one half of inequality between individuals was explained by unequal development of countries and another half by income differences between social classes—that is, essentially between workers and capitalists. How does it compare with the situation today? . . . If we use the same decomposition between location and class today, when our data are much better than for the past, we find that of the global Gini, which amounts to 65.4 points, 56.2 Gini points or 85 percent is due to differences in mean country incomes, and only 9.2 Gini points (15 percent) to "class." Not only is the overall inequality between world citizens greater in the early 21st century than it was more than a century and a half ago, but its composition has entirely changed; from being an inequality determined in equal measures by class and location, it has become preponderantly an inequality determined by location only . . . using Maddison's data, in order to keep comparability with the 1850 results, we find that the top-to-bottom ratio in 2007 was in excess of 100 to 1 (as opposed to 4 to 1 as it was in 1850). (Milanovic, 2012, 127, 129)

The reassertion of race, space and place in capital's cartographies and world-systems geographies

In examining the unfolding of the contemporary African tragedy in comparative perspective, while noting (among other factors) the greater foreign debt of Sub-Saharan Africa, Latin America (North Africa, Eastern Europe and the Middle East), dependence on foreign capital and, to varying extents, natural resource dependence relative to East Asia, Arrighi et al. (2010) instead underscored the limits of such factors as an explanatory framework, arguing instead for the centrality of geohistory. Here, Arrighi et al. (2010) returned to their early landmark critique of the notion that underdeveloped areas are characterized by "unlimited supplies of labor," pointing out that this situation never really applied to Africa.

Moreover, Arrighi (2002) further pointed out that the "import of guns and export of slaves" which was the basis for African-European relations in the modern period and central to the making of the capitalist world-economy, made worse whatever structural shortage of labor then existed in the continent, while also contributing to African overspecialization in the protection industry. Here, as is often noted, West African chiefdoms prospered while Africa bled (Lovejoy, 2012). And yet, as Arrighi

(2002) also noted, even before the devastating consequences of the Atlantic slave trade, in sharp contrast to many other world regions, Africa's shortage was never that of land but instead that of people, or labor. While *parts* of Africa were highly urbanized, populated and prosperous, as Jack Goody (1971; 1976; 1995) pointed out in *Technology, Tradition and the State in Africa* and related works, Africa had long been characterized by a low density of population and related demographic deficit relative to other world regions (Ehret, 2002; 2011; Terreblanche, 2002; Olson and Cole, 2006; Nunn, 2007; Livi-Bacci, 2012, 25; Shillington, 2012).

More recently, Goody (2006, 3) has emphasized the crucial and related point that "Africa never experienced the urban revolution of the Bronze Age." Here, Goody (1971; 1990) drew on his long emphasized broad distinction between the hoe cultures of extensive agriculture in Sub-Saharan Africa versus lands of intensive agriculture via the plough in Eurasia. Following these radical differences, Sub-Saharan African societies tended to be less complex and had less individualized forms of ownership, replete with conjugal unions characterized by the absence of dowries, lateral inheritance and polygyny. This pattern stood in sharp contrast to more pronounced class divisions and stratification, along with vertical inheritance via monogamy, the development of individual private ownership and a corresponding greater degree and complexity of state formations, throughout Eurasia (Goody, 1976; 1995; Anderson, 1990, 75).

Goody's (1971) thesis, widely upheld in the subsequent literature, also relates to another theme of Arrighi's (2007) comparison of Europe, Asia and Africa. As Arrighi (2007) argued, Western Europe and its settler offshoots developed along what Adam Smith (1976 [1776]) called the unnatural path of development, namely an extroverted militarized form of state-corporate capitalism focused on labor saving technology, foreign trade and high finance, relative to Asia's relatively introverted natural path, which in contrast engaged in labor-absorbing rather than labor-saving technology, until the fusion of these paths to a significant extent in the late twentieth and early twenty-first century. Yet even with white-settler colonialism, as Arrighi (2009) emphasized, it was only on the backs of 12.5 million African slaves—some 10 million of which were exported to the Americas—that the lands of new white settlement were built, which, as pointed out earlier, only exacerbated Africa's already pronounced demographic deficit, thus furthering the underdevelopment of the continent's black Africans relative to their white-settler counterparts, both within and outside Africa proper (Blackburn, 2011a; 2011b; D. B. Davis, 2006; Eltis and Richardson, 2010; Nunn, 2010; Rodney, 2011 [1972]).

In addition, there is the often neglected, but centrally related, fact of radically different paths of state and class formation throughout much of Eurasia and Sub-Saharan Africa. Here, as a host of scholarly accounts have stressed, the classical Weberian ideotypical path of state formation, with states exercising monopolies of legitimate violence in given territories, while accurately describing West European state formation with their full containers of people and goods from the early modern period to the present, fail to understand Africa's divergent path. For in Sub-Saharan Africa, with its few people relative to its massive land mass, the important factor was control over people and the means of destruction, and not land, territory or the means of production. As Goody (1971) has recurrently emphasized, this fundamental demographic reality of Africa and related process of state formation ensured that there would be a pronounced emphasis on the control of people and means of destruction rather than control over territory and the monopoly over the means of production, as was typical in Western Europe (Kopytoff, 1989; Herbst, 2000; Hyden, 2006, 65–71; Laitan, 2008).

Subsequent work such as that of Jared Diamond's (2005 [1997]) *Guns, Germs and Steel,* though mostly not explicitly related to the Goody thesis in the literature, has nevertheless significantly expanded our understanding of this fundamental demographic divergence between Eurasia and Sub-Saharan Africa. Diamond (2005) revealed the central role of the lack of large mammals that could be domesticated, as well as the related absence of the wheel and plough, along with poor soils, not to mention related realities of malaria and the like, in Sub-Saharan Africa, along with its sparse population and related demographic deficit and subsequent underdevelopment. This premodern demographic deficit, and subsequent state deformation and overspecialization of the protection industry, then was of course greatly exacerbated by the Atlantic slave trade and European colonial rule, neocolonialism and the legacies of Cold War militarization thereafter.

These insights on the intersection of geography and demography of East Asia versus other world regions were later developed by Arrighi (2002, 16) to explain the bifurcation of the world-system in the period from 1975–1990 and beyond,

> between the deteriorating performance of Sub-Saharan Africa, Latin America, and to a lesser extent the Middle East and North Africa, on the one hand, and the improving performance of East and South Asia on the other ... The African collapse was a particularly extreme manifestation of this divergence.

In explaining how the African crisis of the 1970s turned into the African tragedy of the 1980s and thereafter, simultaneous with the rising wealth of East Asia, Arrighi turned to the crucial importance for both Africa and East Asia of the changing fortunes of the U.S. hegemony in the 1970s, 1980s and beyond. For it was exactly in the context of the U.S. competition on the global capital markets and the reflation of world demand in the West that the crucial geohistorical realities of East Asia and Sub-Saharan Africa discussed earlier came to the fore. The effects of this switch in U.S. policy bifurcated existing geo-economic regions into two groups, those that were able to benefit from producing commodities to meet the reflated demand in the West, and those that were unable to take advantage of this new conjuncture in the global system (Arrighi, 2002, 22).

Thus, with East Asia and to a lesser extent South Asia—India in particular—again being notable exceptions, the counterrevolution of development policy expressed in the rise of the neoliberal Washington Consensus and Wall Street-Treasury nexus saw a generalized collapse of developmental efforts in the 1980s, in what came to be called the lost decade of the (global) South. During this period stretching from 1980 to 1988, Latin America's GNP relative to the organic core dropped some 46%, the Middle East and North Africa by 27%, Western and Eastern Africa by 66% and Southeast Asia by 35% (Arrighi, 1991, 51). When measured by GNP per capita as a percentage of world GNP per capita, the changes from 1960–1999 make Sub-Saharan Africa's collapse the world's worst, with a decline of some 47%, though this is almost entirely due to changes after 1975 (Arrighi, 2002, 15–16).

In terms of GNP per capita as a percentage of the First World's, from 1960–2005, Sub-Saharan Africa's fell from 5.6 to 2.3%, South Africa's share fell from 25.9% to 12.7%, Latin America's from 19.7 to 11.2%, while East Asia's per capita GNP, in stark contrast, rose substantially (Arrighi, et al., 2010, 413; Arrighi and Zhang, 2011, 28). Moreover, between 1960 to 1978 those countries that were the world's poorest grew from 24 to 43 in number so that "[b]eing part of the Fourth World is now the most common category for all regions (except for the West): between 50 and 60 percent of Asian, LAC, and Eastern European/FSU countries belong to the poorest category, as do no fewer than 80 percent of African countries" (Milanovic, 2005). Milanovic (2005, 70–71, 149) refers to this as "plutocracy at the global level," with one of its most notable features being the "Westernization of wealth," reinforcing "the position of the West as the club of the rich," simultaneous with the "Africanization of [global] poverty."

The economic performance of so-called Communist states in Eastern Europe mirrored that of most other world regions, with the mirage of development eventually giving way to the reality of continued underdevelopment and failure to catch up, despite higher levels of welfare than other regions with similar GNP per capita (Arrighi, 1991; Berend, 1996; 2009). And yet, with the application of neoliberal shock therapy in Eastern Europe after the collapse, much of the Second World was relegated once again to its original Third World role, as the numbers of those living in "extreme poverty . . . rocketed from 14 million to 168 million: an almost instantaneous mass pauperization without precedent in history," while poverty in the former USSR increased from some 6–10% of all families to some 60% (Berend, 1996; M. Davis, 2006, 166).

As mentioned earlier, central to East Asia's rising fortunes, in contrast to Africa's increasing misfortunes, were the fundamentally different geo-economic realities, namely the former regions' endowment of healthy, well-educated and seemingly unlimited supplies of labor, a legacy in significant part shaped by the Chinese Communist revolution of 1949. East Asia, then, stood in sharp contrast to Sub-Saharan Africa, burdened by a demographic deficit as well as an exponential increase in epidemic diseases such as AIDS, the combination of the full proletarian condition, migration patterns, poor education and health all combining here to ensure the astonishing median age of death in the region of under-five years, in an astonishing reversal of what has been the near universal increase in life expectancies over much of the twentieth century (Ashforth, 2005; Sen, 2005, xi; Iliffe, 2006; Hunter, 2010; Pepin, 2011). And in fact, over the last three decades some 30 million people have died of AIDS, a large percentage of them in Sub-Saharan Africa.

At the time of the latest International AIDS conference in Washington, D.C. in July of 2012, of the 33.4 million persons who were HIV positive in the world, over 28 million of them, the vast majority, were in Sub-Saharan Africa. The highest burden of AIDS in the world is today in Southern Africa, with deaths in South Africa alone increasing some 100% from 1997 to 2005, when the figure rose to the astonishing figure of over 600,000 deaths annually. Today, South Africa has over 5 million, or some 17.8% of persons infected with HIV, some 17% of the world total, though the country has only 0.7% of the global population. Life expectancy in the country is well under 60 years old. In addition, in many countries of the African diaspora, and in some first world countries too, notably the United States, the disease has reached epidemic proportions in the black community, in the United States in the context of large scale criminalization and imprisonment of poor African American men with little formal education and the larger communities of color of which they are an integral part (Marais, 2011, 262, 281; Iweala, 2012; NPR, 2012a; 2012b; 2012c; PBS, 2012a; 2012b; Reifer, 2012b).

In contrast to Africa, East Asia's economic performance and healthy and well-educated labor force meant that this region, more than any other, came closest to Arthur Lewis's ideal type of unlimited labor supplies. Moreover, East Asia's centuries-old practice, related to rice-cultivation, of an industrious revolution incorporating its large supplies of labor, stood in stark contrast not only with the labor saving industrial revolution in Western Europe and its settler offshoots, but also with the processes of accumulation in the Southern Africa of the labor reserves (Arrighi, 2007). Here, proletarianization via the violent dispossession of the African peasantry through forced removals limiting the African majority to a tiny portion of the land so as to create a labor force for the mines and industry, eventually created massive barriers to capital accumulation and corresponding categorical inequalities of race/class that have actually widened since the fall of apartheid (Terreblanche, 2002; Crais, 2011; Marais, 2011).

Global climate change geographies and future anti-systemic cartographies

In a warmer world . . . socio-economic inequality will have a meteorological mandate [with the rich countries primarily responsible for climate change least affected while those adversely affected are overwhelmingly in the Global South] . . . worldwide adaption to climate change, which presupposes trillions of dollars of investment in the urban and rural infrastructures of poor and medium-income countries, as well as the assisted migration of tens of millions of people from Africa and Asia, would necessarily command a revolution of almost mythic magnitude in the redistribution of income and power. Meanwhile we are speeding toward a fateful rendezvous around 2030, or even earlier, when the convergent impacts of climate change, peak oil, peak water, and an additional 1.5 billion people on the planet will produce negative synergies probably beyond our imagination. (M. Davis, 2010)

In terms of the implications of these trends for the future of the world-system, we must add to this picture the current world's population and future forecasts for its dramatic growth and how this intersects with global climate change in our new geological era of the Anthropocene (Philosophical Transactions of the Royal Society, 2011b). Today, global population stands at 7 billion. Over 1 billion persons across the world today live in slums, a figure expected to double to 2 billion by 2030, while the total world urban population is expected to increase by an additional 3 billion people by 2050, 90% of whom will live in the poor cities of the so-called developing world (M. Davis, 2010, 39). In Africa alone, the total population topped 1 billion in 2009 and is expected to rise to 2 billion by 2050 (UN Habitat, 2003a; 2003b; 2008; 2010). In fact, Africa will account for nearly 50% of all future global population growth to 2050, when it is expected to comprise 25% of total world population, while a recent UN forecast predicted a 2100 world population of some 10 billion, with Africa's share of the global total, 3.6 billion, and Asia's 4.6 billion (Gillis and Dugger, 2011; Science, 2011). Yet whether these demographic trends of increasing numbers and higher densities of especially urban populations in the poor areas of Africa and Asia can be capitalized to reverse Africa's and Asia's tragic underdevelopment, given current global inequalities of wealth and power and interrelated environmental and social crises, is an open question (Arrighi, 2002; M. Davis, 2004; 2006; Mills and Herbst, 2012).

For simultaneous with the rapid urbanization of humanity and the polarization between the global North and South, excepting Chinese-led East Asia and India, experts are also predicting widespread loss of arable land throughout key regions of the so-called developing world, including South Asia, Sub-Saharan Africa, as well as parts of Latin American and the Caribbean, while in the hottest summer on record in 2012 global warming appears to have played a role in devastating crops across the United States, as well as in the destructive wrath of Hurricane Sandy (Hansen et al., 2012). With these trends, in the future hundreds of millions may face increasing hunger, famine and disease, with some 1 to 2 billion facing water shortages, what with food prices having gone up in recent times by 80% (Cline, 2007; M. Davis, 2010; World Bank, 2010, 5). These changes will add greatly to ongoing displacement and migration of hundreds of millions, primarily in the Global South, many of whom will attempt to move to the rich countries of the increasingly fortified global North for refuge and/or employment (Milanovic, 2012).

Today, global climate change, far from decreasing, is increasing faster than ever and some predict that greenhouse gas emissions could triple or more by mid-century, with a recent special issue of the *Philosophical Transactions of the Royal Society* (Philosophical Transactions of the Royal Society, 2011a) considering the implications of an increase in global temperatures of four degrees and beyond (M. Davis, 2010, 33; Atlas, 2012). While some 42 percent of the ecological debt caused by environmental degradation is primarily the result of the industrialization of the rich countries of the global North, the Southern share is increasing and, moreover, it is in the Global South that its primary impacts will be felt, with the rich states bearing only some 3 percent of its global costs (Roberts and Parks, 2006; Srinivasan, quoted in M. Davis, 2010, 39). Thus, the globe seems to be witnessing a perfect storm of human-induced environmental catastrophes, growing socioeconomic polarization and related violent conflict.

To be sure, the growing weight of Southern economies, notably countries such as Brazil, Russia, India, China and South Africa, the so-called BRICS is increasing, opening up, as Arrighi (2007) argued, the prospects for a new Bandung. Yet as has also been pointed out, whether the world will become more equal in terms of the greater representation and weight of the global South, or just as, or even more unequal, though with a greater Southern contribution to global governance and the world political economy, significantly depends on social movements across the global South. And, as the Occupy Movement intimates, it also looks possible that in the context of an increasingly endemic crisis of capitalism envisaged by Marx and Engels, and that of the global ecology unforeseen by them, this could unleash a perfect storm that would herald the transition to a new more egalitarian, democratic and peaceful world-system (Arrighi, 1990b; 1991; M. Davis, 2010; 2011). Of particular importance here is China, with the world's largest working class, arguably "the most dangerous class on the planet" (Silver and Zhang, 2009; M. Davis, 2011, 15).

As the new millennium begins, vast transformations in world-system geographies are laying out trajectories for future anti-systemic cartographies. Here, intersections of race and class remain central. In a landmark article in a special edition of *Race and Class* commemorating the 150th anniversary of the abolition of slavery in the English-speaking Caribbean, Jan Pieterse (1988) posited the possibility of a "triangle of emancipation" that might serve to "redress the historical balance of the triangular trade," going onto acknowledge that the reality is at once "much less and much more than this. Much less because many in the African diaspora exist as a vast underclass . . . Much more because the people of Africa have joined a stream that is far wider than the waters of the Middle Passage, and have carried it further," with rap and hip hop now the dominant forms of youth culture on the planet (see Reifer, 2012b; 2013b). And indeed, one of the key aspects for transforming the world-system is to understand the foundational aspects of anti-black racism in the making of the modern world and the need to move beyond the triangle of emancipation for transforming the global system and remaking it on new and enlarged, and more socioecologically just, social foundations. For despite the centrality of global inequalities today, there are also massive inequalities, especially in terms of race, ethnicity and nation, within all three zones of the capitalist world-economy (Sampson, 2012; Reifer, 2013a; 2013b).

Indeed, Wallerstein (1995) argues that we are returning to "the pre-1848 situation, in which, within the traditional loci of the liberal state (Western Europe and North America), the 'workers' will be poorly paid and outside the realm of political and social rights. Western workers will once again have become the 'dangerous classes,' their skin color will have changed and the class struggle will be a race struggle. The problem of the twenty-first century will be the problem of the color line." Arrighi (1990b, 63), too, noted that capital was increasingly putting social power in the traditionally weak segments of the world proletariat, both by moving to peripheral and semiperipheral locations and increasingly employing women, persons of color and immigrants in the core, arguing that "[t]o the extent that these struggles succeed, the stage will be set for the socialist transformation of the world."

With the combination of uneven global climate change most especially affecting the world's poorest states and the continued polarization of the world's wealth, migratory pressures can also be expected to grow. Take for example, the U.S.-Mexican hyperborder, ground zero for these North American transformations with Mexico and the United States being the largest emigration and immigration countries in the world respectively, with some 11 to 12 million Mexican born citizens now living in the United States, over 6 million of them—the majority—undocumented (Romero, 2007; Massey, 2008, 142). As Douglas Massey (2008, 142) notes: "These figures imply that one of every ten people born in Mexico now lives in the United States," with some 55% of them undocumented, with immigrants now making up a growing percentage of all Mexican-Americans, some 40% in 2005, meaning that about over half of Mexican-born persons and over a fifth of all persons of Mexican descent "lack any social, political, or economic rights in the United States. Mexicans are now more exploitable than at any time since the 1950s," in an economic, political and social context in which capitalism is experiencing its worst economic crisis since the Great Depression (Massey, 2008, 142; Reifer, 2010b). Moreover, although the tightening of border controls, the criminalization of immigration in the United States and the U.S. recession has temporarily stayed immigration, push and pull factors, combined with environmental degradation related to global warming in Mexico—the fifth largest and third most populated state in the Americas—will likely increase migration in the near future (see Huber-Sannwald et al., 2012).

Mexicans are today second largest minority group in the United States, making up some 66% of Latinos, they are—at 28 million—second only to African Americans, which compose 38 million, though this is now less than the entire U.S. Latino population. All this is part of a vast demographic shift that will ensure that some 25% of the U.S. population will be Latinos well before 2050, as part of America's larger transformation into a multicultural majority country (M. Davis, 1999; 2001a; Grosfoguel et al., 2005; Massey, 2008, 115; Salvidar, 2012). While for some time, remittances from foreign Mexican-born workers in the United States were rising, the combination of economic crisis and deportations has led to dramatic declines in these flows over the last few years. Yet this close off of what Albert Hirschman called opportunities for exit may lead to the exercise of more voice by some of Mexico's poorest citizens and add to the social movements which portend the dramatic future transformation of the Mexican politico-economic landscape, not to mention that of the United States as well, as the immigrant workers' freedom rides, and May Day demonstrations of 2006 and thereafter have so powerfully demonstrated (Cockcroft, 1998; 2010; Hamilton, 2011; Voss and Bloemraad, 2011).

Despite these deportations and related processes of immigrant and Latino criminalization, nevertheless in the future, the social foundations for global conflict and cooperation will arguably be remade by America's dramatic and ongoing demographic transformation. In terms of the United States as a whole, the total Latino population is expected to triple from its current numbers of 50 million persons to some 200 million, or almost 30% of the total U.S. population of 438 million by 2050. This demographic upsurge presages the coming of the United States as a majority multicultural, or majority non-white, society, a future that has already arrived in California, not surprising given how often the Golden State presages national trends. Indeed, in an epochal transformation, Latinos are now the majority minority in California, New York, and the nation as a whole. Demographically, moreover, Latinos are today the absolute majority in California's public schools. In fact, today, Latinos make up roughly 37%, or almost 14 million of the state's roughly 34 million persons, and some 16%, or 50 million, out of a total U.S. population of some 300 million. Moreover, Latinos will become California's largest racial/ethnic group by 2020, while by 2050 Latinos will comprise over 30 million of California's inhabitants, or an absolute majority of the state's projected 2050 population of some 60 million (PEW Charitable Trusts, 2008).

The possibilities for a new socioeconomic model and social contract are not some far off dream. As the May Day demonstrations for immigrant and workers' rights in the United States and around the world, as well as the second Arab Revolt, the related Occupy Wall Street protests and the movement against austerity in Europe today reveal, the battle for the future is already underway. Despite some commentary about the unexpectedness of the second Arab Revolt, many analysts have been predicting a regional uprising for some time, given the important changes in the Middle East and North Africa's social structure combined with the continued humiliations of authoritarian rule. Another critical aspect in the social explosions has been an ever-widening divide between the haves and have-nots in the so-called neoliberal era and the related demographic youth bulge. For example, Linda Herrera's (2010, 128) "Young Egyptians' Quest for Jobs and Justice," in *Being Young and Muslim*, notes that:

Arab States that are characterized by a youth bulge contain among the highest regional average of young people in the world, with 65% of the population younger than 25 years old, 20% of whom are in the 15- to 24-year age bracket. The Middle East and North Africa region holds the inauspicious distinction of being the fastest growing labor force, which, since the 1990s, has 25% youth unemployment—the highest regional average and almost double the global average, which is 14%. In the coming decade, some 34 million jobs need to be created in the region to absorb the emerging labor force (World Bank, 2008). In Egypt, unemployment is highest among the young (youth unemployment accounts for 80% of the country's total unemployed population), and among youth, it is proportionately higher among females and the educated; a staggering 95% of unemployed youth have secondary or university education . . .

Indeed, the wave of protests in Tunisia set off by one such high-school-educated youthful street vendor, accompanied by the soundtrack to the revolution via Tunisian hip-hop artist El General, expressed powerfully the dynamics of transformation in the region brilliantly analyzed in a series of recent books by Iranian born Middle-East scholar, Asef Bayat (2007; 2010), in his *Life as Politics: How Ordinary People Change the Middle East* and related works. Significant too is the growing importance for the movements of social media, including Facebook, Twitter, email and satellite television and related forms of electronic communication, long recognized as possible "liberation technologies," though perhaps never as much as today, as Wikileaks and the Arab Revolts revealed. Yet it was nearly two decades ago that Giovanni Arrighi, Terence Hopkins and Immanuel Wallerstein (Arrighi et al., 1992, 236–237) noted that:

> . . . with the means of communication increasingly becoming almost entirely electronic, every movement "local" is equally a movement communications "center," each network nodal point being as able as the next to broadcast (e.g., via electronic bulletin boards) as well as to receive.
> . . . Increasingly, the modern world-system as a whole becomes the terrain of movements world-scale in extent and trans-state in structure. And national arenas thus increasingly become for them so many linked locales in struggles that are not only in fact worldwide but also more and more conceived by activists to be . . . "global."[2]

Moreover, the increased income concentration among the top 1% in the United States and across much of the world has gone hand in hand with astonishing declines in incomes for the vast majority, but most especially for racial and ethnic minorities in the United States, with wealth gaps between whites, blacks and Latinos hitting historic highs in the context of the Great Recession. Between 2005 and 2009,

---

2 On this, see also Castells (2011; 2012).

the median wealth of Latinos, blacks, and Asians in the United States fell by 66%, 53% and 54%, respectively, with the U.S. ranking at the bottom of the scale in terms of social justice and intergeneration mobility in the OECD zone, threatening to make college education increasingly unaffordable for those most in need (Schraad-Tischler, 2011; PEW Hispanic Research Center, 2011; Reifer, 2011; Smeeding et al., 2011; see also Brady, 2009). The global distribution of wealth is even more skewed. As detailed in the UN's study, *The World Distribution of Household Wealth*, the richest 1% of the world's population owned 40% of global assets in 2000, with the richest 10% accounting for 85% of total world wealth, in contrast to the world's bottom half, which owned "barely 1% of global wealth" (Davies et al., 2008). With this increasing wealth divide and related forces encouraging immigration, migrants are today the world's new proletarians (Milanovic, 2012).

Today, the combination of economic crisis, widespread austerity programs, rapid climate change and demographic transformations, with continued massive migration and new forms of immigrant activism, could herald new alternative forms of regional and global cooperation on new and enlarged social foundations, namely a high-wage, education-intensive economic strategy embracing a green Keynesianism and more inclusive model of national, regional and global citizenship. The combination of these intersecting trends has today put on the agenda new and urgent proposals for the making of a more humane world-system, as the revolutions across the Middle East and North Africa, the pink tide in Latin American and related processes of alternative regionalisms from Latin America to East Asia, as well as the global spread of the Occupy Wall Street movement, with its clarion call, we are the 99%, appear to indicate. Naomi Klein's observation here that there no longer seem to be rich nations, only rich people, while indeed exaggerated, is of particular relevance in capturing the present moment in the debate on world inequalities.

Conclusion: The battle for the future has already begun

In an age of rampant greed and the collapse of socialist projects of the past, the endeavor [of creating a more democratic, socially just and ecologically sustainable world-system] naturally looks hopeless. Yet, take another fifteen-year step forward—this time into the future . . . as . . . systemic chaos for the peoples of the West will . . . be much higher. Protection costs . . . will have escalated to the point where the pursuit of oligarchic wealth will begin to appear to many as what it has always been: a highly destructive endeavor that shifts the costs of the prosperity and security of a minority (no more, and probably less, than one-sixth of the human race) onto the majority and onto the future generations of the majority itself. At that point, the addresses croaked by Western "frogs" to the "tadpoles" of the former East and South will sound anachronistic to the "frogs" themselves, or at least to a growing number of them. Western socialists will then face their own moment of truth. Either they will join forces with Eastern and Southern Associates and come up with an intellectual project and political programme capable of transforming systemic chaos into a more equal and solidary world order, or their appeals to human progress and social justice will lose all residual credibility. (Giovanni Arrighi, 1991, 65)

. . . how to think about justice when the increasing salience of transnational and sub-national processes makes state-centric conceptions of social justice less tenable than ever[?] A serious engagement with questions of this kind should be at the top of the agenda for anyone concerned with social justice . . . (Giovanni Arrighi, blurb for Nancy Fraser, 2009)

The inequalities of the modern world-system have been based on oligarchic wealth, in which the exploitation and ecological appropriation of the vast majority by a small oligarchic minority has been the defining feature. Increasingly, in a world of global climate change and related global inequalities of wealth, power, income, and result-ing climactic impacts of global warming, this "climate of injustice" is recognized to be one of the major issues confronting humanity today. Though long divided into core, semiperipheral and peripheral locales, the most sophisticated work on global inequalities, as this chapter has tried to demonstrate, has stressed the centrality of the intersection of race, space and place in the making of the global system and its local/global inequalities. These inequalities are part of humanity's past and a critical issue in the battle for its future.

Increasingly, there is a growing awareness across the world of the inseparabil-ity of struggles for political democracy and democratic wealth, as any remaking of the global system and its geo-economic regions must be based on more sustainable socioecological foundations. Past injustices and current policies that exacerbate these, while speeding up human-induced climate change, confront humanity with arguably its greatest challenges. Questions of the capitalist world-economy and global ecology can no longer be separated; nor can the question of global demo-cratic governance, as well as related collective action and planning to mitigate, stop and ultimately reverse climate change and move to a post-carbon future, something that will cost tens of trillions of dollars and Herculean efforts. And this revolution in values and related wealth and power will not be possible unless the question of global justice and what Hannah Arendt (quoted in Benhabib, 2004) once called "the right to have rights," or what Seyla Benhabib (2004) calls "the rights of others," is ad-dressed and made a reality. Otherwise, in the face of converging crises of resources, climate change and increased global violence and instability, "human solidarity itself may fracture like a West Antarctic ice shelf, and shatter into a thousand shards" (M. Davis, 2010, 40). In the face of these dangers, calls for global and local transforma-tions must be built simultaneously on local and global solidarities, weaving a new politics into a new thread. Questions of transparency, sustainability and increased human control over the means of production, communication and reproduction of the human species, on an egalitarian, democratic and sustainable basis, must be the order of the day. As the old saying goes, there is a future to win. And as demonstrated herein, the battle for a just, democratic and sustainable future—indeed for a future—has already begun.

References

Anderson, Perry. 1990. A Culture in Contraflow-I. *New Left Review,* 180: 41–80.

Arrighi, Giovanni. 1973. "Labor Supplies in Historical Perspectives: A Study of the Proletarianization of the African Peasantry in Rhodesia." In Giovanni Arrighi and John S. Saul (eds.), *Essays on the Political Economy of Africa.* New York: Monthly Review Press.

Arrighi, Giovanni. 1990a. "The Developmentalist Illusion." In William Martin (ed.), *Semiperipheral States in the World-Economy.* New York: Greenwood.

Arrighi, Giovanni. 1990b. Marxist Century, American Century: The Making and Remaking of the World Labour Movement. *New Left Review,* 179: 29–64.

Arrighi, Giovanni. 1991. World Income Inequalities and the Future of Socialism. *New Left Review,* 189: 39–65.

Arrighi, Giovanni. 2002. The African Crisis: World Systemic and Regional Aspects. *New Left Review,* 15: 5–38.

Arrighi, Giovanni. 2007. *Adam Smith in Beijing: Lineages of the Twenty-First Century.* New York: Verso.

Arrighi, Giovanni. 2009. In Retrospect. Interview with David Harvey. *New Left Review,* 56: 61–96.

Arrighi, Giovanni. 2010 [1994]. *The Long Twentieth Century: Money, Power, and the Origins of Our Times.* New York: Verso.

Arrighi, Giovanni, Nicole Aschoff, and Ben Scully. 2010. Accumulation by Dispossession and its Limits. *Studies in Comparative International Development,* 45: 410–438.

Arrighi, Giovanni, Terence Hopkins, and Immanuel Wallerstein. 1992. 1989, the Continuation of 1968. *Review: A Journal of the Fernand Braudel Center for the Study of Economies, Historical Systems, and Civilizations,* XV(2): 243–256.

Arrighi, Giovanni, and Lu Zhang. 2011. "Beyond the Washington Consensus: A New Bandung?" In Jon Shefner and Patricia Fernandez-Kelly (eds.), *Globalization and Beyond.* University Park, Pennsylvania: Pennsylvania State University Press.

Ashforth, Adam. *Witchcraft, Violence and Democracy in South Africa.* Chicago: University of Chicago Press.

Atlas, James. 2012. Is This the End? *New York Times,* November 25.

Balibar, Etienne, and Immanuel Wallerstein. 2011 [1991]. *Race, Nation, Class.* New York: Verso.

Bayat, Asef. 2007. *Making Islam Democratic: Social Movements and the Post-Islamist Turn.* Stanford: Stanford University Press.

Bayat, Asef. 2010. *Life as Politics: How Ordinary People Change the Middle East.* Stanford: Stanford University Press.

Belich, James. 2009. *Replenishing the Earth: The Settler Revolution and the Rise of the Anglo-World, 1783–1939*. Oxford: Oxford University Press.

Belich, James. 2010. "Exploding Wests: Boom and Bush in Nineteenth Century Settler Societies." In Jared Diamond and James A. Robinson (eds.), *Natural Experiments of History*. Cambridge: Harvard University Press.

Benhabib, Seyla. 2004. *The Rights of Others: Aliens, Residents and Citizens*. New York: Cambridge University Press.

Berend, Ivan. 1996. *Central and Eastern Europe, 1944–1993: Detour from the Periphery to the Periphery*. Cambridge: Cambridge University Press.

Berend, Ivan. 2009. *From the Soviet Bloc to the European Union: The Economic and Social Transformation of Central and Eastern Europe since 1973*. Cambridge: Cambridge University Press.

Blackburn, Robin. 2011a. *The American Crucible: Slavery, Emancipation and Human Rights*. London and New York: Verso.

Blackburn, Robin. 2011b. *The Making of New World Slavery: From the Baroque to the Modern, 1492–1800*. New York: Verso.

Bourguignon, François, and Christian Morrison. 2002. Inequality among World Citizens, 1820–1992. *American Economic Review*, 92(4): 727–744.

Brady, David. 2009. *Rich Democracies, Poor People: How Politics Explains Poverty*. New York: Oxford University Press.

Calloway, Colin G. 2003. *One Vast Winter Count: The Native American West before Lewis and Clark*. Lincoln and London: University of Nebraska Press.

Castells, Manuel. 2011. *Communication Power*. New York: Oxford.

Castells, Manuel. 2012. *Networks of Outrage and Hope: Social Movements in the Internet Age*. New York: Polity.

Cline, William R. 2007. *Global Warming and Agriculture*. Washington, DC: Center for Global Development.

Cockcroft, James D. 1998. *Mexico's Hope: An Encounter with Politics and History*. New York: Monthly Review Press.

Cockcroft, James D. 2010. *Mexico's Revolution Then and Now*. New York: Monthly Review Press.

Crais, Clifton. 2011. *Poverty, War, and Violence in South Africa*. New York: Cambridge University Press.

Crosby, Alfred W. 2003. *The Columbian Exchange: Biological and Cultural Consequences of 1492*. 30th anniversary edition. New York: Praeger.

Crosby, Alfred W. 2008. *Ecological Imperialism: The Biological Expansion of Europe, 900–1900*. Second revised edition. Cambridge: Cambridge University Press.

Davies, James B., Susanna Sandstrom, Anthony Shorrocks, and Edward Wolff. 2008. "The World Distribution of Household Wealth." In James B. Davies (ed.), *Personal Wealth from a Global Perspective*. New Yord: Oxford University Press.

Davis, David Brion. 2006. *Inhuman Bondage: The Rise and Fall of Slavery in the New World*. New York: Oxford University Press.

Davis, Mike. 1999. Magical Urbanism: Latinos Reinvent the US Big City. *New Left Review,* 234: 3–43.

Davis, Mike. 2001a. *Magical Urbanism: Latinos Reinvent the US Big City.* New York: Verso.

Davis, Mike. 2001b. *Late Victorian Holocausts: El Nino Famines and the Making of the Third World.* New York: Verso.

Davis, Mike. 2002. *Dead Cities.* New York: New Press.

Davis, Mike. 2004. Planet of Slums. *New Left Review,* 26: 5–34.

Davis, Mike. 2006. *Planet of Slums.* New York: Verso.

Davis, Mike. 2010. Who Will Build the Ark? *New Left Review,* 61: 29–48.

Davis, Mike. 2011. Spring Confronts Winter. *New Left Review,* 72: 5–15.

Diamond, Jared. 2005 [1997]. *Guns, Germs and Steel.* New York: W.W. Norton and Co.

Diamond, Jared. 2012. *The World Until Yesterday: What Can We Learn from Traditional Societies?* New York: Viking.

Du Bois, W.E.B. 1969 [1935]. *Black Reconstruction in America: An Essay Toward a History of the Part Which Black Folk Played in the Attempt to Reconstruct Democracy in America, 1860–1880.* New York: Atheneum.

Ehret, Christopher. 2002. *The Civilizations of Africa: A History to 1800.* Charlottesville: University of Virginia Press.

Ehret, Christopher. 2011. *History and Testimony of Language.* Berkeley: University of California Press.

Eltis, David, and David Richardson. 2010. *Atlas of the Transatlantic Slave Trade.* New Haven and London: Yale University Press.

Fraser, Nancy. 2009. *Scales of Justice: Reimagining Political Space in a Globalizing World.* New York: Columbia University Press.

Gillis, Justin, and Celia D. Dugger. 2011. U.N. Forecasts 10.1 Billion People By Century's End. *New York Times,* May 3. URL: http://www.nytimes.com/2011/05/04/world/04population.html?_r=0 and http://www.nytimes.com/imagepages/2011/05/03/world/20110503_POPULATION_graphic.html?ref=world (accessed March 30, 2014).

Goody, Jack. 1971. *Technology, Tradition and the State in Africa.* New York: Cambridge University Press.

Goody, Jack. 1976. *Production and Reproduction: A Comparative Study of the Domestic Domain.* New York: Cambridge University Press.

Goody, Jack. 1990. *The Oriental, the Ancient and the Primitive: Systems of Marriage and the Family in the Pre-Industial Societies of Eurasia.* New York: Cambridge University Press.

Goody, Jack. 1995. *The Expansive Moment: Anthropology in Britain and Africa, 1918–1970.* New York: Cambridge University Press.

Goody, Jack. 2006. *The Theft of History.* New York: Cambridge University Press.

Grosfoguel, Ramon, Nelson Maldonado-Torres, and Jose David Salvidar. 2005. *Latin@s in the World-System.* Boulder, CO: Paradigm Press.

Hamilton, Nora. 2011. *Mexico: Politics, Social and Economic Evolution.* New York: Oxford University Press.

Hansen, James, Makiko Sato, and Reto Ruedy. 2012. Perception of Climate Change. Proceedings of the National Academy of Sciences, August 6, 2012. URL: http://www.pnas.org/content/early/2012/07/30/1205276109.full.pdf (accessed March 30, 2014).

Herbst, Jeffrey. 2000. *States and Power in Africa: Comparative Lessons in Authority and Control.* New Jersey: Princeton University Press.

Herrera, Linda 2010. "Young Egyptians' Quest for Jobs and Justice." In Linda Herrera and Asef Bayat (eds.), *Being Young and Muslim: New Cultural Politics in the Global South and North.* New Yord: Oxford University Press.

Hoerder, Dirk. 2002. *Cultures in Contact: World Migrations in the Second Millennium.* Durham: Duke University Press.

Huber-Sannwald, Elisabeth, Mónica Ribeiro Palacios, José Tulio Arredondo Moreno, Marco Braasch, Ruth Magnolia Martínez Peña, Javier García de Alba Verduzco, and Karina Monzalvo Santos. 2012. Navigating Challenges and Opportunities of Land Degradation and Sustainable Livelihood Development in Dryland Social-Ecological Systems: A Case Study from Mexico. *Philosophical Transactions of the Royal Society,* 367: 3158–3177.

Hunter, Mark. 2010. *Love in the Time of AIDS: Inequality, Gender, and Rights in South Africa.* Bloomington and Indianapolis: Indiana University Press.

Hyden, Goran. 2006. *African Politics in Comparative Perspective.* Cambridge: Cambridge University Press.

Iliffe, John. 2006. *The African AIDS Epidemic: A History.* Athens: Ohio University Press.

Iweala, Dr. Uzodimna. 2012. *Our Kind of People: A Continent's Challenge, A Country's Hope.* New York: Harpers.

James, C.L.R. 2001 [1938]. *The Black Jacobins.* New York: Penguin.

Kakel, III, Carroll P. 2011. *The American West and the Nazi East: A Comparative and Interpretive Perspective.* New York: Palgrave MacMillan.

Kopytoff, Igor (ed.). 1989. *The African Frontier: The Reproduction of Traditional African Societies.* Bloomington and Indianapolis: Indiana University Press.

Laitan, Daniel. 2008. African Outcomes. *New Left Review,* 51: 136–142.

Livi-Bacci, Massimo. 2012. *A Concise History of World Population.* New York: Wiley-Blackwell.

Lovejoy, Paul E. 2012. *Transformations in Slavery: A History of Slavery in Africa.* 3rd edition. New York: Cambridge University Press.

Maddison, Angus. 2007. *Contours of the World Economy, 1–2020 AD: Essays In Macro-Economic History.* New York: Oxford University Press.

Magubane, Bernard M. 1996. *The Making of a Racist State: British Imperialism and the Union of South Africa, 1875–1910.* Trenton, NJ: Africa World Press.

Marais, Hein. 2011. *South Africa Pushed to the Limit The Political Economy of Change.* London: Zed Press.

Massey, Douglas. 2008. *Categorically Unequal: The American Stratification System.* New York: Russell Sage Foundation Press.

Milanovic, Branko. 2005. *Worlds Apart: Measuring International and Global Inequality.* Princeton, NJ: Princeton University Press.

Milanovic, Branko. 2010. *The Haves and the Have-Nots: A Brief and Idiosyncratic History of Inequality around the Globe.* New York: Basic Books.

Milanovic, Branko. 2012. Global Inequality: From Class to Location, from Proletarians to Migrants. *Global Policy,* 3(2): 125–134.

Mills, Greg, and Jeffrey Herbst. 2012. *Africa's Third Liberation: The New Search for Prosperity and Jobs.* New York: Penguin.

Ndikumana, Leonce, and James Boyce. 2011. *Africa's Odious Debts: How Foreign Loans and Capital Flight Bled a Continent.* New York: Zed Press.

NPR (National Public Radio). 2012a. "Tinderbox": How the West Fueled the AIDS Epidemic. Audio document. February 28, 2012. URL: http://www.npr.org/player/v2/mediaPlayer.html?action=1&t=1&islist=false&id=147491878&m=147496246 (accessed April 19, 2014).

NPR (National Public Radio). 2012b. AIDS in Black America: A Public Health Crisis. Audio document. July 5, 2012. URL: http://www.npr.org/2012/07/05/156292172/aids-in-black-america-a-public-health-crisis (accessed April 19, 2014).

NPR (National Public Radio). 2012c. Our Kind: Unpacking Misconceptions About AIDS in Africa. Scott Simon talks to Dr. Iweala Uzodimna. Audio document. July 21, 2012. URL: http://www.npr.org/2012/07/21/157154279/our-kind-unpacking-misconceptions-about-aids (accessed April 19, 2014).

Nunn, Nathan. 2007. Historical Legacies: A Model Linking Africa's Past to its Current Underdevelopment. *Journal of Development Economics,* 83: 157–175.

Nunn, Nathan. 2010. "Shackled to the Past: The Causes and Consequences of Africa's Slave Trade." In Jared Diamond and James A. Robinson (eds.), *Natural Experiments of History.* Cambridge: Harvard University Press.

OECD. 2010. *Tackling Inequalities in Brazil, China, India and South Africa: The Role of Labour Market and Social Policies.* Geneva: OECD.

Olson, David R., and Michael Cole. 2006. *Technology, Literacy, and the Evolution of Society: Implications of the Work of Jack Goody.* Mahwah, NJ: Lawrence Erlbaum Associates, Publishers.

Pepin, Jacques. 2011. *The Origins of AIDS.* Cambridge: Cambridge University Press.

PEW Charitable Trusts. 2008. *Public Safety, Public Spending: Forecasting America's Prison Population 2007–2011.* URL: http://www.pewtrusts.org/uploadedFiles/wwwpewtrustsorg/Reports/State-based_policy/PSPP_prison_projections_0207.pdf(accessed April 19, 2014).

PEW Hispanic Reasearch Center. 2011. Census 2010: 50 Million Latinos: Hispanics Account for More Than Half of Nation's Decade of Growth. March 24, 2011. URL: http://www.pewhispanic.org/files/reports/140.pdf (accessed April 19, 2014).

Philosophical Transactions of the Royal Society. 2011a. Four Degrees and Beyond: The Potential for a Global Temperature Increase of Four Degrees and Its Implications. Special Issue. *Philosophical Transactions of the Royal Society,* 369(1934). URL: http://rsta.royalsocietypublishing.org/content/369/1934.toc (accessed April 19, 2014).

Philosophical Transactions of the Royal Society. 2011b. The Anthropocene: A New Epoch of Geological Time? Special Issue. *Philosophical Transactions of the Royal Society,* 369(1938).

Pieterse, Jan. 1988. Slavery, and the Triangle of Emancipation. *Race and Class,* 30(2): 1–21.

Reifer, Tom. 2009. Capital's Cartographer: Giovanni Arrighi: 1937–2009. *New Left Review,* 60: 119–130. URL: http://newleftreview.org/II/60/tom-reifer-capital-s-cartographer (accessed April 19, 2014).

Reifer, Tom. 2010a. "Beyond Divide and Rule? From the Washington to the Beijing Consensus." In Sungho Kang and Ramon Grosfoguel (eds.), *Geopolitics and Trajectories of Development.* Berkeley: Institute for East Asian Studies, University of California Berkeley. URL: http://www.tni.org/paper/beyond-divide-and-rule-washington-beijing-consensus and http://ieas.berkeley.edu/publications/rpps45.html (accessed April 19, 2014).

Reifer, Tom. 2010b. Lawyers, Guns and Money: Wall Street Lawyers, Investment Bankers and Global Financial Crises, late 19th to 21st Century. *Nexus: Chapman University Journal of Law and Public Policy,* 15: 119–133. URL: http://www.tni.org/paper/lawyers-guns-and-money-wall-street-lawyers-investment-bankers-and-global-financial-crises (accessed April 19, 2014).

Reifer, Tom. 2011. Global Inequalities, Alternative Regionalisms and the Future of Socialism. *Austrian Journal of Development Studies,* XXVII(1): 72–94. URL: http://www.tni.org/paper/global-inequalities-alternative-regionalism-and-future-socialism (accessed April 19, 2014).

Reifer, Tom (ed.). 2012a. *Global Crises and the Challenges of the 21st Century: Antisystemic Movements and the Transformation of the World-System.* Boulder, CO: Paradigm.

Reifer, Tom. 2012b. "The Social Foundations of Global Conflict and Cooperation: Globalization and Global Elite Integration, 19th to 21st Century." In Salvatore Babones and Christopher Chase-Dunn (eds.), *Handbook of World-Systems Analysis.* New York: Routledge.

Reifer, Tom. 2013a. Legacy: Giovanni Arrighi: Scholarship, Activism and the World-System. *Development and Change,* 44(3): 769–785. URL: http://onlinelibrary.wiley.com/doi/10.1111/dech.12031/pdf (accessed April 19, 2014).

Reifer, Tom. 2013b. The Reassertion of Race, Space and Punishment's Place in Urban Sociology and Critical Criminology. *Environment and Planning D: Society and Space,* 31: 372–380. URL: http://www.envplan.com/epd/fulltext/d31/d311r1.pdf (accessed April 19, 2014).

Roberts, J. Timmons, and Bradley Parks. 2006. *A Climate of Injustice: Global Inequality, North-South Politics and Climate Change.* Cambridge, MA: MIT Press.

Rodney, Walter. 2011 [1972]. *How Europe Underdeveloped Africa.* Baltimore, MD: Black Classic Press.

Romero, Fernando. 2007. *Hyperborder: The Contemporary US-Mexico Border and Its Future.* New York: Princeton Architectural Press.

Salvidar, Jose David. 2012. *Trans-Americanity: Subaltern Modernities, Global Coloniality, and the Cultures of Greater Mexico.* Durham: Duke University Press.

Sampson, Robert J. 2012. *Great American City: Chicago and the Enduring Neighborhood Effect.* Chicago: University of Chicago Press.

Schraad-Tischler, Daniel. 2011. Social Justice in the OECD – How Do The Member States Compare? Gütersloh: Bertelsmann Stiftung. URL: http://www.sgi-network.org/pdf/SGI11_Social_Justice_OECD.pdf (accessed March 30, 2014).

Science. 2011. Population. Special section. *Science,* 333(6042): 538–594.

Sen, Amartya. 2000. *Development as Freedom.* New York: Anchor.

Sen, Amartya. 2005. "Foreword." In Paul Farmer, *Pathologies of Power: Health, Human Rights, and the New War on the Poor.* Berkeley: University of California Press.

Shachar, Ayelet. 2009. *The Birthright Lottery: Citizenship and Global Inequality.* Cambridge: Harvard University Press.

Shillington, Kevin. 2012. *History of Africa.* 3rd edition. New York: Palgrave Macmillan.

Silver, Beverly, and Lu Zhang. 2009. "China as an Emerging Epicenter of Labor Unrest." In Ho-Fung Hung (ed.), *China and the Transformation of Global Capitalism.* Baltimore: Johns Hopkins.

Smeeding, Timothy M., Robert Erikson, and Markus Jantti (eds.). 2011. *Persistence, Privilege, and Parenting: The Comparative Study of Intergeneration Mobility.* New York: Russell Sage Foundation.

Smith, Adam. 1976 [1776]. *An Inquiry into the Nature and Causes of the Wealth of Nations.* Edited by Edwin Cannan. Chicago: University of Chicago Press.

Terreblanche, Sampie. 2002. *A History of Inequality in South Africa, 1652–2002.* Pietermaritzburg: University of Natal Press.

Tilly, Charles. 1999. *Durable Inequality.* Berkeley: University of California Press.

Timberg, Craig, and Daniel Halperin. 2012. *Tinderbox: How the West Sparked the AIDS Epidemic and How the World Can Finally Overcome It.* New York: Penguin.

UN Habitat. 2003a. *The Challenge of Slums: Global Report on Human Settlements.* New York: United Nations Human Settlement Programs.

UN Habitat. 2003b. *Slums of the World: The Face of Urban Poverty in the New Millennium?* New York: United Nations Human Settlement Programs.

UN Habitat. 2008. *The State of African Cities.* New York: United Nations Human Settlement Programs. URL: http://chede.org/chede/wp-content/uploads/2011/08/State-of-African-Cities-in-2008-UN-Habitat.pdf (accessed April 19, 2014).

UN Habitat. 2010. *The State of African Cities, 2010: Governance, Inequality, and Urban Land Markets.* New York: United Nations Human Settlement Programs.

Voss, Kim, and Irene Bloemraad. 2011. *Rallying for Immigrant Rights: The Fight for Inclusion in 21ˢᵗ Century America.* Berkeley: University of California Press.

Wallerstein, Immanuel. 1974. *The Modern World-System I: Capitalist Agriculture and the Origins of the European World-Economy in the Sixteenth Century.* San Diego: Academic Press.

Wallerstein, Immanuel. 1995. Response: Declining States, Declining Rights. *International Labor and Working-Class History,* 47: 24–27.

Williamson, Jeffrey G. 2011. *Trade and Poverty: When the Third World Fell Behind.* Cambridge: MIT.

World Bank. 2010. *World Development Report 2010: Development and Climate Change.* Washington, DC: World Bank.

PART II

World Political Structures and Transformations

7

World War II: What Does It Tell Us about Future Great Power Wars?

Albert J. Bergesen

World War II wasn't primarily between Germany and the United States over who would succeed Britain as the hegemon of the capitalist world-system, as suggested by hegemonic succession theory. Instead it was primarily a war between the land powers Nazi Germany and the Soviet Union and the sea powers Imperial Japan and the United States. Based upon these facts a new framework for understanding great power war is advanced and employed to speculate about possible combatants should there be another great power war in the 21st century.

Introduction

With China predicted to pass the United States as the world's largest economy, it seems reasonable to inquire if the world is headed toward another round of hegemonic succession wars (Wallerstein, 2011),[1] one of the most prevalent world-system theoretical accounts of the underlying dynamics of World War II. The argument is that during the "slow decline of the hegemonic power" rising economic powers emerge as contenders, such as last time around the United States and Germany with Britain being the hegemon in decline (Wallerstein, 2011, xxiii). Eventually "the struggle becomes so acute that order breaks down and there is a 'thirty years' war' [1914–1945] between the contenders for hegemony" (Wallerstein, 2011, xxiii).[2] On the surface this idea seems to fit the data surrounding the Second World War, where

---

1   Hegemonic succession war theory is similar to power transition theory, which argues war tends to break out when a state attains enough power that it begins to threaten the dominant state (Organski and Kugler, 1980). Somewhat similar is the idea of Modelski and Thompson (1996) and Rasler and Thompson (1994) concerning "leadership transitions" where reigning power is not happy with a newer one gaining some breakthrough (usually technological) that allows them to challenge for the global leadership position. In some sense all of these theories are variants of Thucydides' classic comment on the origin of the Peloponnesian War: "What made war inevitable was the growth of Athenian power and the fear which this caused in Sparta."

2   Wallerstein (2011, xxiv) goes on to further argue that "[i]n each case up to now one contender has been primarily land-based and the other primarily sea-based (or today, sea/air)" and that "the land-based power sought to gain dominance by transforming the world-economy into a world-empire" while the sea-based power "sought to become not an imperial but a hegemonic power."

by the end of the nineteenth century Britain was in decline and the United States and Germany were rising economic powers fighting each other during World War I and World War II. And, of course, as everyone knows, after 1945 the United States became the clear-cut hegemon of the capitalist world-system.

End of story. Perhaps. But I would like to suggest that before we move on to apply this theory to potential great power conflicts of the twenty-first century, we take a closer look at the data about who was actually fighting whom during the Second World War. Reference will be made to the First World War as well, but I would like to start out with World War II, what world-system theory considers the most recent hegemonic succession war. In so doing I want to suggest two problems that force a reconsideration of the underlying dynamics of that 1939–1945 conflict.

Nazi Germany vs. Soviet Russia

From this point of view World War II purportedly was a war between the contenders for capitalist hegemony, the United States and Germany. But from the point of view of battle deaths, the war wasn't primarily between these two rising economic powers; nor between, say, Germany rising and Britain declining, or the two contenders in some sort of alliance against the declining hegemon. Four out of five German battle deaths were on the Eastern Front, meaning the Germans were principally fighting the Russians. Here, along the 1000-mile front from the Baltic to the Black Sea was where most of the fighting took place. Here were the huge battles of Stalingrad (1942) and Kursk (1943), the horrendous siege of Leningrad (Leningrad); and the largest number of battle deaths: German and Russian, not German and American, battle deaths. The Soviets suffered 7,500,000 battle deaths and the Germans 3,500,000, compared to only 405,400 American and 418,765 British battle deaths (Sarkees and Wayman, 2010, 121). In fact, more "Russians died in Leningrad alone than British and American soldiers and civilians during the whole of the Second World War" (Roberts, 2011, 172), and even when "the Allies directly encountered the Wehrmacht on the continent after the Normandy landing in June of 1944 they were fighting only 68 German Divisions compared with 173 German divisions fighting the Russians on the eastern front" (Dobbs, 2012, 19). As one historian concluded, "Churchill was correct in concluding that it was the Russians, not the Americans or the British, who had done the main work in tearing the guts out of the German army" (Dobbs, 2012, 19).

There was, of course, fighting between the United States and Germany in North Africa, Sicily, and Italy, but when the U.S. Army finally confronted the Wehrmacht on the continent in 1944, it was only a year before the war was over and the German army was now exhausted from fighting the Red Army on the eastern front. As most historians agree the 1942–1943 battles at Stalingrad and history's largest tank battle at Kursk marked the turning point of the war way before serious German engagements with American forces on the ground. This is not to slight the effect of Allied

Strategic Bombing (Overy, 1995) in weakening the German war effort, but it is to agree with most recent histories of the war that the German war was both fought, and lost, on the eastern front (Weinberg, 1994; Ferguson, 2006; Hastings, 2011; Roberts, 2011; Beevor, 2012).

But according to world-system theory Germany was supposed to be primarily fighting the United States as a contender to succeed Britain as the hegemon of the capitalist world-system; instead Germany decided to invade Russia, no one's idea of a potential successor to hegemony over the capitalist world-system. There is a second problem. This one dealing with whom the United States was fighting, and like Germany it is someone who is not listed at all as one of the contenders by standard versions of world-system theory; that of course is Japan fighting the United States in the 1941–1945 Pacific War.

Imperial Japan vs. the United States

The United States, of course, was at war with Germany and "Britain was given a guarantee that the defeat of Hitler was still the primary ambition, but the Pacific got the lion's share of naval and army resources. By the middle of 1942 there were almost 400,000 American soldiers in the Pacific theatre; against Germany and Italy there were only sixty thousand" (Overy, 1995, 34). But world-system theory makes no mention of Japan as a potential rival of the United States to succeed Britain. That role is reserved solely for Germany. The case of Japan needs to be considered more seriously.

First, like Germany, Japan was a modernizing and industrializing power in the late nineteenth century. Second, and different from Germany, Japan was a distinctly maritime power that had, like Britain, acquired overseas colonial holdings. "After war with China in 1894–95 and Russia 1904–05 Japan acquired first the island of Formosa (now Taiwan), then Korea" and as early as 1904, "the Japanese cabinet pronounced that 'If large numbers of emigrants from our country . . . can penetrate the [Korean] interior . . . we will acquire in a single stroke an emigration colony for our excess population and sufficient supplies of foodstuffs'" (Collingham, 2012, 50, 59). Third, of necessity, sea powers rely upon expeditionary warfare, since large bodies of water separate them from territories they wish to colonize or conquer, and Japan was involved in expeditionary warfare from Manchuria in 1931 to their conquest of Shanghai, Nanking, and other Chinese cities in the Sino-Chinese war of 1937–1945. Also, the weakness of the European colonial powers in 1940 "encouraged the Japanese chiefs of staff to think that they could take over the entire southeast Asian treasure house of [colonial] resources" (Collingham, 2012, 63). And so, in 1941–1942, "Japanese forces landed in the Philippines, on the Malay Peninsula, and on Borneo, Sumatra, and Java. Thailand surrendered on December 9; Hong Kong fell on Christmas Day; Manila on January 2 [1942] . . . Singapore fell on February 15

... In the wake of this ... the Japanese conquered an island empire of more than ten thousand square miles ... (Symonds, 2011, 43).

Compare this with the war activity of Germany, who directly attacked a contiguous land power, Soviet Russia, while Japan, on the other hand, attacked the colonial holdings of fellow sea powers, Britain, France, and the Netherlands, and the navy of her direct sea-power competitor for hegemony, the United States at Pearl Harbor. Successor to Britain was more than just national economic output, for Britain was above all the sea power; it was the very foundation of her global hegemonic role. And, importantly, previous world-system hegemons were also great sea powers, such that any serious study of who was in contention to succeed Britain would have to look and see which sea powers were, in fact, at war over control of the oceanic commons (Posen, 2003). If indeed Japan had "within a matter of weeks crippled the American fleet and eliminated the British and Dutch navies in the Far East" such that "the Indian and Pacific Oceans lay wide open to Japanese sea power . . . [and] none of the world's broad seaways could be safely sailed, or easily defended" (Overy, 1995, 32), then Japan was, in fact, directly contending to lay claim to being the successor to British sea power hegemony.

But fighting the United States for control of the world's oceans was not what Germany was doing; she was, as we have seen, primarily engaged with Soviet Russia in a massive and all encompassing land war. Except for the use of submarines and auxiliary cruisers which mostly attacked merchant shipping, there were virtually no major engagements between German and U.S., or British, surface warships, nor between German and American dive and torpedo bombers launched from aircraft carriers. German innovative use of airpower was in highly coordinated combination with tank and infantry units *(Blitzkrieg)*, while Japanese innovation with airpower came from mixing them with ships, exemplified by the famed *Kido Butai*, or strike force, composed of six large aircraft carriers plus two fast battleships, and screened by a dozen cruisers and destroyers. It was the most powerful concentration of naval air power in the world. The Americans utilized a single carrier in a naval strike force which could launch 60–90 planes; the Japanese *Kido Butai* strike force launched 350 planes at Pearl Harbor (Symonds, 2011).

The irony with Hitler's Germany is that rather than going to war over succession to Britain, it may have been just the opposite. There never seems to have been a German war aim to supplant Britain's leading capitalist role, e.g., to gain a global network of colonies, or to be the center of global finance and dominate world stock markets. Recent historical research (Tooze, 2006; Snyder, 2010; Collingham, 2012) on the economic aims of the Third *Reich* suggests Germany was more interested in developing a more autarkic economic system instead.

> How could a large land empire thrive and dominate in the modern world without reliable access to world markets and without much recourse to naval power? Stalin and Hitler had arrived at the same basic answer to this fundamental question. The state

must be large in territory and self-sufficient in economics, with a balance between industry and agriculture . . . . Both Hitler and Stalin aimed at imperial autarky, within a
large land empire well supplied in food, raw materials, and mineral resources (Snyder,
2010, 158).

Seeking to be the most the most autarkic state in the world is no way to battle the
United States or Britain for the "capitalist" hegemony of the modern world-system.

Hegemony of the capitalist world-system never seemed to have been a German
goal, for "Britain's empire and navy structured a world system that neither the Nazis
nor the Soviets aimed, in the short run, to overturn. Each instead accepted that they
would have to win their wars, complete their revolutions, and build their empires,
despite the existence of the British Empire and the dominance of the Royal Navy"
(Snyder, 2010, 158). In fact, even before the war autarky was on Hitler's mind, writing in the 1920s he argued, "one could either acquire new soil in order annually to
send off the superfluous millions, and thus conserve the nation further on the basis
of a self-sustainment [the land option], or one could set about . . . through industry
and trade, to produce for foreign consumption and to live on the proceeds [the sea
option]" (Hitler, 1941, 178). He concludes that the "healthier" of these options is
"the first." "For Germany, therefore, the only possibility of carrying out a sound territorial policy was to be found in the acquisition of new soil in Europe proper . . .
If one wanted land and soil in Europe, then by and large this could only have been
done at Russia's expense . . ." (Hitler, 1941, 181–182). Bismarck also understood the
geographical constraints of Germany's geopolitical situation when replying to a colonial enthusiast in 1888 he stated, "your map of Africa is really quite nice. But my
map of Africa lies in Europe. Here is Russia, and here . . . is France, and we're in the
middle—that's my map of Africa" (quoted in Feuchtwanger, 2002, 228).

In sum, from 1941 until the end of the war, Germany's primary military engagements were on land, acting appropriately as a land power, against her prime land
power competitor to the east, Russia (McMeekin, 2011). With little in the way of
significant sea power (except commerce raiding) Germany made no serious efforts
to capture colonial holdings of the weakened hegemon, Britain, or other maritime
states (France, the Netherlands, the United States) or directly attack her purported direct competitor the United States. Japan's primary engagements against the
United States were fought as a sea power, and importantly against the holdings
and naval strength of other global sea powers. It needs to be remembered that in
fact the next hegemon after Britain was the major sea power, the United States. As
for Japan's challenge for hegemony of the distinctly capitalist world-system, it also
needs to be remembered that 23 years after defeat in 1945 Japan had become the
world's second largest capitalist economy, a position held until 2012 when Japan
slipped to third behind China. In the light of this it is perhaps appropriate, now,
in something of an Asian Pivot in world-system thinking, to consider that Japan
was, in a very real sense, a legitimate contender to try and succeed Britain. That

she failed doesn't diminish her status as the sea power that fought with the United States over succession to Britain. The post-war economic rise of Japan, South Korea, Taiwan, Singapore, and of course China, suggests that the competitors were indeed from Asia and North America, not North America and Europe. Germany should have been fighting the United States, but was engaged with Russia; the United States should have been fighting Germany (and did some), but was fighting with Japan. Since the United States became the hegemon, and if World War II was a succession war, and if the United States was principally fighting Japan, then it stands to reason that Japan, not Germany, was the U.S. competitor to succeed Britain.

Why are only sea powers hegemons of the world-system?

Along with replacing Germany with Japan in world-system theory as the hegemonic contender fighting the United States, we can also entertain the proposition that, in fact, all hegemons will be sea powers and hence all hegemonic succession wars will be between sea powers; not sea and land, or land and land, powers. What this in turn suggests is that there are two sets of dynamics for land vs. land power, and sea vs. sea power wars.

Let's start at sea first. It may be an accident, although I don't think so, but upon a moment's reflection it becomes clear that all of the hegemons of the modern world-system since its inception in the sixteenth century have been not just maritime states, but sea powers, and usually the dominant, or hegemonic, sea power at that. The usual list of world-system hegemons, Imperial Spain (for some Portugal; see Modelski and Thompson, 1996), the Netherlands (although some think not; for a dissenting view, see Wilkinson, 2012), Britain, and the United States were also, in their time, the dominant sea power. Notice: There are no land powers on this list. No Czarist, Imperial, Soviet, or Republic of, Russia; no Austro-Hungarian Empire; no French or Napoleonic Empire; no Bismarckian, Wilhelmite, Nazi, or Federal Republic of, Germany. The issue isn't that these weren't capitalist powers. Certainly Germany and France were and Czarist Russia showed tremendous growth prior to World War I. Geopolitically, the birth of the modern world-system (Wallerstein, 1974) is tied to the emergence of European sea power, such that with the onset of "Iberian-based maritime ventures there was the start of, in Mahan's words, 'authority based on the control of the seas'" (Kennedy, 1976, 18), and a chronology of world-systemic hegemonic succession wars would look something like this. There is general agreement about sixteenth century Imperial Spain. Spanish decline combined with the emergence of Dutch and English sea powers, which are also growing capitalist powers, the Anglo-Dutch Naval Wars of 1652–1674, constitute the sea-power struggle to succeed economic and sea power hegemon, Spain. The Napoleonic Wars are often seen as the key struggle to succeed Spain (Wallerstein, 2011) but like the Nazi Germany vs. Soviet Union war these were mostly land wars similar to France vs. Austria, Prussia, Italy, Russia and so forth. There were, of course, naval battles, like the Battle of the Nile (1798) and Trafalgar (1805), but in general the Napoleonic War years 1792–1815 were largely comprised of ground campaigns, Ulm (1805), Austerlitz (1805), Jena (1806), Eylau (1807), Friedland (1807), Wagram (1809), Borodino (1812), Waterloo (1815). The Napoleonic Wars simply did not involve a significant challenge to British sea power, and so it wasn't really a hegemonic succession war. They were more about the logic of land, and as such more similar to the 1941–1945 German-Russian War. If one adds World War I to the mix then all these land wars are basically driven by expanding and contracting land empires/states which, given the territorial proximity of land powers, raises the risks of war (Turchin et al., 2006; Levy and Thompson, 2010). Contracting, declining, weakening land powers generate vacuums into which expanding states are drawn, as in the case of Habsburg Spain for the Thirty Years' War and the Ottoman Empire for World War I (McMeekin, 2010). Land wars are not about competing to replace an ocean spanning empire of a trade-oriented, export- and import-dependent economy that operates on a world-systemic scale. It wasn't the goal of those who fought in the Thirty Years' War, nor of Napoleon, Bismarck, Kaiser Wilhelm II, Czar Nicholas II, Hitler, or Stalin. It was, though, the goals of those who fought in the Anglo-Dutch Naval Wars and the American-Japanese Pacific War.

Viewing the seventeenth and twentieth centuries more broadly then we see two sets of major wars; one on land; one at sea. On land, and not primarily involving the English or Dutch sea powers, is the Thirty Years' War (1618–1648) and also on land is the twentieth century German Russian War (1941–1945). This too does not primarily involve the sea powers Japan or the United States. Conversely, at sea were the Anglo-Dutch Wars (1652–1674) and the Japanese American Pacific War (1941–1945), in which the land powers of the time were not major participants.

Oceanic foundations of capitalist development

Economic production on a continent, no matter how expansive and no matter what the relations of production under which it is executed, does not, per se, make a "world"-economic system without the products of said production being consumed by markets on other continents, or without much of the raw materials for such production being imported from other continents. If, say, Russia produces more goods than any other country, and all of that is consumed by the Russian domestic economy, that makes for the largest national economy, but it doesn't make for a world-economy. Conversely, a lower level of output that does involve raw material imports and finished goods exports from continent to continent would, in fact, comprise a world-economy. This seems obvious, of course, but for this to happen aquatic sinews linking continents of producers and consumers, importers and exporters, and the military force that guarantees the hierarchal structure of these aquatic relations, are required. And this is as true today as yesterday, for 90 percent of all goods in today's international economy move by sea.

I think theory has not emphasized this point because since the nineteenth century it has generally followed the land-based model of Marx; where relations in production (class relations) are paramount and trade or exchange relations are secondary. You can't exchange it if you haven't produced it, in effect. Understood. But on a world-scale the presumptive priority of production can be questioned, for land-based continental production devoid of oceanic transport not only eliminates additional consumption on additional continents, but more seriously de-globalizes, or de-world-economizes, the overall economic process. If inter-continental relations are required for a world-economy to be world, then aquatic relations are absolutely essential, otherwise there would be no "world" or "system" in the capitalist world-system. What the global would mean is just the aggregation of separate, discrete, national/continental economies with their own internal production and exchange relations.

If this is so, then the political component of the concept of the political economy of the world-system is less the night watchman state of army, police, courts, jails, and more the maritime state of a blue water navy for the transport and reinforcement of expeditionary forces to establish colonies, ports of call, refueling stops, and police trade routes, thus enforcing the unequal exchange involved in maintaining the core-periphery hierarchal structure. Virtually none of the more abstract properties of the capitalist world-economy can be enforced and reproduced without the presence of sea power. The night watchman for the world-economy is naval sea power. No national economy exists without the political to structure and enforce its economic relations and globally the political is manifest as the naval presence to structure, enforce, and reproduce the intercontinental oceanic trade/transport relations that make the distinctly world-economy possible. From this point of view the world-system's hegemon has to be, and hence has always been, and for the near future will continue to be, at one and the same time, the dominant military sea power and the leading capitalist economic power.

Shallow and deep hegemony

There is an old saying that in elections political parties compete, contend, and go to war with each other, but that in the end it is always money that wins. The same holds here. It is sea, not land power that is the geographical constant, for at a very deep geopolitical level the globe's sea-ring of colonial dependencies, refueling stations, friendly ports of call, expeditionary placed troops, naval ships of war and the merchant shipping they protect, is always hegemonic. It is why there have been no land power hegemons so far. Water, sea, oceans, no matter how you put that, as 70 percent of the earth's surface not only surrounds but connects the remaining 30 percent of the world that is continents and islands. Deep hegemony is that of the oceans over the continents as the foundation for capitalist hegemony.

From the point of view of this deep geographical hegemony there will never be a land power that will exercise hegemony within the capitalist world-system. What we have till now called "hegemonic succession struggles" are really struggles for shallow hegemony; nothing more than shifts in geo-locale of the next sea power who, after a struggle with a peer, will go on to assume the mantle of dominating world-system. Historically, there was Imperial Spain; up and then down, with Britain and the Netherlands fighting those seventeenth century sea-battles over who would assume Spain's mantle as the joint capitalist/sea power hegemon. Britain won. Then it was Britain up and then down, with the void filled by the twentieth century Pacific war between Japan and the United States. The United States won. Then the United States went up, and now it is slipping down, and we again think of future sea power/ capitalist challengers to fill the void in controlling the World Ocean. This brings us to the first sentence of this chapter, the prediction that China will shortly pass the United States as the world's largest economy, and with that a new speculative interest in who might participate in another set of great power wars, amongst land or sea, or possibly between land and sea. The future of global conflict is, of course, a guessing game, but given the geopolitical perspective introduced here we can explore some possible scenarios.

Scenario 1: Land power vs. land power

China vs. Russia

As noted, some international conflict is just among land powers, as we saw with the Thirty Years' War, Napoleonic Wars, World War I, and the German-Russian part of World War II. If land powers follow logics dictated by their continental status, domestic expansion may start with the more powerful dominating weaker neighbors. But eventually stronger land powers, given land's finite nature, will have expanded enough to have no choice but to confront each other. Think of the centuries-long expansion of Imperial Russia and the more recent expansion of Imperial Germany after unification in 1871. Land being finite makes great power war almost inevitable at some point. This may very well have been what World War I and World War II were about. If so the zone of dynamic growth on the Eurasian continent has shifted east to China where there are Russian concerns over migrations of Chinese migrants into Russian Siberia. For that matter Chinese migration into her own western provinces can also pose a potential threat to India to the south and Russia to the west and north. If we look at World War I as centering upon expanding and contracting land powers (the German, Austro-Hungarian, Russian, and Ottoman empires) with World War II as a continuation of that war now centered upon just two empires, Nazi Germany and Soviet Russia, perhaps World War III will involve a similar mix of expanding, contracting, and static great land powers; perhaps the EU, or just Germany, Russia, China, or India. Here the Arab Middle East and Central

Asia of Iran, Afghanistan, and Pakistan could very well constitute the Balkans tinderbox, or void, where Russia, China, and India meet or contend, or are drawn into.

Germany + Russia vs. China

A second scenario centers upon the continued disintegration of the EU and the emergence of a more formal German/Russian entente. Already, over 60 percent of Germany's gas imports come from Russia and Nord Stream pipeline brings Siberian gas directly to Germany. This was Mackinder's great fear in 1905, but control of his heartland at the center of Eurasia seems, devoid of any control over the World Ocean, a particularly pre-1914 British anxiety of a combination, rather than opposition, of the two great land powers of his time. A Russian/German entente would seemingly informally dominate the rest of western Europe and it seems doubtful that, if it should turn to overt conflict, the United States would this time around come to participate in that conflict, particularly since Britain is no longer central to the maintenance of oceanic hegemony. It is possible that Russia will secure her western front in ties to Germany before seriously engaging China in the east. Ironically, the same strategy Germany used in World War I and World War II before marching east into Russia.

Germany vs. Russia

A re-run of World War II is always possible, but it seems much less likely. But again, nothing can be ruled out. A cautionary note here on all these possible scenarios. While there are known unknowns, the real danger is unknown unknowns. Think for a moment about World War II. Given German control over much of western Europe, and at the very same time bombing Britain, who would have thought that Hitler's real war aims centered upon invading Russia, or that Japan, so deeply invested in a war with China was to be primarily involved for the rest of the war with fighting the United States.

Scenario 2: Sea power vs. sea power

China vs. the United States

Japan's 1941–1945 oceanic challenge was perhaps premature, but in retrospect Japan was clearly on her way to global economic prominence, as seen in its dramatic economic growth after 1945. China, though, seems on a different trajectory. First, its economic rise has preceded the present military rise, which is more the British, than American, model of hegemonic ascendance. Second, whereas Japan was highly dependent upon American imports prior to the war, it is China that holds a large portion of American government bonds and sells much to the United States. China to the United States seems, now at least, more like the United States to Britain earlier. Which would mean allies during another outbreak of global war.

Nonetheless there is discussion about the growth of Chinese military spending and the development of a blue water navy along with territorial claims in the South China Sea (Friedberg, 2011). Again using the American model, this could be their version of a Monroe Doctrine as part and parcel of coming on line as a great power. The British eventually abandoned military outposts in North America—some in direct exchange for aid during World War II—and one could imagine something similar in future conflicts where the United States abandons the island bases of Guam, or Tinian for Chinese aid. On the surface the rise of a competitor to American naval power is no one but China and for that reason alone China may initiate an abrupt challenge to dominate the Indo Pacific, although that seems highly unlikely. More likely China will inherit from the United States, as the United States did from Britain, control of the World Ocean and with that the irreplaceable aquatic sinews of the capitalist world-economy.

Scenario 3: Sea power vs. land power

This is perhaps the most controversial scenario and is based upon the tensions and dynamics inherent in tensions between land and sea powers. The colonial holdings of sea powers are weakly held because expeditionary forces, which by their nature have to be transported by sea, can only carry so many troops and supplies. While sea power's expeditionary forces are weak compared to the ground forces of land powers, they are nonetheless capable of dominating even weaker land forces, again, usually on other continents—what we know of as colonies. What this means is that sea powers, if they are to expand, can only do this *vis-à-vis* weaker land powers, which has meant searching other continents for less developed areas to conquer or subvert. Land powers don't have the sea resources to acquire the same number of colonies and, given domestic economic growth, their expansion is more likely to be at the expense of their immediate neighbors, for they have no large bodies of water that would stop the massive advances of their ground forces (Mearsheimer, 2001).

The result of these two different geopolitical logics is two kinds of empires generated by security concerns in general, and something like a Hobson/Lenin dynamic whereby economic growth pushes for wider markets to absorb production and requires increased raw material imports from other areas. Land empires faced with the Hobson/Lenin trap have the capacity to march into their neighbors' territory, and hence tend to expand their domestic territory at the expense of other land powers. Witness the growth of the extensive Russian, Austro-Hungarian, German, and Ottoman Empires. Sea powers, though, face the stopping power of water and so they turn their bordering body of water to their advantage and advance further abroad by sea routes, but with admittedly lesser forces than their land power peers have on land. The overall land/sea geopolitical structure is stable as long as the more slowly growing land powers have yet to reach their oceanic bound continental frontier. At that point we witness Imperial Russian threats to British India from Russian-controlled Persia and the threat of the Berlin-Baghdad railroad coupled with a spur to Basra and from there down the Persian Gulf to the Arabian Sea and then British India. Whitehall worried much about both prior to World War I, for at this point the sea power's weaker expeditionary forces, which could defeat colonial locals, could not defeat the larger ground forces of the approaching land power. Was this what happened to Britain who, rather than allow the German 1914 invasion of Belgium become just another Franco-Prussian War, set up a trip wire for poor Belgium and used that as a pretext to enter the war against Germany?

Sea power defends the sea access front of colonial or weaker allies, but it is vulnerable to land access from the backside. When the slower growing, but stronger, land power's expansion finally reaches the wider ring of weaker held sea power colonial outposts, instability results.

Conclusion and summary

Hegemonic decline does seem associated with the outbreak of conflict between rising economic powers. But there is a geopolitical intervening variable; is it a land or a sea power? The mistake we have all made till now is to just focus upon being a rising power, regardless of geopolitical status, which has led in turn to conflating land wars and their own logic with sea power succession wars and their own logic. The dramatic case was the data from World War II: four out of five German battle deaths in World War II were incurred on the eastern front. Germany, rising economically as she was, was not, as theorized, primarily fighting her purported rival the United States. And if that wasn't enough there has been virtually no discussion of Japan's role in any sort of mid-twentieth century succession struggle with the United States even though they fought the Pacific War.

So, first, at minimum, theory should substitute Japan for Germany as the primary opponent of the United States in this succession struggle.

Second, Germany was certainly fighting in World War II but not for hegemony. It appears she desired insulation from the predations of blockading sea powers doing what Britain had done to Germany in World War I. As a land power Germany, and for that matter the Soviet Union, sought self-sufficiency within Eurasia as economically autarkic land powers. The pioneering historical scholarship of Tooze (2006), Snyder (2010) and Collingham (2012) now make all of this quite clear.

Third, world-system theory is now faced with another set of axial global divisions to go along with the well-researched hierarchal core-periphery economic dependency structure, as the world is also divided into stronger and weaker land and sea powers. How the global economic and global geopolitical interrelate will be the subject of future research, but initially it seems clear that sustaining a core-periphery economic structure that is trans-continental relies upon global sea power strength to enforce those relations, leading to the working hypothesis that the hegemon of the oceans is at one and the same time the hegemon of the capitalist world-economy. The preliminary evidence here is the fact that those states that have been so far identified as world-system hegemons have all been at the same time dominant sea powers. And, of course the observation that as China's economic ascent continues so does the development of her blue water navy.

Fourth, if land powers are not contenders for hegemony they do nonetheless engage in international conflicts of great ferocity and violence, and their causal logic seems different from the sea power's hegemonic succession wars. Continental land is bound by water, constituting something of a global sea-ring, and land power territorial expansion, for whatever reason, is a somewhat zero-sum game coming at the expense of a weaker land power. Stronger on weaker we call conquest; stronger vs. stronger we call great power war. How and to what degree these logics of land expansion and sea power expansion influence one another is another question that will have to be settled by future research.

Fifth, the fact of these different types of land and sea wars points to an underlying deep geopolitical structure that characterizes the globe as a whole. Oceans surround continents, the sea-ring idea, and land constitutes a continental core of this geographical complex. How this architecture affects the states which arise within the geographical structure we are just beginning to understand and what has been asserted here is very preliminary and will no doubt be revised by future research. World War II suggests at least two dynamics. First is conflict within the sea-ring amongst maritime states over hegemonic succession within the capitalist world economy (the Anglo-Dutch, and Japanese-American Wars). Second, there are conflicts within the continental core (the Thirty Years' War and the German-Russian War). What is at this point least understood is the interaction dynamics of sea-ring and continental core.

References

Beevor, Antony. 2012. *The Second World War.* New York: Little Brown.

Collingham, Lizzie. 2012. *The Taste of War: World War II and the Battle for Food.* New York: The Penguin Press.

Dobbs, Michael. 2012. *Six Months in 1945: From World War to Cold War.* New York: Knopf.

Ferguson, Niall. 2006. *The War of the World: Twentieth-Century Conflict and the Descent of the West.* New York: Penguin.

Feuchtwanger, Edgar J. 2002. *Bismarck.* London: Routledge.

Friedberg, Aaron L. 2011. *A Contest for Supremacy: China, America, and the Struggle for Mastery in Asia.* New York: Norton.

Hastings, Max. 2011. *Inferno: The World at War, 1939–1945.* New York: Vintage.

Hitler, Adolf. 1941. *Mein Kampf.* Complete and unabridged and fully annotated. New York: Beynal and Hitchcock.

Kennedy, Paul M. 1976. *The Rise and Fall of British Naval Mastery.* London: Macmillan.

Levy, Jack, and William Thompson. 2010. Balancing on Land at sea: Do States Ally against the Leading Global Power? *International Security,* 35: 7–43.

McMeekin, Sean. 2010. *The Berlin-Baghdad Express: The Ottoman Empire and Germany's Bid for World Power.* Cambridge: Harvard University Press.

McMeekin, Sean. 2011. *The Russian Origins of the First World War.* Cambridge: Harvard University Press.

Mearsheimer, John. 2001. *The Tragedy of Great Power Politics.* New York: W.W. Norton.

Modelski, George, and William Thompson. 1996. *Leading Sectors and World Powers.* Columbia: University of South Carolina Press.

Organski, A.F.K., and Jacek Kugler. 1980. *The War Ledger.* Chicago: University of Chicago Press.

Overy, Richard. 1995. *Why the Allies Won the War.* New York: W.W. Norton.

Posen, Barry. 2003. Command of the Commons: The Military Foundation of U.S. Hegemony. *International Security,* 28(1): 5–46.

Rasler, Karen A., and William R. Thompson. 1994. *The Great Powers and Global Struggle, 1490–1990.* Lexington, KY: University of Kentucky Press.

Roberts, Andrew. 2011. *The Storm of War: A New History of the Second World War.* New York: Harper.

Sarkees, Meredith Reid, and Frank Whelon Wayman. 2010. *Resort to War: A Data Guide to Inter-State, Intra-State, and Non-State Wars, 1816–2007.* Washington, DC: CQ Press.

Snyder, Timothy. 2010. *Bloodlands: Europe between Hitler and Stalin.* New York: Basic Books.

Symonds, Craig L. 2011. *The Battle of Midway.* New York: Oxford University Press.

Tooze, Adam. 2006. *The Wages of Destruction: The Making and Breaking of the Nazi Economy.* New York: Viking.

Turchin, Peter, Jonathan M. Adams, and Thomas D. Hall. 2006. East-West Orientation of Historical Empires and Modern States. *Journal of World-Systems Research,* XII(II): 219–229.

Wallerstein, Immanuel. 1974. *The Modern World-System: Capitalist Agriculture and the Origins of the European World-Economy in the Sixteenth Century.* New York: Academic Press.

Wallerstein, Immanuel. 2011. *The Modern World-System II: Mercantilism and the Consolidation of the European World-Economy, 1600–1750.* With a New Prologue. Berkeley: University of California Press.

Weinberg, Gerhard L. 1994. *A World at Arms: A Global History of World War II.* New York: Cambridge University Press.

Wilkinson, David. 2012. "Authenticating seventeenth century 'hegemonies': Dutch, Spanish, French, or none?" In Salvatore J. Babones and Christopher Chase-Dunn (eds.), *Routledge Handbook of World-Systems Analysis.* Abingdon: Routledge.

8

United States and China in the Twenty-First Century: The Costs of the War on Terror and the Shifting in Asymmetric Interdependence

Bruno Hendler and Antonio José Escobar Brussi

The chapter's main objective is to promote the academic debate on Sino-American relations in the last decade and to identify possible connections between the costs of the War on Terror for the United States and relative gains for China. Based on Giovanni Arrighi's framework of hegemonic transitions in the modern world-system, we intend to analyze the relation between declining hegemonies and associated rising powers from the perspective of Joseph Nye's concepts of sensibility (quantitative base) and vulnerability (qualitative base). Based on the premises of American financial expansion and Chinese material expansion associated with American capital, technology and markets, the preliminary hypothesis points to the increasing quantitative interdependence (sensibility) with qualitative changes (in vulnerability) in favor of China since the rapprochement between the two countries in the late 1970s. It is intended to demonstrate from the collected data that since the bilateral rapprochement in the late 1970s the China-U.S. relations gained complexity and became progressively less asymmetric. The reduction of asymmetries was accelerated in the last decade by the costs of the War on Terror to the United States—costs which can be compared to the increasing vulnerability of the past hegemonies to their respective associate rising power, due to damages caused by the War of Spanish Succession to the Dutch hegemony and by World War I to the British hegemony.

Hegemonic transitions in the modern world-system

The rise and fall of great powers is one of the most fascinating and intriguing phenomena within social science debates and central to this is the relationship between the rising and declining powers in times of global turmoil. As relevant as understanding the competitive advantages that lifted the United Provinces, Britain, and the United States to the condition of hegemonic powers of the modern world-system is the study of the relationship between these "complexes" in periods of transition from one to another. Thus, to understand the mechanisms of the modern world-system and its current trends, it is necessary to push the boundaries of individual analysis of each of these arrangements and identify, by their interactions, possible continuities and ruptures within the system.

The first section of this chapter presents an empirical analysis of the past hegemonic transitions from the perspective of systemic cycles of accumulation (SCAs)[1] developed by Giovanni Arrighi (1996) and the pattern also identified by Chase-Dunn (1989). It follows that: a declining hegemony (A) in the process of financial expansion is pressed by a revisionist emerging power (B) which, dissatisfied with the current international order, tends to increase the systemic chaos culminating in a period of widespread conflict; the hegemon (A) is induced to form alliances with another emerging power (C) to combat the military threat of (B); (A) and (C) win the war and (C) emerges as the new hegemon from a *tertius gaudens*[2] position.

Thus, we argue that since the bilateral approach between the United States and China in the late 1970s, there has been a process of reducing asymmetries between the two countries. Chinese vulnerability in the 1970s and 1980s started to reduce due to an increase in U.S. vulnerability since the mid-1990s. At this conjuncture, the War on Terror[3] can be seen as a conflict of the American hegemony (A) against the emerging revisionist (B), which makes China, in the position of the associated emergent (C), the major winner.

However, a number of peculiarities should be borne in mind if such reasoning is taken into consideration.

(1) Although the United States faces deep challenges, it remains the largest and most dynamic economy in the world and the only military superpower, so that no single state can replace them so soon (Chase-Dunn and Inoue, 2012, 158).

---

1   Giovanni Arrighi in his work develops the concept of systemic cycles of accumulation (SCA) in analyzing the long-term structures of historical capitalism and associates the rise and fall of global hegemonies. The author realizes that these cycles follow a pattern of "prosperity/material expansion" and "depression/financial expansion" according to the law of capitalist appreciation by Marx (money - commodity - more money). The phase of prosperity or material expansion of the capitalist center occurs when the innovations of the capital-alliance hegemon are absorbed by the real economy and the available capital is invested in productive and commercial sectors leading the system to a new spatial fix, which creates conditions for the emergence of divisions of labor broader or deeper (Arrighi, 2008, 241). Since the phase of depression/financial expansion coincides with the decline or hegemonic "autumn" when the material bases of the regime of capital accumulation and hegemonic power of the state are exhausted, i.e., no longer provide earnings expectations in its extraordinary productive structures, a growing volume of capital in its liquid form, and more flexible, will seek its recovery in the financial sphere (Arienti and Filomeno, 2007, 120–121).

2   "Tertius gaudens" is a Latin expression that means "the third who rejoices." It refers to occasions when a third agent takes advantage of a dispute between other two, and by not taking sides he ensures his own interests regardless of the outcome of the clash (Birnbaum, 1995, 258).

3   The term "War on Terror" is used in this chapter as a reference to the campaign led by the United States, under the Administrations of George W. Bush and Barack Obama, to fight global terrorism networks and states that supposedly support them—according to official documents published by the U.S. Department of State, such as the National Security Strategy of the United States of America of 2002, 2006, and 2010.

(2) The associated emerging power, China, has its own characteristics that make the process even more intricate, like the complex and rooted relations within Asia and its non-Western nature, easing the vulnerability to the West;

(3) In the case of the United States, the emerging revisionist power (B) is not an expansionist state or a specific organization, but a relationship of constant conflicts with a variety of enemies, where growing spending on defense is combined with an economic conjuncture of financial expansion and rupture of institutions created by the hegemony itself. This relationship started in the 1970s with the economic crisis in the United States associated with the growing of military spending in the Vietnam War, continued in the so-called "Second Cold War" during the Reagan Administration and since 2001 has the Islamic terrorism as its *raison d'être*.

According to Fiori (n.d., 48), the current Sino-U.S. relationship is simultaneously complementary and competitive, political and economic, driving the world-system back to the logic of endless search for power and wealth. The period of the Cold War was an exception, when the United States carried on a military competition with the Soviet Union—a country that barely affected the U.S. economy—and maintained dynamic and competitive economic relations with countries without military autonomy, like Germany and Japan.

What makes China a complex puzzle for the Americans is the fact that the country has, at the same time, political and military autonomy like the Soviet Union did, as well as a deep economic impact on the United States like Japan and Germany in the postwar decades. Therefore, the relevance of this work is justified by the dynamism and prominence of Sino-U.S. relations in the course of the modern world-system.

Sensitivity and vulnerability in asymmetric interdependence

The relationship "declining hegemon - associated emerging power" is a fundamental object of study in the modern world-system analysis, and the dialogue with Joseph Nye Jr. and Robert Keohane's concepts of sensitivity and vulnerability can facilitate its understanding. As two countries strengthen the different types of economic ties, there is a tendency for their business agents to create a relationship of mutual dependence, also known as interdependence. Since these changes are included in a capitalist world-economy and affected by unequal power relations between states, it is natural that asymmetries will come up. Thus, interdependence is rarely balanced, and the asymmetries are real sources of power that can be measured by the sensitivity and vulnerability of each agent (Nye, 2011, 55).

Sensitivity is a quantitative parameter defined as "the amount and pace of the effects of mutual dependence; that is, how quickly does change in one part of the system bring about change in another part?" (Nye, 2011, 54). Vulnerability is qualitative and has varying degrees. Nye (2009, 254; 2011, 54) defines it as the ability to minimize the costs of mutual dependence, i.e., the ability of a particular agent to minimize the costs imposed by changes elsewhere in the system.

Since perfect symmetry in economic interdependence is quite rare, the asymmetries in interdependence are important sources of power. Thus, two countries, A and B, that are very sensitive to each other can gain mutual benefits in absolute terms, but it is the ability to react to actual or potential costs imposed by B that guarantees a surplus of power to A. So A has the challenge to deepen ties with B, raising mutual sensitiveness but preventing this interdependence from resulting in higher vulnerability in relative terms.

Emerging economies that have become global hegemonies have had a special relationship with the hegemonic power that preceded them, hence the term "associated emerging power" (AEP). In periods of transition, the AEP managed to reduce its vulnerabilities towards the declining hegemon which, in turn, gradually became weaker and more reliant on the AEP until finally being replaced.

Changes in asymmetrical interdependence between the United Provinces and Britain (1688–1815)

Although the military superiority of the United Provinces is questionable even at its peak during the mid-seventeenth century, it is acceptable to use the term "Dutch hegemony" because of Amsterdam's centrality in trade and financial networks in the world-economy. Furthermore, the role of the Dutch trading companies in generating wealth, dismissing the protection of large monarchical states, such as Habsburg Spain and Bourbon France, and producing their own protection was a notorious evolution from the Italian city-states. However, the deficit of the United Provinces' coercive power made it vulnerable to its main competitors, France and England, which through "wars of adjustments" weakened the Dutch hegemony just a few decades after its ascension.

The hegemonic transition from the United Provinces to England began in the late seventeenth century and ended in 1815, after the Napoleonic Wars. Although many aspects should be mentioned, our focus is to identify the changes in vulnerabilities between them. After three Anglo-Dutch wars of short duration—the last (1672–1674) resulted from the Anglo-French alliance against the United Provinces—England and Holland began a long process of closer political and economic ties and in both aspects the British came out strengthened and the Dutch more vulnerable.

In European geopolitics, the French commercial and continental expansionism catalyzed the Anglo-Dutch alliance (Arrighi and Silver, 2001, 55), strengthened by the rise of the Dutch William of Orange to the English throne in the "Glorious Revolution" in 1688. With its Navy weary after three wars, the Netherlands began to play a secondary and exhausting role in aiding the British struggle against France (Boxer, 1965, 111).

During the Anglo-French rivalry in the War of Spanish Succession (1701–1713), the Dutch provided 3/8 of the sea power to Britain's 5/8 and an army of 102,000 men to join the British Army of 40,000 men. According to Mahan (in Arrighi and Silver, 2001, 57), "this geostrategic division trapped the Netherlands in land warfare, undermining its strength and allowing Britain to concentrate on its naval power." In short, the Dutch expenditure in the war weakened its naval force and increased the domestic debt, forcing its leaders to seek financial resources with the associated emerging power (Britain) to honor their commitments.

The Dutch indebtedness due to military spending was associated with the demographic deficit, productive and commercial competition with Britain, and the wave of protectionism in the Baltic which limited privileged access to primary products. If at the end of the seventeenth century the Netherlands were already vulnerable to British naval superiority, the mid-eighteenth century witnessed declining profitability of Dutch trading companies in the face of British competitors, reducing the economic weight of Amsterdam in manufacturing and global trade.

Nevertheless, the Dutch cycle of accumulation reached its phase of financial expansion in the 1740s, when the excess of idle capital in the stock market of Amsterdam found in British companies the required profitability to recycle. Thus, Dutch maritime power was reduced to the extent that Britain's was expanded, and the Dutch retreated to the role of funders of the British state and its military activities. Soon, the sources of wealth in the Netherlands came to depend increasingly on Britain, making the former immensely more vulnerable to the latter.

In contrast, Britain, whose trading companies and first industries had developed with Dutch capital, reduced its vulnerability to Holland as looting and colonial conquests, especially in India, brought an influx of wealth sufficient to repay its foreign debt (Arrighi, 1996, 215). So when in 1780 the British power was freed from Dutch capital, the vulnerabilities had been reversed completely. The Netherlands were no longer a major naval power and their sources of wealth, once sovereign and powerful, were at the mercy of England, which eliminated them. Britain, which had long needed the military and financial support of the Dutch, defeated them in a brief confrontation in 1782–1783 and subsequently subjugated Napoleonic France by forming a coalition of European states and relying solely on its own material resources, thus becoming the world hegemon in the nineteenth century.

Unlike the Dutch hegemony, the British disposed, during the nineteenth century, of considerable military superiority and became the world's economic center by internalizing agribusiness production and spreading the vision of liberalism according to its own interests. Thus, while the Dutch innovated in the commercial sphere, the British innovated in the productive sphere, bringing to the sovereignty of the empire both agricultural production from the colonies and industrial production from the metropolis. Moreover, while the military and economic superiority of the United Provinces was challenged soon after its hegemonic consolidation, the British leadership began to face real rivalries and competition only half a century after its consolidation in 1815, with the German unification in 1871 and the victory of the Northern states in the American Civil War (1861–1865).

Changes in asymmetric interdependence between Britain and the United States (1865–1918)

Unlike the turbulent Anglo-Dutch political relationship in the seventeenth and eighteenth centuries, the Anglo-American relationship after 1812 was marked by peace and very few disagreements. This "special relationship" of political, cultural, religious, and linguistic affinities (Zhu, 2006, 56), was transformed by the American continental-scale industrialization and the financial expansion centered in London—both interlinked phenomena of the second half of the nineteenth century.

On the other hand, the economic closeness between the hegemon and the AEP is similar in both transitions. Just like Britain canalized Dutch capital and copied the trading companies' model to further develop the industrial/imperial model with its own resources, the United States also canalized British capital and copied the model of familiar industry to further develop the model of great corporations with its own resources (Arrighi and Silver, 2001, 152). Thus, the U.S. economic vulnerability toward Britain was higher in the early stages of development, decreasing gradually during the *Belle Époque* (1870–1914) and more quickly in the period between the two world wars.

From Independence to the Civil War the United States was quite vulnerable to Britain, performing peripheral activities such as the export of primary products to British industries and participating in triangular trade with Central America and other European countries. The incipient industries in the northern states reproduced the British familiar style and depended on capital goods and technologies which largely came from Britain.

With the North's victory in the Civil War, measures were taken to protect the domestic industry, to stimulate the arrival of immigrants for land use, promote a market for domestic consumption, centralize the banking systems and to create a transcontinental railroad and telegraph system (Arrighi, 1996, 300). The main capitalist innovation in this period was the model of large, vertically integrated corporations (Cury, 2006, 98) which, less dependent on British capital, overcame the family industries aiming at the domestic market as the final destination of their products—setting the basis for what would become the first mass consumption society in history.

Due to developments in business organizations and their alliance with the state, the United States became, in a short time, the largest industrial nation in the world. Possessing a vast territory rich in natural resources, an equitable occupation of lands by an immigrant population, a booming domestic market and individual liberty guaranteed by a democratic constitution and a federalist government, the capitalist groups prospered as they never had.

> In the following decades of the Civil War, the agricultural and artisanal economy was replaced by the industrial world of coal, steel and steam. Small familiar firms were replaced by large industrial complexes, which took advantage of the wide availability of raw materials, extensive and cheap labor, technological innovation, a growing consumer market and favorable state policies to transform the United States by far, in the largest industrial nation in the world at the turn of the twentieth century. (Karnal, 2007, 177)

Across the Atlantic, Britain headed down the "no-way-back" path of financial expansion. The falling rate of profit in the agroindustrial sector and the excess of speculative capital pushed Britain firms to financial and trade intermediation (Arrighi and Silver, 2001, 139). According to the data presented by Hobsbawm (2003), since 1850 the national income of Britain depended increasingly on interest and dividends earned from foreign loans and financial services, such as loan sharking and exchange, in contrast to the increase in the deficit of foreign trade.

From 1870 to 1913 Britain accounted for 41.8% of all global foreign investment, followed by France and Germany, with 19.8% and 12.8% respectively (Daudin et al., 2008, 27). The main destination for British capital was the United States (20%)—more than double the other major destinations like Canada, Argentina, Australia and India. The proportion of British capital in the U.S. public sector between 1883 and 1913 rose from 32.2% to 48.6% (Esteves, n.d., 31). Thus, even though the American private sector reduced its dependence on British capital, the public sector was highly vulnerable to Britain—a fact that would be changed by the First World War.

The costs of the "Great War" to Britain were far beyond the military spending. Raising taxes and increasing state intervention in the economy on behalf of the war effort played a decisive role not only in the loss of competitiveness of British family firms, but mainly in changing from U.S. creditor to debtor (Arrighi, 1996, 278–279).

Thus, the British model was deteriorated by the attrition of war, the costs of which burdened the real economy and forced the British government to raise its vulnerability and dependence on the United States.

Therefore, we see a return to the script of hegemonic transitions exposed in the introduction. The British hegemony in the process of financial expansion and increased economic interdependence with the AEP, the United States, deepens this bilateral relationship disadvantageously in order to counter the threat of an emerging revisionist power (Imperial Germany). The reduction in disparities of power and wealth between Britain and the United States had already been lessened since the mid-nineteenth century, but what destroyed the centrality and vitality of British capitalism and, therefore, accelerated the concentration of power and wealth in the United States was not market competition, but military confrontations (Arrighi and Silver, 2001, 143). At the end of World War I the Anglo-American interdependence had changed, with Britain becoming the more vulnerable side. However it would take World War II to define the United States as the new world hegemon and definitively place Britain in a supporting role.

Not by coincidence, the two cases discussed characterize the process of hegemonic transition in the modern world-system. In common, they share:

(1) A conjuncture of gradual reduction of asymmetric interdependence between declining hegemon (A) and associated emerging power (C). This reduction of asymmetries occurs in favor of (C), which undergoes a process of material expansion linked to the financial expansion centered on (A);

(2) A revisionist, expansionist and continental power (B) acts as a catalyst for the (A-C) alliance, triggering a period of systemic chaos marked by military clashes;

(3) Such conflicts as the War of Spanish Succession for the United Provinces and World War I for Britain, meant struggles for security and vital interests of both sovereign countries, which came out as official winners. However, the economic costs of these military and political victories accelerated the cyclical process of increased vulnerability and dependence on the AEP that eventually became the new hegemon under the logic of the *tertius gaudens.*

We assume that the United States can be characterized, since the 1970s, as a hegemon in decline (A), since it is undergoing a process of identifiable financial expansion; and China can be characterized as an AEP (C), as it has been living since the late 1970s in a process of economic liberalization and material expansion associated, to some extent, to capital, technologies and U.S. markets. As mentioned in the introduction, the emerging revisionist (B) is not an expansionist state, but a relation of constant conflict with a variety of U.S. enemies, Islamic terrorism being the ultimate opponent.

Despite the numerous differences between the relations of "Holland - Britain" in the seventeenth and eighteenth centuries, "Britain – United States." in the nineteenth and twentieth centuries, and "United States - China" over the past four decades, it is reasonable to say that in all cases there was a quantitative increase in interdependence, i.e., each side became more sensitive to each other, and that the vulnerabilities were gradually changed in favor of the AEP.

The numerous peculiarities of Sino-U.S. relations make risky any prediction that China might replace United States as the most relevant nation in the world-system. Nevertheless, even though a hegemonic transition similar to the historical pattern is unlikely, we argue that the Chinese dependence on the United States, most evident in the 1970s and 1980s, has become a relationship of mutual dependence in balanced levels, and that this process was accelerated after 2001 with the election of George W. Bush and his War on Terror.

The following sections cast a closer glance at specific spheres of Sino-U.S. relations to validate or invalidate the hypothesis that the costs of the War on Terror increased U.S. vulnerabilities, opening strategic rooms for China and reducing asymmetries, formerly pro-United States, in Sino-American interdependence.

United States and China: Conjuncture and rapprochement

The United States from 1973 to 2001

The attacks of 09/11 and the subsequent War on Terror are embedded in a context of American hegemonic decline, characterized by the process of financial expansion that began in the 1970s and was in many aspects similar to what happened with Britain and the United Provinces in their hegemonic "autumn." That conjunctural process resulted in the profitability crisis of large U.S. corporations, caused by sharp German and Japanese competition in the process of "catching up," the model of subcontracting informal networks and manufacturing economies of East Asia, and the financial and military costs of the Vietnam War (Arrighi, 2008).

In order to respond to the downward pressure on profit rates caused by German and Japanese competition, the U.S. government found a Keynesian solution, through federal deficits, monetary flexibility and the end of the fixed exchange rate system created in Bretton Woods, thus sustaining global economic expansion from a bloated and little regulated financial system. However, this expansion, driven by public debt, generated an unsustainable long-term demand and increased the vulnerability of the United States with regards to foreign creditors.

Seeking to regain the competitiveness of American firms, restore confidence in the dollar and center the money of the world again in the United States, the Republican Administrations of Reagan and Bush I sought: a) to raise the interest rate so that the government could compete for circulating capital in the world; b) the deregulation of the financial system to encourage the free flow of capital; and c) the indebtedness of the government because of the military sector, either with the reheating of the Cold War—Reagan's "Star Wars" being the best known example—or by a series of military expeditions in Third World, "unfriendly" countries, such as Grenada, Libya, Panama and Iraq (Arrighi, 1996, 328).

In general, these actions have achieved their goals as the fall of corporate profit rates was shared with Germany and Japan; East Asia, especially China, started to receive capital and technology from large corporations seeking to exploit the local production advantages, and the United States experienced a period of strong economic growth.

However, the unsustainable character of this recovery culminated in the financial bubble in the second half of the 1990s, during the Clinton Administration. The strengthening of the dollar in 1995, made possible by the inverted Plaza Accord, allied to the regime of the Federal Reserve's easy credit and expansion of public and private debt, caused a massive inflow of foreign capital to the United States. The result was a financial bubble where the main active force was non-financial American companies, each seeking to "greatly expand its debt in order to buy shares in colossal volume" (Arrighi, 2008, 151).

Therefore, the United States reaches the turn of the century with an increasing reliance on foreign investment to subsidize the public debt, private consumption and the current account deficits. If only these investments were largely productive, ponders Dorn (2008, 161), the United States could incur "healthy" deficits. However, speculative capital in this period came to US$1.6 trillion, compared with about US$900 billion in productive investments (Brenner, 2003, 275).

China from 1978 to 2001

The changes that took place in China since its opening by Deng Xiaoping in the late 1970s are characteristic of a material expansion experienced by an AEP. In political terms, the rapprochement with the United States, since the last years of the Mao era, meant the containment of the Soviet Union and the international recognition of Communist China, represented by the right to a permanent seat on the UN Security Council.

In economics, Deng's Four Modernizations (industry, agriculture, technology, and military) began a process of linking China to the United States and the capitalist world. Inspired by Japan and the Asian Tigers, the Chinese leadership started to see a cooperative macro-environment with the United States as a crucial factor for the country's economic development (Deng and Wang, 2005, 204).

In the United States, the rapprochement with the East Asian countries meant more than containing the Soviet Union. Closer economic ties secured access to a supply of cheap and disciplined labor from rural areas and accustomed to intensive labor (Mariutti, 2011, 32). This supply of cheap labor would fit the U.S. companies' need for lower production costs since they were facing increasing competition from German and Japanese companies. Thus, the U.S. strategic imperative coupled with economic changes and the shifting paradigms of the Chinese state have made China the locus of an Asian material expansion—initiated by Japan—which placed the country on the map of global capitalist networks.

Indeed, not only China's exports now depended on American household consumption, but many other factors were crucial to the rise of the Asian country in the international division of labor in Asia-Pacific: Import of capital goods and technology; attracting capital from the United States, Europe and Japan; and human resources development with Chinese youth exchanges with U.S. universities (Deng and Wang, 2005, 205–214). Even though a considerable amount of productive investment in China came from the Chinese diaspora scattered in neighboring countries, since the 1980s we perceive a first sign of Sino-American interdependence, still extremely asymmetric in favor of the Western side, i.e., a bilateral relationship in which China is more vulnerable and dependent on the United States than the opposite.

The international division of labor in Asia-Pacific in the 1980s was shaped up as follows: Japan concentrating on the areas of information technology, automotive, robotics and other leading sectors; the Asian Tigers ascending in the sectors of steel production, shipbuilding, automobiles, motors and electrical products; and China joining this movement by receiving investments of industrial plants from Japanese and Western companies through the Special Economic Zones (SEZs), competing with Southeast Asian nations (ASEAN) and playing a similar role to that of the Tigers in previous years (Vizentini, 2007, 57).

The Japanese model of political stability, economic development and preferential partnership with the United States signaled the emergence of a new world power in the 1980s. But the primacy of the dollar, the U.S. military dependence and Sino-American rapprochement blocked these perspectives. (Pecequilo, 2009, 123–125; Mariutti 2011, 33).

In contrast, after a decade of economic and social reforms, China starts the 1990s as a double pole in global capitalism (Medeiros, 2008, 256)—a fact attributed either to the role of foreign trade or to public investments in heavy industry (steel, heavy chemicals, aluminum) and in sectors such as infrastructure, roads and construction (Mariutti, 2011, 38).

On the one hand, China has become the major absorber of Asian exports by receiving American and Japanese transnational corporations and adding value to primary products derived from its neighbors. On the other hand, through a developmentalist Keynesianism associated with foreign capital and technology (Carvalho and Catermola, 2009, 248), China became the largest producer in the manufacturing of low unit value goods, as much in traditional goods as in electronics, which, through devaluation, began to flood the markets of developed countries. In this sense, Chinese innovation so far is not based as much on technological advances as on organizational changes—substituting the model of vertically integrated corporations, such as General Motors, with subcontractor networks spread throughout East Asia and commanded by the Chinese Diaspora overseas, which has the Wal-Mart retail type as the final destination for its products (Arrighi, 2008, 352).

Mariutti (2011, 34–35) points out two contradictions in Sino-American articulation that have become more apparent in the 1990s. In the United States, the relocation of productive investment to China coupled with financial and credit expansion had consequences, as the surge of speculative bubbles and hypertrophy of the services sector of luxury and entertainment occurred at the expense of jobs in the industrial sector. For China, it engendered an export model that attracted productive investment but remained vulnerable to the United States since it binds the country's development to American and other rich countries' consumers and to financial markets. Moreover, it has created or intensified a number of internal problems in China, such as the increase in inequality between industrial elites in coastal cities (*urban bias*) and peasants in the countryside, compression of wages and domestic consumption in favor of corporate profits and foreign markets, and an unprecedented rural exodus (Hung, 2009, 13).

This vulnerability becomes reciprocal as, in the United States, household consumption, credit growth and public deficit in current account became possible by the purchase of government bonds by foreign creditors, mostly from China, Japan and other parts of East Asia. On the other hand, the creditors were hostages of the dollar and the U.S. consumer market, becoming vulnerable to crises and protectionist outbreaks in this country.

This tension is, in other words, the phenomenon (previously discussed) of shifting vulnerabilities between the declining hegemon and the AEP. In the past transitions, the AEP reduced its dependencies on the hegemon as it sank in financial expansion and military confrontations. In the current U.S.-China relationship the big question to be answered is whether the attrition the United States faced in the War on Terror resulted in increasing or decreasing China's vulnerability. It is clear that both countries have become more sensitive to each other in absolute terms, but the question is whether the change in qualitative terms was really damaging to the United States and beneficial to China.

United States and China: Costs and gains related to the War on Terror

The costs of the War on Terror for the United States

The rise of the neoconservatives with George W. Bush's election is embedded in a context that deserves a deeper analysis of U.S. *momentum* in the 1990s, when the belief in the victory of democracy, the virtues of globalization and the superiority of free market over authoritarian socialist regimes prevailed. In this chapter, we limit ourselves to emphasizing the conservative groups that preached theses like the "American exceptionalism" and the "clash of civilizations" and had strong influence and financial support in the decision-making process of U.S. foreign policy, either by donations to the campaigns of 2000 and 2004 or in the figures of key policymakers like Dick Chaney, Donald Rumsfeld and Paul Wolfowitz (Burbach and Tarbell, 2004, 80). Avoiding a chronological description of the wars that followed the attacks of 09/11, we seek to understand how the costs of these military developments impacted on the U.S. economy (and hegemony) and increased its vulnerability to China, having in mind the context of growing interdependence between the two countries.

Figure 1 below shows the defense spending of the U.S. government. The three leaps are related, respectively, to the Vietnam War, the "Second Cold War" in Reagan's Administration, and the War on Terror. Although the military spending relative to GDP has suffered only a small rise compared to the 40% of GDP during the Second World War and 10% during the Vietnam War (from 3.5% in 1999 to 6% in 2009), the conjuncture of financial expansion in the last decade has exposed the weaknesses of the U.S. economy.

Figure 1: U.S. defense spending (in U.S. billion dollars at their 2005 value)

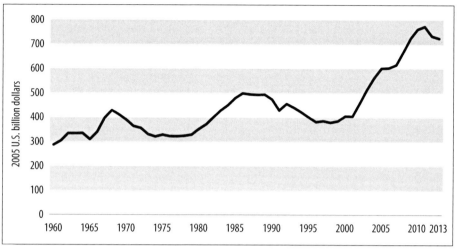

Source: UsGovernmentSpending (2013a).

According to official data of the U.S. Congress, the nominal costs of the Department of Defense in ten years of the War on Terror are estimated at around US$1.3 trillion, of which about US$800 billion was spent in Iraq, US$450 billion in Afghanistan, and tens of billions have had secondary destinations also linked to operations in these countries (Belasco, 2011, 3).

Table 1 below shows that the costs directly associated with the War on Terror occupied a considerable part of the Pentagon budget, 2007 and 2008 being the peak years of the insurgency in Iraq and Afghanistan, requiring about 1/4 of the total budget. Although not counted as a cost of war, a considerable portion of the base spending is also linked to the fight against terrorism, such as the increase in the recruitment of soldiers and marines, and the development of specific combat equipment for scenarios like Iraq and Afghanistan. In this sense, Wheeler (2011) says that, in 2011 values, the costs could reach almost US$2 trillion.

Apart from the defense sector, Figure 2 below shows the relation income/spending of past U.S. Administrations. Coincidentally, all Republican Administrations had higher expenditures than revenue, but in none was the disparity as striking as in the G. W. Bush era, a fact that is due not only to the War on Terror but also to a series of tax cuts that reduced the revenues of the state and led to a total deficit of US$7 trillion in 2011.

In order to fund the military incursions in the Greater Middle East, Bush had four options and chose two (Arrighi, 2008, 206–209). The president chose not to raise taxes, because it would undermine his political base and go against his political

Table 1: Percentage of the U.S. defense budget for the war on terror (2011 U.S. billion dollars)

	2001	2002	2003	2004	2005	2006	2007	2008	2009	2010	2011	Total
Wars spending (A, bn $)	21.7	21.1	96.6	87.4	118.7	130.8	179.4	188.4	153.4	156.4	159.1	1313.0
Base DOD budget (B, bn $)	385.6	421.0	444.6	476.3	437.6	466.0	472.7	520.1	536.4	548.9	529.5	5238.7
Total (C, bn $)	407.3	442.1	541.2	563.7	556.3	596.8	652.1	708.5	689.8	705.3	688.6	6551.7
Relation (A/C, %)	5.3	4.8	17.8	15.5	21.3	21.9	27.5	26.6	22.3	22.2	23.1	20.0

Source: Wheeler (2011).

platform, and failed to make the war pay for itself, since the Iraqi oil did not come even close to covering the costs of the conflict.

The chosen options were to take loans abroad and to print money. The loans came as purchases of the Federal Reserve's public bonds, and the main creditors were no longer private investors but foreign governments, mostly East Asians, that gained influence over U.S. economic policy, making it more vulnerable to external factors. This phenomenon resembles the Dutch demand for British capital to collaborate in the fight against France in the War of Spanish Succession and the British pursuit of American funding to fight World War I against Germany.

The rampant issuance of money to close the government accounts generated a major devaluation of the dollar (35% against the euro and 24% against the yen, from 2001 to 2004) and served as a "soft default" on creditors since it reduced the value of the bonds in their hands. Thus, the adjustment between the weaker dollar and the appreciation of currencies from countries with large current account surpluses,

Figure 2: Change in average revenue and spending by administration

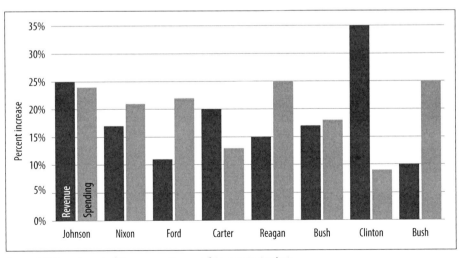

Source: US Department of Commerce: Bureau of Economic Analysis.

Figure 3: George W. Bush administration policies: U.S. public debt as a percentage of GDP

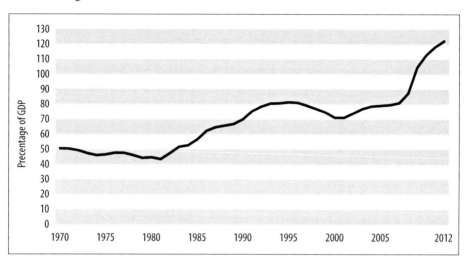

Source: UsGovernmentSpending (2013b).

such as those of East Asia, resulted in a long-term decline in the dollar's role as the international means of payment and reserve currency. Therefore, this excess of capital temporarily covered the U.S. public deficits, rolling the debt at the cost of increasing vulnerability to lenders across the Pacific. And inside the country, the flood of liquidity was combined with low interest rates and lax banking regulations which in turn helped fuel the housing bubble (IEP, 2011, 16).

Continuing the trend of public debt with military spending—softened in short periods—the U.S. public debt exceeded 100% of GDP in 2009.

James Dorn (2008, 152) draws attention to the growing gap between revenues and spending in the United States, not only in government accounts but also at the level of household consumption and income. For him, "living beyond their own means" has increased the vulnerability of Americans with regards to creditors abroad. From 2002 to 2011, the participation of foreign capital in U.S. public debt rose from 1/6 to 1/3, mostly being controlled by central banks in East Asia.

The relative gains for China from the War on Terror

If the United States and China consolidated deep economic ties in the 1990s, the following decade was marked by a vital interdependence between them, creating another type of mutual assured destruction (MAD)—the so-called mutually assured economic destruction (MAED) which links economic vulnerabilities of both countries. The main difference is that the old MAD between the United States and

Table 2: Major foreign holders of U.S. treasury bonds (in U.S. billion dollars)

	2000	2001	2002	2003	2004	2005	2006	2007	2008	2009	2010	2011
China	60.3	78.6	118.4	159.0	222.9	310.0	396.9	477.6	727.4	894.8	1160.1	1151.9
Japan	317.7	317.9	378.1	550.8	689.9	670.0	622.9	581.2	626.0	765.7	882.3	1058.0
Oil exporters	47.7	46.8	49.6	42.6	62.1	78.2	110.2	137.9	186.2	201.1	211.9	258.3
Brazil			12.7	11.8	15.2	28.7	52.1	129.9	127.0	169.2	186.1	226.9
Carib. central banks	37.4	27.6	50.3	47.3	51.1	77.2	72.3	116.4	197.9	128.2	168.4	226.0
Taiwan	33.4	35.3	37.4	50.9	67.9	68.1	59.4	38.2	71.8	116.5	155.1	177.3
Total foreigners	1015.2	1040.1	1235.6	1523.1	1849.3	2033.9	2103.1	2353.2	3077.2	3685.1	4435.6	4996.4
Gross public debt			6405.7	6998.0	7596.1	8170.4	8680.2	9229.2	10699.8	12331.3	14025.2	15222.8

Source: Made by the author and based on US Treasury data (U.S. Department of the Treasury, 2012).

the Soviet Union was defined in terms of military capabilities, the "balance of terror," while in the current MAED, also called "balance of financial terror" (Dorn, 2008, 154), vulnerability is measured in economic terms. These impacts are both political-military and economic—recalling Fiori's statement above on the mutual causality between economics and politics in the current Sino-U.S. relationship.

The typical deficit lifestyle of American families and the government since the 1970s was augmented by the War on Terror and found in China its main guarantor in recent years. The thrifty character of Chinese society and the developmentalism based on exports has ensured large reserves in foreign currencies for the Chinese state, which end up returning to the United States through purchases of government bonds, financing both the government deficits and the consumption (of Chinese products) by American families. For Wallerstein (2012),

> The situation in which the world finds itself today is that China has a significant balance of payments surplus with the United States, much of which it invests in U.S. Treasury bonds, thereby underwriting the ability of the U.S. government to continue to spend vast amounts of resources on its multiple military activities around the globe (and particularly in the Middle East), as well as to be a good customer for Chinese exports.

Table 2 and Table 3 show the increasing importance of China as a holder of U.S. public debt. In December 2011 the bonds in Chinese hands amounted to about US$1.1 trillion and, despite the monthly oscillation, since 2009 China controls about 8% of U.S. total debt. Regarding the amount controlled by foreigners (about US$5 trillion or 1/3 of the total in 2011), China alone holds around 25%, followed by Japan with around 20%.

China's rising share of U.S. debt represents a gain in potential power. Since its opening, China has been dependent on and vulnerable to American consumption and, as Hung (2009, 22) argues, this relationship remains to this day. However, until the 2000s, households and the U.S. government could go into debt and maintain a high standard of consumption without resorting to borrowing from China: today, the U.S. economy does not work without the credit of that country.

Table 3: China's role in U.S. total debt and in total foreign holders of U.S. debt (%)

	2000	2001	2002	2003	2004	2005	2006	2007	2008	2009	2010	2011
Total foreign holders	5.93	7.55	9.58	10.43	12.38	15.24	18.87	20.29	23.63	24.28	26.15	23.05
Total public debt			1.84	2.27	2.93	3.79	4.57	5.17	6.79	7.25	8.27	7.56

Source: Made by the author and based on US Treasury data (U.S. Department of the Treasury, 2012).

The geopolitical impacts of this change in asymmetries clearly show that China has benefited in relative terms from the War on Terror. China's power projection in East Asia, either in multilateral organizations or in military training, as well as the growing economic influence in both central and peripheral countries, occurs simultaneously with the crisis of U.S. hegemonic appeal in the world. China's rapprochement with countries in Africa, Latin America, the Middle East and Central Asia deserves attention, especially with regard to the impacts on regional power arrangements historically made by the United States.

Furthermore, it is clear that the costs of the War on Terror to the United States turned into relative benefits to China. The reduction of asymmetries between the two countries, which was accelerated in the last decade, does not turn China into a self-sufficient nation or one with only internal vulnerabilities. However, from a historical perspective, the ever-decreasing asymmetric interdependence with the United States can be seen as a considerable gain.

Conclusion

A historical analysis of the relationship "declining hegemon - AEP" is quite helpful to understand the current U.S.-China relationship. Like the War of Spanish Succession for the United Provinces and World War I for Britain, the War on Terror takes place within the context of financial expansion and "hegemonic autumn," leaving the U.S. economy more vulnerable to an AEP like China.

Like Britain in the eighteenth century and the United States in the nineteenth and early twentieth century, China had its economic development, from the 1970s onwards, in many ways associated and dependent on the hegemon of its time. However, since the 1990s this unbalanced dependence was gradually replaced by a series of innovative alliances between productive capital and the Chinese state. With a society bearing a saving mindset and a state surplus on budget, China has become in the 2000s, the most suitable country to fund a consumer society and a state with high deficits (and high costs of war) like the United States. Analogies can also be made with the British loans to the Netherlands in the War of Spanish Succession and the U.S. loans to Britain in the First World War.

So if these analogies are possible, why can we not expect a hegemonic transition from the United States to China according to the patterns of the past? Why does the United States not seem to sink as quickly as Britain did during and after the two

World Wars? And why does China not look like a new hegemon capable of reorganizing the modern world-system in its image and likeness?

Although the United States faces deep challenges, it remains the largest and most dynamic economy in the world and the only military superpower. Also, even though global wealth is gradually moving to Asia, Fiori (n.d., 59) reminds us of the States' relentless pursuit for global power—a pursuit facilitated by the fact their submarines, aircraft carriers, tanks and fighters remain far more effective than the arms of any other nation. Moreover, al-Qaeda or Iran is less threatening to the United States than Imperial Germany was to Britain or monarchical France was to Holland.

Nevertheless, the great mystery still lies in China's role. On the one hand, its vulnerability to the United States has been reduced in terms of investment, technology, human resources and protection. On the other hand, China remains extremely vulnerable to the U.S. consumer market and the fate of the dollar, triggering a relationship of mutual hostage or MAED with the United States and contradicting the historical pattern of total inversion of vulnerabilities. In a few words, we conclude that instead of a *total inversion* of vulnerabilities between the hegemon and the AEP, both countries have developed a relation of *mutual dependences in balanced terms*.

With regard to becoming less vulnerable, China's prospects are more optimistic than America's. While in recent years the Chinese government has sought to expand the range of trading partners, foster the domestic market and widen possibilities of investment and reproduction of natural resources, the Obama Administration continues to encourage long-term credit, rescues "trash" bonds from private banks and only slowly reduces defense and war spending. Between the uniqueness of the present and the similarity with the past, the challenge for social scientists is to understand such a complex relationship as the Sino-American one, given the cyclical processes of the past four decades and the events of the past eleven years.

Acknowledgements

We would like to thank the Political Economy of the World-Systems Section of the American Sociological Association and the World Society Foundation Award of Excellence Program for Research Papers on World Society for the financial support to attend the 37th PEWS UC-Riverside, April 2013. The first author received a graduate scholarship from CAPES (Brazilian Federal Agency for High Education).

References

Arienti, Wagner L., and Felipe A. Filomeno. 2007. Economia política do moderno sistema mundial: as contribuições de Wallerstein, Braudel e Arrighi. *Ensaios FEE,* 28(1): 99–126.

Arrighi, Giovanni. 1996. *O longo século XX: dinheiro, poder e as origens de nosso tempo.* Rio de Janeiro and São Paulo: Contraponto and Editora Unesp.

Arrighi, Giovanni. 2008. *Adam Smith em Pequim: origens e fundamentos do século XXI.* São Paulo: Boitempo.

Arrighi, Giovanni, and Beverly J. Silver. 2001. *Caos e governabilidade no moderno sistema mundial.* Rio de Janeiro: Contraponto.

Belasco, Amy. 2011. *The Cost of Iraq, Afghanistan, and Other Global War on Terror Operations Since 9/11.* Washington: Congressional Research Service.

Birnbaum, Pierre. 1995. "Conflitos." In Raymond Boudon (ed.), *Tratado de sociologia.* Rio de Janeiro: Jorge Zahar Ed.

Boxer, C.R. 1965. *The Dutch Seaborne Empire (1600–1800).* New York: Alfred A. Knopf.

Brenner, Robert. 2003. *O boom e a bolha: os Estados Unidos na economia mundial.* Rio de Janeiro: Record.

Burbach, Roger, and Jim Tarbell. 2004. *Imperial Overstretch: George W. Bush and the Hubris of Empire.* New York: Palgrave Macmillan.

Carvalho, Cecília, and Fabrício Catermola. 2009. Relações econômicas entre China e EUA: resgate histórico e implicações. *Revista do BNDES,* 16(31): 215–252.

Chase-Dunn, Christopher K. 1989. *Global Formation: Structures of the World-Economy.* Cambridge, MA: Library of the Congress.

Chase-Dunn, Christopher K., and Hiroko Inoue. 2012. Accelerating Democratic Global State Formation. *Cooperation and Conflict,* 47(2): 157–175.

Cury, Vania M. 2006. *História da industrialização no século XIX.* Rio de Janeiro: UFRJ.

Daudin, Guillaume, Matthias Morys, and Kevin O'Rourke. 2008. Globalization, 1870–1914. Department of Economics Discussion Paper Series, 395, University of Oxford. URL: http://www.economics.ox.ac.uk/Research/wp/pdf/paper395.pdf (accessed August 05, 2012).

Deng, Yong, and Fei-Ling Wang (eds.). 2005. *China Rising: Power and Motivation in Chinese Foreign Policy.* Lanham, MD: Rowman & Littlefield Publishers.

Dorn, James A. 2008. The Debt Threat: A Risk to U.S.–China Relations? *Brown Journal of World Affairs,* 14(2): 151–164.

Esteves, Rui P. n.d. Between Imperialism and Capitalism: European Capital Exports Before 1914. Unpublished paper. URL: http://users.ox.ac.uk/~econ0243/Imperialism.pdf (accessed April 08, 2012).

Fiori, José Luis. n.d. The Global Power of United States: Formation, Expansion and Limits. URL: http://www.ie.ufrj.br/pesquisa/politica/jlfiori/ARTIGOS_arquivos/Microsoft%20Word%20-%20The%20Global%20Power%20of%20United%20States.pdf (accessed March 03, 2012).

Hobsbawm, Eric. 2003. *Da Revolução Industrial inglesa ao imperialismo.* 5th ed. Rio de Janeiro: Forense Universitária.

Hung, Ho-Fung. 2009. America's head servant? The PRC's Dilemma in the Global Crisis. *New Left Review,* 60: 5–25.

IEP (Institute for Economics and Peace). 2011. Economic Consequences of War on the U.S. Economy. Institute for Economics and Peace (IEP), Sydney, New York and Washington. URL: http://economicsandpeace.org/wp-content/uploads/2011/09/

The-Economic-Consequences-of-War-on-US-Economy.pdf (accessed November 15, 2012).

Karnal, Leandro. 2007. *História dos Estados Unidos: das origens ao século XXI.* São Paulo: Editora Contexto.

Mariutti, Eduardo Barros. 2011. Ordem e desordem internacional: tendências do capitalismo contemporâneo. *Observatório da Economia Global – textos avulsos,* 9, CECON, Unicamp.

Medeiros, Carlos. 2008. "Desenvolvimento econômico e ascensão nacional: rupturas e transições na Rússia e China." In Carlos Medeiros, José L. Fiori, and Franklin Serrano (eds.), *O mito do colapso do poder americano.* Rio de Janeiro: Record.

Nye, Joseph S. 2009.*Cooperação e conflito nas Relações Internacionais.* São Paulo: Editora Gente.

Nye, Joseph S. 2011. *The Future of Power.* New York: The Perseus Books Group.

Pecequilo, Cristina S. 2009. *Manual do candidato: política internacional.* Brasília: Fundação Alexandre de Gusmão.

UsGovernmentSpending. 2013a. Government Spending Chart. URL: http://www.usgovernmentspending.com/spending_chart (accessed September 05, 2012).

UsGovernmentSpending. 2013b. Government Debt Chart. URL: http://www.usgovernmentspending.com/debt_chart (accessed September 05, 2012).

U.S. Department of the Treasury. 2012. Major Foreign Holders of Treasury Securities. Data. URL: http://www.treasury.gov/resource-center/data-chart-center/tic/Documents/mfhhis01.txt (accessed November 13, 2012).

Vizentini, Paulo F. 2007. *As relações internacionais da Ásia e da África.* Petrópolis, RJ: Vozes.

Wallerstein, Immanuel. 2012. China and the United States: Rivals, Enemies, Collaborators? Commentary 321, January 15, 2012. URL: http://www.iwallerstein.com/china-united-states-rivals-enemies-collaborators/ (accessed September 20, 2012).

Wheeler, Winslow T. 2011. Unaccountable: Pentagon Spending on the Post-9/11 Wars. URL: http://costsofwar.org/sites/default/files/WheelerPentagonSpending.pdf (accessed November 15, 2012).

Zhu, Zhiqun. 2006. *US-China Relations in the 21ˢᵗ Century: Power Transition and Peace.* New York: Routledge.

9

Antisystemic Movements in Periods of Hegemonic Decline: Syndicalism in World-Historical Perspective

Robert MacPherson

Since 2010, the eurozone debt crisis has resulted in unprecedented social upheaval in the states of Southern Europe. The crisis provided an opening for syndicalist unions, organizing on a radically democratic basis, to join with urban movements against austerity. This chapter attempts to place syndicalist coalitional prospects in long-term historical perspective, analyzing syndicalism as an antisystemic movement which can be best understood by charting the movement as it has been affected by, and in turn helped shape, the processes and institutions of the world-economy. Using the incorporated comparative method and detailed process-tracings of syndicalist mobilization in Chile and Spain, the syndicalist movement of the 1920s is compared with the current upwelling. The results reveal how the regulative liberalism which undercut syndicalist prospects in the early twentieth century only prepared the ground for the current crisis. The institutionalized unions and liberal states that "solved" the interwar crises of global capitalism are now unraveling, encouraging coalitions of syndicalist and popular democratic movements.

Systemic crisis and antisystemic response

The ongoing crisis in Europe, one manifestation of the wider set of convulsions that has beset the world-economy since 2008, has seen harsh austerity measures imposed upon the people of Spain, Greece, Italy, Portugal and Ireland. This attempt to push the costs of the crisis onto poor and working populations amounts to nothing less than the reperipheralization of the weaker regions of Europe, where "austerity marks the violent conclusion of the Keynesian/social democratic compromise" (Peet, 2011, 397).

The result has been the rise of movements for popular democracy that have brought hundreds of thousands into the streets, and have retaken public space for large participatory assemblies. In this environment, one important element has received relatively little attention: the syndicalist unions whose democratic organizational tenets and penchant for direct action mirror the practices of the popular movements. Indeed, the crisis has proved to be a singular opportunity for syndicalists in the European semiperiphery. In 2011–2012, a coalition of syndicalist federations undertook a series of strike actions against both the Spanish state and the reformist unions; these recurring waves included the most prominent syndicalist federations in Spain, the General Workers' Confederation (*Confederación General del Trabajo*—CGT) and the National Workers' Confederation (*Confederación Nacional del Trabajo*—CNT).[1] Working closely with the popular occupation movement, the actions drew millions of participants across several major Spanish cities accompanied by solidarity actions across Europe.

The CNT and CGT share a set of core democratic and revolutionary precepts with the mass syndicalist unions that appeared worldwide during the early twentieth century. What has been called syndicalism's "glorious period" ranged from the mid-1890s to the mid-1920s; an era in which syndicalists built revolutionary union federations and attempted to "establish a collectivized, worker-managed social order resting on union structures" (Hirsch and van der Walt, 2010, xxxvii). The 2012 strikes recall the mass actions of the "glorious era," being the first time in decades that syndicalists have spearheaded general strikes that recruit broad swathes of the population. The rebirth of mass syndicalist action, then, has deep world-historical roots. It may hold the potential for advancing what Immanuel Wallerstein (2011b) has termed "the spirit of Porto Alegre": the movements aiming to reconstruct the current world-system along "relatively democratic and relatively egalitarian" lines.

Research into the forms of social mobilization that could implement systemic change on a global scale is urgently needed. World-systems scholars have advanced the concept of *antisystemic movements* to ground investigations of movements whose goals or practices stand opposed to the structural imperatives of global capitalism. This chapter uses the antisystemic analytic framework to compare the "glorious era" of syndicalism with the current situation. One major determinant of the movement's trajectory in the early twentieth century was the syndicalists' ability to construct, maintain and utilize coalitions with other institutions and social movement organizations. Thus, this analysis will focus on the ways in which syndicalist coalitional activity has been conditioned by both the movement's own strategic choices and the prevailing state of the capitalist world-system in which it operates.

Syndicalism as an antisystemic movement

In recent years, antisystemic movement analysis has benefited from much-needed theoretical elaboration and is now being used fruitfully in empirical studies (Martin, 2008; Moghadam, 2012; Reese et al., 2012; Smith and Wiest, 2012). This is a useful corrective to some social movement scholarship that until recently neglected the impact of large-scale capitalist processes on movements (Goodwin and Hetland, 2009). Designating a movement as antisystemic suggests two broad areas of analytic focus: first, the aspects of the movement's ideology, organizational logic or tactical

---

1   See also Appendix for abbreviations.

repertoire that make it antagonistic to the requisites of global capitalism and, second, the impact of world-systemic processes on the movement's development itself.

Syndicalism makes a crucial subject for antisystemic movement study for two reasons. First is the important role syndicalism played in the era of late British hegemony. The "glorious era" was one of the few times that mass unions combining explicitly revolutionary aims with participatory democratic structures recruited large parts, and in some regions the majority, of the organized working class (Hirsch and van der Walt, 2010). While the best-known syndicalist organizations of the "glorious era" arose in Spain and France, large syndicalist unions also arose in Italy, Ireland, Mexico, Chile, Argentina, Brazil, Peru, South Africa, Russia and China; the movement was thus global in scope.[2] As such, syndicalism played a central part in the massive post-World-War-I strike wave of 1918–1922. This upwelling heralded an era of increasing instability in the world-economy and political tumult as the old institutions of British hegemony eroded and those of the United States only haltingly took their place.

This globalized understanding of syndicalism, in which the movement is characterized by Benedict Anderson as "the dominant element in the self-consciously internationalist radical left," is a result of a recent explosion in scholarship on syndicalism and the broader anarchist tradition from which it descends (quoted in Hirsch and van der Walt, 2010, xxxviii; Graeber, 2004; Anderson, 2006; Darlington, 2008; Damier, 2009, Schmidt and van der Walt, 2009; Berry and Bantman, 2010; el-Ojeili, 2014). The syndicalism of the early twentieth century can trace a lineage back to the federalist sections of the First International and the earliest anarchist attempts at constructing mass organizations (McKay, 2012).

A second reason for syndicalism's importance as an area for antisystemic study is its unique organizational and tactical logic, which serve to differentiate it from many antisystemic movements sharing its goal of a postcapitalist future. The syndicalist commitment to direct action and democracy means that coalition building, whether with other organizations or with the state, is a complex undertaking with unique dynamics. While socialist parties looked to capture the state, syndicalist organizations hoped to replace the state entirely with the free federation of councils. In most organizations the aim was to use recallable delegates and minimize permanent union staff. This meant that syndicalists were wary of any institutionalization of their organizations *vis-à-vis* the state and generally preferred to win even short-term political goals by direct action in the workplace.[3]

---

2   Scholars also identify the U.S. Industrial Workers of the World as part of the broad syndicalist tradition.

3   The majority of syndicalist organizations, influenced by anarchist *political* organizations, often had defined short-term political aims, took stands on state policy, and fought for such aims via "general or 'political' strikes" (Damier, 2009, 10).

Thus both syndicalism's historical presence and its unique organizational and tactical logic make it a fitting subject for study as an antisystemic movement. Accordingly, analysts of social transformation should pay careful attention to the resurgence of syndicalist organizing during the current crisis.

Antisystemic movements and the comparative method

Adequately capturing syndicalism as an antisystemic movement requires a clear understanding of the dynamics of global capitalism within and against which the movement develops. The value of this approach is in the very fact that it "presumes an analytic perspective about a system" (Arrighi et al., 1989, 1). The world-economy, organized around the endless accumulation of capital, continually reproduces uneven development via a worldwide division of labor between high and low value extraction activities. Within this long-term structural condition of global capitalism a series of hegemonic states have managed to come to preeminence in the world-economy and successively reorganize the rules of the interstate system (Arrighi, 1994). It is this conceptualization of capitalism at the larger geographic and longer temporal levels that is the point of departure for study of antisystemic movements.

Much social movement research has studied localized movements and has adopted a "movement centric" analytic approach which sees each movement's history as largely a function of the movement's own qualities and strategic choices (McAdam, 1982; McAdam et al., 2001). Recently, comparative and historical analysis of movements sought to remedy the limitations of this approach by stressing the need to see movements as developing in relation to the surrounding political and institutional context (Amenta et al., 2005; Giugni and Yamasaki, 2009; Halfmann, 2013). This constitutes a clear advance, yet this approach often privileges shorter-term analyses and adopts a stance which, while able to richly specify the particulars of state-movement interaction, often assumes states to be independently developing units. This results in difficulty in capturing the ways that the political environment in which movement battles play out is conditioned by larger world-systemic processes.

Even studies of transnational movements often lack a clear model of the workings of these world-economic processes and interstate developments (Marks and McAdam, 1999; Della Porta et al., 2004). In contrast, when analyzing antisystemic movements these global forces are not conceived of as "context" but rather as active conditioning factors. This dialectical relationship influences the movement's own qualities as well as the shape and powers of the political institutions that respond to movement activity, and the outcomes of these struggles can then in turn become important in determining the development of the world-system itself.

Antisystemic analysis is well-served by a method of "incorporated comparison" which "reveals the world historical character of local processes while giving historical content to the concept of world economy through the concrete analysis of particular phenomena" (Tomich, 1990, 6). Incorporating comparisons take as their point of departure the recognition that global processes are always instantiated in the form of local particularities, and it is the interconnection of these historical particularities that form totalities at larger levels. One way this methodological guideline can be used is to analyze an object of analysis from several levels of abstraction, progressively moving across different spatial levels of analysis to achieve a "zoom effect" (Trouillot, 1982, 383). These spatial levels can also correspond to temporal levels of abstraction, such that event-level, cyclical and long-term dynamics can all be drawn into a rich explanatory narrative. The result is levels of analysis that nest within each other like a set of Russian dolls (Tomich, 1990).[4]

This study uses a framework for cross-time hegemonic comparison modeled after McMichael (2000) and Arrighi and Silver (2003) combined with the nested model of multiple levels of abstraction. This will allow us to compare syndicalist coalitional activity in the period of late British hegemony with the current recomposition of syndicalism as U.S. hegemony dissolves. Within the analysis of each of the two periods, syndicalism will be situated within three progressively finer levels of analysis. At the most fine-grained level of analysis, this study will trace the coalitional activities of syndicalists in Chile during 1921–1925 and in Spain in 2010–2012. These periods parallel each other in their deflationary character, pressures by elites on wage levels, and the general tenor of a "short stop" in external capital financing. The incorporated comparative method will allow us to capture these periods not only as similar analytic units, but also to uncover their "difference in unity" as parts of a singular world-historical process.

In crisis periods, coalitions become crucial to resisting attempts by capital to push costs off onto the masses. Antisystemic analysis aims to capture the way that coalitional practice is a function of both the movement's specific properties and the movement of the world-system. The next section's multilevel analysis of syndicalism in the "glorious era" can yield substantive content along both axes. By uncovering crucial determinants of syndicalist coalitional capability in the past we can proceed, in the final section, to using these findings to better understand the movement's current situation.

---

4   This "nested" model is different from even the variants of social movement theory that analyze contexts in terms of "nested political opportunity structures" (Meyer, 2003; Smith, 2004). Here, these levels are levels of *abstraction* and not necessarily concretely existing political arenas. The emphasis here is on the ways in which world-systemic processes are both actively at work *within* and in part formed *by* the causal narrative of local events. In other words, "these dimensions exist simultaneously and condition one another" (Tomich, 1990, 7).

The "glorious era"

Syndicalism and the long-term trajectory of the workers' movement

Syndicalist organization in southern Europe, Latin America and the colonial world grew considerably in the "glorious era," encompassing large proportions of the urbanized workforce in many areas (Hirsch and van der Walt, 2010). These mass organizations gained positions of structural power within the regions' economies and caused major transformations in the social life and political economy of the region. Despite this, by the late 1930s almost all of these mass organizations were crushed and much of the labor movement's energy was drained off into institutionalized unions allied with socialist or Communist parties (Thorpe, 1989; van der Linden and Thorpe, 1990).

Wallerstein's (1989; 2011a) extensive work detailing the birth of world-historical ideologies emphasizes the way in which both conservatism and radicalism came to accept the gradualist and state-administered conception of social change that was a hallmark of centrist liberalism. The majority of conservatives and radicals, even while espousing antisystemic goals, became "avatars of liberalism" in their tactical and organizational approaches. This disjuncture between the long- and middle-term logics of the left led, after the abortive and disorganized revolutionary attempts of 1848, to both reformist and revolutionary anticapitalists focusing the majority of their energies on capturing the state.

Syndicalism grew out of a minority current that never fully embraced the state-centric tactical consensus. As early as the French Revolution a segment of the left calling for direct democracy can be identified, and these approaches matured into the Proudhonist and federalist strains of anarchism that formed a large part of the First International. Syndicalism explicitly drew on this tradition as it emerged in the 1890s in Europe and early 1900s in Latin America. It focused on building "counter-power" rooted in the democratic control of work, opposing the parliamentarian strategies adopted by many other antisystemic movements.

The course of nineteenth-century syndicalist predevelopment sketched above coincides with the period in which the institutional framework of the liberal state was coalescing under British hegemony. The gold standard, even when not formally adopted, comprised a set of institutional assumptions ensuring that unbalanced trade and capital flows or sudden changes in world-market prices would work to the advantage of core capital. Inflationary or deflationary adjustments would be borne by the dependent economies. In this way the international financial system protected the ability of London to invest safely, even outside of its formal colonial network. The period from 1880 to World War I saw massive investment on the part of Britain, the United States and Germany in Latin America as "gentlemanly finance" led the world-economy out of the depression of the 1870s (Cain and Hopkins, 1993).

The postwar conjuncture

After World War I the weakening of British hegemony and increasing economic turbulence led to a massive worldwide strike wave lasting until the mid-1920s (Silver, 2003). The syndicalist coalitions analyzed here formed a part of this world-wide upwelling.

Several large syndicalist organizations were created in the WWI period, many of them having roots in anarchist-led movements that took on a more structured and labor-oriented direction. Syndicalist federations in France and Spain at times encompassed hundreds of thousands of workers, with smaller but lively syndicalist organizations throughout Europe. In the Southern Cone, the syndicalist organizations grew to be some of the largest and most militant, with the Argentine Regional Workers' Federation (*Federación Obrera Regional Argentina*—FORA) organizing 200,000 workers in the early 1920s and the Chilean Industrial Workers of the World (IWW) encompassing 25,000 workers and wholly controlling their country's ports in the same period.

In Chile, anarcho-syndicalist unions predominated in Santiago and the bustling port cities of Valparaiso, Iquique and Antofagasta. By the end of World War I the largest syndicalist unions, such as the Bakers' Union (*Unión Syndical de Panaderos*—USP) and the shoeworkers' federation made tentative steps toward multicity federations. This expansion was given a boost when contact with U.S. sailors led to the founding of the Chilean IWW. From 1919 the IWW became a lynchpin of syndicalist power in the cities, ubiquitous among the ports' stevedores and lightermen and organizing the construction trade in Santiago and Valparaiso (DeShazo, 1983). This paralleled developments in Argentina, Brazil, and Peru as well as in other peripheral areas such as South Africa. In this period large syndicalist umbrella organizations began to organize multiple industries. Most of these growing syndicalist federations shared a basic syndicalist tactical and organizational logic: participatory and democratic, committed to direct action as a means of "revolutionary gymnastics."

However, social protest tactics were in the middle of a decades-long progression toward increasingly state-centric forms. The Second International had turned increasingly to parliamentarian politics, and the resulting institutional pressures pushed the parties to adopt increasingly hierarchical forms quite at odds with the direct democratic methods espoused by the syndicalists. Unions that allied with the parties followed suit, and began to distance themselves from direct action tactics. This process was most advanced in Europe, where strong states could begin the process of incorporation even before 1914. In Latin America this process played out with a slight delay; after the War reformist and socialist parties were brought into power-sharing arrangements. Even the revolutionary factions within the left parties, such as the Bolsheviks, shared this hierarchical organizational logic and tactical focus on the state.

These developments contributed to a pincer movement that squeezed the syndicalists over the interwar period. On one side were the parties: social democrats sought to domesticate syndicalists toward similar reformist status, and from 1921 the Profintern branch of the Third International sought to subordinate unions to the centralized direction of the Soviet state.

On the other side, capitalists themselves became more formally interventionist, dropping the pretense of self-adjusting markets in favor of a range of approaches that sought to undercut syndicalism with either the "stick" of discipline or the "carrot" of populism. Merchant associations formed across Latin America to fight wage increases in times of inflation and push wages down during deflationary periods. The tentative pro-labor approach of reformists such as Presidents Hipolito Yirigoyen in Argentina and Arturo Alessandri in Chile formed the softer side of this interventionism, though these regimes eventually allied with the merchant associations to impose both repressive measures and basic social welfare provisions. By the end of the 1920s these interventions often came at the hands of the military, moving toward policies of import substitution industrialization *avant la lettre*.

The same world-systemic processes that strengthened the hand of hierarchical parties and interventionist states gave impetus to increased syndicalist mobilizations. The most important of these was the general breakdown of the rules governing international property that had underlain the previous four decades of financialized British hegemony (Lipson, 1985). While the Depression of the 1930s would wipe away the system's final remnants, the fracturing of the gold standard in 1914 had already ushered in "the interwar crisis in capital markets" in which "the center of the world capital market gradually shifted from London to New York . . . but the American capacity to supply funds to the rest of the world did not as rapidly fill the void left by the British" (Taylor, 2006, 81). Remaining "open" sites for capital investment made Latin America extremely vulnerable.

The coalitional drives examined in the next section took place when the postwar inflation ended, revealing the interwar period's true deflationary dynamic. The result was a contraction across Latin America that struck just as the 1917–1919 inflation-induced strikes began winning wage increases and elements of workers' control. The nub of the issue in the 1921–1925 depression became just who would pay the price. British, U.S. and other European capitalists sought to ensure continuing payments on their loans to Latin American states as well as protect the profits of their export firms. Foreign investors combined efforts with local employers to pressure the state, aiming to use the period's high unemployment to attack unions with an eye toward reversing wage gains and dissolving working-class organizations.

Capital's short-term concerns were dominated by the need to keep wages down as inflation took hold, or to break down wages as deflation set in. Underlying this was a more fundamental concern with the level of worker organization and, specifically, the level of workers' control that unions were able to wrest away from capital. Syndicalist organizations were uniquely positioned to fight on the wage front via advancing workers' control at the very site of employers' direct domination and were thus viewed as uniquely dangerous.

Syndicalist coalition-making on the ground

Given these long-term and conjunctural dynamics, how did syndicalist organizations approach coalitions during the depression of the 1920s? We can illustrate this by examining one cycle of syndicalist mobilization in detail, one which involved building alliances with state organs and other movements. The aim here is simply to sketch the manner in which the processes of declining British hegemony in the world-system served to condition the coalitional prospects of concrete syndicalist organizations.[5]

In Chile, 1921 saw the reformer Arturo Alessandri take office as the representative of a new class coalition of "forward thinking" elites and the growing urban white-collar sector. This incomplete break with the older oligarchs paralleled similar developments in Argentina and throughout Latin America. Relying on populist appeals to secure his election, the Administration's Labor Offices spent the first half of 1921 attempting to construct a détente between the powerful syndicalist unions, the socialist-party-affiliated Chilean Workers' Federation (*Federación Obrera de Chile*—FOCh) and the large export capitalists.

By mid-year the IWW had emerged as the only multicity organization for Chile's syndicalists. The IWW had increasingly allied with the most militant independent syndicalist unions, such as the bakers' USP, as well as the FOCh. Through these struggles the IWW won both wage gains and vital mechanisms of workers' control, such as a multicity work-sharing and hiring system called the *redondo*. The combination of Labor Office neutrality and their structural power at the ports allowed them to begin using boycotts and sympathy strikes as an effective means of organizing factories within the city of Valparaiso. Given that the long-term logic of their antisystemic stance was that democratic unions must take the place of both capitalist firms and the parliamentary state, inroads into employer prerogatives like the IWW's hiring system were perceived by both domestic and foreign capitalists to be an unacceptable danger.

By March 1921 the depression had begun. Chile's state revenues in this period were completely dependent upon export fees on nitrates and tariffs on imported consumer goods, both sectors long controlled by British mining, shipping and manufacturing firms that repatriated the bulk of profits. Nitrate prices slumped and imports contracted just as incoming capital flows dried up. Export capitalists saw this as their opportunity to check the wage and workers' control gains. The merchant

---

5   This account primarily draws on Breslin (1980), Monteón (1981), DeShazo (1983), and Deutsch (1999).

associations unleashed a series of lockouts, hoping to use the depressed volume of business to their advantage. The first few lockouts were weathered by a coalition of the USP, IWW and FOCh, and secured Alessandri's personal intervention to stave off the attempts.

One significant member of this coalition was missing, however: the community outside the unions themselves. Three years earlier moves were made in this direction when the syndicalists and the FOCh cooperated in creating the Workers' Assembly on National Nutrition (*Asamblea Obrera de la Alimentación Nacional—AOAN*). This short-lived organization united broad swathes of the urban population of Santiago and Valparaiso to pressure the government to control rising food prices. Syndicalists, including the largest urban unions, were centrally involved in its creation. In 1918 and 1919 the AOAN struck fear into the governing elites, with one multicity protest drawing nearly 100,000 participants. However, this organization failed to develop into a permanent set of organs that could complement syndicalist workplace democracy with deliberative bodies within the community itself. Instead, it channeled its energies into legislative demands and dissolved by 1920.

As the lockout continued into the winter of 1921 the coalition began to fracture. When the IWW and USP struck in sympathy with a FOCh-directed tobacco worker action, the FOCh ended their strike as soon as wage increases were promised while the IWW and USP stayed out and continued pushing for partial hiring control. When the Valparaiso Merchants Association made their biggest move, a lockout at the port, their explicit target was the IWW and the *redondo*. The Association, relying on a recent influx of unemployed nitrate workers as replacements, spread the lockout to several other port cities and the IWW and other syndicalist unions responded by calling a multicity general strike.

Whereas two years earlier the AOAN had forced the state to postpone repression, by the time of the 1921 lockouts and strike the most active non-union movements on the ground were rightist militias, who attacked the unions and the small student movement while pressuring Alessandri at every turn. The IWW had begun to rely on the personal contacts it had built up with Alessandri and his appointees, at one point requesting he intervene in the strike as it became apparent the Associations had the upper hand. After the general strike collapsed in September, the Administration allied with a significant national employers' association to promote a series of employer-controlled welfare measures, using the proposals as cover while abolishing the *redondo*. This defeat was crushing for the IWW and associated syndicalists. It was capped by a FOCh strike the following February in which the FOCh quickly took the smallest of concessions and cut short the strike, hanging the now weakened syndicalists out to dry once again.

The workers movement in Chile deteriorated further over the next two years, with the IWW shrinking by 75%. In the past, when syndicalism had been repressed it had come roaring back, but when the next labor resurgence occurred in the mid-1920s the movement was unable to capture its former power in the face of welfarist policies and parties. This pattern was repeated throughout the semiperipheral regions of Latin America. In Argentina the mass syndicalist federation, the FORA IX, allied with other anarchist and syndicalist organizations but failed to develop community organizations even as its workplace power increased. The largest union within the FORA, the Maritime Workers' Federation (*Federación Obrera Maritima*—FOM), gradually outdistanced reformist allies in terms of workers' control demands, cultivated ties with state agencies that were eventually severed, and succumbed to a combination of repression and cooptation by basic welfare measures (Rock, 1975; Horowitz, 1995).

These patterns illustrate the importance of a "dual structure" of unions and community councils, something envisaged, but rarely achieved, by early syndicalists (Schmidt and van der Walt, 2009). Syndicalist coalitions with state agents and reformist unions seem inherently unstable; the radically democratic methods of the syndicalists in Chile ensured they would "push past" the FOCh until the reformist organization begun to peel away. Meanwhile, the very non-parliamentary stance that ensured syndicalist focus on workers' control often shaded into a "workerism" that neglected community democracy in favor of workplace battles.

It is probably too much to cast this as a fundamental contradiction between the short-term tactical logic of syndicalists, battling in the workplace, with the middle- and long-term goals of a democratized society. Rather, it was the historically specific processes playing out in the world-system that made certain this lack of community support was fatal.

The decisive factor was increasing state interventionism, a conjunctural expression of the long-term ascendance of liberalism. Though Arrighi and Silver (1999, 197) are correct that "[w]ith the political credibility of high finance and liberal governments destroyed . . . and with no alternative world-hegemonic project on the horizon, internationalism was abandoned in favor of purely national hegemonic projects," their definition of "liberal governments" is too narrow in light of Wallerstein's long-term reconceptualization. The operational logic of liberalism toward a regulating set of state institutions persisted even as the purpose to which it had been heretofore put, world market integration on self-adjusting terms, fell apart in the interwar period. Interventionist statism, thus partially freed from the strictures of the previous world-scale regime of accumulation, took a local form. In Chile military juntas took power in 1924 and again in 1932 and enacted many of the reformists' welfare and labor provisions which were drafted during parliamentary periods. In Argentina and Brazil, state intervention took on a decidedly welfare cast in key industries throughout the 1920s and even the rightist military regimes that prevailed in both areas in the 1930s continued these measures (Bergquist, 1986).

These measures combined with the increasing institutionalization of left parties and reformist unions. All of these factors were already at work in the depression years of the early 1920s, and were only boosted after the collapse of 1929.[6] The rise of the interventionist state and recuperated left parties and unions was made possible by the larger dissolution of British financial bonds and their replacement by U.S. capital.[7]

Latin American states were not only granted more freedom of movement by the still immature networks of U.S. capital; the tenor of U.S. dominance already differed from that of its predecessor. Vertically integrated firms, such as the Guggenheim Brothers' copper operation in Chile, imported methods of business unionism and encouraged semiperipheral states in their moves toward national welfare provisions. Further, the increased efficiency of the new U.S.-style firms over the horizontal and fissile British model allowed the sorts of surpluses required for welfare outlays. This was amplified in turn by the gradual disappearance of international finance capital and its attendant *rentier*-like drains on state revenues. These developments prepared the ground for the national development projects that would characterize later U.S. hegemony, and strengthened the state against movements such as syndicalism.

The coalitional patterns of syndicalist organizations in the semiperiphery can thus be understood as the confluence of two factors: the movement's antisystemic tactical and organizational logic and the unfolding state of the world-system. This logic, especially its tendency toward unstable state and party coalitions and need for community support, played out in a context defined by the opportunities for statist cooptation afforded by the change from British to U.S. hegemony. The following section will apply our three-level nested method of analysis to the current U.S.-led era, charting the ways in which these two factors are once again interacting to determine the path of syndicalist coalitional activity.

Syndicalism at the end of U.S. hegemony

The workers' movement and U.S. hegemony

Syndicalism was a muted presence in the world workers' movement during much of the rest of the twentieth century. Keynesian economic measures and social democratic and state-socialist political forms privileged institutionalized unions and parties worldwide. However, two long-term changes under U.S. hegemony would be of

---

6   New scholarship on Latin America has undermined the conventional view that moves toward ISI began with the Great Depression. Instead, analysis of domestic manufacturing combined with the welfarist reformers policy shows that "the import-substitution phase of Chilean industrialization had commenced with the First World War" (Palma, 2000, 44).

7   From this perspective, the prestige which the Bolsheviks attracted was due to both having been seen as completing the first successful revolution against capitalism and, later in the 1920s, the fit of Bolshevik institutional forms with the general tenor of the interventionist state.

major importance for syndicalism: the gradual reappearance of participatory forms of social movement organization outside the labor movement, and the transformation of the governing policy regime of the world-economy from a social democratic model toward neoliberalism.

In the aftermath of World War II, the United States backed the creation of a new global order revolving around "[t]he cooptation of the 'responsible' elements of the labor movements through institutional reforms and mass consumption" (Arrighi and Silver 1999, 206). This model was implemented in the global South via developmentalism, though there the promises of mass consumption rang false and many times development took on a decidedly militarized and repressive cast. In both cases, the United States strategically recycled its considerable capital surpluses to support the rebuilding of the world-system as a type of carefully administered capitalism that was the epitome of centrist liberalism (Varoufakis, 2011). Where nominally revolutionary unions and parties remained strong, such as in parts of Europe and Latin America, they often took on all the trappings of entrenched political players.[8]

Where formally syndicalist unions survived, they dropped much of their antisystemic tactical repertoire and their demands for workers' control. The prefigurative politics demanded by syndicalism could not be sustained in the rising social democracies of Europe, with the French General Workers' Confederation (*Confédération Générale du Travail*—CGT) throwing overboard its syndicalism and the Central Organization of the Workers of Sweden(*Sveriges Arbetares Centralorganisation*—SAC) beginning a long period of moderation beginning in the 1950s (Damier, 2009). In Spain, Portugal, Italy and Greece formerly powerful syndicalist federations were all but erased at the hands of fascism and Stalinism, becoming a negligible presence for decades afterward.

The upheavals of the late 1960s revived anarchist-inspired forms of participatory organization which found fertile ground within the new movements for gender, racial and sexual equality. The phrase used to describe the resulting proliferation of movements, the "social movement society," captures the importance of these post-1968 changes (Meyer and Tarrow, 1998). More fundamentally, Wallerstein has identified this period as the breakdown of the liberal statist logic that governed right, left and center since 1848. The growth of these "new social movements" (NSMs) and their democratic forms of organization had world-historical import; "centrist liberalism had been dethroned" while the statist "Old Left movements were destroyed as mobilizers of any kind of fundamental change" (Wallerstein, 2011b, 137).

However, the new experiments in organizational logic in the NSMs were largely unable to "reseed" the established union movement with more democratic and revolutionary principles. The prewar situation for syndicalism had been reversed; from

---

8   The United States, whose own syndicalist IWW had been destroyed by the 1930s, went furthest in domesticating its labor movement thanks to McCarthyism and the resources for cooptation afforded by its position at the heights of the world-economy (Lichtenstein, 2002).

radically democratic workers' organizations without complementary organizations of community support the long-term trend has been toward increasingly participatory forms of social movement and community organization with little meaningful counterpart in the world of labor.

This situation was only exacerbated as the character of global capitalism transformed in reaction to the overaccumulation crisis of the 1970s. Neoliberalism as a policy regime would undermine the capital-labor pact by boosting capital's mobility and the United States would move into permanent deficit, remaining the financial *entrepot* by recycling the massive amounts of surplus capital flowing in from both Europe and the global South. Union density in the United States, Europe and Latin America registered sharp declines throughout the 1980s and 1990s, as employers empowered by legislative changes and emboldened by their new spatial freedom mounted attacks on even established unions (Munck and Vaterman, 1999).

One unifying mechanism enabled the various elements of neoliberalism: a move toward financialization as capital sought returns in finance rather than production (Arrighi, 1994; Peet, 2011). This entailed not only the deregulation and expansion of the financial services sector, but the proliferation of a vast array of new investment instruments and the explosive growth of international bond and currency markets. Despite debate over the exact trajectory of rate of profit since the 1970s, most analysts agree that core profits recovered from the 1980s though they failed to reach the levels of the Keynesian years (Li et al., 2007; Nichter, 2008; Duménil and Levy, 2011). Neoliberalism as a world-scale regime of accumulation thus mirrored late British hegemony, seeking to offload costs and risks onto workers in order to recoup profits.

The conjunctural crisis in the eurozone

Neoliberalism fundamentally conditioned both the post-2008 crisis and the delegitimation of European states and traditional unions that opened the door to possible syndicalist resurgence. This section will trace the contours of the crisis as they bear on syndicalism, and the subsequent section will offer a brief survey of the ongoing syndicalist presence in the current protests against austerity.

While formally syndicalist organizations remained on the margins in the later neoliberal period, the gap between the NSMs and the democratic workers' movement was narrowed from the late 1990s by the global justice movement (GJM). The GJM brought together the increasing population of non-governmental organizations with activist networks coalescing against neoliberal globalization initiatives. Foreshadowed by the Zapatista uprising in 1994 and gaining momentum after the globalization protests in 1999 and 2001, the movement has been marked by a concern with democratic and participatory decision making (Smith, 2008; Pleyers, 2010). The formation of the World Social Forum and a myriad of regional Social Forums facilitated a global convergence of movement organizational practices, as "horizontalist" practices prevalent in the global South spread to movement actors in the North (Reese et al., 2012).

Despite these challenges, neoliberalism continued its advance throughout the 1990s and 2000s, with both global and national inequalities increasing as financialized accumulation created ever larger bubbles within the world market. Superficially, the 2008 crisis was the popping of a housing bubble in the United States. In reality, as the entire Byzantine structure of debt unwound it would be the institutional changes put in place earlier in the neoliberal era that would ensure the crisis' generalization.

Features of the crisis can be traced to the earliest days of the eurozone's formation in the 1980s. Spain and Portugal, and to a later and lesser extent Greece, became initial stops for Northern European capital as it relocated basic parts of production chains (Holman, 1996). This industrial growth was due to careful wage suppression and was cut short when, after joining the European Exchange Rate Mechanism, both incoming and domestic capital diverted toward speculative debt and construction activity (Overbeek, 2012). With the formalization into the European Monetary Union (EMU) this process of credit-based expansion was boosted and between 1998 and 2008 Spain, Greece and Ireland saw rapid GDP increases in what many observers proclaimed was a "catching up" to the level of the European core (Rothschild, 2009).

Each successive stage of "Europeanization" pressured Southern Europe to privatize and liberalize its external trade, damaging the small and medium sized productive enterprises that formed the bulk of the region's employers. At the same time, the large urban-based unions that were affiliated with socialist and Communist parties were relatively insulated from these changes. Spain's organization here was typical; the institutionalization of workplace bargaining via state-financed works councils became the large unions' main source of funding. The General Union of Workers (*Unión General de Trabajadores*—UGT), associated with the Spanish Socialist Workers' Party (*Partido Socialista Obrero Español*—PSOE), and the formerly-Communist Workers' Commissions (*Comisiones Obreras*—CCOO), concentrated their energies on winning council elections so as to maintain a flow of state funding. Since European unification began in the early 1980s their membership numbers have barely kept pace with the increase in employment, with their density remaining around 18% (Köhler and Jiménez, 2010, 284). Most importantly, they were often cajoled by the state into supporting neoliberal reforms in return for institutional concessions (Royo, 2006).

This pattern played itself out throughout Europe as the social democratic left was brought into the structures of state power in the decades after WWII and then faced with a seemingly inexorable turn to neoliberalism (Hyman, 2005). The result has been a general loss of party membership and legitimacy in many European governments, with the links between the large union federations and the parties increasingly strained (Preece, 2009; Taylor et al., 2011; van Biezen et al., 2012).

Syndicalist organizations remained small except in Spain, where the legacy of the Spanish Civil War and revolution of the 1930s helped syndicalists to establish a foothold after Franco's death. The 1970s witnessed a brief flowering of democratic workers' councils; though the CNT reestablished itself, it was subject to splits over the question of participation in state work councils, forming the General Workers' Confederation (CGT) and a smaller federation that retained the CNT moniker. Both were small in comparison to the "glorious era," when the CNT spearheaded a social revolution in Catalonia while battling both Stalinism and fascism. Still, the syndicalist federations grew slowly and steadily from the 1990s. By 2005 the CGT had grown to become Spain's third largest union federation with 60,000 members and representing over two million workers via council delegates (Alternative Libertaire, 2004). The CGT retained its commitment to syndicalist practice throughout, attempting to democratize the councils and organize direct action outside the control of the UGT and CCOO (Loris, 2011; Ferraro et al., 2011). At the same time, the CNT, while a much smaller union presence, took on a role in reviving the international syndicalist umbrella organization, the International Workers' Association (IWA), which had been founded in 1922 but had little impact during the movement's early existence. This groundwork, resulting in the relinking of smaller anarcho-syndicalist activist groups throughout Europe, was well in place if not widely visible when the crisis struck.

The spread of the crisis from the United States after 2008 resulted in a deeply indebted European periphery, an incitement to neomercantilist beggar-thy-neighbor responses from the Northern European core states, and a nearly irresistible predatory opportunity for the banks. The indebtedness of the Southern European states and Ireland was a function of the way the EMU enabled unified interest rates and thus increased freedom for capital flows over the previous decade. These regions saw the inflow of speculative capital slow and the crisis begin in earnest by 2010, with a disappearance of the credit needed to rollover existing public debt (Greece), prop up asset price bubbles (in Spain and Portugal), and finance public debt incurred by the complete bailout of the private banks (Ireland). In almost all cases it was the transfer of private debt to the state which marked the most recent phase of the crisis, thus "the 'sovereign' debt crisis was nothing but the other face of the private debt crisis, which, as in the United States, began first" (Bellofiore and Halevi, 2011). Instead of being forced to restructure, overexposed banks "loaded up on eurozone public debt in the years that followed—raking in considerable profits for themselves in the process, by borrowing at practically zero rates and buying government bonds paying 3 to 4 percent interest" (Aglietta, 2012, 17).

Northern Europe, represented by France and Germany, supported this turn of events. French and German banks held roughly US$500 billion in public debt each, and the French and German states had shared in the fusion of financial capital and state interests that had characterized the neoliberal era. Moreover, the EMU had become a vehicle for enabling Germany to embark on the most extensive wage-suppression campaign in Europe, building up large capital surpluses that were then redirected to Southern Europe (Bellofiore and Halevi, 2011; Overbeek, 2012). Indeed, when the crisis caused the United States to falter in its role as a sink for net European surplus, the neomercantilist orientation of the North toward the European South was only strengthened. From the point of view of Northern capital, the costs of the crisis would have to be borne by the populations of Southern Europe and Ireland. The end result was a seemingly endless series of austerity measures that sought to push down wages and slash social spending. To protect finance capital, two decades of growth in Southern Europe would be erased and the regions repositioned as semiperipheral players in the world-economy.

Both the debt-based value extraction of the banks and the neomercantile intransigence of Northern capital were possible due to the particular structure of the EMU. The EMU was a child of neoliberalism, and it was thus no surprise that the International Monetary Fund (IMF) became involved in the debt rescue plans and the ensuing austerity. The fundamental flaw of the EMU was its lack of any mechanism for handling the uneven development and thus unbalanced surpluses that are inescapable features of capitalism (Varoufakis, 2011; Hadjimichalis, 2011). This arrangement, benefiting the Northern neomercantilists and banks, recalls the days of British hegemony since "as a system the euro is akin to the gold standard: an external currency whose overall supply was out of reach of national governments" (Aglietta, 2012, 20).

Syndicalism and the movement against austerity

During the crisis syndicalists found new footing and forged alliances with the newly powerful and widely-coordinated mass movements agitating for democracy and against austerity. This process is most easily visible in Spain, where sizable syndicalist unions still have formal existence, but can also be discerned in Greece, Portugal and Ireland where radically democratic unions focused on workers' control are growing through linkages with the wave of popular protests. This section charts some of the dynamics of this synergy between syndicalist unions and the new movements.[9]

Throughout the recent struggles the specific coalitional properties of syndicalism have played a major role in destabilizing alliances with reformist unions and the state. By early 2010 the unwinding debt of Spanish banks and credit contraction across the eurozone pushed unemployment toward 20%. GDP shrank more than 4% and a downgrading of Spanish bonds soon followed (Martín and Urquizu-Sancho, 2012, 351). The PSOE government turned toward austerity in an effort to protect Spanish finance capital and remain in good standing with the Northern EMU pow-

---

9   The following section draws on Hughes (2011), Publico.es (2011), Bohigas (2012), Déclos (2012), Durgan and Sans (2012), Declós (2012), El País (2012a; 2012b; 2012c), Gómez (2012), Martín and Urquizo-Sancho (2012), Morell (2012), Pastor (2012), and Roos (2012).

ers, unveiling a package of spending and public employee wage cuts followed by a set of antilabor provisions in early 2010. As the PSOE's popularity plummeted, the UGT and CCOO convened a general strike in late September and, though successful, the unions decided to move directly to negotiate a compromise. The situation resembled a much accelerated replay of the previous decade's pattern of creeping neoliberalism via collaborationist unionism. However, a breaking point came when the UGT and CCOO agreed to a retirement age hike in January 2011; the package once again included measures for labor market "flexibility." In response, both a smaller coterie of labor federations—including the syndicalists—and the general population embarked on an explosive mobilization against the state that jeopardized the institutionalized unions' control.

In January of 2011, the CGT and CNT put aside some of their organizational differences and joined with smaller radical unions to take an unprecedented step: invoking a general strike *without* the UGT or CCOO. While the January strike was small, it marked the first independent mass action by radical unions against both the state and hierarchical unions, setting in motion a series of increasingly large protests. The general strikes of 2011 and 2012, as well as a series of smaller municipal and regional general strikes occurring in Catalonia and the Basque region, have featured large CGT-CNT-led demonstrations with autonomy from the more routinized UGT and CCOO marches. One important ally in these actions has been the regional unions such as the Basque Left Union Convergence (*Ezker Sindikalaren Konbergentzia*—ESK), which calls to mind Hirsch and van der Walt's (2010) findings that early twentieth century syndicalists were an important part of early anticolonialist and nationalist struggles. A second and larger ally was found in the unprecedented mass movement for popular democracy, an anti-austerity movement that is at the same time an expression of a worldwide phenomenon.

This mass movement for democracy, named 15-M for its initial May 15th 2011 urban occupations, was a child of the GJM and the legitimacy crisis of the social democratic state. Many of the initial communications networks used by the movement, as well as the initial core of activists, were forged in GJM struggles. Huge numbers participated in protests based around popular assemblies, occupying public squares in Madrid and Barcelona and calling for an end to austerity and a reformulation of politics via a "completely open horizontal working policy, based on the assembly system in order to generate consensus" (Roos, 2012). Similar to the GJM, the movement has maintained a dense network of links between regional and municipal occupations and councils, as well as constant communication and collaboration with similar movements throughout Europe. Indeed, the 15-M is but one regional manifestation of what is quickly becoming a Europe- and world-wide phenomenon. At the movement's core is a call for direct democracy, and this practice of *asamblearismo* ("assembly-ism") permeates the many protests and occupations. Crucially, during a lull in protest activity in the summer of 2011, the mass assemblies made a series of decisions to move into regional and neighborhood councils. The aim was to plant the seeds of a permanent, multilevel council structure.

The alliance between syndicalist organizations and the 15-M has several important components. First, the radical unions have provided cover for the 15-M actions that paralyzed Madrid and Barcelona; under Spain's 1978 law "political" strikes are prohibited and thus the backing of a labor federation is a prerequisite to calling city-wide occupations that amount to a general strike. Within the last year, as the newly-elected conservative government has stepped up calls to label the 15-M actions political strikes and thus ban them, the official support of the syndicalists has provided a measure of protection. At the same time, the 15-M's presence gives a major boost to CGT democratizing drives in the workplace. The 15-M movement, with deep support among the unemployed and youth, reaches segments of the population that the formal union organizations have trouble organizing. Many elements of the 15-M are increasingly critical not only of the austerity measures, but of capitalist organization of the social world itself.

By the spring of 2012, the syndicalists were integral in drawing out the larger unions to participate in actions even against the UGT and CCOO leadership's will. In one of many examples, pushed by public sentiment the UGT reluctantly called for a multicity general strike on March 29th but then attempted to scuttle the action. Despite media predictions of only 18% adherence, a concerted support campaign by the 15-M and syndicalist bloc resulted in 81% participation and widespread hostility to UGT and CCOO coordination attempts. Time and again, as the UGT and CCOO have negotiated austerity agreements with the state or stopped at one-day strike actions, the CGT and CNT have been at the forefront of calls for refusing the cuts and extending the strikes into occupations and extended action campaigns. In the most recent actions, the CGT-CNT alliance sought to expand general strikes in September and November, calling explicitly for social revolution and the extension of *asamblearismo* to the workplaces as well as neighborhoods. The 15-M, meanwhile, have progressed to "Surround the Parliament" actions in which hundreds of thousands swarmed Madrid and Barcelona, itself a climbdown from even more ambitious calls to "occupy" parliament. State violence and arrests of key union and movement activists have been ramped up in response.

Greece, Portugal, and Ireland are subject to the same IMF-style debt regime, in which the imposition of austerity measures makes the debt crisis worse and unleashes a slew of antilabor initiatives. All have seen mass social protest along 15-M lines, with the most widespread and continuous in Greece. With wages slashed by more than 25% since 2009, skyrocketing youth unemployment, and a precipitous fall in living standards, the protests there have been the most frequent and violent in Europe. At the same time, Socialist party control of the major union federations is tighter than Spain's, and though the Communist party-affiliated federation All Workers' Militant Front (*Panergatiko Agonistiko Metopo*—PAME) has been at the forefront of strike action it is clear they maintain a tightly controlled, top-down approach that is at odds with the "assemblyism" of the social protests (Leontidou, 2012, 310–311n). Closer affinities exist among the multitudes of urban syndicalist unions that sprung up in the 2000s as the Greek workforce was increasingly casualized. These unions, often involving anarchists, have been active in fomenting opposition to the larger federations' capitulations (Kaplanis, 2011; Kretsos, 2011). This pattern can also be seen in Portugal and Ireland, with syndicalist groups working both within existing unions and through the newly revitalized anarcho-syndicalist IWA to coordinate simultaneous, multiregion actions (Secretariat of the International Workers Association, 2012a; 2012b).

Meanwhile, the European Central Bank, the IMF and Northern European politicians have worked to shore up pro-austerity EU elites in the South. The EMU has thus become a trap from which there seems to be no escape; the requisites of financial capitalism, predominant within the structures of the world-economy and EMU for decades, allow no escape from the debt-driven destruction of the Southern European semiperiphery. At the same time, the political mediation that would allow this extraction to continue is falling apart, as both social democratic and conservative parties are discredited in the generalizing "electoral chaos" (Bosco and Verney, 2012).

Conclusion

In order to understand the contours of syndicalist mobilization within the current crisis, this chapter examined the first wave of syndicalist mobilization in the 1920s. In both periods, the deflationary impact of world-economic crisis created a situation in which capital and the state attempted to offload the costs onto workers. However, these parallel instances are not isolated "cases" but rather an interconnected world-historical process, in which the interventionist solutions that solved the crisis of late British hegemony laid the groundwork for the latter era's extreme institutionalization of unions and left parties. The complicity of these organizations with the neoliberal turn and the deflation-driven austerity drive in post-2008 Europe has deeply eroded their legitimacy; the cracking of this hollowed-out institutional shell has revealed "another world" populated by the movement for global justice and radical democracy.

Analyzing syndicalism across two linked periods of world-systemic history demonstrates the efficacy of the antisystemic analytic framework. The two analytic axes of the framework, while here yielding theoretical and historical gains specific to syndicalism, may be usefully applied to a range of other movements.

The first axis, charting of the antisystemic ideology of the movement, includes the manner in which the movement's tactical, organizational and prescriptive logics conflict with the structure of capitalism. Here, radically democratic syndicalist practice led the movement to form unstable coalitions with state and reformist organizations, pushing towards goals of workers' control while at the same time limiting the capacity for syndicalist organizations to be accommodated by institution-alized structures. In turn, this created a need for mass social movement support through democratic community organizations.

Second, and no less important, is the historical reconstruction of the movement as a constitutive component of the world-system. This requires going beyond any national or regional history of a given movement. For syndicalism, the formation of interventionist liberalism during the twilight of British hegemony and its subsequent erosion under neoliberalism was central, providing the analytic key to understanding the movement's early twentieth century decline and its resurgence today.

Acknowledgements

The author wishes to thank Julee Gardner, David A. Smith and Mark Frezzo for their assistance in the preparation of this text.

References

Aglietta, Michel. 2012. The European Vortex. *New Left Review,* 75: 15–36.

Alternative Libertaire. 2004. Spain: CGT is Now the Third Biggest Union. In *Common Struggle/Lucha Común.* URL: http://nefac.net/node/1398 (accessed November 20, 2012).

Amenta, Edwin, Neal Caren, and Sheera Joy Olasky. 2005. Age for Leisure? Political Mediation and the Impact of the Pension Movement on Old-Age Policy. *American Sociological Review,* 70: 516–538.

Anderson, Benedict. 2006. *Under Three Flags: Anarchism and the Anti-Colonial Imagination.* London: Verso.

Arrighi, Giovanni. 1994. *The Long Twentieth Century: Money, Power and the Origin of Our Times.* New York: Verso.

Arrighi, Giovanni, Terence K. Hopkins, and Immanuel Wallerstein. 1989. *Antisystemic Movements.* New York and London: Verso.

Arrighi, Giovanni, and Beverly J. Silver. 1999. *Chaos and Governance in the Modern World System: Comparing Hegemonic Transitions.* Minneapolis, MN: University of Minnesota Press.

Arrighi, Giovanni, and Beverley Silver. 2003. Polanyi's "Double Movement": The Belle Époques of British and US Hegemony Compared. *Politics and Society,* 31: 325–355.

Bellofiore, Riccardo, and Joseph Halevi. 2011. "Could Be Raining": The European Crisis After the Great Recession. *International Journal of Political Economy,* 39(4): 5–30.

Bergquist, Charles W. 1986. *Labor in Latin America: Comparative Essays on Chile, Argentina, Venezuela, and Colombia.* Stanford: Stanford University Press.

Berry, David, and Constance Bantman. 2010. *New Perspectives on Anarchism, Labour and Syndicalism.* Newcastle Upon Tyne, UK: Cambridge Scholars Publishing.

Bohigas, Oleguer. 2012. Las piezas están sobre el tablero, juguemos para ganar y ya veremos qué pasa. *En Lucha,* July 6, 2012. URL: http://enlucha.org/articulos/las-piezas-estn-sobre-el-tablero-juguemos-para-ganar-y-ya-veremos-qu-pasa/#.Ur-ROLp3zm71 (accessed November 20, 2012).

Bosco, Anna, and Susannah Verney. 2012. Electoral Epidemic: The Political Cost of Economic Crisis in Southern Europe, 2010–11. *South European Society and Politics,* 17(2): 129–154.

Breslin, Patrick Edward. 1980. The Development of Class Consciousness in the Chilean Working Class. PhD dissertation, Department of Political Science, University of California, Los Angeles.

Cain, P.J., and A.G. Hopkins. 1993. *British Imperialism: Crisis and Deconstruction, 1914–1990.* London and New York: Longman.

Damier, Vadim. 2009. *Anarcho-Syndicalism in the 20th Century.* Canada: Black Cat Press.

Darlington, Ralph. 2008. *Syndicalism and the Transition to Communism.* London: Ashgate Publishing Company.

Declós, Carlos. 2012. General Strike Marks Another Step Forward for Indignados. In Roarmag.org, March 30, 2012. URL: http://roarmag.org/2012/03/general-strike-spain-barcelona-police-indignados/ (accessed November 30, 2012).

della Porta, Donatella, Masimiliano Andretta, Lorenzo Mosca, and Herbert Reiter. 2006. *Globalization from Below: Transnational Activists and Protest Networks.* Minneapolis, MN: Minneapolis University Press.

DeShazo, Peter. 1983. *Urban Workers and Labor Unions in Chile, 1902–1927.* Madison, WI: University of Wisconsin Press.

Deutsch, Sandra McGee. 1999. *Las Derechas: The Extreme Right in Argentina, Brazil, and Chile, 1890–1939.* Stanford, CA: Stanford University Press.

Duménil, Gérard, and Dominique Lévy. 2011. *The Crisis of Neoliberalism.* Cambridge, MA: Harvard University Press.

Durgan, Andy, and Joel Sans. 2012. "No One Represents Us": the 15 May Movement in the Spanish State. *Sozial.Geschichte Online,* 7: 93–113. URL: http://duepublico.uni-duisburg-essen.de/servlets/DerivateServlet/Derivate-30291/06_Durgan_Spanien.pdf (accessed November 20, 2012).

el-Ojeili, Chamsy. 2014. Anarchism as the Spirit of Contemporary Anti-Capitalism? A Critical Survey of Recent Debates. *Critical Sociology,* 40 (3): 451–468.

El País. 2012a. Union Leaders Call for Government Consensus after Thursday's Strike. *El País,* March 30, 2012. URL: http://elpais.com/elpais/2012/03/30/inenglish/1333130737_176104.html (accessed November 20, 2012).

El País. 2012b. La CNT llama a continuar con las movilizaciones tras la huelga general. *El País,* November 17, 2012. URL: http://economia.elpais.com/economia/2012/11/17/agencias/1353177051_020299.html (accessed November 20, 2012).

El País. 2012c. Movilizaciones en defensa del trabajo y de los derechos socials. *El País,* November 20, 2012. URL: http://ccaa.elpais.com/ccaa/2012/11/20/paisvasco/1353429664_685413.html (accessed November 20, 2012).

Ferraro, Angel, Iván Gordillo, and Saturnino Mercader. 2011. Los sindicatos tienen que pasar a la ofensiva. *El Viejo Topo*, 276: 55–61.

Giugni, Marco, and Sakura Yamasaki. 2009. The Policy Impact of Social Movements: A Replication through Qualitative Comparative Analysis. *Mobilization: An International Journal*, 14(4): 467–484.

Gómez, Manuel V. 2012. Outrage on the Streets of Spain after Latest Austerity Measures. *El País*, July 20, 2012. URL: http://elpais.com/elpais/2012/07/20/inenglish/1342797489_509247.html (accessed November 20, 2012).

Goodwin, Jeff, and Gabriel Hetland. 2009. The Strange Disappearance of Capitalism from Social Movement Studies. Paper presented at the American Sociological Association Annual Meeting. San Francisco, USA, August 8, 2009.

Graeber, David. 2004. *Fragments of an Anarchist Anthropology.* Chicago, IL: Prickly Paradigm Press.

Hadjimichalis, Costis. 2011. Uneven Geographical Development and Socio-Spatial Justice and Solidarity: European Regions after the 2009 Financial Crisis. *European Urban and Regional Studies*, 18(3): 254–274.

Halfmann, Drew. 2013. *Doctors and Demonstrators.* Chicago, IL: University of Chicago Press.

Hirsch, Steven, and Lucien van der Walt (eds.). 2010. *Anarchism and Syndicalism in the Colonial and Postcolonial World, 1870–1910: The Praxis of National Liberation, Internationalism and Social Revolution.* Boston, MA: Brill.

Holman, Otto. 1996. *Integrating Southern Europe, EC Expansion and the Transnationalisation of Spain.* London: Routledge.

Horowitz, Joel. 1995. Argentina's Failed General Strike of 1921: A Critical Moment in the Radicals' Relations with Unions. *The Hispanic American Historical Review,* 75(1): 57–79.

Hughes, Neil. 2011. "Young People Took to the Streets and all of a Sudden all of the Political Parties Got Old": The 15M Movement in Spain. *Social Movement Studies: Journal of Social, Cultural and Political Protest,* 10(4): 407–413.

Hyman, Richard. 2005. Trade Unions and the Politics of the European Social Model. *Economic and Industrial Democracy,* 26(1): 9–40.

Kaplanis, Yiannis. 2011. "An Economy that Excludes the Many and an 'accidental' Revolt." In Antonis Vradis and Dimitris Dalakoglou (eds.), *Revolt and Crisis in Greece: Between a Present Yet to Pass and a Future Still to Come.* Oakland, CA: AK Press.

Köhler, Holm-Detlev, and José Pablo Calleja Jiménez. 2010. Organizing Heterogeneity: Challenges for the Spanish Trade Unions. *Transfer: European Review of Labour and Research,* 16(4): 541–557.

Kretsos, Lefteris. 2011. Grassroots Unionism in the Context of Economic Crisis in Greece. *Labor History,* 52(3): 265–286.

Leontidou, Lila. 2012. Athens in the Mediterranean "Movement of the Piazzas." Spontaneity in Material and Virtual Public Spaces. *City: Analysis of Urban Trends, Culture, Theory, Policy, Action,* 16(3): 299–312.

Li, Minqi, Feng Xiao, and Andong Zhu. 2007. Long Waves, Institutional Changes, and Historical Trends: A Study of the Long-Term Movement of the Profit Rate in the Capitalist World-Economy. *Journal of World-Systems Research,* 13(1): 33–54.

Lichtenstein, Nelson. 2002. *State of the Union: A Century of American Labor.* Princeton, NJ: Princeton University Press.

Lipson, Charles. 1985. *Standing Guard: Protecting Foreign Capital in the Nineteenth and Twentieth Centuries.* Berkeley, CA: University of California Press.

Loris, Sergio. 2011. Compartimos la idea de asamblearismo y la de unidad de los y las trabajadoras con el 15M. *En Lucha.* URL: enlucha.org/diari/compartimos-la-idea-de-asamblearismo-y-la-de-unidad-de-los-y-las-trabajadoras-con-el-15m/ (accessed February 11, 2014).

Marks, Gary, and Doug McAdam. 1999. "On the Relationship of Political Opportunities to the Form of Collective Action: The Case of the European Union." In Donatella della Porta, Hanspeter Kriesi, and Dieter Rucht (eds.), *Social Movements in a Globalizing World.* New York: St. Martin's Press.

Martín, Irene, and Ignacio Urquizu-Sancho. 2012. The 2011 General Election in Spain: The Collapse of the Socialist Party. *South European Society and Politics,* 17(2): 347–363.

Martin, William G. (coord.). 2008. *Making Waves: Worldwide Social Movements, 1750–2005.* Boulder, CO and London: Paradigm Publishers.

McAdam, Doug. 1982. *Political Process and the Development of Black Insurgency, 1930–1970.* Chicago: University of Chicago Press.

McAdam, Doug, Sidney Tarrow, and Charles Tilly. 2001. *Dynamics of Contention.* Cambridge: Cambridge University Press.

McKay, Iain. 2012. Syndicalism, Anarchism and Marxism. *Anarchist Studies,* 20(1): 89–105.

McMichael, Philip. 2000. World-Systems Analysis, Globalization, and Incorporated Comparison. *Journal of World-Systems Research,* 6(3): 68–99.

Meyer, David S. 2003. Political Opportunity and Nested Institutions. *Social Movement Studies: Journal of Social, Cultural and Political Protest,* 2(1): 17–35.

Meyer, David S., and Sidney Tarrow (eds.). 1998. *The Social Movement Society: Contentious Politics for a New Century.* London: Rowan & Littlefield.

Moghadam, Valentine M. 2012. "Anti-systemic Movements Compared." In Salvatore J. Babones and Christopher Chase-Dunn (eds.), *Routledge International Handbook of World-Systems Analysis.* New York: Routledge.

Monteón, Michael. 1981. *Chile in the Nitrate Era: The Evolution of Economic Dependence, 1880–1930.* Madison, WI: University of Wisconsin Press.

Morell, Mayo Fuster. 2012. The Free Culture and 15M Movements in Spain: Composition, Social Networks and Synergies, Social Movement Studies. *Journal of Social, Cultural and Political Protest,* 11(3–4): 386–392.

Munck, Ronaldo, and Peter Vaterman. 1999. *Labour Worldwide in the Era of Globalization: Alternative Union Models in the New World Order.* New York: Palgrave.

Nichter, Matthew. 2008. Capital Resurgent? The Political Economy of Gérard Duménil and Dominique Lévy. *Journal of World-Systems Research,* XIV(1): 75–84.

Overbeek, Henk. 2012. Sovereign Debt Crisis in Euroland: Root Causes and Implications for the European Integration. *The International Spectator,* 47(1): 30–48.

Palma, Gabriel. 2000. "From an Export-Led to an Import-Substituting Economy: Chile 1914–39." In Rosemary Thorp (ed.), *An Economic History of Latin America, Volume 2: Latin America in the 1930s.* New York, NY: Palgrave.

Pastor, Jaime. 2012. La crisis, el 15-M y la izquierda en España. *Le Monde Diplomatique en Español,* 201: 3.

Peet, Richard. 2011. Inequality, Crisis and Austerity in Finance Capitalism. Cambridge *Journal of Regions, Economy and Society,* 4(3): 383–399.

Pleyers, Geoffrey. 2010. *Alter-Globalization.* Cambridge, MA: Polity.

Preece, Daniel V. 2009. *Dismantling Social Europe: The Political Economy of Social Policy in the European Union.* Boulder, CO: First Forum Press.

Publico.es. 2011. Hoy huelga en Euskado, Navarra, Galicia y Catalunya. In Publico.es, January 27, 2011. URL: http://www.publico.es/dinero/358382/hoy-huelga-en-euskadi-navarra-galicia-y-catalunya (accessed November 20, 2012).

Reese, Ellen, Ian Breckenridge-Jackson, Edwin Elias, David W. Iverson, and James Love. 2012. "The Global Justice Movement and the Social Forum Process." In Salvatore J. Babones and Christopher Chase-Dunn (eds.), *Routledge International Handbook of World-Systems Analysis.* New York: Routledge.

Rock, David. 1975. *Politics in Argentina, 1890–1930: The Rise and Fall of Radicalism.* London: Cambridge University Press.

Roos, Jerome. 2012. Occupy Congress: Indignados Encircle Parliament. In Roarmag. org, September 25, 2012. URL: http://roarmag.org/2012/09/occupy-congress-spains-indignados-radicalize-resistance/ (accessed November 20, 2012).

Rothschild, Kurt W. 2009. Neoliberalism, EU and the Evaluation of Policies. *Review of Political Economy,* 21(2): 213–225.

Royo, Sebastián. 2006. Beyond Confrontation : The Resurgence of Social Bargaining in Spain in the 1990s. *Comparative Political Studies,* 39: 969–995.

Schmidt, Michael, and Lucien van der Walt. 2009. *Black Flame: The Revolutionary Class Politics of Anarchism and Syndicalism.* London and Oakland, CA: AK Press.

Secretariat of the International Workers Association. 2012a. IWA External Bulletin, May 01, 2012. Oslo: Secretariat of the International Workers Association. URL: http://libcom.org/files/BI0810_ait_iwa-external-bulletin-no-1-may-2012.pdf (accessed February 11, 2014).

Secretariat of the International Workers Association. 2012b. IWA External Bulletin 3, October 01, 2012. Oslo: Secretariat of the International Workers Association. URL: http://libcom.org/files/IWA%20external%20bulletin%20no%203%20October%20 2012.pdf (accessed February 11, 2014).

Silver, Beverly J. 2003. *Forces of Labor: Workers' Movements and Globalization since 1870.* New York, NY: Cambridge University Press.

Smith, Jackie. 2004. *Transnational Processes and Movements.* Malden, MA: Blackwell Publishing.

Smith, Jackie. 2008. *Global Movements for Global Democracy.* Baltimore, MD: Johns Hopkins University Press.

Smith, Jackie, and Dawn Wiest. 2012. *Social Movements in the World-System: The Politics of Crisis and Transformation.* New York: Russell Sage Foundation.

Taylor, Alan M. 2006. "Foreign Capital Flows." In Victor Bulmer-Thomas (ed.), *The Cambridge Economic History of Latin America, Volume II.* New York: Cambridge University Press.

Taylor, Graham, Andrew Mathers, and Martin Upchurch. 2011. Beyond the Chains That Bind: The Political Crisis of Unions in Western Europe. *Labor History,* 52(3): 287–305.

Thorpe, Wayne. 1989. *"The Workers Themselves": Revolutionary Syndicalism and International Labor 1913–1923.* Dordrecht: Kluwer Academic Publishers.

Tomich, Dale W. 1990. *Slavery in the Circuit of Sugar: Martinique and the World Economy, 1830–1848.* Baltimore, MD: Johns Hopkins University Press.

Trouillot, Michel-Rolph. 1982. Motion in the System: Coffee, Color, and Slavery in Eighteenth-Century Saint-Domingue. *Review (Fernand Braudel Center),* 5(3): 331–388.

van Biezen, Ingrid, Peter Mair, and Thomas Poguntke. 2012. Going, Going … Gone? The Decline of Party Membership in Contemporary Europe. *European Journal of Political Research,* 51(1): 24–56.

van der Linden, Marcel, and Wayne Thorpe (eds.). 1990. *Revolutionary Syndicalism: An International Perspective.* New York: Scolar Press.

Varoufakis, Yanis. 2011. *The Global Minotaur: America, the True Origins of the Financial Crisis and the Future of the World Economy.* London: Zed Books.

Wallerstein, Immanuel. 1989. *The Modern World-System III: The Second Era of Great Expansion of the Capitalist World-Economy, 1730–1840s.* New York: Academic Press.

Wallerstein, Immanuel. 2011a. *The Modern World-System IV: Centrist Liberalism Triumphant.* Berkeley, CA: University of California Press.

Wallerstein, Immanuel. 2011b. Structural Crises. *New Left Review,* 62: 133–142.

Appendix: Acronyms and abbreviations

AOAN   *Asamblea Obrera de la Alimentación Nacional*—Workers' Assembly on National Nutrition

CCOO   *Comisiones Obreras*—formerly-Communist Workers' Commissions

CGT   *Confederación General del Trabajo*—General Workers' Confederation

CGT   *Confédération Générale du Travail*—French General Workers' Confederation

CNT   *Confederación Nacional del Trabajo*—National Workers' Confederation

EMU   European Monetary Union

ESK   *Ezker Sindikalaren Konbergentzia*—Basque Left Union Convergence

FOCh *Federación Obrera de Chile*—Chilean Workers' Federation
FOM *Federación Obrera Maritima*—Maritime Workers' Federation
FORA *Federación Obrera Regional Argentina*—Argentine Regional Workers' Federation
GJM Global Justice Movement
IMF International Monetary Fund
IWA International Workers' Association
IWW Industrial Workers of the World
NSM's New social movements
PAME *Panergatiko Agonistiko Metopo*—All Workers' Militant Front (Greece)
PSOE *Partido Socialista Obrero Español*—Spanish Socialist Workers' Party
SAC *Sveriges Arbetares Centralorganisation*—Central Organization of the Workers of Sweden
UGT *Unión General de Trabajadores*—General Union of Workers
USP *Unión Syndical de Panaderos*—Bakers' Union

10

Globalization and Industrial Relations in Affluent Democracies, 1970–2005: A Cross-National Analysis of Corporatism and Industrial Conflict

Anthony Roberts

The persistence of cross-national variation in the industrial relation systems of advanced capitalist countries during a period of rapid global political and economic integration has been a heavily disputed issue in the extant literature. This study sets out to adjudicate this contention in the literature by examining the direct and indirect effects of economic and political globalization on corporatism and industrial conflict in the industrial relation systems of advanced capitalist countries. I apply fixed-effects and random-coefficient models to an unbalanced panel dataset of 18 OECD countries observed over a 35-year period (1970–2005) for estimating the direct and indirect effects of globalization along with the variance of these effects across countries. Findings from the models indicate that Southern import penetration indirectly reduces corporatism and industrial conflict through processes of deindustrialization and deunionization. Participation in intergovernmental organizations is directly associated with a decline in industrial conflict, while the ratification of International Labour Organization conventions is associated with a direct decline in corporatism. Overall, the findings suggest that both economic and political globalization induce a transition toward more flexible and less contentious industrial relation systems, but these processes are conditioned by unobserved national-level processes.

Introduction

Over the last thirty years researchers have produced an extensive literature on globalization and industrial relation systems in the advanced capitalist countries.[1] In this extant literature, researchers have debated whether economic globalization has reduced cross-national variation in industrial relations and whether countries are converging toward a "neoliberal" model characterized by weak corporatist institutions and labor politics (Traxler et al., 2001; Kollmeyer, 2003; Campbell, 2004; Mills et al., 2008; Hall and Thelen, 2009; Baccaro and Howell, 2011; Kristensen and Morgan, 2012). In this debate researchers have given little consideration to the effect of *political* globalization on industrial relation systems even though advanced capitalist countries are increasingly participating in and committing to internation-

---

1   See Baccaro and Howell (2011) and Molina and Rhodes (2002) for a review of this literature.

al institutions (Meyer et al., 1997; Meyer, 2000; Cao, 2009; Beckfield, 2010). More importantly, the paucity of comparative *and* systematic research on the effects of globalization on industrial relations has perpetuated this debate. This chapter contributes to this extant literature on globalization and industrial relation systems by assessing the effects of economic and political globalization on corporatism and conflict in the industrial relation systems of eighteen OECD countries over a thirty-five year period (1970 to 2005).

In order to account for the main characteristics of industrial relations, I utilize a two-dimensional conceptualization of industrial relations: corporatism and industrial conflict (Baccaro and Howell, 2011). Broadly defined, corporatist industrial relations are based on the tripartite decision-making between employer associations, trade unions, and state agencies over collective bargaining agreements, industrial policy, and social insurance programs. This definition captures both the "structure of interest representation" and "the form of policy making" in corporatist industrial relations (Schmitter, 1982). In studying corporatist industrial relations, researchers have primarily focused on the centralization, coordination, and the involvement of states in wage bargaining. Centralization refers to "the level(s) at which wages are bargained or set" (Kenworthy, 2001, 59). Wage coordination is defined as the "degree of intentional harmony in the wage-setting process—or, put another way, the degree to which minor players deliberately follow along with what the major players decide" (Kenworthy, 2001, 76). Finally, state involvement in a collective bargaining agreement significantly varies across developed economies, where the state can play an active role by passing legislation requiring collective agreements and defining the structure the bargaining process. In contrast, the state can play an indirect role by enacting labor regulations, such as national minimum wage and payroll taxes. Overall, these are the main institutional characteristics of corporatism that have received the most attention in the theoretical and empirical literature on industrial relations. However, this exclusive focus on the "form of policy making" ignores other characteristics of corporatism.

In addition to wage-setting, corporatist industrial relations are facilitated by the interests of organized labor and the development of social programs. Unions are the primary institution for representing the interest of workers. More importantly, the establishment and persistence of wage-setting institutions are partially determined by the organizational strength of unions since the political objective of unions is to institutionalize the practice of collective bargaining in labor markets (Alquhist, 2010). Additionally, organized labor is a strong advocate of social policy. A common feature of corporatist systems is the presence of strong welfare programs aimed at providing social safety nets for workers and strong unions aimed at promoting the interest of labor over capital (Pampel and Williamson, 1988; Esping-Andersen, 1990; Pierson, 1994).

Since the 1970s an extensive literature has been directed at explaining cross-national variation in corporatism and its effects on economic development and labor market performance (Schmitter, 1974; Harrison, 1980; Calmfors and Driffill, 1988; Wallerstein et al., 1997; Traxler et al., 2001; Blau and Kahn, 2002; Molina and Rhodes, 2002). In more recent years, researchers have begun to assess whether corporatist institutions are being replaced by neoliberal policies designed to improve economic competitiveness through labor market flexibility (Regini, 1995; Therborn, 1998; Glyn, 2001; Rhodes, 2001; Traxler et al., 2001; Baccaro and Howell, 2011). On one hand, researchers have argued that corporatist institutions have been not been replaced, but rather re-purposed to allow for a degree of flexibility in labor markets by reducing the centralization of wage bargaining (Traxler, 1995; Traxler and Kittel, 2000; Crouch, 2000; Baccaro and Howell, 2011). On the other hand, researchers have argued that corporatist institutions are not viable in a volatile and global economy, where macroeconomic shocks increase unemployment in countries with "rigid" labor markets (Grahl and Teague, 1997; Blau and Kahn, 2002; Baccaro and Howell, 2011). Given the paucity of systematic and comparative research on the relationship between globalization and corporatism, this argument continues to persist in the literature. In addition to the lack of systematic and comparative research, the inattention to the structural mechanisms linking globalization to corporatism has also fueled this disagreement. Based on the current status of the literature, this chapter contributes to this debate by evaluating the direct and indirect effects of economic globalization on corporatism.

While wage corporatism is an important facet of industrial relations in advanced capitalist countries, this exclusive focus on corporatism ignores the contentious nature of capital and labor relations. Conflict-based industrial relations are characterized by collective disputes between interest groups representing capital and labor. Instead of engaging in cooperative negotiations over wages, working conditions, and other policies, firms and organized labor engage in strikes, lock-outs, and work stoppages for gaining concessions from each other. Arguably, this strategy relies on the associational power of unions because unions often utilize industrial strikes during periods of collective bargaining to combat the asymmetrical power in the relations between capital and labor. In this view, industrial strikes are one of the main mechanisms for institution building, where labor directly confronts employers with the intention of establishing restraints on the ability for the market and firms to set wages and working conditions through disrupting the work process (Korpi and Shalev, 1979). However, several studies have noted the recent decline of industrial strike activity in advanced capitalist countries (Shalev, 1992; Edwards and Hyman, 1994; Hamann et al., 2012), but the proximate causes are unclear. While globalization has been recognized as a contributor to the decline of industrial strikes, the mechanisms underlying this relationship remain unaddressed. Therefore, this study aims to examine the direct and indirect effects of globalization on industrial conflict. While an extensive literature on industrial conflict exists, to date, this study provides the first comprehensive and systematic account of cross-national variation in cooperative (corporatist) and conflict-based industrial relations.

One of the main arguments of the chapter is that economic globalization indirectly promotes the decline of corporatism and industrial conflict through its effects on the industrial labor force and union membership. Specifically, the globalization of production reduces the incentive for manufacturing firms to engage in corporatist policy making since they are no longer dependent on industrial labor in advanced capitalist countries. More importantly, through processes of outsourcing and offshoring, the demand for unskilled and semi-skilled manufacturing labor declines, reducing the bargaining power of labor. As a consequence, national governments are continually pressured by employer associations and multinational firms to deregulate labor markets by limiting collective bargaining, employment protection legislation, and eliminating social insurance programs. Additionally, since multinational firms have increased their bargaining power via global production, they are able to effectively reduce industrial conflict by deterring workers from participating in unions. Since membership is the primary resource of unions for enacting effective bargaining tactics (Ahlquist, 2010), a decline in union membership reduces the frequency, intensity, and worker involvement in industrial conflict. These processes of deindustrialization and deunionization have induced a shift toward "flexible" labor market policies, which aims to limit wage-setting institutions and conflict in industrial relation systems. A less understood process of globalization for explaining cross-national variation in industrial relation systems has been the emergence of international institutions. Given the rapid growth of international governmental organizations (IGOs) over the last sixty years (Boli and Thomas, 1997; Meyer, 2007; Cao, 2009; Beckfield, 2010), international institutions, such as the International Labour Organization (ILO), are playing an increasingly important role in national policy-making. Accordingly, this emerging world polity has caused national institutions to become articulated by global culture and norms that emerge from interactions within international organizations (Meyer et al., 1997). For example, between 1919 and 2007, the ILO has been the major organization dedicated to improving national labor regulation through the development and promotion of 188 conventions and 199 recommendations. Countries voluntarily adopt and implement these conventions and recommendations to signify their commitment to improving labor regulations and rights.

Recently, researchers have argued that the construction of global culture and norms are the product of intense struggles between multinational firms, states, professional associations, and transnational labor within international institutions (Beckfield, 2003; Henisz et al., 2005). Given the asymmetrical power of global capital relative to labor and national governments (see Robinson, 2004), it's likely that global norms and culture promotes flexible labor markets. Therefore, whether IGOs, and specifically the ILO, promote or hinder the persistence of corporatist industrial relations and industrial conflict remains unclear.

The institutional trajectory of corporatism and industrial conflict

In a recent study on the institutional trajectory of industrial relations in advanced capitalist countries, researchers found that labor market institutions have been fundamentally transformed through processes of deregulation and re-purposing (Baccaro and Howell, 2011). According to these researchers, paradoxically while cross-national variation in industrial relation systems persists, these institutions increasingly promote neoliberal policies. However, this research does not address the causal factors behind this "common neoliberal trajectory." Therefore, this chapter first examines the trajectory and cross-national variation in industrial relation systems amongst advanced capitalist countries. Next, the chapter empirically evaluates the causal factors driving institutional change in industrial systems.

As seen in Figure 1, over the last thirty-five years, there has been an average downward trend in corporatism and industrial conflict. During the early 1970s, the average rate of industrial conflict was relatively high in response to economic crises and the struggle to impose a strong corporatist framework for regulating industrial

Figure 1: LOWESS trends in corporatism and industrial conflict, 1970–2005

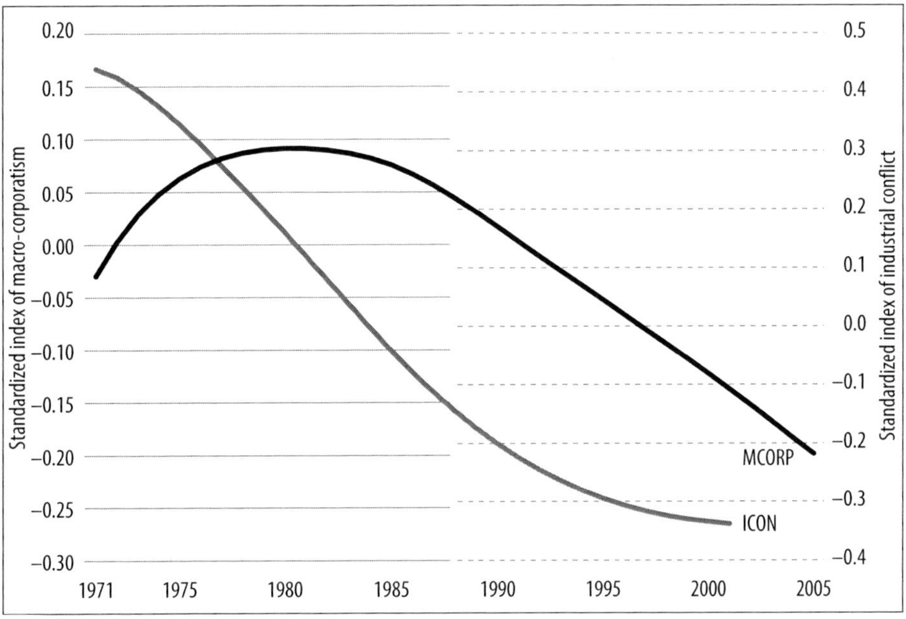

Notes: MCORP=standardized index of macro-corporatism (left scale); ICON=standardized index of industria la conflict (right scale).
Sources: Visser (2011) and ILO (2011).

Figure 2: Cross-national variation in corporatism, 1970–2005

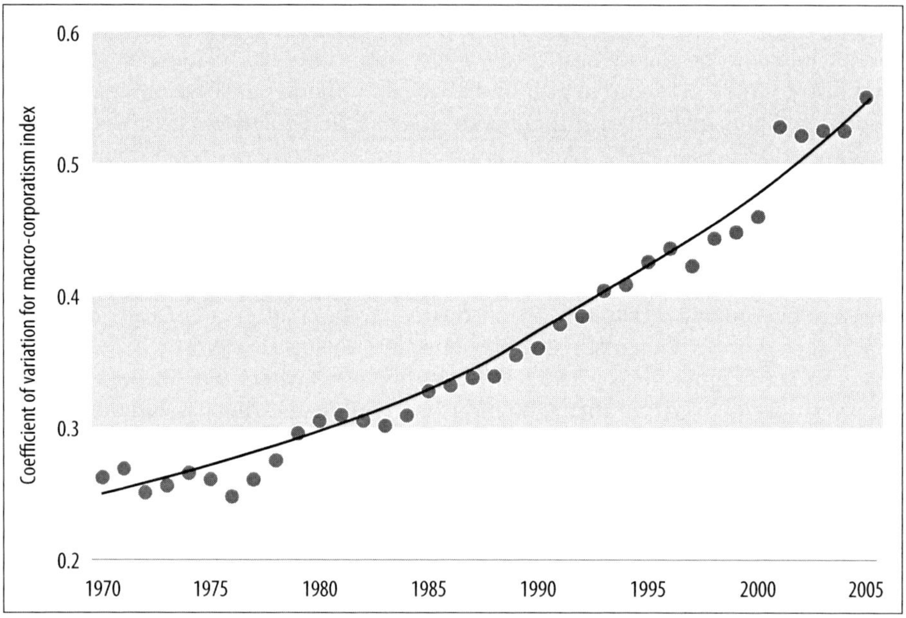

Source: Visser (2011).

relations. However, over the late 1970s and 1980s, there was a dramatic decline in industrial conflict. Similarly, with the peak of industrial conflict, there was a noticeable increase in corporatism in the 1970s and early 1980s. However, with the steady decline of industrial conflict, there has been a corresponding decline in corporatism. Overall, both the average decline in corporatism and industrial conflict represents a significant transition toward greater labor market flexibility in advanced capitalist countries.

While advanced capitalist countries are exhibiting an average trajectory toward less corporatism, Figure 2 shows that over the same period there has been a steady increase in the variation of corporatism across these same countries. Even though, on average, countries are deconstructing corporatist industrial relations, it appears that countries are exhibiting institutional change at differing rates. What remains unanswered is whether cross-national variation in global political and economic integration explains this persistent diversity and whether unobserved factors condition the effects of globalization on corporatism.

While variation in corporatism has increased over the last forty years, cross-national variation in industrial conflict has steadily decreased over this period. However, the degree of cross-national variation is substantially greater than variation in corporatism. This steady decline in variation of industrial conflict (exclud-

Figure 3: Cross-national variation in industrial conflict, 1970–2000

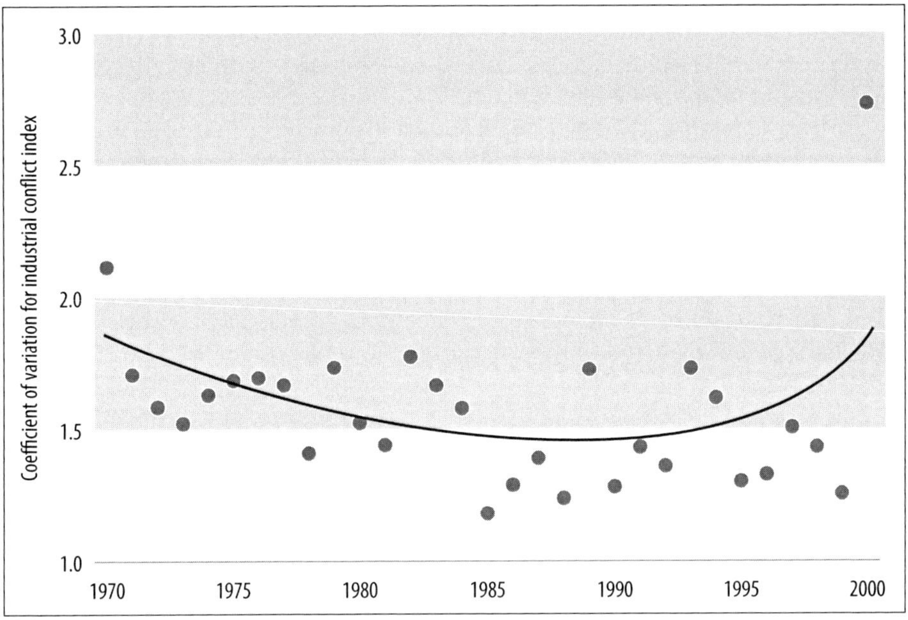

Source: ILO (2011).

ing the mass unrest in 1999–2000) appears to signify the decline in conflict-based tactics in negotiating capital-labor relations. Whether this decline in cross-national variation is indicative of a neoliberal convergence induced by globalization remains unanswered.

Globalization and industrial relations

Perhaps the most significant processes for explaining the institutional trajectory of industrial relations in advanced capitalist countries have been the emergence of globalized production, deindustrialization, and deunionization. These interrelated processes are primarily driven by the emergence of a new mode of industrial organization that integrates both developed and developing countries in vast networks of economic production processes (Dicken, 2003; Gereffi et al., 2005). Within global production networks, a complex division of labor develops where firms in advanced capitalist countries specialize in high-value activity, such as retail, design, and research, while firms in developing countries tend to specialize in low-value activity, such as component production and assembly (Mahutga, 2012). A direct consequence of this new organization of production has been the steady decline of the manufacturing employment in advanced capitalist countries as firms outsource and offshore production (Alderson, 1999; Kollmeyer, 2009).

Multinational firms have begun offshoring and outsourcing parts of the production process to developing countries in order to specialize in their core competencies—distribution, retail, design, and development (Gereffi et al., 2005; Contractor et al., 2010; Mudambi and Venzin, 2010). This restructuring of industrial production has significantly reshaped the profile of trade between developed and developing economies, where developed countries are increasingly importing manufacturing goods from developing countries (Kaplinsky, 2005; Krugman, 2008). The increase in manufacturing imports from developing countries has decreased the relative demand for unskilled and semi-skilled manufacturing employment since labor-intensive production processes are more cost effective in developing countries with an abundance of unskilled and semi-skilled labor (Revenga, 1992; Wood, 1994; Mion and Zhu, 2012).

Indeed, over the 1970–2005 period, on average, imports from developing countries have increased from about 6% of total manufacturing imports to 25% of total manufacturing imports while, on average, the share of the labor force in manufacturing declined from 37% to 23% (OECD, 2011). This shift towards globalized production appears to have established a new manufacturing base in developing countries through reducing industrial employment in developed countries. Since semi-skilled manufacturing labor has been the primary economic group advocating for corporatist relations, manufacturing imports from low-wage countries should indirectly reduce corporatism through its negative effect on industrial employment. Additionally, since semi-skilled manufacturing workers were the primary members of trade unions, manufacturing imports from low-wage countries should indirectly reduce industrial conflict through its negative effect on unionization.

Over the last thirty-five years, there has been a substantial growth in IGO memberships from an average of 60 in 1970 to an average of about 95 in 2005. Similarly, on average, countries ratified around seven ILO conventions in 1970 compared to about eight conventions in 2005. Overall, this suggests that countries are increasingly becoming integrated into the world polity. The major question is whether the ILO and IGOs are promoting the corporatism and conflict in industrial relation systems or whether the global model of labor regulation is directed at increasing the flexibility of labor markets and reducing industrial conflict.

The emergence of the ILO, as an international institution dedicated to the promotion of labor rights, has been a significant force in the development of a global model of labor regulation. In general, ILO conventions and recommendations tend to prescribe stronger collective bargaining, greater representation of labor, and improvements in working conditions. Since the ILO lacks any coercive mechanism, the organization has relied on normative and learning mechanisms for pressuring states into adopting conventions and implementing recommendations (Standing, 2008). The ILO pressures member countries into ratifying new conventions and implementing new legislation through strategic campaigning and reporting. Additionally, the ILO provides technical assistance to countries trying to implement new legislation. These isomorphic pressures to adopt common models of labor regulation are not only exerted by the ILO, but also by other IGOs in the world polity. Previous studies have shown that participation in the world polity has facilitated the convergence in welfare spending (Cao, 2009) and privatization policies in international industries (Henisz et al., 2005).

While the ILO is the most significant international organization for the development of a global model of labor regulation, other intergovernmental organizations are sites for the production and diffusion of this global model. Drawing on the work of DiMaggio and Powell (1983), the primary mechanisms driving the emergence and diffusion of global models of economic regulation are coercive, mimetic, and normative processes (Meyer et al., 1997; Cao, 2009). Coercive mechanisms rely on the asymmetry of power between member states, where advanced capitalist countries are able to dictate the development and implementation of policies by exploiting political and economic dependence. Mimetic mechanisms occur during periods of uncertainty which cause member countries to adopt similar policies without consideration of their effectiveness in a given context. Finally, normative mechanisms rely upon the advocacy of policies and the diffusion of information on its effectiveness. Overall, the general mechanisms suggest that political globalization could reduce and increase both corporatism and conflict, depending on the nature of the global model of labor regulation.

In addition to these general mechanisms, participation in international institutions provides opportunities for other national labor movements to exploit international opportunity structures (Keck and Sikkink, 1998; Kay, 2011). The most immediate consequence of this scalar change in labor activism is the subsequent decline in the utilization of industrial strikes to affect collective bargaining. Therefore, while IGO participation (especially in the ILO) promotes corporatism in industrial relations, it should also reduce conflict in industrial relations.

Globalization and the persistence of institutional diversity

In the comparative political economy literature, the persistent disagreement over the isomorphic effect of globalization has generally revolved around two general perspectives: (1) the "path dependence" perspective (Dobbin, 1994; Milner and Keohane, 1996; Fligstein, 2001; Hall and Soskice, 2001; Campbell, 2004) and (2) the "global convergence" perspective (Sassen, 1996; Meyer et al., 1997; Harvey, 2005; Baccaro and Howell, 2011). In regard to the former perspective, researchers argue that national-level factors condition the impact of globalization on the decision making of state and economic actors in designing and implementing economic policy (Campbell, 2004, 129). The latter perspective argues that national institutions are converging toward a common neoliberal model aimed at increasing competitiveness in the global economy through greater market flexibility. Overall, this contention remains unresolved because evidence for either perspective is largely derived from case-study methodology, which restricts the analytical capacity to examine variation in the effects of globalization on institutions across a few countries without the ability to control for multiple processes.

In the path dependence perspective, one of the most paramount theories is the "varieties of capitalism" perspective which generally argues that institutional change is *incremental* and economic globalization causes a greater *divergence* between coordinated and liberal economies, because of the "bounded experimentation" of firms and the general path dependence of national institutions (Stopford, 1997; Swank, 1998; Scruggs and Lange, 2002; Hall and Thelen, 2009; Kristensen and Morgan, 2012). Accordingly, this process of institutional experimentation and inertia are significantly limited by the pre-existing formal and informal prescriptions of national institutions, because actors utilize local resources, cognitive frames, and ideas to develop solutions for resolving the disruptive effects of economic globalization (Campbell, 2004; Hall and Thelen, 2009). Given the distinctiveness of national institutions, the effects of globalization should significantly vary across countries.

The global convergence perspective includes a myriad of arguments with a common theme: economic globalization requires national governments, firms, and labor organizations to develop flexible labor systems in order to adequately compete in the global economy. In general, this perspective argues, while cross-national variation in institutions persists, competitive pressures from the world economy are causing structural changes in national economies, namely the deindustrialization, and manufacturing employment has significantly decreased (Wood, 1994; Kollmeyer, 2009). As a result of this significant structural change to industrial sectors, national governments are implementing neoliberal policy scripts (Sassen, 1996; Harvey, 2005) and union participation is significantly declining because of decreasing manufacturing employment (Western, 1997; Lee, 2005). Based on these arguments, the effects of globalization should not significantly vary across countries.

Data and analysis

Data on 18 countries (Australia, Austria, Belgium, Canada, Denmark, Finland, France, Germany, Ireland, Italy, Japan, the Netherlands, Norway, New Zealand, Sweden, Switzerland, United Kingdom, and the United States) over a 35-year period (1970 to 2005) is compiled to analyze the effects of economic and political globalization on industrial relation systems.[2] Overall, the sample for the analysis on corporatism contains 544 country-year observations. Since data on industrial conflicts is

---

2   See appendix for a list of country and years in the sample.

only available until 2001, I utilize a second sample of 464 country-year observations for analyzing the effects of globalization on industrial conflict.

Data on corporatism, industrial conflict, trade openness, outward foreign direct investment, and controls is drawn from three sources: the Institutional Characteristics of Trade Unions, Wage Setting, State Intervention and Social Pacts (ICTWSS) database (Visser, 2011); the World Development Indicators (WDI) database (World Bank, 2011); and the Comparative Welfare States (CWS) database (Huber et al., 2004). Data on economic and institutional globalization is drawn from three different sources. First, the number of ILO ratifications is obtained from the ILOLEX database (ILO, 2010). Second, data on IGO memberships is drawn from the Correlates of War database (Pevehouse et al., 2004). Finally, data on imports from non-OECD countries is drawn from OECD trade statistics (OECD, 2011).

Based on the measurement model developed by Baccaro and Howell (2011), corporatism and industrial conflict are measured using two indices derived from an exploratory factor analysis (EFA) of eight variables: (1) wage coordination scale; (2) centralization index; (3) government involvement scale; (4) union density; (5) social security transfers; (6) number of labor disputes; (7) workers involved in labor disputes; and (8) number of working days lost due to disputes. Data on wage coordination, government intervention, centralization, and union density was drawn from the ICTWSS database. Wage coordination is measured as a five-category rank variable where lower ranks indicate fragmented bargaining at the firm-level, while higher ranks indicate nation-wide bargaining (Kenworthy, 2001). Government involvement is measured as a five-category rank variable where lower ranks indicate the state was not involved or minimally involved in wage bargaining, while higher ranks indicate the state was actively participating to either sponsors or imposes wage standards. Centralization is measured with an index that accounts for union authority and union concentration at multiple levels (Iversen, 1999). The centralized index ranges from 0 to 100, where 0 indicates highly decentralized bargaining while 100 indicates highly centralized bargaining. Data on union density is drawn from both the ICTWSS and the CWS. Union density is measured as the net union membership as a proportion of all waged and salaried employees. Social security transfers were measured as the total value of transfers as a percentage of GDP. Data on social security transfers is drawn from both the CWS and OECD databases. Finally, data on the number of industrial disputes, the number of workers involved in disputes (in thousands), and the number of working days lost to labor disputes was drawn from the ILO's *LABORSTA* database and the CWS.

Table 1 shows the factor loadings and eigenvalues of the EFA from a varimax rotated solution. Overall, variables 1–5 load on a single factor (corporatism) while variables 6–8 loaded on a second factor (industrial conflict). The variables are combined into two standardized indices where items are weighted by their factor loading. The corporatism index ranges from –1.52, indicating weak corporatist industrial relations, to 1.40, indicating relatively high levels of corporatism in industrial

Table 1: Exploratory factor analysis – factor loadings and eigenvalues

Variables	Factor 1 Macro-corporatism	Factor 2 Industrial conflict
Government involvement	0.56	–
Wage coordination	0.67	–
Wage centralization	0.86	–
Union density	0.64	–
Social security transfers	0.48	–
Number of labor disputes	–	0.77
Workers involved in strike	–	0.69
Working days lost	–	0.82
Eigenvalue	2.24	1.13

Notes: N=18 (countries), n=464 (country years). Only indicators with factor scores greater than .40 were retained.
Sources: See detailed information in section "Data and analysis."

relations. The industrial conflict index ranges from a rate of –.47, indicating no labor disputes, to 4.73, indicating many intensive and impactful labor disputes. Production globalization is measured with three variables: (1) direct investment outflow; (2) trade openness; and (3) total manufacturing imports from non-OECD countries. Both trade openness and direct investment outflow are drawn from the WDI database, while Southern import penetration is drawn from OECD data. Direct investment outflow measures the net outflow of foreign direct and portfolio investment as a percentage of GDP. Overall, countries range from an outflow of 0% to 26.83% of GDP. Trade openness is measured by total imports and exports as a percentage of GDP. Countries range from 11.25% to 184.42% of GDP. Southern import penetration is measured as the total imports from non-OECD countries as a percentage of total manufacturing imports. Countries range from 2.18% to 56.74% of total manufacturing imports from developing countries. Given the non-normal distribution of all three variables, I use the natural log of each variable in the analysis.

Political globalization is measured with two variables: (1) the number of intergovernmental organization memberships and (2) the total number of ILO ratifications. IGO membership is a total count of full membership in a population of IGOs for a given year. Countries range from 44 memberships to 129 memberships. ILO ratifications are the total count of labor standards ratified by a country. Countries range from 0 to 17 conventions ratified.

In the analysis, I include developmental and political measures in the model as control and mediating variables. First, I include a measure of economic development. Data on GDP per capita (current US$) was drawn from the WDI database. Second, I include measures of labor market performance, namely the labor force participation rate and the unemployment rate. Both variables are drawn from the WDI database and the CWS database. Third, I include a measure of industrializa-

Table 2: Summary statistics of outcomes and covariates

Variable	n	Mean	Standard deviation	Minimum	Maximum
Macro-corporatism index	544	−0.03	0.74	−1.52	1.40
Industrial conflict index	464	−0.002	0.82	−0.47	4.73
Southern import penetration	544	12.82	9.07	2.18	56.74
Outward foreign direct investment	544	2.28	3.24	0.00	26.83
Trade openness	544	60.05	28.81	11.25	184.42
Number of ILO ratifications	544	8.46	5.07	0.00	17.00
Number of IGO memberships	544	86.30	16.49	44.00	129.00
Industrial labor force	544	27.71	5.93	1.50	46.69
Labor force participation	544	47.64	5.26	34.53	59.98
Unemployment rate	544	6.17	2.99	0.10	15.70
GDP per capita	544	19 360.93	10 872.50	2 221.40	65 324.15
Cumulative leftists seats	544	14.50	11.63	0.00	50.61

Sources: See detailed information in section "Data and analysis."

tion based on the percentage of labor force in manufacturing sectors. Data on industrial employment is drawn from the WDI database. Finally, to account for the effect of leftist political parties on both outcomes, I include the cumulative number of seats of leftist political parties. Data on the cumulative number of seats is drawn from the CWS database and updated to 2005 using annual issues of the *European Journal of Political Research*. Table 2 provides summary statistics for both outcomes and covariates.

Analytical strategy

In order to estimate the effects of the covariates on both outcomes and the cross-national variation in the effects, I utilize fixed-effects (FEM) and random-coefficient models (RCM). Since the hierarchical structure of the panel data violates the necessary conditions for B.L.U.E. estimation using ordinary least squares, I use a generalized least squared estimator adjusted for unobserved time- and country-invariant heterogeneity in the FEMs and random unobserved heterogeneity in the RCMs. For estimating the level of the total effects, I use a two-way fixed-effects estimator with robust-cluster standard errors. These models provide the most robust estimation by controlling for unobserved country and period heterogeneity using fixed intercepts for n−1 countries and t−1 periods (Wooldridge, 2002). For two-way fixed-effects models (FEMs) the regression equation was as follows:

$$y_{it} = \alpha_{it} + \sum \beta_{kit} X'_{kit} + \varepsilon_{it} + u_i + j_t$$

where y_{it} is the level of macro-corporatism or industrial conflict in country i at time t, which is a function of k covariates ($\beta_{kit} X'_{kit}$), an overall intercept(α_{it}), residuals (ε_{it}), a vector of country-specific intercepts (u_i) and a vector of period-specific intercepts (j_t).

I utilize random-coefficient models (RCMs) for estimating both the level of, and variation in, the effects across the countries. This model applies a dual data generating process to the data, which estimates an intercept measuring cross-national variation in country-specific means (e.g., random-effects) and a parameter measuring cross-national variation in the coefficients based on country-specific means of covariates (Rabe-Hesketh and Skrondal, 2012). For random-coefficient models, the regression equation is as follows:

$$y_{it} = \alpha_{it} + \Sigma\, \beta_{kit} X'_{kit} + \zeta_{1i}\, \alpha_{it} + \zeta_{2i} X_{it} + \varepsilon_{it}$$

where y_{it} is the level of corporatism or industrial conflict in country i at time t, which is a function of the summation of k covariates ($\beta_{kit} X'_{kit}$), an overall intercept (α_{it}), the product of the overall mean and the unit variance in means (ζ_{1i}), residuals (ε_{it}), and the product of country-specific variation of a parameter (ζ_{2i}) and the covariate. The significance of ζ_{2i} indicates whether the key parameter, e.g., the effect of a single co-variate, varies across countries. If the effect of a covariate significantly varies across countries, it suggests that the effect of the covariate is conditioned by unobserved country-specific heterogeneity.

Results

Table 3 shows the results of the two-way FEMs for corporatism and industrial employment. Models 1–4 provide estimates of the partial effects of production globalization, political globalization, strength of leftist parties, and macroeconomic conditions on corporatism. Model 5 estimates the partial effects of production globalization on industrial employment net of the developmental controls from Model 2. Overall, the models suggest that production globalization has a negative indirect effect on corporatism through deindustrialization. Political globalization has a negative direct effect on corporatist relations.

According to Model 1, net of investment outflow and trade openness, Southern import penetration is negatively associated with macro-corporatism. For every 1% increase in the share of manufacturing imports from developing countries, corporatist relations decline by a score of –.291. However, the inclusion of macroeconomic controls in Model 2 dramatically decreases the coefficient of Southern import penetration from –.291 to –.07 and the coefficient is no longer significant ($p > .1$). Based on the theoretical discussion earlier, this substantial change in the coefficient of Southern import penetration is primarily caused by the inclusion of industrial employment in the model. In fact, only industrial employment had a significant effect in Model 2 ($p < .1$). For a 1% increase in the manufacturing share of the labor force, corporatist industrial relations increase by a score of .04 in the corporatist

Table 3: Two-way fixed-effects models of corporatism and industrial employment, 1970–2005

	1 MC	2 MC	3 MC	4 MC	5 IE
Southern import penetration (ln)	−0.291*	−0.069			−1.229*
	(0.138)	(0.202)			(0.591)
Trade openness (ln)	−0.058	0.199			−3.938
	(0.288)	(0.277)			(2.409)
Outward FDI (ln)	−0.017	−0.006			−0.249
	(0.039)	(0.034)			(0.201)
Industrial employment		0.041+			−
		(0.020)			−
Labor force participation rate		−0.025			−0.129
		(0.018)			(0.113)
Unemployment rate		0.023			−0.557***
		(0.019)			(0.117)
GDP per capita (ln)		0.134			−3.579**
		(0.161)			(1.247)
Number of ILO ratifications			−0.322**	−0.331***	
			(0.092)	(0.083)	
Number of IGO memberships			−0.008*	0.002	
			(0.004)	(0.006)	
Strength of leftist parties				0.034+	
				(0.017)	
Constant	0.876	−2.029	3.385***	3.034***	64.600***
	(0.900)	(2.480)	(0.716)	(0.667)	(10.910)
R^2	0.170	0.273	0.156	0.234	0.613

Notes: Period indicators not shown. Robust-cluster standard errors in parentheses. N=18 (countries), n=544 (country years). MC=Macro-Corporatism Index; IE=Industrial Employment. + $p<.05$ (1-tail), * $p<.05$, ** $p<.01$, *** $p<.001$.
Sources: See detailed information in section "Data and analysis."

relations index. This suggests that the mechanism explaining the relationship between Southern import penetration and corporatism in Model 1 is the size of the industrial labor force.

Model 5 directly tests whether production globalization significantly reduces the share of the labor force in the manufacturing sector. Based on the results, only Southern import penetration adversely affected the size of the industrial labor force. Net of trade openness and capital outflow, a 1% increase in the share of manufacturing imports from developing countries was associated with a 1.2% decrease in the manufacturing share of the labor force. Even though all three measures of economic globalization were negatively associated with industrial employment, only manufacturing imports from developing countries appears to have an indirect relationship with corporatist relations. In order for a mediation effect to exist, the indirect variables need to have a significant association with the outcome when the mediating variable is not included in the model and an insignificant association when the mediating variable is included in the model (Baron and Kenny, 1986). While outward foreign direct investment and trade openness exhibit negative relationships with industrial employment and corporatism, only Southern import penetration exhibits significant relationships with corporatism and industrial employment. In order to test whether industrial employment mediates the effects of production globalization, I conduct a Sobel test (Sobel, 1982)[3] using the coefficients and standard errors for Southern import penetration and industrial employment from Models 1, 2, and 5. Based on the results (t=6.43, p<.001), it appears that industrial employment mediates the effects of production globalization on corporatism. Overall, evidence from the corporatism and industrial employment models and the Sobel test suggests that production globalization indirectly reduces corporatism through its negative effect on industrial employment.

Models 3 and 4 estimate the partial effects of IGO memberships and ILO convention ratifications, net of each other and the strength of leftist political parties. Based on the results, the number of ILO convention ratifications is the most robust effect of political globalization on corporatism. However, the coefficient of ILO convention ratifications is negatively signed which indicates that for every additional ratification corporatist relations declined by an index score of .32. Even when controlling for strength of leftists parties, the coefficient remains relatively the same. Surprisingly, the number of IGO memberships had no significant effect on corporatist relations when controlling for strength of leftist parties. Even when only controlling for ILO ratifications, the effect of IGO memberships was small, where for every additional membership the corporatist relations declined by an index score of less than .01. Not surprisingly, when controlling for political globalization, strength of leftist parties is positively associated with corporatist relations, where for every additional cumulative seat held by leftist parties, the corporatist relations increased by an index score of .03.

Overall, according to the results, political globalization negatively affects corporatist relations. I argue, the normative and mimetic pressures of ILO conventions are ineffective for promoting corporatism because the ratification of these agreements is purely ceremonial and symbolic. Since the ILO lacks coercive mechanisms for ensuring the implementation of labor policy, national governments are able to legitimate themselves in the world polity through ratifying conventions while never enacting more industrial policy that promotes corporatist decision-making.

---

3   I used the following test: $t=(\tau-\tau')/SE$, where τ is the coefficient for Southern import penetration in Model 1 and τ' is the coefficient for Southern import penetration in Model 2. The SE is calculated using the following equation: $\sqrt{(\alpha2\ \sigma2\beta + \beta2\sigma2\alpha)}$, where α is coefficient of Southern import penetration in Model 5 and $\sigma\alpha$ is the standard error of the coefficient in Model 5. β is the coefficient of industrial employment in Model 2 and $\sigma\beta$ is the standard error of the coefficient in Model 2. Significance was determined using a t-distribution.

Table 4: Two-way fixed-effects models of industrial conflict and union density, 1970–2000

	1 IC	2 IC	3 IC	4 IC	5 UD
Southern import penetration (ln)	−0.745[+]	−0.033			−0.754*
	(0.364)	(0.259)			(0.367)
Trade openness (ln)	−0.520	−0.492			−4.083
	(0.741)	(0.570)			(4.074)
Outward FDI (ln)	−0.103	0.024			−0.261
	(0.132)	(0.138)			(0.809)
Industrial employment		−0.034			1.026*
		(0.063)			(0.487)
Labor force participation rate		0.108**			−0.604
		(0.036)			(0.358)
Unemployment rate		−0.089			0.717*
		(0.053)			(0.315)
GDP per capita (ln)		−0.860**			1.706
		(0.287)			(2.871)
Union density		0.056**		0.055**	
		(0.017)		(0.015)	
Number of ILO ratifications			−0.020	−0.034	
			(0.240)	(0.211)	
Number of IGO memberships			−0.042***	−0.049**	
			(0.010)	(0.013)	
Strength of leftist parties				0.052	
				(0.040)	
Constant	9.106**	9.645	8.986***	6.560**	63.960**
	(2.553)	(5.550)	(2.057)	(1.657)	(18.290)
R^2	0.109	0.254	0.164	0.250	0.279

Notes: Period indicators not shown. Robust-cluster standard errors in parentheses. N=18 (countries), n=464 (country years). IC=Industrial Conflict Index; UD=Union Density. + p<.05 (1-tail), * p<.05, ** p<.01, *** p<.001.
Sources: See detailed information in section "Data and analysis."

Table 4 shows the results of two-way FEMs for the industrial conflict index and union density. Models 1, 2, and 5 estimate the direct effects of production globalization on industrial conflict and union density, while Models 3 and 4 estimate the direct effects of political globalization on industrial conflict. Overall, production globalization indirectly influences industrial conflict through its negative effect on union density, while political globalization directly reduces industrial conflict.

Model 1 provides the estimates for the partial effects of production globalization. Similar to the corporatism models, out of the three measures of production globalization, only Southern import penetration had an effect on industrial conflict, where for every 1% increase in the share of manufacturing imports from developing countries industrial conflict decreases by an index score of .75. However, in Model

2, with the inclusion of developmental measures and union density in the model, this effect was reduced to zero in the population. In Model 2, only the labor force participation rate, economic development, and union density had significant effects on industrial conflict.

Based on the theoretical discussion, the effect of Southern import penetration should be mediated by union density. In Model 5 union density is regressed on the measures for production globalization and the developmental controls. Based on the results, the only measure of production globalization that is significantly associated with union density is Southern import penetration. In fact, for every 1% increase in the share of manufacturing imports from developing countries, the proportion of waged and salaried workforce in unions decreased by nearly 1%. Based on a Sobel test using the standard errors and coefficients from Models 1, 2, and 5, it appears that Southern import penetration was mediated by union density (t=28, p<.001). Given the positive effect of union density on industrial conflict, as manufacturing imports from developing countries erode the industrial base of developed economies, union membership suffers significant decline. The decline of union representation reduces the associational power of labor and its capacity to enact conflict-based strategies for institution building. I argue that globalized production increases the risk of acquiring union membership, which, in turn, reduces the capacity for unions to engage in collective labor disputes and work stoppages.

Similar to its effect on corporatism, political globalization reduces industrial conflict. More specifically, the number of IGO memberships is negatively associated with the industrial conflict index, where for every additional membership, industrial conflict decreases by an index score of .05. Even when controlling for both union density and the strength of leftist parties, IGO memberships reduces the industrial conflict. The mechanism underlying this effect is based on the idea that as countries increasingly engage in international institutions, the scale of capital-labor relations fundamentally shifts from national contexts to international contexts (Keck and Sikkink, 1998; Kay, 2011). Given the infancy of the international labor movement, this scalar shift substantially favors international capital over labor. Whether this signifies a scalar change in industrial conflict or the decoupling of a global model of labor regulation and national legislation remains unanswered and would require further research.

Table 5 shows the results of the random-coefficient models for both corporatism and industrial conflict. For the purpose of evaluating cross-national differences in the effects of economic and political globalization, the most important parameters in Models 1–4 are the standard deviations of the coefficients for Southern import penetration, ILO ratifications, and IGO memberships. According to the results, each effect significantly varied across countries. The average difference between the mean effect and country-specific effects of Southern import penetration is a score of .42 for corporatism and .12 for industrial conflict. The average difference between the mean effect and the country-specific effect of ILO ratification is about a score

Table 5: Random-coefficient models of corporatism and industrial conflict

	1 MC	2 IC	3 MC	4 IC
Southern import penetration (ln)	−0.169* (0.079)	−0.410* (0.202)		
Trade openness (ln)	0.085 (0.104)	−0.880* (0.399)		
Outward FDI (ln)	−0.037* (0.018)	−0.069 (0.075)		
Number of ILO ratifications			−0.051* (0.025)	0.131 (0.084)
Number of IGO memberships			−0.009*** (0.001)	−0.049*** (0.011)
Constant	0.176 (0.430)	9.521*** (1.838)	1.688*** (0.455)	8.075*** (1.363)
σ_β (Southern import penetration)	0.422*** (0.084)	0.119*** (0.026)		
σ_β (ILO ratifications)			1.845*** (0.394)	
σ_β (IGO memberships)				0.055*** (0.011)
Between-country standard deviation	0.871*** (0.172)	5.964*** (1.193)	1.711*** (0.396)	6.044*** (1.093)
Log likelihood	−94.089	−624.749	−168.076	−729.855
n	544	464	544	464

Notes: MC=Macro-Corporatism Index; IC=Industrial Conflict Index. * p<.05, ** p<.01, *** p<.001.
Sources: See detailed information in section "Data and analysis."

of 1.85 for corporatism, which is substantial compared to the overall range of the index. Finally, the average difference between the mean effect and country-specific effects of IGO memberships is about a score of .06 for industrial conflict. Compared to the average effects, the standard deviation of the effects are, for the most part, larger, which suggests that the effects of economic and political globalization on corporatism and industrial conflict substantially vary across advanced capitalist countries.

Overall, the results of Table 5 provide strong evidence for how unobserved country-specific heterogeneity moderates the effects of economic and political globalization on corporatism and industrial conflict. This evidence provides support for the main contention of the path dependence perspective, where institutional change is caused by national-level actors and institutions employing a diverse range of strategies developed from local resources, cognitive frames, and ideas to cope with the disruptive effects of exogenous shocks (Hall and Thelen, 2009). Whether this difference in effect is the product of institutional inertia or national experimentation remains unresolved. More importantly, the proximate national-level processes conditioning the effects of production and political globalization are unclear. Future research needs to unpack these country-specific factors and examine how they condition the isomorphic effects of political and economic globalization.

Discussion and conclusion

Returning to the question of whether economic globalization affects the industrial relation systems of advanced capitalist countries, the evidence suggests that manufacturing imports from developing countries indirectly reduces corporatism and industrial conflict. Consistent with the hypothesis on the indirect effects of production globalization, size of the industrial labor force and unionization mediates the effects of Southern import penetration. Estimates from fixed-effects models and Sobel mediation tests suggest that the globalization of production induces processes of deindustrialization and deunionization which reduce the bargaining and associational power of organized labor (Sassen, 1996; Alderson, 1999; Brady and Denniston, 2006; Kollmeyer, 2009). I argue this asymmetry in power between capital and labor results in a neoliberal reform of industrial relation systems, which aims to increase market flexibility through dismantling corporatist institutions and reduce collective disputes.

The global dispersion of production and the integration of unskilled and low-waged manufacturing labor from developing economies into global production networks have significantly affected labor markets in developed economies. Specifically, the relative demand for low- and semi-skilled manufacturing labor in developed economies declines, with an increase in the imports of cheap component and final manufacturing goods from low-waged developing countries (Wood, 1994). As a consequence, the decline of industrial employment in advanced capitalist countries reduces the marketplace bargaining power of manufacturing labor. As firms in developed countries specialize in their core competencies, the incentive to engage in corporatist decision making declines, since these firms are not reliant on maintaining cooperative relations with organized labor.

According to the results, the globalization of production causes a reduction in industrial conflict through the process of deunionization. The offshoring and outsourcing of labor-intensive production processes to low-wage economies increases the risk of participating in unions, because firms are able to utilize the threat of relocation to deter workers from joining.

Further, the globalization of production causes a decline in industrial employment, which forces workers to migrate into traditionally non-union service sectors which further reduce the unionization of the workforce (Western, 1995; Ebbinghaus and Visser, 1999). The total effect is the continued decline in union membership. Since membership is the main determinant of successful collective disputes (Ahlquist, 2010), a decline in membership reduces the rate of industrial conflict.

One of the most significant empirical gaps in the literature is the paucity of analysis examining the effect of political globalization on industrial relation systems.
Based on the regression analysis, as countries integrate into the world polity through
joining IGOs and ratifying ILO conventions, industrial relation systems are becoming increasingly less corporatist and industrial conflict is becoming less common.
Even though ILO conventions promote collective bargaining and corporatist relations, in general, the evidence suggests there is a significant decoupling between the
ceremonial ratification of conventions and actual policy implementation. Arguably,
this decoupling process is not caused by a lack of public resources, as in developing
countries (see Meyer et al., 1997, 154). It appears that advanced capitalist countries are able to resist the isomorphic pressure of global norms and culture. Given
the increasing demand for consumer-based and non-governmental regulation of
labor (Bartley, 2007) and the ILO's lack of enforcement mechanisms for ensuring
implementation (Cao, 2009), it's not too surprising that ILO convention ratifications are associated with declining corporatist relations. Often these conventions
fail to prescribe specific policy reforms and, further, have no requirement to institute particular policies that effectively promote collective bargaining. While states
are concerned with their international reputation, it seems they are also concerned
with maintaining global competitiveness through implementing neoliberal reforms
for labor market institutions. Therefore, these countries are able to improve their
international reputation while failing to institute effective policy reforms.

An alternative explanation for the decoupling between ceremonial ratification
and policy implementation is based on the interpretation of international institutions as fields of power struggles between capital and labor (Boswell and Chase-
Dunn, 2000; Robinson, 2004). Drawing upon a "conflict perspective" of the world
polity (Beckfield, 2003; 2010), international institutions are viewed as domains of
material and ideational struggle between nation-states and transnational conflict
groups. In regard to industrial relations, this struggle is primarily between global
capital and national labor. Given the proclivity of global capital to advocate and pursue neoliberal reform, it's not surprising that the policy scripts promoted by international institutions suppress corporatism and the capacity for labor to disrupt work
processes as a strategy in bargaining over wages and working conditions. Since the
international labor movement is nascent, it has yet to obtain adequate support in
international institutions and is unable to effectively promote the interest of labor
over capital in international institutions. Therefore, the asymmetry of power in the
world polity is expected to continue the general trend toward liberalized industrial
relation systems.

Additionally, the results can be interpreted as tentative evidence for the rescal-
ing of opportunity structures from national to international institutions (Kay, 2011),
which means sector- or industry-level strikes might be ineffective for gaining concessions from multinational firms. Until labor starts to develop an international
strategy based on the formation of cross-border alliances, it's unlikely that they can

exploit the emergence of a new international structure of opportunity. Thus, at least in the short-term, international institutions and the development of global models will primarily promote the interest of global capital. This finding substantiates the need to include the world polity perspective into analysis on global integration and institutional change (Meyer, 2000; 2007; Cao, 2009). More importantly, these findings suggest that future research needs to theorize and empirically elucidate how specific mechanisms of the world polity operate to advance neoliberal policy scripts and whether emerging world culture is the product of asymmetries in institutional power.

The second part of the analysis aims to provide evidence for adjudicating the long-standing debate on the persistence of cross-national variation in industrial relation systems. According to the path dependence perspective, the effects of globalization vary across countries because of differences in the institutional configurations, culture, and histories (Hall and Soskice, 2001; Campbell, 2004). For example, globalization should have a more disruptive effect on industrial relations in liberal market economies because labor markets are more exposed to, and articulated by, macroeconomic exogenous shocks induced by the global economy. According to the random-coefficient models, the effects of Southern import penetration, IGO participation, and the ratification of ILO conventions on corporatism and industrial conflict significantly vary across advanced capitalist countries. What remain unanswered are the historical, institutional, and structural factors that moderate processes of political and economic globalization. Given the findings of this chapter, it's imperative that future research accounts for the interactive nature of international and national processes. More importantly, these findings call for a new integrative perspective on globalization and institutional change that explains how economic and political processes restructure national institutions to induce new institutional experimentation amongst national actors.

The general purpose of the chapter is to determine whether globalization induces institutional change in the industrial relation systems of advanced capitalist countries. Based on the results of two-way FEMs and RCMs, Southern import penetration indirectly reduces corporatism and industrial conflict, while political globalization directly reduces corporatism and industrial conflicts. However, rather than assume that these effects are homogenous across countries, the chapter finds significant variation in these effects across advanced capitalist countries. Furthermore, this chapter contributes to the literature by providing evidence from systematic and comparative analysis for the adjudication of the ongoing debate over whether globalization is causing a rapid neoliberal reform of industrial relation systems. Consistent with previous research (Baccaro and Howell, 2011), the negative effects of political and economic globalization on corporatism and industrial conflict, as well as the heterogeneity of effects, suggest that corporatist institutions are being reconfigured to increase labor market flexibility and reduce collective disputes and work stoppages. Overall, the findings should be interpreted as a call for more systematic and comparative research on the relationship between globalization and industrial relations.

Acknowledgements

I thank Matthew C. Mahutga and other participants in the UCR PEGSC Workshop for helpful comments on an earlier draft.

References

Ahlquist, John. 2010. Building Strategic Capacity: The Political Underpinning of Coordinated Wage Bargaining. *American Political Science Review,* 104(1): 171–188.

Alderson, Arthur. 1999. Explaining Deindustrialization: Globalization, Failure, or Success? *American Sociological Review,* 64(5): 701–721.

Baccaro, Lucio, and Chris Howell. 2011. A Common Neoliberal Trajectory: The Transformation of Industrial Relations in Advanced Capitalism. *Politics and Society,* 39(4): 521–563.

Baron, Reuben, and David Kenny. 1986. The Moderator-Mediator Variable Distinction in Social Psychological Research: Conceptual, Strategic, and Statistical Considerations. *Journal of Personality and Social Psychology,* 51(6): 1173–1182.

Bartley, Tim. 2007. Institutional Emergence in an Era of Globalization: The Rise of Transnational Private Regulation of Labor and Environmental Conditions. *American Journal of Sociology,* 113(2): 297–351.

Beckfield, Jason. 2003. Inequality in the World Polity: The Structure of International Organization. *American Sociological Review,* 68(3): 401–424.

Beckfield, Jason. 2010. The Social Structure of the World Polity. *American Journal of Sociology,* 115(4): 1018–1068.

Blau, Francine, and Lawrence Kahn. 2002. *At Home and Abroad: U.S. Labor-Market Performance in International Perspective.* New York: Russell Sage Foundation.

Boli, John, and George Thomas. 1997. World Culture in the World Polity: A Century of International Non-Governmental Organization. *American Sociological Review,* 62(2): 171–190.

Boswell, Terry, and Christopher Chase-Dunn. 2000. *The Spiral of Capitalism and Socialism: Toward Global Democracy.* Boulder, CO: Lynne Rienner.

Brady, David, and Ryan Denniston. 2006. Economic Globalization, Industrialization, and Deindustrialization in Affluent Democracies. *Social Forces,* 85(1): 297–329.

Calmfors, Lars, and John Driffill. 1988. Bargaining Structure, Corporatism, and Macroeconomic Performance. *Economic Policy,* 6: 13–61.

Campbell, John. 2004. *Institutional Change and Globalization.* Princeton: Princeton University Press.

Cao, Xun. 2009. Networks of Intergovernmental Organizations and Convergence in Domestic Economic Policies. *International Studies Quarterly,* 53: 1095–1130.

Contractor, Farok, Vikas Kumar, Sumit Kundu, and Torben Pedersen. 2010. Reconceptualizing the Firm in a World of Outsourcing and Offshoring: The Organizational and Geographical Relocation of High-Value Company Functions. *Journal of Management Studies,* 47(8): 1417–1433.

Crouch, Colin. 2000. The Snakes and Ladders of Twenty-First-Century Trade Unionism. *Oxford Review of Economic Policy,* 16(1): 70–83.

Dicken, Peter. 2003. *Global Shift: Reshaping the Global Economic Map in the 21ˢᵗ Century.* 4ᵗʰ edition. London: Sage.

DiMaggio, Paul, and Walter Powell. 1983. The Iron Cage Revisited: Institutional Isomorphism and Collective Rationality in Organizational Fields. *American Sociological Review,* 48(2): 147–160.

Dobbin, Frank. 1994. *Forging Industrial Policy: The United States, Britain, and France in the Railway Age.* New York: Cambridge University Press.

Ebbinghaus, Bernhard, and Jelle Visser. 1999. When Institutions Matter: Union Growth and Decline in Western Europe, 1950–1995. *European Sociological Review,* 15(2): 135–158.

Edwards, Paul, and Richard Hyman. 1994. "Strikes and Industrial Conflict: Peace in Europe?" In Richard Hyman and Anthony Frener (eds.), *New Frontiers in European Industrial Relations.* Oxford, UK: Blackwell.

Esping-Andersen, Gosta. 1990. *Three Worlds of Welfare Capitalism.* Princeton: Princeton University Press.

Fligstein, Neil. 2001. *The Architecture of Markets: An Economic Sociology of 21ˢᵗ Century Capitalist Societies.* Princeton: Princeton University Press.

Gereffi, Gary, John Humphrey, and Timothy Sturgeon. 2005. The Governance of Global Value Chains. *Review of International Political Economy,* 12(1): 78–104.

Glyn, Andrew (ed.). 2001. *Social Democracy in Neoliberal Times. The Left and Economic Policy Since 1980.* New York: Oxford University Press.

Grahl, John, and Paul Teague. 1997. Is the European Social Model Fragmenting? *New Political Economy,* 2(3): 405–426.

Hall, Peter, and David Soskice (eds.). 2001. *Varieties of Capitalism: The Institutional Foundation of Comparative Advantage.* Oxford: Oxford University Press.

Hall, Peter, and Kathleen Thelen. 2009. Institutional Change in the Varieties of Capitalism. *Socio-Economic Review,* (7): 7–34.

Hamann, Kerstin, Alison Johnston, and John Kelly. 2012. Unions against Governments: Explaining General Strikes in Western Europe, 1980–2006. *Comparative Political Studies,* 46(9): 1030–1057.

Harrison, Reginald J. 1980. *Pluralism and Corporatism: The Political Evolution of Modern Democracies.* London: Allen & Unwin.

Harvey, David. 2005. *A Brief History of Neoliberalism.* Oxford: Oxford University Press.

Henisz, Witold, Bennet Zelner, and Mauro Guillen. 2005. The Worldwide Diffusion of Market-Oriented Infrastructure Reform, 1977–1999. *American Sociological Review,* 70(6): 871–897.

Huber, Evelyne, Charles Ragin, John Stephens, David Brady, and Jason Beckfield. 2004. Comparative Welfare States Data Set. Northwestern University, University of North Carolina, Duke University, and Indiana University.

ILO (International Labour Organization). 2010. Information System on International Labour Standards. URL: http://www.ilo.org/dyn/normlex/en (accessed April 29, 2010).

ILO (International Labour Organization). 2011. Laborsta Database. URL: http://laborsta.ilo.org/ (accessed February 11, 2011).

Iversen, Torben. 1999. *Contested Economic Institutions: The Politics of Macroeconomics and Wage Bargaining in Advanced Democracies.* Cambridge: Cambridge University Press.

Kaplinsky, Raphael. 2005. *Globalization, Poverty and Inequality.* Malden: Polity Press.

Kay, Tamara. 2011. *NAFTA and the Politics of Labor Transnationalism.* Cambridge: Cambridge University Press.

Keck, Margarita, and Kathryn Sikkink. 1998. *Activists beyond Borders: Advocacy Networks in International Politics.* Ithaca: Cornell University Press.

Kenworthy, Lane. 2001. Wage-Setting Measures: A Survey and Assessment. *World Politics,* 54(1): 57–98.

Kollmeyer, Christopher. 2003. Globalization, Class Compromise, and American Exceptionalism: Political Change in 16 Advanced Capitalist Countries. *Critical Sociology,* 29(3): 369–391.

Kollmeyer, Christopher. 2009. Explaining Deindustrialization: How Affluence, Productivity Growth, and Globalization Diminish Manufacturing Employment. *American Journal of Sociology,* 114(6): 1644–1674.

Korpi, Walter, and Michael Shalev. 1979. Strikes, Industrial Relations, and Class Conflict in Capitalist Societies. *British Journal of Sociology,* 30(2): 164–187.

Kristensen, Peer Hull, and Glenn Morgan. 2012. From Institutional Change to Experimentalist Institutions. *Industrial Relations,* 51(1): 413–437.

Krugman, Paul. 2008. Trade and Wages, Reconsidered. *Brooking Papers on Economic Activity,* Spring 2008: 103–137.

Lee, Cheol-Sung. 2005. International Migration, Deindustrialization and Union Decline in 16 Affluent OECD Countries, 1962–1997. *Social Forces,* 84(1): 71–88.

Mahutga, Matthew. 2012. When Do Value Chains Go Global? A Theory of the Spatialization of Global Value Chains. *Global Networks,* 12(1): 1–21.

Meyer, John. 2000. Globalization: Sources and Effects on National States and Societies. *International Sociology,* 15(2): 233–248.

Meyer, John. 2007. Globalization Theory and Trends. *International Journal of Comparative Sociology,* 48(4): 261–273.

Meyer, John W., John Boli, George Thomas, and Francisco O. Ramirez. 1997. World Society and the Nation-State. *American Journal of Sociology,* 103(1): 144–181.

Mills, Melinda, Hans-Peter Blossfeld, Sandra Buchholz, Dirk Hofäcker, Fabrizio Bernardi, and Heather Hofmeister. 2008. Converging Divergences? An International Comparison of the Impact of Globalization on Industrial Relations and Employment Careers. *International Sociology,* 23(4): 561–595.

Milner, Helen, and Robert Keohane. 1996. "Internationalization and Domestic Politics: An Introduction." In Robert Keohane and Helen Milner (eds.), *Internationalization and Domestic Politics.* New York: Cambridge University Press.

Mion, Giordano, and Linke Zhu. 2012. Import Competition From Offshoring to China: A Curse or Blessing for Firms? *Journal of International Economics,* 89(1): 202–215.

Molina, Oscar, and Marthin Rhodes. 2002. Corporatism: The Past, Present, and Future of a Concept. *Annual Review of Political Science,* 5: 305–331.

Mudambi, Ram, and Markus Venzin. 2010. The Strategic Nexus of Offshoring and Outsourcing Decisions. *Journal of Management Studies,* 47(8): 1510–1533.

OECD (Organization for Economic Cooperation and Development). 2011. *Main Economic Indicators Database.* Paris: OECD Statistics.

Pampel, Fred, and John Williamson. 1988. Welfare Spending Advanced Industrial Democracies, 1950–1980. *American Journal of Sociology,* 93(6): 1424–1456.

Pevehouse, Jon, Timothy Nordstrom, and Kevin Warnke. 2004. *Intergovernmental Organizations, 1815–2000: A New Correlates of War Data Set.* URL: http://www.correlatesofwar.org/COW2%20Data/IGOs/IGOv2-1.htm (accessed March 07, 2010).

Pierson, Paul. 1994. *Dismantling the Welfare State? Reagan, Thatcher, and the Politics of Retrenchment.* Cambridge: Cambridge University Press.

Rabe-Hesketh, Sophia, and Anders Skrondal. 2012. *Multilevel and Longitudinal Modeling Using Stats, Volume 1.* College Station: Stata Press.

Regini Mario. 1995. *Uncertain Boundaries: The Social and Political Construction of European Economies.* Cambridge, UK: Cambridge University Press.

Revenga, Ana. 1992. Exporting Jobs? The Impact of Import Competition on Employment and Wages in U.S. Manufacturing. *The Quarterly Journal of Economics,* 107(1): 255–284.

Rhodes, Martin. 2001. "The Political Economy of Social Pacts: 'Competitive Corporatism' and European Welfare State Reform." In Paul Pierson (ed.), *The New Politics of the Welfare State.* Oxford, UK: Oxford University Press.

Robinson, William. 2004. *A Theory of Global Capitalism: Production, Class, and State in a Transnational World.* Baltimore: The Johns Hopkins University Press.

Sassen, Saskia. 1996. *Losing Control: Sovereignty in an Age of Globalization.* New York: Columbia University Press.

Schmitter, Phillippe. 1974. Still the Century of Corporatism? *The Review of Politics,* 36: 85–131.

Schmitter, Philippe. 1982. "Reflections On Where the Theory of Neo-Corporatism has Gone and Where the Praxis of Neo-Corporatism May Be Going." In Gerhard Lembruch and P.hilippe Schmitter (eds.), *Patterns of Corporatist Policy Making.* London: Sage.

Scruggs, Lyle, and Peter Lange. 2002. Where Have All the Members Gone? Globalization, Institutions, and Union Density. *Journal of Politics,* 64(1): 126–153.

Shalev, Michael. 1992. "The Resurgence of Labour Quiescence." In Mario Regini (ed.), *The Future of Labour Movements*. London: Sage.

Sobel, Michael. 1982. Asymptotic Confidence Intervals for Indirect Effects in Structural Equation Modeling. *Sociological Methodology*, 13: 290–312.

vanced Industrialized Countries. *Oxford Review of Economic Policy*, 6: 36–61.

Standing, Guy. 2008. The ILO: An Agency of Globalization. *Development and Change*, 39(3): 355–384.

Stopford, John M. 1997. "Implications for National Governments." In J.H. Dunning (ed.), *Governments, Globalization, and International Business*. New York: Oxford University Press.

Swank, Duane. 1998. Funding the Welfare State: Globalization and the Taxation of Business in Advanced Market Economies. *Political Studies*, 46(3): 671–692.

Therborn, Goran. 1998. Does Corporatism Really Matter? The Economic Crisis and Issues of Political Theory. *Journal of Public Policy*, 7(3): 259–284.

Traxler, Franz. 1995. "Farewell to Labour Market Associations? Organized Versus Disorganized Decentralization as a Map of Industrial Relations." In Colin Crouch and Franz Traxler (eds.), *Organized Industrial Relations in Europe: What Future?* Aldershot, UK: Avebury.

Traxler, Franz, Sabine Blaschke, and Bernhard Kittel. 2001. *National Labour Relations in Internationalized Markets*. New York: Oxford University Press.

Traxler, Franz, and Bernhard Kittel. 2000. The Bargaining System and Performance: A Comparison of 18 OECD Countries. *Comparative Politics*, 33(9): 1154–1190.

Visser, Jelle. 2011. *Database on Institutional Characteristics of Trade Unions, Wage Setting, State Intervention and Social Pacts in 34 Countries Between 1960 and 2007.* Code Book. Amsterdam: Amsterdam Institute for Advanced Labour Studies. URL: http://www.uva-aias.net/208 (accessed October 15, 2011).

Wallerstein, Michael, Miriam Golden, and Peter Lange. 1997. Unions, Employers' Associations, and Wage-Setting Institutions in Northern and Central Europe, 1950–1992. *Industrial and Labor Relations Review*, 50(3): 379–401.

Western, Bruce. 1995. A Comparative Study of Working-Class Disorganization: Union Decline in Eighteen Advanced Capitalist Countries. *American Sociological Review*, 60(2): 179–201.

Wood, Adrian. 1994. *North-South Trade, Employment and Inequality: Changing Fortunes in a Skill-Driven World*. New York: Oxford University Press.

Wooldridge, Jeffrey. 2002. *Econometric Analysis of Cross Section and Panel Data*. Cambridge, MA: MIT Press.

World Bank. 2011. *World Development Indicators Database*. Washington, DC: The World Bank.

Appendix: Country and years in samples

Corporatism sample		Industrial conflict sample	
Australia	1970–2005	Australia	1970–2000
Austria	1971–2005	Austria	1971–2000
Belgium	1975–2005	Belgium	1975–2000
Canada	1971–2005	Canada	1971–2000
Denmark	1976–2005	Denmark	1976–2000
Finland	1976–2004	Finland	1976–2000
France	1976–2005	France	1976–1999
Germany	1972–2005	Germany	1972–2000
Ireland	1982–2005	Ireland	1982–2000
Italy	1971–2005	Italy	1971–2000
Japan	1978–2005	Japan	1978–2000
Netherlands	1970–2005	Netherlands	1970–2000
New Zealand	1973–2005	New Zealand	1973–2000
Norway	1976–2005	Norway	1976–2000
Sweden	1971–2005	Sweden	1971–2000
Switzerland	1984–2005	Switzerland	1984–2000
United Kingdom	1971–2005	United Kingdom	1971–2000
United States	1971–2005	United States	1971–2000

11

Global and Local: Elites and the Dynamics of Nominal Democratization in South Korea and Nigeria

Rakkoo Chung

Many democracy scholars note the paradox of contemporary democracy: an increase in the quantity and a decrease in the quality of global democracy. Previous theories of democratization cannot explain, and did not predict, the massive emergence of low-quality democracies. To fill this gap, this chapter defines *nominal democratization* as the transition of a nondemocratic regime to a low-quality democracy, and develops theories of nominal democratization through the comparative historical analysis of South Korea and Nigeria. Employing the elite conflict theory, this chapter investigates when, why, how and by whom nominal democratization occurred in response to the pressures from various domestic and international actors, as well as under the particular structural and institutional settings. This chapter demonstrates the ways in which domestic elites and the core countries (notably, the United States and the United Kingdom) contributed to producing such nominal democratizations in South Korea and Nigeria.

Introduction

The last decades of the past millennium witnessed two seemingly incompatible trends: an increase in the quantity and a decrease in the quality of global democracy. While democracy spread across the globe, intermediate cases (i.e., countries that were neither fully democratic nor fully autocratic) rapidly increased in number (Markoff, 1996; Nyerere, 1997; Diamond, 1999; 2002; 2008; Sandbrook, 2000; also see Collier and Levitsky, 1997; Collier and Adcock, 1999). Such is a paradox of contemporary democracy, in that the worldwide spread of democratic institutions is related to the increasing shallowness of such (electoral) democracies (Diamond, 1996; Kim, 2003; Rogers, 2005). Zolo (1992) also criticizes this form-oriented democratization and argues that a façade of democratic institutions and procedures of periodic election of representatives through parties not only hides the decline in the substance of democracy but also provides a false legitimacy for elite control and dominance in the current regime.

Nevertheless, previous theories of democratization mainly focus on how to consolidate democracy and cannot explain the emergence of such hollow democracies. I argue that it is important to explain how and why such nominally democratic countries emerged, not only because it can uncover the global and local contexts underlying the rapid spread of hollow democracy, but also because it can give clues to the question of how to improve those nascent democracies. Thus, this chapter aims to investigate the conditions and mechanisms that produced such democratic shams, and to develop the theories of democratization through comparative historical analysis of two carefully selected cases, South Korea (Korea, hereafter) and Nigeria.[1]

Nominal democracy and nominal democratization

I define a nominal democracy as a regime that works undemocratically but runs some democratic institutions, such as multiparty election, which are minimal, but often enough to look democratic. By nominal democratization I mean the transition of a nondemocratic regime to such a low-quality democracy. I assume that nominal democratization is relatively easier and quicker to occur than substantive democratization, and that the trend of nominal democratization is related to the spread of the third wave.

This form-oriented nature of contemporary democratization raises an important question: Who wants such a hollow democracy? It is known that the wealthy, or the governing class, do not want full democracy, while the goal of the working class, or those ruled, is full democracy (see Collier, 1999; Boix, 2003; Acemoglu and Robinson, 2006). Further, elites do not passively resist democratization but often actively welcome it as far as its benefit outweighs its cost. Huntington (1984, 212) posits that "[democratic] institutions come into existence through negotiations and compromises among political elites calculating their own interests and desires." Markoff (1996, 116) also mentions that "[the governing elites] may protect or even enhance their own positions under democratic auspices."

Democratization usually involves struggles between the ruling who resist it and the ruled who demand it (see Tilly, 2007). Thus, the less the ruling elites resist democratization, the easier it is to occur. Studies on third-wave democratizations report the increased roles of elites in democratization and reduced conflict between the ruling and the ruled. Huntington (1991, 192) concluded that "most third wave democratizations were relatively peaceful compared to other regime transitions." Mason and Kluegel (2000) reported that transitions to liberal democracy in post-communist states were almost entirely directed by political and economic elites, often with the help of Westerners. Of the 67 cases of democratic transitions in Karatnycky and Ackerman (2005), the driving forces of 32 transitions involved (at least a fraction of) powerholders without "strong" civic coalitions, and even 15 out of the 32 cases were primarily driven by powerholders or outside elites.

---

1   Official names are the Republic of Korea (ROK) and the Federal Republic of Nigeria.

However, when ruling elites take the leading role in democratization, its consequence can be adverse, even if democratic transition can be easier and quicker to occur. Karatnycky and Ackerman (2005) conclude that top-down transitions, which are launched and led by elites, tend to produce lower-level democracies than bottom-up transitions. In a sense, nominal democracy became an option for ruling elites to respond to the demands for democracy without losing too much. Often, ruling elites decide to democratize in an attempt to alleviate civil unrest and forestall serious confrontation (see Acemoglu and Robinson, 2006; Ziblatt, 2006).

Theoretically, nominal democratization is best explained by *decoupling* (Meyer and Rowan, 1977). The trend of nominal democratization can be regarded as a process of decoupling of third-wave democracies from the normative models of democracy. The third wave accelerated in the late 1980s when adopting some institutions of democracy became the routinized response to ever-increasing global normative pressure for democracy, which did not necessarily require deep societal changes in existing undemocratic practices. Moreover, in the context of increasing global culture, the signal of democratization may be maximized, so that civil unrest or pressure for democracy from below could be more easily handled by even democratic appearance. Therefore, the growing legitimacy of democracy on a global scale might have paradoxically contributed to the proliferation of nominal democracies.

As Meyer et al. (1997, 154) noted, "Decoupling is endemic because . . . [w]orld culture contains a good many variants of the dominant models, which leads to the eclectic adoption of conflicting principles." The political elites of third-wave countries were creative in eclectically adopting modern democratic institutions. The range of variants of nominal democracy shows the examples of such eclectic adoptions.

Further, the powerholders could utilize the formal rules of democratic institutions to shrewdly suppress popular mobilization by installing illusory avenues for open expression (Markoff, 1996). Zolo (1992) also warns that electoral institutions can falsely legitimate elite control and dominance. Accordingly, even if such a top-down transition does not produce substantive shift towards democracy but only symbolic changes or changes in the institutional appearance, its value to ruling elites is real: It helps ruling elites justify their regime by masking some undemocratic features and practices. Therefore, once nominal democratization became an option, powerholders should find fewer reasons to resist it and more incentives to welcome it.

This chapter particularly pays attention to the effects of world society on local elites of third-wave democracies. Clearly, those elites of fledgling democracies did not invent democracy independently (Whitehead, 1996) but adopted the ideas and forms of democracy from developed democracies in various ways. The fact that so many countries in the world suddenly converged on democracy during the short period of the third wave, despite their great historical and political diversity, implies the significance of transnational diffusion of democracy. Robinson (1996) insightfully demonstrates that the roles of the United States changed in the early 1980s when it began supporting such limited democratization in the peripheral and semi-peripheral countries in an attempt to facilitate the expansion of global capitalism. However, this chapter shows that democracy diffused not only during the third wave but also in much earlier and longer years. In addition, I argue that democracy was not simply diffused by external forces but also strategically adopted and modified by local elites. Existing democratic countries, including such core countries as the United Kingdom and the United States, were not always pro-democracy but they were inconsistent and often adverse forces of democratization and contributed to the emergence of nominal democracies in less-developed countries. It was partly because the developed countries supported the elites of less-developed countries to implement democratic institutions to stabilize the politics, while such institutions and the elites who run them did not guarantee full democracy. Regarding democratizations in Korea and Nigeria, this chapter shows how the powerholders of the former authoritative military regimes still maintained power after democratic transitions in both countries, and how the United Kingdom and the United States are related to it.

Theoretical framework

I investigate the ways in which local political elites chose to adopt the institutions of democracy (say, electoral democracy) under the rubric of constraints and opportunities, which were created by structural and institutional settings and various (competing and cooperating) actors, both domestically and globally.[2] Democratization was viewed as an option for local and global elites to stabilize the local political systems and maintain their economic interests.[3] In other words, low-quality democracy was spread across many less-developed countries by the hands of local and global elites rather than by civil society. Thus, I look into the ways in which local elites of less-developed nondemocratic countries (here, Korea and Nigeria) decide to shift to low-quality democracies.

---

2   As opposed to the structuralist approach, Samuel Huntington (1991, 108) notes that "the emergence of social, economic and external conditions favorable to democracy is never enough to produce democracy. Whatever their motives, some political leaders have to want it to happen."

3   John Markoff (1996, 103) excellently expresses this point from the local elite's perspective: "Why bother with such a farcical, meaningless 'democratic' political structure? . . . [Because] powerholders often need to justify their power—sometimes to their own people, sometimes to potential foreign benefactors, perhaps to themselves." In addition, democratization of developing countries also concerned international financial organizations and the core countries (most notably, the United States). David Harvey defines neoliberalization as "a *political* project to reestablish the conditions for capital accumulation and to restore the power of economic elites" (2005, 19) and argues that "[neoliberalization] after 1979 had to be accomplished by democratic means" (2005, 39).

I borrow the elite conflict theory of the middle range (Lachmann, 1989; 1990; 2000; 2003; 2009). Elites are defined in terms of power (Lachmann, 2000). I lay the major focus on critical episodes, such as political crises and significant institutional changes, in which elites exert their power to make changes for their own sake. Such an episode marks the end of the elite dynamics of the immediately preceding period and, at the same time, sets the path dependence for subsequent changes in the elite structure. Indeed, structure is the "artifacts of past chains of agency" (Lachmann, 2000, 14). Current structural settings put constraints on some elites, give opportunities to others, and thus generate competition (both conflict and alliance) among elites, which will cause structural changes. Thus, I inquire: (1) for what purposes and under what (both domestic and international) conditions the key actors make what decisions at a critical moment; and then (2) how their actions shape the subsequent structural/institutional changes.

Dynamics of nominal democratizations in Korea and Nigeria

How does a democratic transition occur? It must occur through elections. Obviously, a democratic regime could not arise in a coup or a revolution during the third wave. Of course, election is not everything about democracy. As Table 1 shows, many democratic elections were held under the autocratic and military dictatorial regimes in Korea, and those elections never replaced the dictators.[4] Nevertheless, election has been a necessary condition of democratic transition.

The 1987 elections in Korea and the 1999 elections in Nigeria marked the last democratic transition in each country. However, prior to those last transitions, there were multiple critical moments when democratic transitions could have occurred or actually occurred. Those moments came along with political crises, or a lack of legitimacy of the current regime. When faced with such crises, Korean and Nigerian ruling elites showed different responses: Korean elites resisted (or tried to avoid) a democratic transition, while Nigerian elites officially prepared for it. Accordingly, the primary driving force of democratization in Korea was the people (led by student organizations, labor unions, and nongovernmental organizations), while Nigerian democratic transitions were basically driven by the ruling elites. Ironically, though Korea and Nigeria took very different routes of democratization, their outcomes were not very different, no better than nominal democracy: Those ruling elites of the former military regimes continued to possess state power after elections. I describe Korean transitions as a stolen victory, Nigerian ones as elite-driven democratization.

---

4   Matt Golder (2005, 103) also finds that "there have been almost as many elections under dictatorship as there have been under democracy."

Table 1: Korean presidents after independence in August 15, 1945

President	Elected on	Body[a]	Regime[b]	Civ.-mil.[c]	Party	How he lost power[d]	Republic
Rhee Syngman	7/20/1948	NA	A	C	NSRRKI		1st
Rhee Syngman	8/5/1952	DPV	A	C	LP		1st
Rhee Syngman	5/15/1956	DPV	A	C	LP		1st
Rhee Syngman	3/15/1960[e]	DPV	A	C	LP	April revolution in 1960; Rhee resigned 4/26/1960	1st
Yun Boseon	8/12/1960	NA	D	C	DP	Park's coup 5/16/1961; Yun resigned 3/22/1962	2nd
Park Chunghee	10/15/1963	DPV	M	M	DRP		3rd
Park Chunghee	5/3/1967	DPV	M	M	DRP		3rd
Park Chunghee	4/27/1971	DPV	M	M	DRP		3rd
Park Chunghee	12/23/1972	EC[f]	M	M	DRP		4th
Park Chunghee	7/6/1978	EC[f]	M	M	DRP	Park assassinated 10/26/1979	4th
Choi Kyuhah	12/6/1979	EC[f]	M	C	Indep[g]	Chun's coup 12/12/1979; Gwangju uprising in May, 1980; Choi resigned 8/16/1980	4th
Chun Doohwan	8/27/1980	EC[f]	M	M	DJP		5th
Chun Doohwan	2/25/1981	EC	M	M	DJP	June democratic uprising in 1987	5th
Roh Taewoo	12/16/1987	DPV	D	M	DJP		6th
Kim Youngsam	12/18/1992	DPV	D	C	DLP	IMF bailout from December, 1997	6th
Kim Daejung	12/18/1997	DPV	D	C	NCNP[h]		6th
Roh Moohyun	12/19/2002	DPV	D	C	MDP[h]		6th
Lee Myungbak	12/19/2007	DPV	D	C	GNP		6th
Park Geunhye	12/19/2012	DPV	D	C	NFP		6th

Notes: Dashed line shows the occurrence of a democratic transition. Party abbreviations : NSRRKI=National Society for the Rapid Realization of Korean Independence, LP=Liberal Party, DP=Democratic Party, DRP=Democratic Republican Party, DJP=Democratic Justice Party, DLP=Democratic Liberal Party, NCNP=National Congress for New Politics, MDP=Millennium Democratic Party, GNP=Grand National Party, NFP=New Frontier Party.
a: NA=National Assembly, DPV=Direct popular vote, EC=Electoral college; b: Regime types: Autocracy (A), Military dictatorship (M), and Democracy (D) (see Oh, 1999); c: President was either a civilian (C) or a military personnel (M); d: The incident that either forced the president to step down or that occurred at the end of each regime is noted. Unless the date of resignation or assassination is noted, the president finished the term; e: The 1960 election was annulled; f: National Council for Unification, an electoral college under the Yushin Constitution; g: Independent; Choi was the Prime Minister of the Park regime; h: Traditionally opposition parties.

When? Political crisis

Though there were many differences between Korea and Nigeria, there were also many commonalities, one of which was that a crisis of political legitimacy of the current regime was always the sign of a democratic transition. I define the political crisis of a regime as the time when the political legitimacy of the current regime is severely damaged and the governing elites find it difficult to continue to stay in power because a revolution or a coup is likely to occur against them, or because their parties are likely to lose in the upcoming elections. Such a political crisis is caused by many factors, including an economic crisis, corruption, state violence against the people, human rights violation, and so forth, but the most direct cause is a ruler's illicit attempt to stay in power longer than he is supposed to. Whenever a ruler illicitly tried to extend his power, he was faced with strong opposition from the people, opposition leaders, and often a faction of his fellows. Such a political crisis often led to significant political changes, either a regime transition or a democratic transition.

Korea

When Rhee Syngman illegitimately amended the constitution to allow himself to run for the presidential election multiple times and used fraudulent counting of the votes on March 15, 1960, the April Revolution[5] occurred and forced him to annul the election, resign and live in exile. Then a new government was established, which was deemed to be a democratic transition, but it was soon reverted by Park Chunghee's military coup on May 16, 1961.

Park Chunghee was elected as president five times, meanwhile he also amended the constitution (so-called, the Yushin Constitution of the Fourth Republic) and paved the way to prolong his one-man rule for his lifetime. Under the Yushin Constitution, the president was to be elected by an electoral college, namely the National Council for Unification, which was under Park Chunghee's control. His Yushin system was criticized by many, but most notably by the two opposition leaders, Kim Daejung and Kim Youngsam. When the ruling party passed a bill to deprive Kim Youngsam (the president of the New Democratic Party) of his membership in the National Assembly, popular uprisings occurred in Busan and Masan where Kim Youngsam was popular. Park Chunghee discussed the measures to handle the Busan and Masan Uprisings with his closest associates, Cha Jicheol and Kim Jaekyu. Park and Cha favored repression, while Kim wanted moderate measures. On October 26, 1979, Park Chunghee and Cha Jicheol were shot by Kim Jaekyu.[6]

After Park's assassination, the public expectation for democratization was higher than ever, but soon Chun Doohwan, one of Park Chunghee's loyal subordinates, took power in a military coup on December 12, 1979. Massive antigovernment protests occurred in Gwangju in 1980, but it was bloodily repressed by the army, and people had to wait for democracy again. Under the repressive military regimes of Park and Chun, democratization movements grew in quality through alliance

---

5   A protest against the sham election was sparked in a small city, Masan, on March 15, 1960 when the members of the Democratic Party exposed the electoral fraud. The government brutally repressed the protest, and a high school student, Kim Ju-yul's body was found (with a tear gas grenade stuck on his eye) in a river by a fisherman. It outraged Koreans and eventually provoked a nationwide popular uprising on April 19 against the Rhee regime (see Kim, 1992; Seo, 2007).

6   The reasons why Kim Jaekyu killed Park Chunghee and Cha Jicheol are not certain.

formation among various social groups (Chang, 2008). Meanwhile, when Chun Doohwan adopted a so-called appeasement policy,[7] the democratization movement began to gain organizational power rapidly. Near the end of Chun Doohwan's tenure and the next presidential election, the government was faced with a strong demand for constitutional amendment to elect the president by direct popular votes. Yet, Chun Doohwan rejected the demand and designated Roh Taewoo, Chun's closest subordinate, as the next presidential candidate of his party. Soon, the largest democratic coalition (Choi, 1989) was formed, allied with the opposition leaders Kim Daejung and Kim Youngsam, and fought for direct popular votes. In addition to multiple cases of human rights violations committed by the Chun regime, the torture death of a university student, Park Jongcheol, eventually triggered the June Democratic Uprising in 1987, which lasted until the government made significant democratic concessions on June 29, the June 29 Declaration. Since October 29, 1987, the Korean president must be elected by direct popular vote.

Unfortunately, this people's victory did not lead to a victory in the upcoming presidential election in December, 1987: Because the votes from those who were sick of military rulers were split into two (one for Kim Daejung and another for Kim Youngsam), Roh Taewoo was elected.[8] In the 1992 presidential election, Kim Youngsam was elected, but he was then allied with those beneficiaries of the former military regimes. Citizen punishment of Kim Youngsam's betrayal of their expectation was weak (Kim, 1994). It was as late as 1997 that the opposition party took power for the first time in Korea. When Korea was severely struck by the Asian Financial Crisis and necessitated the International Monetary Fund (IMF) bailout in 1997, which severely illegitimated the governing party, people voted for Kim Daejung, the opposition candidate.

Nigeria

In Nigeria, the three biggest ethnic groups—Hausa-Fulani, Yoruba, and Igbo—have dominated Nigerian politics. Their political parties were identified with their regions and ethnicities, even if there are a number of ethnic groups in each region. For instance, during the Nigerian First Republic, there were three political parties: the Northern People's Congress (NPC), the Action Group (AG), and the National Council of Nigeria and the Cameroons (NCNC). NPC was the political party for the North, but Hausa-Fulani dominated the NPC. Likewise, Yoruba dominated the AG of the West and Igbo dominated the NCNC of the East. Among these big three, the

---

7   The Chun regime did so, "because they concluded that their rule had been stabilized to some degree [and they] also needed to make an ostentatious display of domestic peace in order to successfully hold the 1986 Asian Games as well as the 1988 Seoul Olympic Games, both of which had been promoted to cover up their lack of legitimacy" (Jung and Kim, 2008, 10).

8   Roh Taewoo won 36.64% of the votes, while Kim Daejung gained 27.04% and Kim Youngsam 28.03% (Republic of Korea National Election Commission, n.d.).

Table 2: Nigerian leaders after independence in October 1, 1960

Tenure	Head of state	Ethnicity[a]	Party	How he rose to power	Republic[b]
1960–1964	Abubakar Tafawa Belawa[c]	Hausa	NPC	Elected in 1959	1st
1964–1966	Abubakar Tafawa Belawa[c]	Hausa	NPC	Re-elected in 1964	1st
1966	Johnson Aguiyi-Ironsi	Igbo	–	Coup 1/15/1966	–
1966–1975	Yakubu Gowon	(Mid)	–	Coup 7/29/1966	–
1975–1976	Murtala Mohammed	Hausa	–	Coup 7/29/1975	–
1976–1979	Olusegun Obasanjo[d]	Yoruba	–	Mohammed assassinated 2/13/1976	–
1979–1983	Shehu Shagari	Fulani	NPN	Elected 8/11/1979	2nd
1983	Shehu Shagari	Fulani	NPN	Re-elected 8/6/1983	2nd
1983–1985	Muhammad Buhari	Fulani	–	Coup 12/31/1983	–
1985–1993	Ibrahim Badamasi Babangida (IBB)	(North)	–	Coup 8/27/1985	–
–	M. K. O. Abiola	Yoruba	SDP	Elected 6/12/1993; election annulled by IBB	3rd
1993	Ernest Shonekan	Yoruba	–	IBB resigned 8/27/1993	–
1993–1998	Sani Abacha	(North)	–	Coup 11/17/1993	–
1998–1999	Abdulsalami Abubakar	(North)	–	Abacha died 6/8/1998	–
1999–2003	Olusegun Obasanjo	Yoruba	PDP	Elected 2/27/1999	4th
2003–2007	Olusegun Obasanjo	Yoruba	PDP	Re-elected 4/19/2003	4th
2007–2010	Umaru Musa Yar'Adua	Fulani	PDP	Elected 4/21/2007	4th
2010–2011	Goodluck Jonathan[e]	(South)	PDP	Yar'Adua died 5/5/2010	4th
2011–now	Goodluck Jonathan	(South)	PDP	Elected 4/16/2011	4th

Notes: Dashed line shows the occurrence of a democratic transition. Party abbreviations : NPC=Northern People's Congress, NPN=National Party for Nigeria, SDP=Social Democratic Party, PDP=People's Democratic Party.

a: Only major tribes are noted here; b: Nigeria's Republics; Hyphens mean military regimes; c: Balewa was the Prime Minister of the First Republic; d: Obasanjo was the Vice President of the Mohammed regime; e: Jonathan was the Vice President of the Yar'Adua regime. Because of Yar'Adua's health issues, Jonathan was the acting president from February 9 until he assumed the office in May 6, 2010.

military elite from the North have almost always prevailed in the Nigerian politics, whether the government was military or civilian (see Table 2).

Postindependent Nigeria started with a functioning democratic system, but the First Republic posed many political problems and was unable to solve them. Johnson Aguiyi-Ironsi took power in a coup in January 1966, but he hailed from the South. Soon Yakubu Gowon took power in a counter coup in July 1966. After the Nigerian Civil War (1967–1970), Gowon promised to transfer power to a civilian government by 1976, but he announced in October 1974 that he would delay it without specifying the deadline. Because the military became much bigger through the Civil War and his government became so corrupt through the oil boom (1973–1976), Gowon and his fellows wanted to enjoy power and wealth as long as possible. After his speech in 1974, not only the general public but also prominent politicians turned their backs on Gowon, and his regime was overthrown by his rival, Murtala Mohammed, in a bloodless coup in 1975.

Murtala Mohammed and his successor, Olusegun Obasanjo, successfully carried out the transition programs, disengaged the military from the political scene, and transferred power to an elected civilian president, Shehu Shagari in 1979. Yet, the Shagari regime was so corrupt and incompetent that it lost popularity, but Shagari was re-elected in the 1983 election, which was neither free nor fair. Opposition leaders and the mass media criticized the electoral sham, and antigovernment movements were being formed. Muhammad Buhari took power in a military coup in 1983, but he did not announce a transitional plan or specify when he would leave. The Buhari regime was soon overthrown by Ibrahim Badamasi Babangida in a bloodless coup on August 27, 1985.

During his tenure, Babangida adopted the IMF Structural Adjustment Program (SAP), which exacerbated the economic problems. Meanwhile, he delayed the elections to 1992 and again to 1993, though he initially promised to hold elections in 1990 to elect a civilian government. Contrary to Babangida's scheme, the 1993 presidential election was won by Chief M. K. O. Abiola from the South. Northern military elites did not welcome this outcome, because they feared having to share with (or transfer to) the South their power in the federal government and their access to the oil money (Falola, 1999). Thus, Babangida annulled the election, which provoked immediate backlash from the opposition parties and the people. Unable to handle the situation, Babangida installed an Interim National Government led by Chief Ernest Shonekan and stepped down in disgrace on August 26, 1993. Yet, Shonekan had no power to handle the situation but to wait for another military leader.

Sani Abacha took the office on November 17, 1993, and announced a new transition program to bring true democracy to Nigeria by August, 1998. Many people, including politicians such as Abiola, believed that Abacha would keep his word. However, he had strong personal ambitions: He became a despot and brazenly tried to consolidate his personal dominance; he kept Abiola in detention; he even invented coups against himself to incarcerate, detain, punish and silence people who were critical to his regime, including Olusegun Obasanjo (Falola, 1999). Abacha also turned his back on the Northern Nigerian Elders, who once had backed the Abacha regime but officially opposed Abacha's self-succession scheme (see Mbeke-Ekanem, 2000, 257–259). On the one hand, he looted Nigeria. On the other, he used force and bribery to suppress opposition forces and co-opt politicians and even pro-democracy activists. Near the promised date of election, Abacha was the only presidential candidate that was nominated by five different parties. His transition plan already turned out to be a sham. Abacha was found dead early in the morning on June 8, 1998. There was a conspiracy theory that Abacha was murdered by Kaduna Mafia (Mbeke-Ekanem, 2000).

Abacha's sudden death could have caused a serious crisis for the Northern military elites, because Abacha had significantly illegitimated the military rule and because he caused a split within the military (i.e., pro- and anti-Abacha).[9] Yet, the military quickly summoned Abdulsalami Abubakar to the Aso Rock[10] to assume the office. In the eyes of the military elites, Abubakar was a suitable alternative, because he was loyal to the military and, contrary to Abacha, lacked personal ambitions. Abubakar proclaimed that his regime would be short and promised to hand power over to an elected president. As he promised, he adopted a new constitution on May 5, 1999 (i.e., Nigeria's Fourth Republic), held elections, and transferred power to the elected president, Olusegun Obasanjo on May 29, 1999. Since then, Nigeria's Fourth Republic has survived, and the People's Democratic Party (PDP) has won all the subsequent elections in 2003, 2007 and 2011. Indeed, the Fourth Republic has provided the ruling elites with greater stability than ever.

How? Rulers' responses to political crisis

When faced with a political crisis, Korean and Nigerian rulers responded to it differently: Korean rulers exercised repressive measures to suppress the opposition forces and tried hard to remain in power until they were faced with a formidable democratization movement, while Nigerian elites used regime transitions to pacify the opposition. Much of the history of Nigerian political changes shows an endless loop of hope and disillusionment: A new regime promised democratic reforms, gave the people and opposition politicians hope, and obtained a grace period; yet, the regime failed to keep its promise and disillusioned them. Permanent transition was a virtual strategy of military control in Nigeria (Diamond et al., 1997; Lewis, 1999). It is interesting to note that most years of military rule in Nigeria were officially spent in preparing for elections. Among the seven military rulers—except Aguiyi-Ironsi whose regime lasted only six months—only Buhari did not announce any plan of democratic transition, partly because of which his regime was short lived. In Korea, on the contrary, rulers fought the public and the opposition parties in an attempt to extend their presidency, often via illegal constitutional amendment. Consequently, Park Chunghee had to resort to repressive measures, and Rhee Syngman and Chun Doohwan were faced with strong popular uprisings at the end of their rules. Thus, a political crisis opened up a great moment of democratic transition, and rulers' different responses to it determined how the transition occurred, either people-driven bottom-up democratization in Korea or elite-driven top-down democratization in Nigeria.

---

9   Later in the 1999 elections, the pro-Abacha faction formed the All People's Party (APP) while the anti-Abacha faction formed the People's Democratic Party (PDP).

10   The Aso Rock is the official residence and principal workplace of the President, located in Abuja, the capital city of Nigeria.

This section explains why Korean and Nigerian rulers responded to political crises differently. First, the structural characteristics of the ruling elites mattered. In Nigeria, the military heads of state were not the kind of individual dictators but, in a sense, the representatives of the Northern military elites as a whole, and the heads of state were usually chosen among the senior generals.[11] When the current ruler was illegitimated, then another general rose to power in a coup and then promised reforms to give false hope to the people and to restore legitimacy temporarily. This was how the Northern elites maintained power and accumulated money through repeated regime shifts in mostly bloodless coups. In this sense, Abacha was an aberration, in that he pursued personal rule and eventually caused a crisis not only in his own regime but also in the entire group of Northern military elites.

On the other hand, Korean dictators were similar to Abacha, in that they were charismatic despots with strong personal ambition. While Nigerian heads were kind of representatives of the Northern military elites and were supposed to consult the Northern Nigerian Elders with important issues, Rhee Syngman, Park Chunghee and Chun Doohwan were at the center of the ruling elites and at the very top of state power. Consequently, when faced with a political crisis due to the lack of legitimacy, Rhee Syngman and Park Chunghee could not consider regime transition—which was a good option for Nigerian military elites to solve legitimacy crises—but used illegitimate and often repressive means to protect their presidency. Only Chun Doohwan tried a regime transition to his loyal subordinate, Roh Taewoo, in an attempt to legitimate his regime and his party.

Second, there was another difference between Korea and Nigeria in the strength of the democratization movement: Civic coalitions against the authoritarian governments were formidable in Korea and weak in Nigeria. This difference might stem from other differences, such as the level of industrialization, income, education of citizens, the size of the territories, ethnic composition of the population, prior experiences of movements, and so forth. Indeed, there was virtually no nationwide civic coalition against Nigerian governments. Regarding the organizational capacity of social movements and rulers' responses, it is not clear which caused which. On the one hand, the difference in the organizational power of democratization movements might have caused the difference in the rulers' responses to a political crisis between Korea and Nigeria. Because Korean civil society had strong organizational power to demand immediate reforms, Korean rulers had to repress it or lose ev-

---

11   Examples are following: Mohammed justified his coup against the Gowon regime by arguing that "[Gowon] did not consult senior military officers in affairs of state" (Ikpeze et al., 2004, 345); When the 1983 coup successfully ousted the Shagari regime, "Buhari was chosen unanimously to be the new head of state" (Encyclopædia Britannica Online, 2014) by middle and high-ranking military officers; Babangida admitted that he had participated in all major coups in Nigeria except one on January 14, 1966, which was plotted mainly by Igbo officers (Falola, 1999, 116–117; Mbeke-Ekanem, 2000, 32).

erything, while Nigerian rulers were able to strategically handle weak or moderate antigovernment forces. On the other hand, the difference in the rulers' handling of a political crisis might also have caused the different power of democratization movements. While Korean democratization movements grew under repression (see Chang, 2008), Nigerian movements could not grow much under the politics of transition. When a Nigerian military head announced a plan of democratic transition, democratization movements did not grow further but waited (and tried to prepare) for the coming elections.

Third, in relation to the rulers and democratization movements, the opposition politicians also worked differently in Korea and Nigeria. Korean opposition politicians allied themselves with democratization movements and fought against the dictators. Particularly under the Park regime, opposition politicians were vulnerable to state violence and thus often needed support from democratization movements, which in turn reinforced the movement organizations. On the other hand, Nigerian opposition politicians did not ally with social movements or fight against the military regimes as long as the rulers promised to hold elections in the near future. Thus, Nigerian opposition politicians were comparatively cooperative with the military rulers in the preparation of elections, while Korean opposition politicians had to contribute to the growth of democratization movements under the repressive military rulers who resisted elections.

In sum, under those three different conditions, Korean rulers tried hard—often illegitimately—to extend their presidency and resisted a democratic transition, while Nigerian rulers actively and officially prepared for a democratic transition. Accordingly, Nigerian democratic transition was elite-driven top-down democratization, while Korean democratic transition was primarily people-driven bottom-up democratization.

Why democracy? Rules of the game

The previous section explains why Korean dictators officially resisted democratic transition while Nigerian military heads officially pursued it. However, one commonality between Korean and Nigerian rulers was that they both considered elections as a means of justifying their regimes. For Korean rulers, election mattered: Presidents had to be elected, whether the elections were fair or not. Rhee Syngman and Park Chunghee were elected four and five times, respectively (see Table 1). In Nigeria, most military rulers had to announce some plans of elections, whether they really wanted to carry it out or not. When Korean rulers attempted something illegitimate regarding elections, democratization movements arose against them. When Nigerian rulers did not keep their promises, they were replaced with other military rulers in coups.

Why, then, were elections (and democratic transition) the means of justifying their regimes in both countries? Obviously, it was because the people and opposition politicians—and sometimes external actors such as foreign governments and international financial organizations—regarded democracy as legitimate. Why, then, was democracy regarded as legitimate, particularly by the general public and opposition politicians? It was partly because democracy had gained legitimacy globally. Yet, this answer is not good enough: firstly, because they demanded democracy in the 1960s and 1970s when the communist countries were well off and democracy was deemed to be bad for economic development, and secondly, more importantly, because the legitimacy of democracy in the global discourse does not necessarily guarantee the legitimacy of democracy in the domestic politics of each country. Thus, here, I examine why the general public and opposition politicians demanded democracy as the legitimate form of government in Korea and Nigeria after independence.

The general public

In both countries, democracy has been deeply entrenched in their political cultures and widely accepted by the people and political elites as the basic rules of the political game. Both Korea and Nigeria started their postindependent periods with democratically (or seemingly democratically) elected governments, which set path dependence. In Korea, elections have been held almost regularly since independence (see Table 1). In Nigeria, most years after independence were spent in preparing for elections, either under military regimes or civilian ones. In so doing, the general public had repeatedly practiced democratic institutions and ideas, and then regarded elections as the only legitimate way of claiming power. Therefore, multiparty elections became a necessary element of politics, and a democratic transition must occur through elections. This was why the people wanted democracy and demanded fair elections whenever the current regime was illegitimated.

Opposition politicians

Opposition politicians greatly contributed to the entrenchment of electoral institutions in their political cultures, but their roles were ambivalent in terms of democracy. On one hand, they significantly contributed to promoting democratization. Criticizing the ruler and/or the governing party regarding democratic principles, and appealing to the voters during the electoral campaigns, opposition politicians pressurized the rulers and spread the ideas and procedures of democracy to citizens. Under the authoritarian regimes, opposition politicians appeared to be the most ardent advocates of democracy. On the other hand, they wanted democracy only to the extent that it increased their political leverage and/or their chance of achieving power. They demanded elections, but did not want full democracy, which might damage their prerogatives.

In Nigeria, the North has always prevailed in the federal government, partly thanks to its population size: The North, the regional base of the Hausa-Fulani, was bigger than the West of the Yoruba or the East of the Igbo. In terms of elections in

Nigeria, Northern elites had a winning strategy based on the presence of Southern elites: Partnering with one and marginalizing the other. Because Yoruba and Igbo collectively outnumbered Hausa-Fulani, if they had united, the South could have been a good match for the North, and the checks and balances within state power could have been achieved early. However, Western and Eastern elites did not want such democracy. They wanted power in the federal government, because federal government decided on the distribution of national revenue to each region, and, moreover, had direct access to the oil money and foreign companies (see Falola, 1999, 102). Accordingly, Western and Eastern elites respectively wanted to team up with the North. Northern elites also welcomed such an ally in either the West or the East so that they could forestall the possible alliance between the West and the East. Consequently, Southern elites demanded elections but did not seriously challenge the Northern domination, and they exercised their regional power to have better electoral results but not to improve democracy in Nigeria.

In Korea, the opposition leaders, such as Kim Daejung and Kim Youngsam, would not have survived the military regimes, if it were not for the strong democratization movement and their popular support. However, they maintained a strategic alliance with the movement sector in that they were ready to break up with it whenever they were given a better chance to achieve power. A good example was the May-3rd Incheon Protests in 1986. In 1986, the democratization movement against the Chun regime was rapidly growing and gave strong support to the opposition party—which was led by Kim Daejung and Kim Youngsam—that demanded constitutional amendment for direct popular vote. However, when Kim Daejung and Kim Youngsam were given a chance to negotiate with the Chun regime, they announced that they would not cooperate with those radicalized movement forces, which enraged the democratization movement (Jung, 1992).

Rulers

Faced with a strong demand for elections by the people and opposition politicians, and under the political culture that valued elections, Korean rulers were only able to extend their tenures through elections, and Nigerian rulers had to announce their plans for democratic transition. Yet, importantly, such options were not only forced. Rulers also had good reasons to choose them.

Thus, rulers knew that another legitimacy crisis was coming along with the next election when the people would be disillusioned by Korean rulers who resorted to illegitimate means to win elections, or by Nigerian rulers who did not really intend to carry out the transition programs, but the rulers also knew that they would be fine until then. Once the president was elected, or once the plan of elections was announced, people and opposition politicians would wait for the next elections.

Furthermore, the ruling elites had the resources and know-how to win elections. In Korea, the governing party (with different names) won all the presidential elections before 1997. The governing party invented ethnicity, developed regionalism, manipulated the Red Scare, tightly controlled the media, exercised the police and military forces, used money, and took advantage of the support from the United States and Japan to defeat or co-opt opposition forces. As mentioned before, Roh Taewoo was elected in December 1987, even though the majority of Korean voters did not want to see him elected, mainly because the governing party took full advantage of the rivalry between the opposition leaders, Kim Daejung and Kim Youngsam. For the 1992 presidential election, the governing party co-opted Kim Youngsam as its candidate, and this strategy worked well. Likewise, in Nigeria, the ruling parties, which were controlled by the Northern elites, have always prevailed. Elections or democratic transitions have never led to a power shift. The two successful transitions to civilian regimes in 1979 and 1999 never would have occurred unless the president-elect was the candidate of the ruling parties of the North. In 1993 when Abiola won the presidential election, Babangida annulled the election, and Abiola was kept in detention until death.

In sum, election was accepted by not only the general public but also the political elites, which was why election was the only legitimate way of handling a legitimacy crisis of any authoritarian regime. However, election hardly worked as the general public expected. Instead, too much emphasis on election in both cultures gave political elites too much power to opportunistically run the electoral institutions to pursue their personal goals. Election was a game among political elites, often rendering the general public passive voters. Ruling parties and opposition parties competed with each other, but together they shared the interests of the ruling class as opposed to those of the general public. Elections could not lead to democracy, unless there were candidates who represented the voters. Consequently, in both countries, multiparty election has entrenched nominal democracy, which is likely to last for the foreseeable future.

Who? Ruling elites and the core countries

The previous section shows that multiparty election has become the rule of the game among the ruling elites in both countries. Thus, this section investigates where the institutions and the ruling elites came from. This question is important because the initial institutional settings and the practices of the first years have significant legacies.

It was the United States and the United Kingdom that initially installed democratic institutions in Korea and Nigeria upon or prior to independence. The problem was that the United States and the United Kingdom did not want truly democratic governments but docile and dependent ones in Korea and Nigeria. Under the administrations of those world powers, colonial collaborators ran the state apparatuses, accumulated wealth along with comprador capital, and exploited rather than represented their people.

The United Kingdom wanted to benefit from Nigerian oil even after independence, so it carefully led the decolonization processes, from constitutional reforms to elections in 1951 and 1959. Through the decolonization processes and the First Republic, Britain secured its economic interests in postindependent Nigeria, and the elites of the three dominant tribes consolidated their power within their home regions. Meanwhile, regionalism became the paradigm of Nigerian politics, because of the quasi-federal structure of colonial Nigeria and three regionally-based political parties that were controlled by and identified with the three biggest ethnic groups (see Falola, 1999, 108). Nigerian political elites corruptly appropriated national resources in collusion with foreign (particularly British) firms and consolidated their structural role in postindependent Nigeria as the facilitator of extended exploitation of the general public and national resources. This undemocratic relationship between the political elites and the general public was soon consolidated. Elections hardly improved the representation issues, because region, ethnicity and religion were so politicized that the exploitative class relation between the ruling and the ruled was less visible. The public interests were largely estranged from the heated electoral competition under the winner-takes-all politics. Grievances of minority ethnic groups were also largely ignored.

There were no such decolonization processes in Korea, because Japan abruptly left Korea as soon as it surrendered in 1945. Instead, the United States administered Korea (and the Soviet Union administered North Korea) after independence. The United States wanted to see political stability and economic development in Korea as soon as possible, because of Korea's geopolitical significance during the Cold War. The United States supported Rhee Syngman, a pro-American figure, but he did not have enough supporters in Korea, so the United States allied him with mostly pro-Japanese collaborators, who were educated and had resources but lacked popularity and the will to represent their people. After becoming the first President of Korea, Rhee Syngman had to rely on illegitimate means to win three more elections. Rhee Syngman, Park Chunghee, and Chun Doohwan, and their parties, resorted to regionalism and the Red Scare to win elections, and their political legitimacy and financial capability were heavily dependent on the U.S. and Japanese governments. Though Korea saw a rapid economic growth under the Rhee, Park and Chun regimes, Korea experienced many financial crises—which were handled by borrowing money from the United States and Japan—and remained as one of the greatest debtor countries till the end of the last millennium.

In sum, the United States and the United Kingdom installed democratic institutions in Korea and Nigeria, but they were run undemocratically by unrepresentative representatives.

Promoting democratic institutions and delaying democratic growth

In addition, the United States and the United Kingdom often exerted direct and adverse influence on the democratic growth in Korea and Nigeria. As mentioned above, the United States and Japan supported Korea's autocratic and military re-gimes, both politically and economically. Particularly, as the Chun regime became illegitimated by its people, its major source of political legitimacy was the support from the United States and Japan based on the U.S.-Japan-ROK Triangular Security Cooperation System. Later, the U.S. government still showed its support of Chun Doohwan and his designated successor, Roh Taewoo, and, at the same time, pres-sured the Chun regime to open the market. Consequently, anti-America sentiment grew together with the democratization movement.

In Nigeria, the colonial economic structure was perpetuated by the government. The United Kingdom did not want to industrialize Nigeria but to protect British industries. After independence, the Nigerian government neglected industrial di-versification. Accordingly, the oil sector was the single most important and virtually the only lucrative industry in Nigeria. Political power and foreign capital became intertwined with the oil production in corrupt ways. Nigerian elites and Britain pri-oritize their gains at the cost of the Nigerian people and democracy. So, when the Abacha regime was going to execute eight environmental activists in a short trial, the British people demanded that Shell—a British oil company—should stop pro-ducing oil and pressurize the Abacha regime not to execute those activists, but Shell ignored such a demand.

Around 1990 and later, the United States and the United Kingdom tended to be more prodemocratic than before, but still did not contribute to democratic growth in Korea and Nigeria. Concerned about the growing anti-America sentiment and the size of the popular uprising, the U.S. government did not want the Chun regime to use military force to suppress the June Democratic Uprising in 1987, even though the United States supported the Chun regime's brutal repression of the Gwangju Democratic Uprising in 1980. Instead, the United States attempted to find a broad conservative alliance and a pro-U.S. government, as it did in the Philippines in 1986.

The execution of those activists provoked international outrage and was imme-diately followed by the isolation of Nigeria from the international community and the introduction of economic sanctions.[12] Thus, the Abacha regime had to suffer se-rious financial problems, which indirectly indicated how desperately Nigerian rul-ing elites needed foreign financial support when Abacha died. As soon as Abubakar announced a plan of democratic transition, great encouragement and financial in-

---

12 Nigeria's membership in the Commonwealth was suspended, and the United States imposed an embargo against Nigeria. The European Union imposed economic sanctions and banned arms sales to Nigeria. Other countries and international organizations also cancelled or suspended their investment plans.

centives were forthcoming from the international community.[13] However, such financial support did not necessarily promote democratic growth in Nigeria. Instead, the money helped the Abubakar regime and the ruling elites to prepare for the election and to secure their victory. It was only recently that developed countries began to consider supporting nongovernmental sectors.

Discussion and conclusion

This chapter investigates the conditions and mechanisms that produced nominal democracy in Korea and Nigeria. Korean rulers resisted democratic transition until they were faced with formidable popular uprisings. Nigerian rulers prepared for democratic transition. Accordingly, the primary driving forces of democratic transition were the democratization movement in Korea and elites in Nigeria. However, no democratization movement fully achieved its goals in Korea. Soon after the April revolution in 1960 ousted Rhee Syngman, Park Chunghee took power in a coup in 1961. When the June Democratic Uprising in 1987 successfully pressurized the Chun regime, Roh Taewoo was elected in December, 1987. In Nigeria, democratic transitions succeeded as long as the president-elect was not going to change the status quo. Therefore, Korea and Nigeria experienced different processes of democratic transition (i.e., stolen victories in Korea and elite-driven democratization in Nigeria) under different conditions, but they culminated in more or less nominal democracy.

Behind the rise of nominal democracy in Korea and Nigeria were the core countries, notably the United States and the United Kingdom. They installed democratic institutions upon independence and let unrepresentative representatives run the government. Consequently, path dependence was set to pose adverse legacies on democratic growth in Korea and Nigeria.

This chapter confirms the concerns of existing literature, such as the tendency of elite-driven democratization to produce a low-level democracy (see Karatnycky and Ackerman, 2005) and the limitations of form-oriented democratization (see Zolo, 1992). Plus, this chapter highlights the historical roots of nominal democracy—the initial settings and the first members of government of postindependent Korea and Nigeria—and the roles of the core countries in creating such contexts. These findings are expected to help us better understand why so many countries with so diverse political, economic, social, and cultural backgrounds in the world converged on low-level democracy during the short period of the third wave.

13　Between October 1998 and September 1999, for instance, Nigeria was said to have received assistance from the United States amounting to US$27.5 million (Aka, 2002, 256). President Clinton also hinted that "sanctions would be lifted if [democratic] progress continued" (Black, 1998). The EU nations said they would reconsider their economic sanctions against Nigeria.

Acknowledgements

The author thanks Richard Lachmann, Aaron Major, Glenn Deane, Chris Chase-Dunn, Christian Suter, and Sehwa Lee.

References

Acemoglu, Daron, and James A. Robinson. 2006. *The Economic Origins of Dictatorship and Democracy*. Cambridge: Cambridge University Press.

Aka, Philip C. 2002. The "Dividend of Democracy": Analyzing U.S. Support for Nigerian Democratization. *Boston College Third World Law Journal*, 22(2): 225–279.

Black, Ian. 1998. Africa "Looks to Nigeria." *Guardian* September 25, 1998: 19.

Boix, Carles. 2003. *Democracy and Redistribution*. New York: Cambridge University Press.

Chang, Paul Y. 2008. Unintended Consequences of Repression: Alliance Formation in South Korea's Democracy Movement (1970–1979). *Social Forces*, 87(2): 651–677.

Choi, Jangjip. 1989. *Structure and Change of Contemporary South Korean Politics*. Seoul: Ggachi.

Collier, Ruth B. 1999. *Paths toward Democracy: The Working Class and Elites in Western Europe and South America*. New York: Cambridge University Press.

Collier, David, and Robert Adcock. 1999. Democracy and Dichotomies: A Pragmatic Approach to Choices about Concepts. *World Politics*, 2: 537–565.

Collier, David, and Steven Levitsky. 1997. Democracy with Adjectives: Conceptual Innovation in Comparative Research. *World Politics*, 49(3): 430–451.

Diamond, Larry. 1996. Is the Third Wave Over? *Journal of Democracy*, 7(3): 20–37.

Diamond, Larry. 1999. *Developing Democracy: Toward Consolidation*. Baltimore: Johns Hopkins University Press.

Diamond, Larry. 2002. Thinking about Hybrid Regimes. *Journal of Democracy*, 13(2): 21–35.

Diamond, Larry. 2008. *The Spirit of Democracy: The Struggle to Build Free Societies throughout the World*. New York: Henry Holt and Company, LLC.

Diamond, Larry J., Anthony H. M. Kirk-Greene, and Oyeleye Oyediran (eds.). 1997. *Transition without End: Nigerian Politics and Civil Society under Babangida*. Boulder, CO: Lynne Rienner Publishers.

Encyclopædia Britannica Online. 2014. Muhammad Buhari. Encyclopædia Britannica Inc. URL: http://www.britannica.com/EBchecked/topic/83801/Muhammad-Buhari (accessed January 26, 2014).

Falola, Toyin. 1999. *The History of Nigeria*. Westport, CT: Greenwood Press.

Golder, Matt. 2005. Democratic Electoral Systems around the World, 1946–2000. *Electoral Studies*, 24(1): 103–121.

Harvey, David. 2005. *A Brief History of Neoliberalism*. New York: Oxford University Press.

Huntington, Samuel P. 1984. Will More Countries Become Democratic? *Political Science Quarterly,* 99: 193–218.

Huntington, Samuel P. 1991. *The Third Wave: Democratization in the Late Twentieth Century.* Norman: University of Oklahoma Press.

Ikpeze, N. I., Charles C. Soludo, and N. N. Elekwa. 2004. "Nigeria: The Political Economy of the Policy Process, Policy Choice and Implementation." In Charles Soludo, Osita Ogbu, and Ja-Joon Chang (eds.), *The Politics of Trade and Industrial Policy in Africa: Forced Consensus?* Trenton, NJ and Ottawa: Africa World Press and International Development Research Centre.

Jung, Hae Gu. 1992. "The Rise of National Democratization Movement and the Fall of the Fifth Republic." In Hyeonchae Park (ed.), *Contemporary South Korean History for Youth, 1945–1991: National History of Suffer and Hope.* Seoul: Sonamu.

Jung, Hae Gu, and Ho Ki Kim. 2008. Development of Democratization Movement in South Korea. Working Paper. URL: http://iis-db.stanford.edu/pubs/22591/Development_of_Democratization_Movement_in_South_Korea-1.pdf (accessed May 7, 2012).

Karatnycky, Adrian, and Peter Ackerman. 2005. *How Freedom is Won: From Civic Resistance to Durable Democracy.* New York, NY: Freedom House.

Kim, Dongchun. 1992. "National Democratic Revolution, 4 19." In Hyeonchae Park (eds.), *Contemporary South Korean History for Youth, 1945–1991: National History of Suffer and Hope.* Seoul: Sonamu.

Kim, Hee-Min. 1994. A Theory of Government-Driven Democratization: The Case of Korea. *World Affairs,* 156(3): 130–140.

Kim, Samuel S. 2003. *Korea's Democratization.* New York: Cambridge University Press.

Lachmann, Richard. 1989. Elite Conflict and State Formation in 16th- and 17th-Century England and France. *American Sociological Review,* 54(2): 141–162.

Lachmann, Richard. 1990. Class Formation without Class Struggle: An Elite Conflict Theory of the Transition to Capitalism. *American Sociological Review,* 55: 398–414.

Lachmann, Richard. 2000. *Capitalists in Spite of Themselves: Elite Conflict and Economic Transitions in Early Modern Europe.* New York: Oxford University Press.

Lachmann, Richard. 2003. Elite Self-Interest and Economic Decline in Early Modern Europe. *American Sociological Review,* 68: 346–372.

Lachmann, Richard. 2009. Greed and Contingency: State Fiscal Crises and Imperial Failure in Early Modern Europe. *American Journal of Sociology,* 115(1): 39–73.

Lewis, Peter M. 1999. Nigeria: An End to the Permanent Transition? *Journal of Democracy,* 10(1): 141–156.

Markoff, John. 1996. *Waves of Democracy: Social Movements and Political Change.* Thousand Oaks, CA: Pine Forge Press.

Mason, David S., and James R. Kluegel (eds.). 2000. *Marketing Democracy: Changing Opinion about Inequality and Politics in East Central Europe.* Lanham, MD: Rowman and Littlefield Publishers, Inc.

Mbeke-Ekanem, Tom E. 2000. *Beyond the Execution: Understanding the Ethnic and Military Politics in Nigeria.* Lincoln, NE: iUniverse.com, Inc.

Meyer, John W., John Boli, George M. Thomas, and Francisco O. Ramirez. 1997. World Society and the Nation State. *American Journal of Sociology,* 103(1): 144–181.

Meyer, John W., and Brian Rowan. 1977. Institutionalized Organizations: Formal Structure as Myth and Ceremony. *American Journal of Sociology,* 83: 340–363.

Nyerere, Julius. 1997. "External Imperatives: International Donors and Democratization." In E. Conteh-Morgan (ed.), *Democratization in Africa: The Theory and Dynamics of Political Transitions.* Westport, CT: Praeger Publishers.

Oh, John Kie-chiang. 1999. *Korean Politics: The Quest for Democratization and Economic Development.* Ithaca, NY: Cornell University Press.

Republic of Korea National Election Commission. n.d. URL: info.nec.go.kr (accessed October 28, 2012).

Robinson, William I. 1996. *Promoting Polyarchy: Globalization, US Intervention, and Hegemony.* New York, NY: Cambridge University Press.

Rogers, Michael T. 2005. Rethinking the Contemporary Approach to Democracy & Democratization: A Critical Analysis Based on the Spirit/Form Tradition in Political Thought. PhD Dissertation. University at Albany, State University of New York.

Sandbrook, Richard. 2000. *Closing the Circle: Democratization and Development in Africa.* Toronto, Ontario: Between the Lines.

Seo, Joong-Seok. 2007. *Contemporary History of South Korea – 60 Years.* Seoul: Korea Democracy Foundation.

Tilly, Charles. 2007. *Democracy.* New York, NY: Cambridge University Press.

Whitehead, Laurence. 1996. "International Aspects of Democratization." In Guillermo O'Donnell, Philippe Schmitter, and Laurence Whitehead (eds.), *Transitions from Authoritarian Rule: Comparative Perspectives.* Baltimore, MD: Johns Hopkins University Press.

Ziblatt, Daniel. 2006. How Did Europe Democratize? *World Politics,* 58(2): 311–338.

Zolo, Danilo. 1992. *Democracy and Complexity.* Translated by David McKie. University Park, PA: The Pennsylvania State University Press.

12

Global Crisis, Global Police State

William I. Robinson

The worldwide crisis of the 1960s and 1970s opened the way for capitalist globalization. We are now in the throes of a new crisis of hegemony at the world-systemic level; witness to the ongoing breakdown of consensual domination. The current global crisis shares some features of earlier structural crises of the 1970s, the 1930s and the 1870s, but exhibits novel features that raise the stakes and place humanity at grave risk. These novel features include ecological limits to the system's reproduction, the unprecedented scale and concentration of the means of violence and social control, limits to the extension expansion of capitalism, the rise of a vast surplus population, and a disjuncture between a globalizing economy and a nation-state based system of political authority. The immense structural inequalities of the global political economy cannot easily be maintained through consensual mechanisms of domination. We face the specter of a 21st century global fascism, involving the fusion of reactionary political power with transnational capital, militarized accumulation, and a racist and xenophobic mobilization of downwardly mobile working classes.

Introduction: Policing the global crisis

In their classic 1978 study, *Policing the Crisis*, Stuart Hall and his colleagues showed how the restructuring of capitalism in response to the crisis of the 1970s in the United Kingdom and elsewhere led to an "exceptional state," in reference to the term coined by Nicos Poulantzas, characterized by an ongoing breakdown of consensual mechanisms of social control and increasing authoritarianism. As good Gramscians, they wrote:

> This is an extremely important moment: the point where the repertoire of "hegemony through consent" having been exhausted, the drift towards the routine use of the more repressive features of the state comes more and more prominently into play. Here the pendulum within the exercise of hegemony tilts, decisively, from that where consent overrides coercion, to that condition in which coercion becomes, as it were, the natural and routine form in which consent is secured. This shift in the internal balance of hegemony—consent to coercion—is a response, within the state, to increasing polarization of class forces (real and imagined). It is exactly how a "crisis of hegemony" expresses

itself . . . the slow development of a state of legitimate coercion, the birth of a "law and order" society . . . the whole tenor of social and political life has been transformed by [this moment]. A distinctively new ideological climate has been precipitated. (Hall et al., 1978, 320–321)

In my view, this is an accurate description of the current state of world affairs. We are already witnessing transitions around the world from *social welfare* to *social control states*. However, the crucial distinction between the current situation and the 1970s is that world capitalism has undergone a set of transformations in this age of globalization. The "exceptional state" now needs to be seen in terms of global society as a unity, that is, as global political society, and as an exceptional transnational state. Let me, then, turn to the nature of global capitalism and to its current crisis.

I have been writing about world capitalism since the 1980s, about globalization since the early 1990s, and about the notion of a transnational capitalist class (TCC) and transnational state (TNS) apparatuses since the late 1990s, as part of a broader collective agenda in what some of us have referred to as the *global capitalism school*. My thoughts on globalization have congealed over the past decade into a more synthetic theory of global capitalism as a *new epoch* in the ongoing and open-ended evolution of world capitalism characterized by novel articulations of transnational social power (see, *inter alia*, Robinson, 1996; 2004; 2008).

More recently, I have focused on the global crisis (Robinson, 2014). We are facing an unprecedented crisis, given its magnitude, its global reach, the extent of ecological degradation and social deterioration, and the sheer scale of the means of violence. This is truly a crisis of humanity; we have entered a period of great upheavals, of momentous changes and uncertainties. This systemwide crisis is distinct from earlier such episodes of the 1930s or the 1970s, precisely because world capitalism is fundamentally different in the early twenty-first century. How, specifically, is world capitalism different now than during previous episodes of crisis? There have been several qualitative shifts in the capitalist system, four of which I highlight here:

(1) *The rise of truly transnational capital* and the integration of every country into a new globalized production and financial system, into globalized circuits of accumulation. This is new global economic structure.
(2) The appearance of a new *TCC*, a class group grounded in new globalized circuits of accumulation rather than national circuits;
(3) The rise of *TNS apparatuses*, loose networks comprised of supranational political and economic institutions and of national state apparatuses that have been penetrated and transformed by transnational forces. The key point here is that national states and TNS apparatuses promote transnational over national fractions of capital and transnational over national circuits of accumulation;

(4) The appearance of *novel relations of inequality and domination* in global society; in particular, the rise of new transnational social and class inequalities that cut across the North-South divide.

The current crisis shares several aspects with earlier structural crises, such as in the 1970s, before that in the 1930s, and prior to that, in the 1870s. Each major episode of crisis in the world capitalist system has posed the potential for systemic change. Each has involved the breakdown of legitimacy and consensual (hegemonic) mechanisms of domination, escalating class and social struggles, military conflicts, and eventually a restructuring of the system, including new institutional arrangements, class accommodations, and accumulation activities around which the system restabilized and resumed development. We are now in the midst of another deep structural crisis that as well has the potential to become systemic. However, there are several features unique to the current crisis that sets it apart from earlier episodes:

(1) The system is fast reaching the ecological limits of its reproduction; we may have already reached the point of no return, or passed what ecologists refer to as "tipping points" in the Earth system. This dimension cannot be underestimated, although I cannot take it up here;

(2) The sheer magnitude of the means of violence and social control, as well as the magnitude and concentrated control over the means of global communication and the production and circulation of symbols and images, is unprecedented:

(3) Computerized wars, drone warfare, bunker-buster bombs, satellite surveillance, data mining, spatial control technology, and so forth, have changed the face of warfare, and more generally, of *systems of social control and repression.* Warfare has become normalized and sanitized for those not directly on the receiving end of armed aggression. And moreover, we have arrived at the panoptical surveillance society (a point brought home by the Edward Snowden revelations) and the age of thought control by those who control global flows of communication and symbolic production;

(4) We are reaching limits to the extensive expansion of capitalism, in the sense that there are no longer any new territories of significance to integrate into world capitalism. De-ruralization is now well advanced, and the commodification of the countryside and of pre- and non-capitalist spaces has intensified, that is, they have been converted in hot-house fashion into spaces of capital, so that intensive expansion is reaching depths never before seen;

(5) There is the rise of a vast surplus population inhabiting a "planet of slums" (Davis 2006), alienated from the productive economy, thrown into the margins, and subject to sophisticated systems of social control and to destruction, into a *mortal cycle of dispossess-exploit-exclusion.* Let us recall: crises provide capital with the opportunity to accelerate the process of forcing greater productivity out of fewer workers. The processes by which surplus labor is generated has accelerated under globalization. Spatial reorganization has helped transnational capital to break the territorial-bound power of organized labor and impose new

capital-labor relations based on fragmentation, flexibilization, and the cheapening of labor. These developments, combined with a massive new round of primitive accumulation and displacement, have given rise to a *new global army of superfluous labor* that goes well beyond the traditional reserve army of labor.

(6) There is a disjuncture between a globalizing economy and a nation-state-based system of political authority. TNS apparatuses are incipient and have not been able to play the role of "hegemon," or a leading nation-state with enough power and authority to organize and stabilize the system. I do not share the view of most world-systems analysts that we are in the interregnum between hegemonic powers, e.g., a declining United States and rising Chinese hegemon. Rather, we are moving beyond the age of national hegemons in an interstate system, yet world capitalism does not exhibit a political mechanism for hegemonic stability.

Let us now review how the crisis has developed. Emergent transnational capital underwent a major expansion in the 1980s and 1990s involving *hyper-accumulation* through new technologies such as computer and information technology, through neoliberal policies, and through new modalities of mobilizing and exploiting the global labor force, including a massive new round of primitive accumulation that uprooted and displaced hundreds of millions of people, especially in the third-world countryside, who have become internal and transnational migrants. But by the late 1990s stagnation set in. The system faced renewed crisis. Sharp global social polarization and escalating inequalities fueled the chronic problem of over-accumulation. The concentration of the planet's wealth in the hands of the few and the accelerated impoverishment and dispossession of the majority have been extreme under global capitalism. Global inequalities and impoverishment of broad majorities have meant that transnational capital cannot find productive outlets to unload enormous amounts of surplus it has accumulated. By the twenty-first century, the TCC turned to several mechanisms to sustain global accumulation in the face of overaccumulation. What were these mechanisms?

One has been militarized accumulation; making wars and interventions that unleash cycles of destruction and reconstruction and generate enormous profits for an ever-expanding "military-prison-industrial-security-energy-financial complex." We are now living in a global war economy that goes well beyond such "hot wars" as in Iraq or Afghanistan. A second has been the raiding and sacking of public budgets. The TCC has used its financial power to take control of state finances and impose further austerity on the working majority. The TCC employs its structural power to accelerate the dismantling of what remains of the social wage and welfare states. This represents a transfer of value from global labor to transnational capital, a claim by the latter on future wages, and a shift in the burden of the crisis to the working and popular classes. A third has been frenzied worldwide financial speculation, turning the global economy into a giant casino. The TCC has unloaded trillions of dollars into speculation in housing markets, food, energy and other global commodities markets, into bond markets worldwide (that is, into public budgets and state finances), and into every imaginable derivative, ranging from hedge funds to swaps, futures markets, collateralized debt obligations, asset pyramiding, and ponzi schemes.

Responses to the crisis

The crisis has resulted in a rapid political polarization in global society. Both right- and left-wing forces are insurgent. Among others, we can identify three respons- es to crisis that are in dispute. One is *reformism from above* aimed at stabilizing the system, at saving it from itself and from more radical responses from below. Reformist-oriented transnational elites have proposed: regulating global financial markets, state stimulus programs, fomenting a shift from speculative to productive accumulation, and limited redistributive measures. Reformist-oriented elites are guided less by neoclassical than institutional economics and pursue a "global neo- Keynesianism." Nonetheless, in the years following the 2008 collapse of the global financial system, these reformers were unable—or unwilling—to prevail over the power of transnational finance capital. It would seem that the national state has lost its "relative autonomy" in the face of a more direct instrumentalization by the TCC and its political agents, together with the enhanced structural power of transna- tional finance capital under globalization over the direct power of national states.

A second response to global crisis has come from popular, grass-roots, and left- ist resistance from below. As social and political conflict escalated around the world in the wake of 2008, there has been a mounting global revolt, including repeated rounds of national strikes and mass mobilizations in the European Union, uprisings in the Middle East and North Africa, the Chilean students movement, Occupy Wall Street, strike waves among Chinese workers, the spread of such transnational social movements as *Via Campesina*, and so forth. While such resistance appears insur- gent, it does not seem to have achieved hegemony among oppositional forces or to have channeled mass frustration into an antisystemic project that could challenge the hegemony of the system. It is spread very unevenly across countries and regions and faces many problems and challenges.

A third response, and that which concerns me most here, is what I refer to as twenty-first century fascism (Robinson, 2014; see also Robinson and Barrera, 2012). The ultra-right is an insurgent force in many countries. The protofascist right seeks to fuse reactionary political power with transnational capital and to organize a mass base among historically privileged sectors of the global working class—such as white "native" workers in the North and middle layers in the South—now expe- riencing heightened insecurity and the specter of downward mobility. Its discourse and practice involves militarism, extreme or "martial" masculinization, racism and racist mobilizations against scapegoats. This search for scapegoats has included immigrant workers and Muslims, for instance, in North America and Europe. It puts forth mystifying ideologies, often involving race/culture supremacy and xenophobia, embracing an idealized and mythical past. Neofascist culture normalizes, even glamorizes, war and social violence, generating a fascination with domination, which is even portrayed as heroic.

It is important to stress that the need for dominant groups around the world to assure the widespread, organized, mass social control of the world's surplus population and rebellious forces from below gives a powerful impulse to projects of twenty-first century global fascism. Simply put, the immense structural inequalities of the global political economy cannot easily be contained through consensual mechanisms of social control, that is, through hegemonic domination.

I especially want to call attention to the rising tide of surplus labor. States abandon efforts to secure legitimacy among this surplus population and instead turn to repression. In place of incorporating those marginalized, the system tries to isolate and neutralize their real or potential rebellion by criminalization of the poor and the dispossessed, with tendencies towards genocide in some cases. The mechanisms of coercive exclusion include: mass incarceration and the spread of prison-industrial complexes; pervasive policing; repressive anti-immigrant legislation; the manipulation of space in new ways so that both gated communities and ghettos are controlled by armies of private security guards and technologically advanced surveillance systems; and ideological campaigns aimed at seduction and passivity through petty consumption and fantasy. We must recall that fascism, whether in its classical form or possible variants of twenty-first century neofascism, is *a particular response to capitalist crisis*. In my public discussions on twenty-first century fascism I have found a tenacious aversion to raising the term; perhaps such dismissiveness is due in part to the frequent misuse of the term to refer to any situation of state repression and authoritarian system. Yet anyone who has recently spent time in Colombia or in Haiti and understands how those countries are organized and operate, to take but two examples, will no doubt recognize twenty-first century fascism.

It is crucial to stress that a twenty-first century fascism would not be a repetition of its twentieth century predecessor. The role of political and ideological domination through control over the media and the flow of images and symbols would make any twenty-first century project more sophisticated, and together with panoptical surveillance and social control technologies, probably allow it to rely more on selective than generalized repression. These and other new forms of social control and modalities of ideological domination blur boundaries, so that *there may be a constitutional and normalized neofascism, with formal representative institutions, a constitution, political parties and elections ... all the while the political system is tightly controlled by transnational capital and its representatives and any dissent that actually threatens the system is neutralized if not liquidated.* Moreover, fascism in the twentieth century involved the fusion of reactionary political power with *national* capital. In fact, it was the national capitals of core or would-be core countries that lost space in the world capitalist system for international accumulation in the midst of crisis that turned to reactionary militaristic power in an attempt to gain or retain such space. Now, the major concentrations of what were national capitalists have transnationalized under globalization. I do not see a twenty-first century fascism as a mechanism of competition among national capitals but as an expression of the dictatorship of transnational capital.

Policing the global crisis: Lessons from the United States

The division of the world into distinct—if inextricably interconnected—nation-states means that a wide variety of polities may appear in accordance with particular national and regional histories, social forces, and conjunctures, and *within a larger global unity*. However, investigation into twenty-first century fascism in the United States, or in any particular country, is a methodological simplification and epistemological reduction, in that a twenty-first century fascism cannot be understood as a nation-state project in this age of global capitalism. It is more analytically and conceptually accurate to talk of a *global police state*, or in applying Poulantzas' notion, an *exceptional transnational state*. The global order as a unity is increasingly repressive and authoritarian. Particular *forms* of exceptional nation-states or national polities, including twenty-first century fascism, develop on the basis of particular national and regional histories, social and class forces, political cultures, and conjunctures. Yet the militarization of cities, politics, and culture in such countries as the United States and Israel is inseparable from these countries' entanglement in webs of global wars and militarized circuits of global accumulation. The powers that be in the global system must secure social control and defend the global order in each particular national territory, lest the global order itself becomes threatened.

Criminialization and the militarized control of the structurally marginalized constitute one major mechanism of preemptive containment. The drive to contain the real or potential rebellion from the mass of the dispossessed and the disenfranchised replaces, in some respects, the drive to crush socialism from the organized working class that helped drive twentieth-century fascism. The state responds to those expelled from the labor market and locked out of productive labor not with social protection but with *abandonment and repressive social controls and containment strategies*. This involves *racialized* criminalization and the mobilization of the culture industries to dehumanize the victims of global capitalism as dangerous, depraved, and culturally degenerate Others—criminal elements posing a threat to society.

This brings us back to Hall et al. In their 1978 study, they highlighted the highly racialized nature of policing and criminalization of black and immigrant communities in the United Kingdom. They deconstructed the complex ideological processes of fabricating criminalization of the oppressed in function of social control at moments of hegemonic crisis. Here we see the strong parallels between the incipient "exceptional state" in the 1970s and the current drift towards such states in the United States and elsewhere. The displacement of social anxieties to crime and to a racialized "criminalized" population in the United States and elsewhere dates back to the 1970s crisis. In the United States, in the wake of the mass rebellions of the 1960s, dominant groups promoted systematic cultural and ideological "law-and-order" campaigns to legitimate the shift from social welfare to social control states and the rise of the prison-industrial complex. "Law and order" came to mean the reconstruction and reinforcing of racialized social hierarchies and hegemonic order in the wake of the 1960s rebellions. This coincided with global economic reconstruction, neoliberalism, and capitalist globalization from the 1970s and on. Criminalization helps displace social anxieties resulting from the structurally violent disruption of stability, security and social organization generated by the current crisis.

In her shocking expose, *The New Jim Crow*, Michelle Alexander (2010) documents mass incarceration in the United States "as a stunningly comprehensive and well-disguised system of racialized social control." Indeed, the racialized nature of the bogus "war on drugs," caging and social death sentences are so blatant that it shocks the senses. Mass incarceration made "legal" by the "war on drugs" is a frighteningly effective system for: sweeping up surplus labor; fragmenting communities from which this labor comes; locking up those captured in cages; and then sentencing them to permanent social death upon release, thereby generating conditions that at the very least make collective rebellion many times more difficult.

The "war on drugs" ushered in domestic militarization that expanded exponentially with the "war on terrorism." This has included 30 million arrested for drug offenses from 1982–2010 and an increase by 1100 percent in the imprisonment of those arrested for these offenses. By 2007 more than seven million people were behind bars, on probation, or on parole, and some 650,000 were being released from prison annually. Roughly 65 million people now have criminal records as a result, often involving social death sentences for life. This conversion of the African-American population into a tightly controlled mass of surplus labor cannot be underemphasized. Ruth Wilson Gilmore (2007), in her study *Golden Gulag*, shows how California—the epicenter of the strategy of mass incarceration—has led the way in "the biggest prison building project in the history of the world." The defeat of radical struggles alongside the accumulation of surplus capital during the 1960s to the 1980s led to a strategy in California of caging surplus labor—vastly disproportionately from racially oppressed groups. She demonstrates the correlation between the expansion of unemployment and the massive increase in the prison population. In sum, in the wake of the crisis of the 1970s, surpluses were channeled by the state into prison expansion, resolving the state's problem of "surplus capacity," capital's problem of how to profitably unload surpluses into new accumulation activities, and removing potentially destabilizing surplus labor from the general population.

This turn to a "law-and-order" police state helped facilitate the dismantling of the Keynesian welfare state. Far from coincidental, the processes of neoliberalism and capitalist globalization, on the one hand, and a "law-and-order" police state, on the other, are mutually reinforcing, *part of a singular strategy of reconstituting hegemony through new mechanisms and discourses of social control.* The "war on drugs" and "war on terror" facilitate domestic militarization and new patterns of militarized accumulation that lend themselves to coercive modes of mass social control. By the 1990s, police forces across the United States were acquiring millions of pieces of military equipment from the Pentagon for domestic operations, including aircraft for transporting police units, UH-60 Blackhawk and UH-1 Hewy helicopters, and later drones, M-16 automatic rifles, grenade launchers, night-vision goggles, and even tanks and bazookas. Paramilitary units known as Special Weapons and Tactics, or SWAT, teams have been formed in every major U.S. city, first to fight the "drug war," and then to fight "terrorism." In 1972, there were just a few hundred paramilitary drug raids per year. By the 1980s there were some 3000 annual SWAT deployments, by 1996, 30,000, and by 2001, on the eve of 9/11, 40,000. As police forces become paramilitary units they move from "community policing" to "military policing" in urban ghettos that become war zones. In analytical abstraction, mass incarceration takes the place of concentration camps. Suffice it to observe here that the system subjects a surplus and potentially rebellious population of millions to concentration, caging, and state violence; the so-called "war on drugs" and "war on terrorism," as well as the undeclared "war on gangs" and "war on immigrants," must be placed in this context.

In his brilliant yet chilling study, *Cities Under Siege: The New Military Urbanism*, Stephen Graham (2010) shows how structures and processes of permanent militarized social control systems and warfare constitute a global project that is by definition transnational. It is important to note that every country has become enmeshed in policing the global crisis as the global economy becomes ever-more invested in warfare, social violence, and state-organized coercion and repression. It is worth quoting Graham (2010, xviii) at some length:

> The new military urbanism feeds on experiences with styles of targeting and technology in colonial war-zones, such as Gaza or Baghdad, or security operations at international sport events or political summits. These operations act as testing grounds for technologies and techniques to be sold on through the world's burgeoning homeland security markets. . . . Israeli drones designed to vertically subjugate and target Palestinians are now routinely deployed by police forces in North America, Europe, and East Asia. Private operators of U.S. "supermax" prisons are heavily involved in running the global archipelago organizing incarceration and torture that has burgeoned since the start of the "war on terror." Private military corporations heavily colonize reconstruction contracts in both Iraq and New Orleans. Israeli expertise in population control is sought by those planning security operations for international events in the west. And shoot-to-kill policies developed to combat suicide bombings in Tel Aviv and Haifa have been adopted by police forces in Europe and America. . . . Meanwhile, aggressive and militarized policing at public demonstrations and social mobilizations in London, Toronto, Paris and New York are now starting to utilize the same "non-lethal weapons" as Israel's

army in Gaza or Jenin. The construction of "security zones" around the strategic financial cores and government districts of London and New York directly import the techniques used at overseas bases and green zones. Finally, many of the techniques used to fortify enclaves in Baghdad or permanently lockdown civilians in Gaza and the West Bank are being sold around the world as cutting-edge and combat-proven "security solutions" by corporate coalitions linking Israeli, U.S., and other companies and states.

In reading Graham, it seems to me hard to understate the significance of new technologies that allow state and corporate repressive apparatuses to exercise such a degree of surveillance and control over space that threats can often be disarticulated before wholesale, mass repression becomes necessary.

Finally, it is important to remember that militarization and violence become accumulation strategies independent of any political objectives and appear as a structural feature of the new global capitalism. As I have discussed at some length elsewhere (Robinson, 2014), given the extensive and continuing privatization of war and state-sponsored social control and repression, it is in the interests of a broad array of capitalist groups to shift the political, social and ideological climate towards the generation and sustaining of social conflict and the expansion of systems of warfare, repression, surveillance and social control. The generation of conflicts, the criminalization of the dispossessed, and the repression of social movements and vulnerable populations around the world continually regenerate opportunities for accumulation. While transnational capital may not at this time have fused with reactionary political power at the highest level of the U.S. federal government, militarized accumulation underscores a broader feature of both classical and twenty-first century fascism: reactionary political forces in the state open up accumulation opportunities for capital in crisis, and in turn capital develops an interest in a system of violence and coercive control.

In conclusion, the worldwide crisis of hegemony of the late 1960s and early 1970s opened the way for capitalist globalization. We are now in the throes of a new crisis of hegemony at the world-systemic level; witness to the ongoing breakdown of consensual domination. Crises open up space for a wide variety of counter-hegemonic forces and collective agencies. It is because the system is facing a crisis of hegemony and because alternative systems are a real possibility, and *not because the current system of domination is strong or secure*, that policing global capitalism acquires these frightening dimensions.

References

Alexander, Michelle. 2010. *The New Jim Crow: Mass Incarceration in the Age of Color Blindness*. New York: New Press.
Davis, Mike. 2006. *Planet of Slums*. London: Verso.

Gilmore, Ruth Wilson. 2007. *Golden Gulag: Prisons, Surplus, Crisis, and Opposition in Globalizing California.* Berkeley: University of California Press.

Graham, Stephen. 2010. *Cities Under Siege: The New Military Urbanism.* London: Verso.

Hall, Stuart, Chas Critcher, Tony Jefferson, John Clarke, and Brian Roberts. 1978. *Policing the Crisis: Mugging, the State, and Law and Order.* New York: Holmes and Meier Publishers.

Robinson, William, I. 1996. *Promoting Polyarchy: Globalization, U.S. Intervention, and Hegemony.* Cambridge and New York: Cambridge University Press.

Robinson, William, I. 2004. *A Theory of Global Capitalism: Production, Class and State in a Transnational World.* Baltimore: Johns Hopkins University Press.

Robinson, William, I. 2008. *Latin America and Global Capitalism: A Critical Globalization Perspective.* Baltimore: Johns Hopkins University Press.

Robinson, William, I. 2014. *Global Capitalism and the Crisis of Humanity.* Cambridge and New York: Cambridge University Press.

Robinson, William, I. and Mario Barrera. 2012. Global Crisis and Twenty-First Century Fascism: A U.S. Case Study. *Race and Class*, 53(4): 4–29.

PART III

World-Ecology and Global Transformation

13

The End of Cheap Nature Or: How I Learned to Stop Worrying about "The" Environment and Love the Crisis of Capitalism

Jason W. Moore

Does capitalism today face the "end of cheap nature"? If so, what could this mean, and what are the implications for the future? We are indeed witnessing the end of cheap nature in a historically specific sense. Rather than view the end of cheap nature as the reassertion of external "limits to growth," I argue that capitalism has today exhausted the historical relation that produced cheap nature. The end of cheap nature is best comprehended as the exhaustion of the value-relations that have periodically restored the "Four Cheaps": labor-power, food, energy, and raw materials. Crucially, these value-relations are co-produced by and through humans with the rest of nature. The decisive issue therefore turns on the relations that enfold and unfold successive configurations of human and extra-human nature, symbolically enabled and materially enacted, over the longue durée of the modern world-system. Significantly, the appropriation of unpaid work—including "free gifts" of nature—and the exploitation wage-labor form a dialectical unity. The limits to growth faced by capital today are real enough, and are "limits" co-produced through capitalism as world-ecology, joining the accumulation of capital, the pursuit of power, and the co-production of nature as an organic whole. The world-ecological limit of capital is capital itself.

Introduction

What can it mean to speak of "the end of cheap nature"? It is a deceptively simple question, for it begs a series of clarifications. Is "the end" a cyclical phenomenon? (The end of neoliberalism's cheap nature?) Or is the "end" secular? (The end of historical capitalism's cheap nature?) Capitalism, we know, enjoys a long history of overcoming seemingly insuperable barriers to revive accumulation. This is especially true of barriers concerning the Big Four inputs: labor-power, food, energy, and raw materials. Does "cheap nature" refer to the bounty—and eventual exhaustion—of extra-human biological systems and geological distributions? Or does cheap nature signify a historical circumstance created—and later unraveled—by the relations of power, accumulation, and nature specific to the modern world-system? Does cheap nature, and its possible demise, include *human* nature? Perhaps most significantly, are these questions about the end of cheap nature questions about nature as an easy source of resources—either because the "taps" have been tapped out or because the "sinks" have been filled up? Or are they about the end of *a way* of organizing nature premised on endless commodification?

Theoretical frame: Value relations in the capitalist world-ecology

What we are seeing today is the "end of cheap nature" as a civilizational strategy, one born during the rise of capitalism in the "long" sixteenth century (c. 1450–1648). An ingenious civilizational project has been at the core of this strategy, to construct nature as external to human activity, and thence to mobilize the work of uncommodified human and extra-human natures in service to advancing labor productivity within commodity production. The great leap forward in the scale, scope, and speed of landscape and biological transformations in the three centuries after 1450— stretching from Poland to Brazil, and the North Atlantic's cod fisheries to Southeast Asia's spice islands—may be understood in this light (Moore, 2007; 2010a; 2010b; 2013a; 2013b). Such transformations were the epoch-making expressions of a new law of value that reconfigured uncommodified human and extra-human natures (slaves, forests, soils) in servitude to labor productivity and the commodity.

The new law of value was quite peculiar. Never before had any civilization negotiated this transition from land productivity to labor productivity as the decisive metric of wealth. This strange metric—*value*—oriented the whole of west-central Europe towards an equally strange conquest of space. This strange conquest was what Marx (1973, 524) calls the "annihilation of space by time," and across the long sixteenth century we can see a new form of time—abstract time—taking shape (Postone, 1993). While all civilizations in some sense are built to expand across varied topographies—they "pulse" (Chase-Dunn and Hall, 1997)—none represented these topographies as external and progressively abstracted in the ways that dominated early capitalism's geographical *praxis*. The genius of capitalism's cheap nature strategy was to represent time as linear, space as flat, and nature as external (Mumford, 1934; Merchant, 1980; Pickles, 2004). It was a civilizational inflection of the "God-trick" (Haraway, 1988), with bourgeois knowledge representing its special brand of quantifying and scientific reason as a mirror of the world—the same world then being reshaped by early modernity's scientific revolutions in alliance with empires and capitals. With abstract time, in other words, would come abstract space (Lefebvre, 1991). Together, they were the indispensable corollaries to the weird crystallization of human and extra-human natures in the form of abstract social labor. It was this ascendant law of value—operating as gravitational field rather than mechanism—that underpinned the extraordinary landscape and biological revolutions of early modernity. Notwithstanding the fanciful historical interpretations of the Anthropocene argument and its idealized model of a two-century modernity (Steffen et al., 2011), the origins of capitalism's cheap nature strategy and today's biospheric turbulence are to be found in the long sixteenth century. The issue is not one of anthropogenic-drivers—presuming a fictitious human unity—but of the relations of capital and capitalist power. The issue is not the Anthropocene, but the *Capitalocene.*

This early modern transition from land productivity in manifold "tributary" relations to labor productivity in manifold "commodity" relations emerged through a powerful bundle of processes co-produced by human and extra-human natures. In this view, capitalism unfolds in and through the *oikeios,* the creative, generative, and multi-layered relation of species and environment (Moore, 2011a). Humans, like all species, are at once producers and products of our environments (Levins and Lewontin, 1985). Humans, and also the civilizations we co-produce with the rest of nature. We find the spirit the *oikeios* when Wallerstein (1980, 162, 132–133; also 1974, 44, 89) speaks of "ecological exhaustion" as a world-historical movement encompassing *human* natures alongside soils and forests. The health of bodies and environments are indeed dialectically bound (Marx, 1977, 238, 636–638).

To be sure, humans are distinctive in forming historically-specific notions of our place in the web of life. This is the history of ideas of nature (Williams, 1980), which are in fact ideas of everything that humans do. We are amongst the planet's more effective "ecosystem engineers" (Wright and Jones, 2006); and even so, we too—our civilizations also—are made and unmade by the environment-making activities of life. (Does anyone today doubt that disease and climate make history every bit as much as any empire or class or market?) To take this position is to immediately abandon the notion of civilization (or world-system or capitalism) *and* environment, and instead re-focus on the idea of civilizations-*in*-nature, capitalism *as* environment-making process. These environments include factories no less than forests, homes no less than mines, financial centers no less than farms, the city no less than the country. Taking "ecology" as the signifier of the whole in its manifold species-environment relations, I have taken to calling capitalism a "world-ecology," joining the accumulation of capital, the pursuit of power, and the co-production of nature in dialectical unity (Moore, 2011a, 2011b; also Oloff, 2012; Deckard, 2012; Leonardi, 2012; Mahnkopf, 2013; Niblett, 2013; Ortiz, 2013).

In what follows, "nature" is matrix, rather than resource zone and rubbish bin. But such an assertion is insufficient in itself, for two reasons. The first is that the philosophical recognition—humanity-in-nature—must be accompanied by workable analytics that allow us to interpret historical change as actively co-produced by humans and the rest of nature. This transition from holistic philosophy to relational history is the core of the world-ecology argument. Secondly, the argument for nature as matrix must include and explain the idea and *praxis* of external nature, created by modernity's successive knowledge revolutions. For nature could not be rendered "cheap" until it was rendered external. Yes, the distinction between human and extra-human natures has a long history that stretches back, at the latest, to Greco-Roman antiquity (Glacken, 1967). But never before had nature as external object become an organizing principle for a civilization.

This view of nature as external object, while demonstrably false in terms of historical *method*, was an essential moment in the rise of capitalism. Here we can see ideas as "material force" (Marx, 1978, 60). Early capitalism's world-praxis, fusing symbolic coding and material inscription, moved forward an audacious fetishization of nature. This was expressed, dramatically, in the era's cartographic, scientific, and quantifying revolutions. These were the symbolic moments of primitive accumulation, creating a new intellectual system whose presumption, personified by Descartes, was the separation of humans from the rest of nature. For early modern materialism, the point was not only to interpret the world but to control it: "to make ourselves as it were the masters and possessors of nature" (Descartes, 2006, 51). It was a powerful vision, one so powerful that that even today, many students of global environmental change have internalized the early modern view of nature, in which space is flat, time is linear, and nature ontologically external to human activity (e.g., Steffen et al., 2011).

The origins of cheap nature are, of course, far more than intellectual and symbolic. The transgression of medieval intellectual frontiers was paired with the transgression of medieval territoriality. While civilizational expansion is in some sense fundamental to all, there emerged in early modern Europe a specific geographical thrust. While all civilizations *had* frontiers of a sort, capitalism *was* a frontier. The extension of capitalist power to new spaces that were uncommodified became the lifeblood of capitalism. I have elsewhere considered the historical geographies of early capitalism's commodity frontiers (Moore, 2000; 2003; 2007; 2010a; 2010b). For the moment, I wish to highlight two relational axes of these frontiers. First, commodity frontier movements were not merely about the extension of commodity relations, although this was indeed central. Commodity frontier movements were also, crucially, about the extension of territorial and symbolic forms that *appropriated unpaid work in service to commodity production*. This unpaid work could be delivered by humans—women or slaves, for example—or by extra-human natures, such as forests, soils, or rivers. Second, such frontier movements were, from the very beginning of capitalism, essential to creating the forms of cheap nature specific to capitalism: the "Four Cheaps" of labor-power, food, energy, and raw materials (Moore, 2012).

Capitalism's basic problem is that capital's demand for cheap natures rises faster than its capacity to secure them. The costs of production rise, and accumulation falters. This was recognized by Marx long ago, not only in his "general law" of the "overproduction" of machinery and the "underproduction" of raw materials (Marx, 1967, III, 119–121), but also in his perceptive observations that the bourgeois tends to accumulate capital by exhausting "labour-power, in the same way as a greedy farmer snatches more produce from the soil by robbing it of its fertility" (Marx, 1977, 376). The solution? Move to the frontier, so much the better if such frontiers were colonies: thus the salience of Irish workers, Caribbean sugar, Mississippi cotton. For this reason, capital finds itself continually dependent on capitalist power and bourgeois knowledge to locate "external" natures whose wealth can be mapped, reshaped, and appropriated cheaply.

In creating these external and "cheap" natures, capital turned weakness to strength. Through its alliance with state-machineries, imperialist power, and bourgeois knowledge, capital has proven adept at overcoming real, or impending, "bottlenecks" to renewed accumulation. The frontier has therefore been capitalism's way of paying the bills that run up across successive long centuries of accumulation. Is the exhaustion of the cheap natures created through neoliberal capitalism a cyclical phenomenon—such as we saw at the end of the late eighteenth century, or the during the long 1970s—or is it the end of the capitalist road to cheap nature? Is the present *conjoncture*, in other words, a developmental crisis, one open to resolution through renewed rounds of capitalization? Or is it, rather, an epochal crisis, one that will compel fundamentally new relations of wealth, power, and nature in the century ahead?

This line of questioning has been marginal in today's proliferating literature on economic and ecological crisis. Prominent scholars who engage both moments—such as David Harvey and John Bellamy Foster—write as if nature and capitalism are separate, rather than unified, phenomena. Their philosophical insistence that humans are part of nature (e.g., Harvey, 1996; Foster, 2013b) rarely translates to historical analysis. Harvey's powerful argument for the relationality of humanity-in-nature falls by the wayside in his narratives of neoliberalism (Harvey 2003; 2005; 2010); Foster (2009) insists on no necessary connection between accumulation and biospheric crises. Foster and Harvey stand in here for a broader intellectual problem. Even when our philosophical position regards humans as part of nature, the narrative rules, methodological premises, and theoretical frames of world-historical scholars often remain within the confines of a modernist view of nature as external. This may explain some measure of the profound undertheorization of "ecological crisis," and the widespread weakness of critical scholars to explain how nature matters to capitalism, not merely as output, but as constitutive relation.

What would such an explanation—one premised on the co-production of capitalism by humans and the rest of nature—look like?

Nature, limits, and capital: Value and the world-ecological surplus

My answer proceeds from two big issues swirling about nature, capital, and limits today. One is historical. The other is conceptual. In the first instance, we must ask whether the peculiar train of events since 2003, when the present commodity boom began, represents a cyclical or cumulative "end" of the Four Cheaps: food, labor, energy, and raw materials (Moore, 2012). Capitalism since the early nineteenth century has been remarkably adept at overcoming the actual (but temporary)—and averting potential (but quite threatening)—bottlenecks relating to the rising price of the Big Four inputs (Rostow, 1978). This capacity to overcome and avert such bottlenecks can be seen in successive epoch-making agricultural revolutions, expansively reproducing the cheap food/cheap labor nexus (Moore, 2010c). England's late eighteenth century agricultural stagnation and food price woes were resolved through the American farmer's marriage of mechanization and fertile frontiers after 1840. The productivity stagnation of early twentieth century capitalist agriculture in western Europe and North America was resolved through successive "green" revolutions, manifested in the postwar globalization of the hybridized, chemicalized, and mechanized American farm model (Kloppenburg, 1988; Federico, 2004). From this perspective, there is good reason for seeing the post-2008 global conjuncture as a *developmental crisis* of the capitalist world-ecology, one that can be resolved through renewed rounds of commodification, especially but not only in agriculture. But the latest wave of capitalist agricultural revolution—in agro-biotechnology— has yet to arrest the productivity slowdown (Gurian-Sherman, 2009). It is therefore also possible that capitalism has entered into an *epochal crisis*.

Developmental and epochal crises do not represent a "convergence" of ontologically independent environmental and economic crises (e.g., Foster, 2013a). Rather, such crises give expression to the maturing contradictions inscribed in those regimes of value, power, and nature that govern capitalism over the *longue durée*, and through successive long centuries of accumulation (Arrighi, 1994; Moore, 2011b). In place of the converging crises model, we may instead view our era's turbulence as a singular crisis—of capitalism as a way of organizing nature—with manifold expressions. Food and climate, finance and energy represent not multiple, *but manifold*, forms of crisis emanating from a singular civilizational project: the capitalist world-ecology.

We might begin with how capitalism goes about forming and re-forming its specific configurations of wealth, power, and nature: not as three independent boxes but as mutually relational moments in the cumulative and cyclical development of the modern world-system. To pursue this line of inquiry brings us squarely onto the terrain of capitalism's law of value. For it is the emergence, development, and cyclical restructuring of capital, power, and nature that are conditioned decisively by capitalism's value relations.

We might think value relations in two major ways. The first is *value as method* (Moore, 2011a; 2011b). This approach reconstructs historical capitalism through "the production and reproduction of real life" as "distinctions within . . . the organic whole" (Engels, 1934; Marx, 1973, 99–100). This permits a world-ecological recasting of "nature" and "society" in favor of the contradictory unity of "the production and reproduction of real life." It is a unity that cuts across and destabilizes any meaningful historical boundary between human activity and the rest of nature; the "reproduction of real life" includes the extra-human intertwined with the human at every step. Taking the production and reproduction of life as our guiding thread allows us to dissolve the ontological and historical divide between the economic and the ecological, in favor of definite historical configurations of human and extra-human natures. Once freed from the fetish of "the economy," we can focus on the relations of power and (re)production that make possible the endless reproduction of value in its double existence: *as abstract social labor and abstract social nature.* (About the latter, more presently.) Value as method therefore posits historical capitalism not as the zone of commodification but as the contradictory unity of endless commodification and its appropriation of the conditions of reproduction—from the reproduction of human beings to to the reproduction of biospheric stability.

This brings us to a second deployment of value relations. This is *value as historical proposition.* In this, we can think value as a historical project that engages reality as something to be reduced to an interchangeable part. These reductions are at once symbolic and material, and they comprise both "economic" and "non-economic" simplifications (e.g., Braverman, 1974; Worster, 1990; Scott, 1998). Crucially, the generalization of value relations works through a dialectic of capitalizing production and appropriating reproduction. Value is encoded simultaneously through the *exploitation* of labor-power in commodity production, and through the *appropriation* of nature's life-making capacities as unpaid work. This double coding of value is therefore a dialectic of *value/not-value.* This latter, *not-value,* is "produced" through the zone of appropriation: the condition for *value* as the zone of exploitation. It includes, pivotally, the unpaid work of all humans, but especially so-called "women's work."

Historical capitalism has been able to resolve its recurrent crises because territorialist and capitalist agencies have been able to extend the zone of appropriation faster than the zone of exploitation. For this reason, capitalism overcomes seemingly insuperable "natural limits" through coercive-intensive and symbolically-enabled appropriations of cheap natures, cyclically renewing the Four Cheaps. Dramatic enlargements in the zone of appropriation resolve capitalism's crises by effecting a remarkable—and necessarily short-lived—trick: appropriation "works" to the degree that it controls and channels, *but does not capitalize,* the reproduction of life-making as unpaid work. Value only works when most work is not valued. Modernity in this sense is a mighty control project, effecting all manner of quantifying and categorizing procedures oriented towards identifying, securing, and regulating human and extra-human natures in the service of accumulation. This latter is the terrain of *abstract social nature.*

From this standpoint, the development of value relations may be discerned through its chief material expression, the Four Cheaps of labor-power, food, energy, and raw materials. These are the indispensable (but not exclusive) conditions for the long-run revival of accumulation, as we saw in 1846–1873, 1947–1973, and mostly recently, 1983–2007.

The cyclical rise and decline of the Four Cheaps therefore offers a promising point of entry into a deeper, world-ecological, understanding of historical capitalism. "Cheap" signifies the value composition of the Big Four inputs. A low value composition represents a relatively low quantum of average human labor (abstract social labor) in the average commodity—and a relatively higher contribution of unpaid work. "Value," understood as abstract social labor, is measured by average labor-time. The *law* of value, in this reading, is a world-historical tendency that— "modified in its working by many circumstances" (Marx, 1977, 798)—transforms the wealth of nature into *value*, as interchangeable and quantifiable units of wealth, defined by interchangeable and quantifiable units of human labor-time *in commodity production*.

This latter is socially necessary labor-time. While all species "work" in some fashion, only humans create and labor under socially necessary labor-time. *Only* humans, and only *some* humans at that. The law of value—not the *theory* of value but its actual historical operation—is anthropocentric in a very specific sense. Only human labor-power *directly* produces value. A tree, or a horse, or a geological vent cannot be paid. And yet, commodified labor-power cannot produce anything without the unpaid work of the horse or the three. Socially necessary *unpaid* work is the pedestal of socially necessary labor time.

"But wait!" says the environmentalist. "Doesn't that show that value is partial, and doesn't work?" The first part of the objection is entirely correct: value *is* partial. *Necessarily* partial. And, unlike the horse or the tree, unpaid human work *could* be paid. But capitalists do not like to pay their bills, and for good reason. To fully commodify the reproduction of labor-power would do away with the unpaid work that allows accumulation to proceed at acceptable rates of profit. Marxists will sometimes characterize capitalism as a system in which "the bulk of society's work is done by propertyless labourers who are obliged to sell their labour-power" (Wood, 2002, 3). But this is precisely what *cannot* occur under capitalism! If the bulk of the work carried out within capitalism were ever to be monetized, the costs of labor-power would soar, and cheap labor-power would not exist. Only the barest rate of capital accumulation would be possible.

None of this suggests that wage-labor is epiphenomenal. Quite the contrary! Rather, proletarianization may be more adequately understood as a "connective historical process" fundamental to the capitalist world-ecology (McMichael, 1991, 343). In this light, the rise of the law of value is not centered on the rise of the modern proletariat *as such*, but on the uneven globalization of wage-work *dialectically joined to* the "generalization of its conditions of reproduction" (McMichael, 1991, 343). Value, as abstract social labor, works *through*, not in spite of, its partiality.

Life-activity outside commodity production, but articulated with it, is *socially necessary unpaid work*. Strictly speaking, it cannot be quantified in the same fashion as commodified labor-power because the condition of quantifiable abstract social labor is a mass of *un*quantifiable work. What capital strives to achieve is the reduction of necessary labor-time. This reduction is intrinsic to capital's existence: hence capitalism's emphasis on labor productivity over land productivity, and capital's mo-bilization of cheap natures in order to make this emphasis possible. The accelera-tion of landscape change and the emergence of a tentative but tenacious regime of abstract social labor were two sides of the rise of capitalism in the sixteenth century; abstract social labor could only take shape on the basis of a new, sharply accelerated, relation to the unpaid work of cheap natures.

In the conventional narrative (Landes, 1969), rising labor productivity is a story of technological advance and organizational innovation in industrial production. This is true enough. But is it the whole story? New machinery and energy sources at the point of production can only advance labor productivity—reducing necessary labor-time over the long-run—through new technologies of power that reduce the value-composition of the Big Four inputs. The Four Cheaps could be restored only partly through innovations within established zones of commodity production; his-torically, they also depended on new strategies of appropriation, on new frontiers. Here we find a systemic connection between the accumulation of capital and the rise of capitalist power in making possible a civilization cohered by the law of value. In order to reduce necessary labor-time, capital sets in motion—and struggles to create through varied combinations of coercion, consent, and rationalization—a civilization that aims to maximize the unpaid "work" of life outside circuit of capital, but within reach of capitalist *power*.

The reduction of socially-necessary labor time through commodification is what I have been calling *capitalization*; the maximization of unpaid work in ser-vice to capitalization, is *appropriation*. There is some overlap, to be sure. Where the Cartesian frame presumes separation of humanity *and* nature, the world-ecology argument presumes a dialectical unity that proceeds from the distinctiveness of hu-mans (amongst many other species) within the web of life. So my focus is directed towards the ways that capitalization and appropriation work together as patterns and rules of reproducing value and power in the web of life. This gives us a way to identify and to explain patterns of environment-making across the *longue durée* of historical capitalism. It is a simplified model, a "first cut" if you will. We are excavat-ing the fundamental historical dynamics of capital accumulation as a pattern that operates through the *specifically* bundled relations of human and extra-human na-ture governed by the law of value.

We can begin with capitalization and appropriation as relations of reproduction. From there, we may consider the relations between the two moments. First, while the capitalization of reproduction assumes many forms, it has occurred most con-spicuously through proletarianization. This was historically prior to the large-scale capitalization of extra-human natures, and indeed historically prior to large-scale industrialization in the nineteenth century (Seccombe, 1995). "Proletarianization" is another way of saying that the reproduction of labor-power flows through capital, largely in the form of paid work.[1] Of course, even proletarian households in the Global North continue to rely upon the significant expenditure of unpaid work (laundry, cooking meals, raising children, etc.). Humans transform the rest of nature only through the labor process, and the commodification of work—directly and indirectly—is therefore historically pivotal to the capitalization of extra-human natures.

But it is not just the reproduction of labor-power that has become capitalized; it is also the reproduction of extra-human natures. Over the past five centuries, capitalist agriculture reveals the dependence of agro-ecosystems on global capital flows (especially through credit) every bit as much as nutrient and hydrological cycles. The extraordinary shift that occurred in the twentieth century—through successive hybridization, chemical, and biotechnological "revolutions"—has been the capitalization of agro-ecological relations (unpaid work) that were previously outside the commodity system (Kloppenburg, 1988). The twenty-first century capitalist farmer must buy new seeds every year rather than save seeds; she must buy more pesticides and herbicides every year to protect the yield; the farming family must strive to produce more and more to satisfy the debt obligations of an agro-ecological model that is increasingly "reproduced within the circuits of capital accumulation" (Boyd et al., 2001, 560). Flows of nutrients, flows of humans, and flows of capital make a historical totality, in which each flow implies the other—a point frequently missed by green critics of capitalism (e.g., Foster et al., 2010).

Accumulation by appropriation also transcends and disrupts the Cartesian binary. The really meaningful distinction is not between humanity and the rest of nature, but between two spheres: life-activity within the commodity system and life-activity outside the zone of commodification, but still ensnared within capitalist power. The movements of both spheres contribute, decisively, to the determination of socially necessary labor time. The first movement occurs within the "organic whole" of commodity production, comprising distribution, exchange, and distribution, alongside immediate production (Marx, 1973, 100). The other is the "organic whole" of appropriating unpaid work in the service of advancing labor productivity. In other words, the rate of exploitation under the law of value is determined not only by the class struggle within commodity production (between capitalists and the direct producers), and not only by the tools, organization, and value composition of commodity production. *It is also determined by the contribution of unpaid work*, performed by human and extra-human natures alike. (There is a class struggle here, too.)

Successive regimes of abstract social labor therefore turn on the active reconfiguration of worlds of production and reproduction. In this view, value relations

---

1   I say "*largely* in the form of paid work," because the relation of bourgeois and proletarian assumes many concrete forms, including master and slave in the early modern sugar plantation (Mintz, 1978); for the late twentieth century, Lewontin (1998) suggests (with some exaggeration) that the farmer has become a proletarian.

unfold through the dialectic of value/not-value, in which "not-value" is directly productive of the conditions necessary for a regime of abstract social labor. This means that capitalism's *technics*—understood as specific crystallizations of tools, nature, and power (Mumford, 1934)—do more than pick the "low-hanging fruit" (Cowen, 2011). Capitalist *technics* seek to mobilize and to appropriate the (unpaid) "forces of nature" so as to make the (paid) "forces of labor" productive in their modern form (the production of surplus value). This is the significance of the *production* of nature; nature is not a pre-formed object for capital, but a web of relations that capital reshapes so as to advance the contributions of unpaid biospheric "work" for capital accumulation. Capital, in so doing, is reshaped by nature as a whole.

The appropriation of unpaid work—represented historically through the cyclical rise and decline of the Four Cheaps—is therefore a central issue for anyone who wants to take seriously the question of limits. This is because the *real* historical limits of capitalism derive from capital as a relation of capitalization and appropriation. The "limits to growth" (Meadows et al., 1972) are not external, but derive from relations internal to capitalist civilization. Why internal? Clearly, we are not speaking of internal as a fixed boundary—much less in a Cartesian sense of "social" limits and "natural" limits—but rather capitalism as an *internalizing* civilization. Here, *internal* is methodological premise, not historical statement. Economists often speak of how capitalism "externalizes" costs. The conversion of the atmosphere to a dumping ground for greenhouse gases is a good example. What bears emphasizing is that the externalization of costs is also the internalization of spaces necessary for capital accumulation: waste frontiers matter, too.

When capitalists can set in motion *small* amounts of capital and appropriate *large* volumes of unpaid work, the costs of production fall and the rate of profit rises.[2] In these situations, there is a *high world-ecological surplus* (or simply, "ecological surplus"). The ecological surplus is the ratio of the systemwide mass of capital to the systemwide contribution of unpaid work. A growing relative contribution of unpaid work tends to reduce the systemwide organic composition of capital, especially within the new centers of accumulation. Over the course of an accumulation cycle, the contribution of unpaid work tends to fall, relative to the mass of capital seeking investment. Every great wave of accumulation therefore begins with a high ecological surplus, which is created through combinations of *capital* (value-in-motion) and *capitalist power* (territorial but also cultural). Together, these movements of capital and capitalist power secure new and greatly expanded sources of unpaid work in service to accumulation. This is the dialectical counterpoint to the traditional rendering of primitive accumulation as a process of class formation in production (bourgeois and proletarian). Primitive accumulation is *equally* about the restructur-

---

2   This is a simplified model of capital and nature. One would naturally wish to elaborate the simple model into a series of world-historical specifications and revisions based on richer totalities of many determinations.

ing of the relations of reproduction—human and extra-human alike—so as to allow the renewed and expanded flow of "cheap" labor, food, energy, and raw materials into the commodity system.

The problem for capital is that the strategies that create the Four Cheaps are "one-off" affairs. You cannot discover something twice. The idea of nature as external has worked so effectively because capital must constantly locate natures external to it. Because these natures are historical and therefore finite, the exhaustion of one historical nature quickly prompts the "discovery" of new natures that deliver yet untapped sources of unpaid work. Thus did the Kew Gardens of British hegemony yield to the International Agricultural Research Centers of American hegemony, which in turn were superseded by the bioprospecting, rent-seeking, and genomic mapping practices of the neoliberal era (Brockway, 1978; Kloppenburg, 1988; McAfee, 1999; 2003.) This means that not only is capitalism bound up with a historically-specific nature; so are its specific phases of development. Each long century of accumulation does not "tap" an external nature that exists as a pre-given warehouse of resources. Rather, each such long wave creates—and is created by—a historical nature that offers a new, specific set of constraints and opportunities. The accumulation strategies that work at the beginning of a cycle—creating particular historical natures through science, technology, and new forms of territoriality and governance (abstract social nature)—progressively exhaust the relations of reproduction that supply "cheap" labor, food, energy, and raw materials. At some point, this exhaustion registers in rising commodity prices.

From peak appropriation to the tendency of the ecological surplus to fall

Exhaustion encompasses the physical deterioration of human and extra-human natures (e.g., health problems, soil erosion), but cannot be reduced to such depletion. Deterioration is an empirical reality that speaks to a relational dynamic: the relation between the shares of unpaid work (appropriation) and paid work (capitalization) in world accumulation. Exhaustion is the flipside of "boom." Both turn on the capacity of particular species, ecosystems (including humans), and even geological formations, to deliver unpaid work. That capacity is not, however, "just there." It is actively co-produced through the relations of capital, capitalist power, and class struggle. Exhaustion in this sense signifies the erosion of those historically-specific *accumulation strategies* that remake the specific forms of capital, power, and nature in successive long centuries of accumulation. The error of much critical discourse on "natural limits" is to confuse the depletion of substances for the exhaustion of accumulation strategies (e.g., Foster et al., 2010). They *are* related. And substances *do* matter. But, as any student of resource economics will tell you, the issue for capital is not energy returned on energy invested, but energy returned on *capital* invested: EROCI, not EROEI. What matters, in capitalist history, is the ratio between the mass of unpaid work and the mass of surplus capital. Stated formally, the *mass* of unpaid work may rise even as its *share* declines relative to accumulation by capitalization. This is probably what has occurred over the past decade since the onset of the 2003 commodity boom.

Several examples illustrate this counter-intuitive theoretical picture. Labor productivity growth may continue, but at a much slower rate than previously. This has been the case with world agriculture since the 1980s (Moore, 2010c). Productivity growth has continued, but at a pace that is too slow to meet capital's need for cheap food. A slowing rate of growth indicates exhaustion, if the need for unpaid work rises, and the agro-food regime fails to restore cheap food. At the same time, rising food prices cannot be reduced to productivity in an era characterized by an unprecedented financialization of commodities (Moore, 2012; Tang and Xiong, 2012).

A second mirage appears in contemporary discussions of global energy. Advocates of "peak everything" point to an impending decline in oil—and eventually, coal—production (Heinberg, 2003). Such declines will occur, although it is far from clear that they will be geologically-driven. The geological dimensions *are* crucial, but a too-narrow focus easily misses the historical reality. This reality turns on the law of value. The "peak" that capitalism cares about is peak *appropriation*: the moment when the contribution of unpaid work is highest, relative to the abstract social labor (capital) deployed. Peak appropriation can be identified both cyclically, in successive accumulation cycles, and cumulatively, since the sixteenth century. Cumulative peak appropriation for coal was reached sometime in the early twentieth century; peak appropriation for oil, sometime around 2000. Output may rise as the ecological surplus falls, as seems to be the case with coal production today. Rising output will restore cheap energy only if the share of unpaid work (here, geological "work") increases relative to the capital necessary to produce it. In this light, post-peak appropriation registers capital's declining capacity to appropriate nature cheaply (with less and less labor-power). The problem is not whether more oil—for example—can be extracted on an abstract supply curve, but whether more oil (or its equivalents) can be extracted with less labor.

And what of human natures? Labor-power is exhausted too. The American working class today, for instance, is not exhausted in the sense of imminent physical breakdown; it is exhausted in its capacity to deliver a rising volume of unpaid work to capital. Its potential for delivering unpaid work is maxed out. The proliferation of "shifts"—a second and third shift in paid and unpaid work—and the neoliberal extension of the workweek provide good reason to think that American workers cannot work much more or much harder (e.g., Hochshild, 1989; Schor, 1991; 2003). (On the margins, perhaps, but not more than this.) Sociophysical "breakdown" *is* implicated in exhaustion. This can be seen in the dramatic rise of mental health problems in the Global North since the 1980s (HHS, 2010), along with rising cancer rates (Davis, 2007). Beyond mounting health problems, one could also look at the "baby strike" of declining fertility, carried out by proletarian women across the North Atlantic in recent decades, now extending to industrialized East Asia (Livingston and Cohn, 2010; The Economist, 2013). Over the course of an accumulation cycle, relations of reproduction once outside the cash nexus become progressively monetized. This capitalization of reproduction delivers a middle-run boost to accumulation through multiple shifts. But the middle-run boom is achieved at a price. As reproduction becomes channeled through commodity relations, the share of *un*paid work stagnates or declines. When this occurs, the expanded accumulation of capital becomes increasingly dependent on the *commodified*, rather than the uncommodified, reproduction of life, and the costs of accumulating capital rise.

This dynamic is the tendency of the ecological surplus to fall.

The most obvious indicator of a declining ecological surplus is the rising price of the Big Four inputs. Labor, food, energy, and raw materials become more and more expensive. The Four Cheaps stop being cheap. This usually doesn't happen all at once, although this is in fact what we have seen since the start of the 2003 commodity boom. The point at which the Four Cheaps stop becoming cheaper and cheaper and start to become more and more expensive is the *signal* crisis of a phase of capitalism. Such crises signal the exhaustion of an accumulation regime (Moore, 2012). For the neoliberal phase of capitalism, this signal crisis—far more important than the near-meltdown of the financial system in 2008—began around 2003. Since that time, the ecological surplus has been falling, and there are few signs that the decline will be reversed soon, if ever. Why? Largely because the greatest frontiers have been exhausted, and because, at the same time, the mass of surplus capital continues to rise. What seems to be occurring is a vicious circle. Finding frontiers few and far between, a growing mass of surplus capital has sought refuge in commodity markets, pushing *up* the very prices of food, energy, and raw materials at the moment when capitalism (as a system) needs those prices to go *down*. This in turn exacerbates the surplus capital absorption problem, which finds partial and temporary resolution in renewed financialization. This in turn further "short-circuit[s] flows of production and trade . . . at the expense of what might have been long-term social surplus" (Blackburn 2006, 67).

This points towards a decisive lacuna in the Marxist theory of capital accumulation. The resolution of cyclical overaccumulation crises—crises defined by a rising mass of "surplus" capital that cannot be reinvested profitably—has depended upon the cyclical restoration of the Four Cheaps. The falling ecological surplus, representing a contraction of capital's opportunities for appropriating unpaid work, is closely linked to the contraction of profitable opportunities for investment in the real economy (M-C-M').[3] Cheap oil, or cheap labor, or cheap metals, *make possible* new products—such as, in their respective eras, the railroad and steam engine, or

---

3   Here I lean of Arrighi's simplified model of Marx's general formula of capital. In "M-C-M' . . . [m]oney capital (M) means liquidity, flexibility, freedom of choice. Commodity capital (C) means capital invested in a particular input-output combination in view of a profit. Hence, it means

the automobile. The production systems, urban spaces, and infrastructures implied by these new products absorbed giant volumes of surplus capital. Indeed, the successive industrializations in the North Atlantic between 1790 and 1960—spanning the first, second, and Fordist industrial revolutions—can be told through the ways these epochal inventions (steam/coal, auto/oil) reworked the capitalist *oikeios* and its rising relative contribution of unpaid work over this period. Intriguingly, the information technology "revolution" of the past forty years has been manifestly inadequate in absorbing surplus capital (Foster and McChesney, 2012, 38).

The Four Cheaps, in making possible those great waves of industrialization, are central to the resolution of recurrent overaccumulation crises in historical capitalism—crises characterized by rising volumes of capital that cannot be invested profitably. Consequently, the cyclical "end" of the Four Cheaps, in successive accumulation cycles, corresponds to a growing mass of surplus capital with no place to go. As accumulation in the real economy falters, a growing mass of capital becomes involved in financial rather than productive activities (M-M' rather than M-C-M') (Arrighi, 1994; Leyshon and Thrift, 2007).[4] The exhaustion of commodity frontiers—and the systemwide stagnation of unpaid work that such exhaustion implies—appears to be closely linked to the peculiar forms of financialization that have emerged since the 1970s.

The rise and demise of cheap nature: The neoliberal moment

Can the tendency of the ecological surplus to fall be seen during the neoliberal era? We may recall that a high world-ecological surplus represents a ratio of low capitalization to high appropriation. This is a necessary condition for the revival of accumulation. For good reason, the neoliberal "boom" that commenced after 1983 was accompanied—or preceded—by a significant cyclical decline in food, energy, and resources prices. Commodity prices for metals fell by nearly half between 1975 and 1989; for food by 39 percent; while oil stabilized by 1983, for the next twenty years, at a price per barrel about twice that of the postwar era (McMichael, 2005; Radetzki, 2006; van der Mensbrugghe et al., 2011).

---

concreteness, rigidity, and a narrowing down or closing of options. M' means expanded liquidity, exibility, and freedom of choice" (Arrighi, 1994, 5).

4   M-M' comes into play during what Arrighi calls financial expansions, such as the one that has characterized the capitalist world-ecology since the 1970s. Such financial expansions are "symptomatic of a situation in which the investment of money in the expansion of trade and production [M-C-M'] no longer serves the purpose of increasing the cash flow to the capitalist stratum as effectively as pure financial deals can. In such a situation, capital invested in trade and production tends to revert to its money form and accumulate more directly, as in Marx's abridged formula MM'" (Arrighi, 1994, 8–9).

But it was not only extra-human natures that became cheap.

The 1980s revival of accumulation also turned on a cheap *labor* regime. This entailed producing a regime of cheap human nature that could supply both paid and unpaid work in sufficient volumes to restore accumulation. In formal terms, establishing a new cheap labor regime meant reducing the value of labor-power. This was not easy to accomplish. There were five key dimensions of the neoliberal project to restore cheap labor after 1973. The first was "wage repression" (Harvey, 2010, 12). Bourgeoisies across the Global North began to "organize as a class" (Moody, 1988), and moved aggressively against trade unions following the 1974–1975 recession. Wage repression was especially important as labor productivity growth sagged in the 1970s, a deceleration that increasingly looks permanent (Gordon, 2010). Second, the falling rate of profit in American industry—induced both by labor's class power and the rising organic composition of capital—led American and other capitalists to move rapidly towards the "global factory" in the 1970s (Barnet, 1980; Gordon et al., 1982). This was a tectonic shift in world history that entailed the simultaneous de-industrialization of core zones and the rapid industrialization of the Global South (Arrighi et al., 2003). Third, the global factory depended upon the "great global enclosure" (Araghi, 2000) that commenced in the early 1980s. These global enclosures, realized through structural adjustment programs and market liberalization, restructured agrarian class relations worldwide, dispossessing hundreds of millions of peasants worldwide. In China alone, some 200–300 million migrants moved from countryside to city (Webber, 2012). The new global proletariat dwarfed any that came before it. In concert with the opening of Russia, China, and India to the world market, the world proletariat doubled after 1989 (Freeman, 2010). Fourth, this great doubling represented an even greater expansion of the female proletariat, adding paid work on top of unpaid work on an unprecedented scale. Neoliberal proletarianization was, in this reckoning, an unprecedented global expansion of Hochschild's (1989) "second shift," an audacious expansion of absolute surplus value. Finally—and almost universally ignored by environmentalists—cheap labor was made possible through a new regime of "forced underconsumption" (Araghi, 2009), such that hunger and nutrient deficiencies today affect nearly three billion people, including 50 million people in the United States (Keats and Wiggins, 2010).

By 2003, the world-ecological surplus had stopped rising, and began to decline. Registered by the slow-, then fast-moving, commodity boom (Jacks, 2013), this was the *signal* crisis of neoliberalism as a way of organizing nature (Moore, 2010c). This expression of crisis signals the beginning of a cyclical contraction of the ecological surplus. The clearest indicator of this signal crisis was the rising price of metals, energy, and food commodity prices. But this was not just any commodity boom, not least because of its unusual durability, now ten years and counting. What does this seemingly endless commodity boom indicate? At a minimum, the peculiar character of this boom—which includes more primary commodities, has lasted longer, and has seen more price volatility than any previous commodity boom in modern world history (World Bank, 2009)—indicates an exhaustion of neoliberalism's cheap nature strategy. Notably, neoliberalism's strategies for reducing the Big Four input prices began to falter at least five years prior to the financial events of 2008. Economists talk of this very long commodity boom as a "supercycle"—a decades-long increase in basic commodity prices. But so far, they have invoked an abstract "world of scarcity" (Jacks, 2013) rather than consider the possibility that today's supercycle represents a historical limit to capitalism's *longue durée* regime of "cheap ecology" (Araghi, 2010).

Even cheap labor may be fading fast. In other words, the signal crisis of neoliberalism is not merely a question of extra-human natures—reflected in the commodity boom—but of human nature too. In China, real wages increased 300 percent between 1990 and 2005 (Midnight Notes, 2009, 4). Manufacturing wages grew six times faster than the rate of inflation, and unit labor costs rose 85 percent between 2000 and 2011 (USDC, 2013). Meanwhile, the usual strategy of moving to cheap labor frontiers—seeking new streams of unpaid work in support of low-wage workers—is in motion, but with rapidly diminishing returns. Within China, the government's "Go West" policy, which has aimed to attract industry to the interior, has narrowed labor costs between interior and coastal regions to a "surprisingly . . . paltry wage differential" (Scott, 2011, 1). Rural-to-urban migration has slowed considerably in recent years (Fegley, 2013). By 2012, per capita foreign investment in Cambodia moved ahead of China (Bradsher, 2013). But Cambodia is much smaller than China, which is part of the broader problem: the frontiers are shrinking at the very moment when capital needs ever-greater commodity frontiers to resolve the overaccumulation problem. Meanwhile, the very information and communication technologies that have made possible global production are now also being used in the class struggle:

> Workers in Cambodia today have begun syndical action after only a few years, not after twenty-five. There are strikes and pressure for higher wages and benefits, which they are receiving. This of course reduces the value for the multinationals of moving to Cambodia, or Myanmar, or Vietnam, or the Philippines. It now turns out that the savings of moving from China are not all that great. (Wallerstein, 2013)

The ongoing erosion of cheap labor is not exclusively an East Asian story. Less well understood, but no less significant, is the transition across the Global North to a "second (and third) shift"—wage work plus unpaid reproductive labor. This transition enacted and embodied one of the last great commodity frontiers of historical capitalism. Unpaid household labor has been a pillar of endless commodification since the sixteenth century (Mies, 1986). What happened in the Global North, and especially in North America, after 1970 was the accelerated proletarianization of women. This marked the demise of the Fordist one-income family and the rise of the "flexible" two-income household. This 1970s acceleration had been prefigured by Soviet developmentalism (Sacks, 1977), and also by the fast entry of American women into paid work since the 1930s (Goldin, 2008). This too was a commodity frontier, marked by the progressive commodification of work-potential and the progressive appropriation of (human) nature's "free" gifts. Hence the imposition of multiple "shifts," and the double squeeze on women's time via the simultaneously operating pressures of capitalization and appropriation; even as early as the mid-1960s a growing number of married American women had traded in their 55-hour work week at home for the 76-hour work week at home *and* work (Hartmann, 1981). If this were all—as in Hochschild's (2002) rendering of the commodity frontier—there would be little to add. What the theory of the commodity frontier illuminates is not only the pattern of successively paired commodifying/appropriating movements, but the finite opportunities inscribed in each such movement (Moore, 2013a; 2013b). In the United States, the extraordinarily rapid increase in mothers' labor force participation—50 percent between 1975 and 1995 (BLS, 2009)—was not only a powerful moment of neoliberal wage repression while maintaining effective (consumer) demand. It was also a *one-shot deal*. The commodity frontier is a one-way ticket. Frontiers, once appropriated and commodified, are no longer frontiers—they do however move on, as we've seen in the roll out of the proletarian relation for women across the Global South since the 1980s (Kabeer, 2007; McMichael, 2012).

Capitalism as frontier: Abstract social natures

Commodity frontiers may roll onwards, but only to a point. Capitalism not only *has* frontiers; it is fundamentally *defined by* frontier movement. The conceit of early modern cartographic revolutions was to conceive of the Earth as abstract space rather than as concrete geographies. The latter, abolished (or at least controlled) in theory, would continually reassert itself, as geographical particularities (climates, soils, topographies, diseases) entered into dynamic tension with bourgeois fantasies of abstract space. The great advantage of mapping the world as a grid and nature as an external object was that one could appropriate the wealth of nature in a fashion profoundly efficient for the accumulation of capital. The very dynamism of capitalist production is unthinkable in the absence of frontier appropriations that allowed more and more materials to flow through a given unit of abstract labor time: value's self-expanding character depends on an exponential rise in the material volume of production without a corresponding rise in the abstract labor implied in such production. This incessant reduction of labor-time can occur, however, only to the extent that cheap energy, cheap food, cheap raw materials, and yes, cheap labor can be secured through strategies of appropriation *outside the immediate circuit of capital*. This can only occur through the continual enlargement of the geographical arenas for appropriation. Thus are capital and capitalist power joined in the co-production of cheap natures.

For this reason, frontiers are much more central to the expanded reproduction of capital and capitalist power than commonly recognized. When Harvey (2003, 131) opines that capitalism, confronting the end of frontiers, might "actively manufacture" such frontiers, he reflects the common sense of the contemporary radical critique. But this is a misinterpretation. The processes of privatization and finance-led dispossession, insofar as they operate within the domain of capitalized relations, cannot revive accumulation by themselves; indeed, these processes worked in the neoliberal era because they were bound to the release of cheap labor-power, food, energy, and raw materials *into* the circuits of capital from *outside* those circuits.

Historically, frontier zones of low or minimal commodification have provided capital's greatest opportunities to reduce the Big Four input prices: labor, food, energy, and raw materials. These costs directly or indirectly reflect the value composition of commodity production as a whole, in their variable, fixed, and, above all, circulating moments. (Note that *circulating* capital refers to the inputs used up in a given production cycle; it is different from the circulation of capital.) Frontiers are pivotal to long waves of accumulation for an elementary reason: they check the rising organic composition of capital, and therefore the tendency of the rate of profit to fall. The reduction of the value composition of these four inputs is significant because it is inversely related to the formation of a global rate of profit, and therefore to world accumulation. In Marx's rarely-cited "general law" of underproduction, the overproduction of machinery tends to lead to the underproduction of raw materials, which in turn enter into the determination not only of the value composition of non-human labor (raw materials) but also, over the course of successive accumulation cycles, of fixed capital itself. Cheap coal, for example, reduced not only the costs of circulating capital (energy costs) but also the costs of manufacturing steam engines and other vital forces of production in the second half of the "long" nineteenth century.

Depeasantization, the reorientation of peasant agriculture towards the world market, the extraction of abundant energy and mineral wealth—these great movements of modern world history have been frontier movements, some more obvious than others. These movements of appropriation have enlarged the reserve army of labor; expanded food supplies to the world proletariat; directed abundant energy flows to, and boosted labor productivity within, commodity production; and channeled gigantic volumes of raw materials into industrial production, driving down the value composition of both fixed and circulating capital even as the technical composition of capital rose mightily (Moore, 2011a; 2011b). Put simply, the Great Frontier that opened the capitalist epoch did so by making nature's free gifts—human natures' too—more or less cheaply available to those with capital and power. The end of the frontier today is the end of nature's free gifts, and with it, the end of capitalism's free ride.

Frontier appropriations occur not only on the horizontal edges of the capitalist system—as in world-historical reckonings of incorporation (e.g., Hopkins and

Wallerstein, 1987)—but also on the "vertical" axis of socio-ecological reproduction within the heartlands of commodification. Although the horizontal and vertical moments of these frontier appropriations unfolded in distinct geographical zones with specific socio-ecological inflections, they were unified through their relation to the accumulation process. Commodity frontiers worked in both heartlands and hinterlands by appropriating and transferring unpaid work from the zones of socio-ecological reproduction towards zones of commodification. In the heartlands, the appropriation of women's unpaid work was central to the cheap reproduction of labor-power; in the hinterlands, the appropriation of extra-human natures (forests, soils, mineral veins) was often primary. The secret of the law of value is in this epochal synthesis of the exploitation of labor-power and the appropriation of the unpaid work of human and extra-human natures. The formation of abstract social labor occurs only partly, not wholly, within the zone of commodification. The regime of abstract social labor—premised on socially necessary labor-time—emerged historically, and restructured cumulatively, through the formation of regimes of *abstract social nature*.

The argument here is that abstract social nature—understood as a systemic family of processes aimed at rationalizing, simplifying, standardizing, and otherwise mapping the world—is directly constitutive of producing external natures that can be cheaply appropriated. In this, abstract social nature is immanent to the law of value; the praxis of external nature was pivotal to the generalization of commodity production and exchange. The cascading and converging processes of commodification, capital accumulation, and symbolic innovation constituted a virtuous circle of modern world development, beginning in the long sixteenth century. I do not propose a revision of Marx's law of value in a strict sense: the substance of capital is abstract social labor. But neither an adequate history of capitalism, nor a sufficiently dynamic theory of capitalist limits, is possible without taking value relations as a methodological premise focused on the trinity of capital/power/nature.

In this perspective, value relations are grounded historically in successive configurations of abstract labor and nature. Those configurations may be called *historical natures*. Each historical nature, co-produced by the law of value, enables the renewed exploitation of labor-power and the renewed appropriation of life-activity as unpaid work. The appropriation of unpaid work must outstrip the exploitation of labor-power, else the Four Cheaps cannot return, and neither can capitalist prosperity. Abstract social nature names those processes that extend, through new forms of symbolic praxis and knowledge formation, the frontiers of accumulation—both accumulation by capitalization and, especially, accumulation by appropriation.

Value is therefore *not* an economic form with systemic consequences. It is, rather, a systemic relation with a pivotal "economic" *expression* (abstract social labor). One cannot think the accumulation of capital without abstract social labor and the struggle to reduce socially-necessary labor-time. By the same measure, one cannot think the accumulation of capital without the symbolic praxis of abstract social nature, allowing for the appropriation of unpaid work on a scale that dwarfs the exploitation of labor-power. Unifying these two moments calls for a mode of inquiry that brings together the circuit of capital with the appropriation of life, and this necessitates a *world-ecological* framework for interpreting the history of capitalism and value's contingent and fluctuating gravities of nature, power, and capital.

Early modernity's epoch-making abstractions—constituting a vast but weak regime of abstract social nature—were registered through the era's new cartographies, new temporalities, new forms of surveying and property-making, schools of painting and music, accounting practices, and scientific revolutions. These abstractions marked the birth of abstract social nature (Mumford, 1934; Merchant, 1980; Harvey, 1993; Crosby, 1997; Pickles, 2004; Cosgrove, 2008). The infant would begin to walk by the close of the sixteenth century. We find the new face of world money- and credit-creation in the rise of the Amsterdam Bourse after 1602. Here, not only were shares of the Dutch East India Company traded, but also, very soon, a growing number of commodities (360 different commodities by 1639!) and even futures. The Bourse's material coordinations and symbolic "rationality provided the basis for a universalisation and intensification of world credit practices which served to set the Dutch[-led world] financial order apart from pre-modern world finance" (Langley, 2002, 45; also Petram, 2011).

Of course, abstract social nature is still with us.

For the history of capitalism may be read, in part, as a succession of scientific revolutions that actively co-produced distinctive historical natures in and through successive phases of capital accumulation. In every significant respect, these scientific revolutions not only produced new conditions of opportunity for capital and states, but transformed our understanding of nature as a whole, and perhaps most significantly, of the boundaries between humans and the rest of nature. The point has been underscored most dramatically by neoliberalism's systematic combination of shock doctrines with revolutions in the earth system and life sciences, tightly linked in turn to new property regimes aiming to secure not only land but life for capital accumulation (Klein, 2007; Mansfield, 2009). This has unfolded at the nexus of the global and molecular scales (McAfee, 2003). On the one hand, the new life sciences emerging after 1973 (with the invention of recombinant DNA) became a powerful lever for producing new conditions of accumulation premised on redistribution and speculation—patenting life forms, starting with the microorganisms recognized in 1980 by the U.S. Supreme Court. The ambition has been to enclose "the reproduction of life itself within the promissory accumulation of the debt form" (Cooper, 2008, 31). On the other hand, the Earth system sciences, aided considerably by the mapping sciences (e.g., remote sensing, geographic information systems, etc.), have sought to reduce

the Earth ... to little more than a vast standing reserve, serving as a ready resource supply center and/or accessible waste reception site ... [They] aspire to scan and appraise

the most productive use of . . . [the] resourcified flows of energy, information, and matter as well as the sinks, dumps, and wastelands for all the by-products that commercial
products leave behind. (Luke, 2009, 133)

This is what Luke (2009) calls "planetarian accountancy." But planetarian accountancy is more than biophysical. It is also about the production of new financial
techniques premised on the same worldview of "scanning and appraising" the most
profitable opportunities for capital accumulation.

> [Beginning] in the 1970s, an "arms race" to develop new financial techniques for com-
> modifying uncertainty spurred innovators competing for profits to ever-new heights,
> and by the 1990s terms such as "financial product" and "financial products division"
> were enjoying an unprecedented vogue. The relevant mode of "production" was what
> might be called "quantism": the material and social processes of isolating, laying claim
> to, objectifying, simplifying, abstracting, quantifying, commensurating, pricing and re-
> aggregating masses of unknowns by which derivatives were manufactured and finan-
> cial uncertainty commodified. Computers and top mathematical talent were given free
> rein in greatly expanded efforts to break down, reframe, mathematise, diversify across,
> appropriate and charge rent for the future. (Lohmann, 2009, 19)

Both "scanning and appraising" the world and the scramble to produce ever-more
exotic financial instruments may be read as efforts to transcend the problems of a
capitalism that has entered uncharted territory: the terrain of post-peak appropriation, which is to say, the end of cheap nature.

By way of conclusion

The rise of capitalism launched a new way of organizing nature, mobilizing for the
first time a metric of wealth premised on labor productivity rather than land productivity. This was the originary moment of today's fast-fading "cheap nature." This
strange law of value, taking shape out of the vast frontier appropriations and productive innovations of the long sixteenth century, allowed for capitalism's unusual
civilizational dynamism: appropriating the whole of nature within its grasp to advance the rate of exploitation of labor-power. From the 1450s, there commenced a
succession of movements of productivity and plunder, joining the vast appropriation of nature's free gifts with extraordinary technical innovations in production
and transport. Each wave of capitalism that followed depended on great frontier
movements, the agrarian counterpart to the spatial and productive "fixes" of capital accumulation in the metropoles. Together these movements of accumulation
by appropriation and accumulation by capitalization constituted world-ecological
revolutions through which new opportunities for peak appropriation were realized,
and capital accumulation maximized. These world-ecological revolutions—and the

organizational structures they implied—encompassed innovations in industry and finance no less than agriculture and resource extraction. These innovations at first liberated accumulation, only to fetter it over time, as the great windfalls of frontier expansion and accumulation by appropriation gradually—sometimes rapidly—disappeared: newly proletarianized workers began to organize, farming regions became exhausted, coal seams were mined out. The tendential result has been a lurching movement towards a rising organic composition of capital and a declining ecological surplus, squeezing the rate of accumulation as opportunities for new productive investment dried up. These developments were, at all turns, linked closely with rising costs of inputs (circulating capital) and with them, the amplified tendency of the rate of profit to fall.

This is of course a provisional model for taking nature seriously in the theory of capital accumulation. It is an invitation. To what? To a conversation over how we might elaborate a more radical, dialectical, and historical *synthesis* of capitalism-in-nature: a synthesis suggested by O'Connor (1998) and Burkett (1999), but whose implications have scarcely been explored.

How to move forward? Certainly, any synthesis worthy of the name will go beyond the Cartesian dualism of "nature" and "society." In this respect, I am struck by Marx's (1973, 748) insight that the fertility of the soil could "act like an increase of fixed capital." The English agricultural revolution had proceeded on precisely this basis, "cashing in on reserves of nitrogen under permanent pasture for short-term gain" (Overton, 1996, 117), and stagnating after 1760. Much the same process of "cashing in" occurred in the American Midwest between 1840 and 1880, after which yield growth slowed until the 1930s (Kloppenburg, 1988; Friedmann, 2000). The same arc of peaking and post-peak appropriation could be seen in South Asia's Green Revolution between the 1960s and 1980s (Moore, 2010c). Capitalism's agricultural revolutions—is it so different for energy and other "modes of extraction"? (Bunker, 1985)—are always premised on such appropriations, combining cutting-edge industrial production with frontier enclosures. In this way, food could be produced cheaply and a double-gift presented to capital: peasant dispossession and cheaper reproduction costs for those already proletarianized. Thus we might extend Marx's observation to all forms of "fertility."

Capitalism's *longue durée* cheap nature strategy has aimed at appropriating the biological capacities and geological distributions of the earth in an effort to reduce the value composition of production, thereby checking the tendency towards a falling rate of profit. As opportunities for accumulation by appropriation contract, we would expect to see a profound shift from spatial to temporal fixes (Harvey, 1989), moving from the appropriation of space to the colonization of time: the greatest strength of neoliberal financialization. By the early twenty-first century, the end of cheap nature was in sight. More violence, more biopower, and more guns restored the Four Cheaps for two decades after 1983. But the bloom was off the rose by the early years of the new millennium. Appropriation was faltering. Rising costs of production and extraction in agriculture, energy, and mining began. The price move-ment was made official by 2003, with the onset of the seemingly endless commodity boom. Labor-power seemed cheap for a time, but here too the cheap labor regime showed signs of wear. Cheap labor became less cheap. The "Great Doubling" no lon-ger seemed so great. But the rising capitalized composition of nature did not stop there. Appropriation not only faltered in all the old ways; it now carried forth a new stench of unfathomable toxification: hydro-fracked aquifers, mountaintop remov-als, the overnight devastation of the Gulf of Mexico.

The problem today is the end of the *Capitalocene*, not the march of the Anthropocene. The reality is not one of humanity "overwhelming the great forces of nature" (Steffen et al., 2011), but rather one of capitalism exhausting its cheap nature strategy. (This is the small kernel of truth in the otherwise absurd discourse on eco-system services.) That process of getting extra-human natures—and humans too—to work for very low expenditures of money and energy is the history of capitalism's great commodity frontiers, and with it, of capitalism's long waves of accumulation. The appropriation of frontier land and labor has been the indispensable condition for great waves of capital accumulation, from Dutch hegemony in the seventeenth century to the rise of neoliberalism in the 1970s and 1980s (Moore, 2010b; 2012). The crucial "work" of these commodity frontiers has been *unpaid*; on that basis, the cheap nature strategy has renewed the Four Cheaps.

With frontiers fast closing, the cheap nature strategy is failing in a double sense. On the one hand, new streams of unpaid work are materializing slowly, if at all. On the other hand, the accumulation of waste and toxification is now threatening the unpaid work that *is* being done. Climate change is the greatest example here. It is increasingly certain that global warming constitutes an insuperable barrier to any new capitalist agricultural revolution—and with it, any return of "cheap food" (Kjellstrom et al., 2009; Zivin and Neidell, 2010). From this perspective, the greatest problem of the twenty-first century may well not be one of resource "taps" at all. The end of cheap garbage cans may loom larger than the end of cheap resources (Parenti, 2012). The shift towards financialization, and a deepening of commodity relations in the sphere of reproduction, has been a powerful way of postponing the inevitable blowback of modernity's cheap nature strategy. It has allowed capitalism to survive. But for how much longer?

Acknowledgments

Special thanks to Diana C. Gildea, and also to Henry Bernstein, Holly Jean Buck, Alvin Camba, Phil Campanile, Giuseppe Cioffo, Christopher Cox, Sharae Deckard, Joshua Eichen, Sam Fassbinder, John Bellamy Foster, Kyle Gibson, Matt Huber, Rebecca Lave, Emmanuel Leonardi, Ben Marley, Phil McMichael, Michael Niblett, Roberto José Ortiz, Christian Parenti, Andy Pragacz, Michael Niblett, Shehryar Qazi, Stephen Shapiro, Dale Tomich, Jeremy Vetter, Richard Walker, Tony Weis,

Anna Zalik, and Xiurong Zhao for conversations and correspondence on the themes explored in this essay.

References

Araghi, Farshad. 2000. "The Great Global Enclosure of Our Times." In Fred Magdoff, John Bellamy Foster, and Frederick Buttel (eds.), *Hungry for Profit*. New York: Monthly Review Press.

Araghi, Farshad. 2009. Accumulation by Displacement. *Review*, 32(1): 113–146.

Araghi, Farshad. 2010. The End of "Cheap Ecology" and the Crisis of "Long Keynesianism." *Economic & Political Weekly*, 45(4): 39–41.

Arrighi, Giovanni. 1994. *The Long Twentieth Century*. London: Verso.

Arrighi, Giovanni, Beverly Silver, and Benjamin Brewer. 2003. Industrial Convergence, Globalization, and the Persistence of the North-South Divide. *Studies in Comparative International Development*, 38(1): 3–31.

Barnet, Richard. 1980. *The Lean Years*. New York: Simon and Schuster.

Blackburn, Robin. 2006. Finance and the Fourth Dimension. *New Left Review*, 36: 39–70.

BLS (Bureau of Labor Statistics). 2009. Labor Force Participation Rate of Mothers, 1975–2007. *The Editor's Desk*, January 08, 2009. URL: http://www.bls.gov/opub/ted/2009/jan/wk1/art04.htm (accessed May 01, 2013).

Boyd, William, Scott Prudham, and Rachel Schurman. 2001. Industrial Dynamics and the Problem of Nature. *Society & Natural Resources*, 14(7): 555–570.

Bradsher, Keith. 2013. Wary of China, Companies Head to Cambodia. *New York Times*, April 8. URL: http://www.nytimes.com/2013/04/09/business/global/wary-of-events-in-china-foreign-investors-head-to-cambodia.html?_r=0, (accessed March 10, 2014).

Braverman, Harry. 1974. *Labor and Monopoly Capital*. New York: Monthly Review Press.

Brockway, Lucile. 1978. *Science and Colonial Expansion*. New York: Academic Press.

Bunker, Stephen. 1985. *Underdeveloping the Amazon*. Urbana: University of Illinois Press.

Burkett, Paul. 1999. *Marx and Nature*. New York: St. Martin's.

Chase-Dunn, Chistopher, and Thomas D. Hall. 1997. *Rise and Demise*. Boulder: Westview.

Cooper, Melinda. 2008. *Life as Surplus*. Seattle: University of Washington Press.

Cosgrove, Denis. 2008. *Geography and Vision*. London: I.B. Taurus.

Cowen, Tyler. 2011. *The Great Stagnation*. New York: Penguin.

Crosby, Alfred W. 1997. *The Measure of Reality*. Cambridge: Cambridge University Press.

Davis, Devra. 2007. *The Secret History of the War on Cancer*. New York: Basic.

Deckard, Sharae. 2012. Mapping the World-Ecology. Unpublished paper. School of English, Drama, and Film, University College Dublin, Ireland.

Descartes, René. 2006. *A Discourse on the Method of Correctly Conducting One's Reason and Seeking Truth in the Sciences.* Oxford: Oxford University Press.

Engels, Fredrick. 1934. Engels to J. Bloch in Berlin, London, September 21, 1890. *New International*, 1(3): 81–85.

Federico, Giovanni. 2004. The Growth of World Agricultural Production, 1800–1938. *Research in Economic History*, 22: 125–181.

Fegley, Bryce. 2013. End of an Era: 30 Years of Double-Digit Chinese Growth. *From The Yardarm*, 7(1).

Foster, John Bellamy. 2009. *The Ecological Revolution.* New York: Monthly Review Press.

Foster, John Bellamy. 2013a. Marx and the Rift in the Universal Metabolism of Nature. *Monthly Review*, 65(7): 1–19.

Foster, John Bellamy. 2013b. The Epochal Crisis. *Monthly Review*, 65(5): 1–12.

Foster, John Bellamy, Brett Clark, and Richard York. 2010. *The Ecological Rift.* New York: Monthly Review Press.

Foster, John Bellamy, and Robert McChesney. 2012. *The Endless Crisis.* New York: Monthly Review Press.

Freeman, Richard. 2010. What Really Ails Europe (and America): The Doubling of the Global Workforce. *The Globalist*, June 3. URL: http://www.theglobalist.com/what-really-ails-europe-and-america-the-doubling-of-the-global-workforce/   (accessed February 10, 2014).

Friedmann, Harriet. 2000. What on Earth is the Modern World-System? *Journal of World-Systems Research*, 6(2): 480–515.

Glacken, Clarence. 1967. *Traces on the Rhodian Shore.* Berkeley: University of California Press.

Goldin, Claudia. 2008. "Gender Gap." In David R. Henderson (ed.), *The Concise Encyclopedia of Economics.* URL: http://www.econlib.org/library/Enc/GenderGap.html (accessed May 1, 2013).

Gordon, David, Richard Edwards, and Michael Reich. 1982. *Segmented Work, Divided Workers.* Cambridge: Cambridge University Press.

Gordon, Robert. 2010. Revisiting U.S. Productivity Growth over the Past Century with a View of the Future. Working Paper, 15834. National Bureau of Economic Research, Washington, DC.

Gurian-Sherman, David. 2009. *Failure to Yield.* Cambridge, MA: Union of Concerned Scientists.

Haraway, Donna. 1988. Situated Knowledges. *Feminist Studies*, 14(3): 575–599.

Hartmann, Heidi. 1981. The Family as the Locus of Gender, Class, and Political Struggle. *Signs*, 6(3): 366–394.

Harvey, David. 1989. *The Condition of Postmodernity.* Oxford: Blackwell.

Harvey, David. 1996. *Justice, Nature, and the Geography of Difference.* Oxford: Blackwell.

Harvey, David. 2003. *The New Imperialism.* Oxford: Oxford University Press.

Harvey, David. 2005. *A Brief History of Neoliberalism.* Oxford: Oxford University Press.

Harvey, David. 2010. *The Enigma of Capital and the Crises of Capitalism.* London: Profile.

Harvey, P.D.A. 1993. *Maps in Tudor England.* Cambridge: Cambridge University Press.

Heinberg, Richard. 2003. *The Party's Over.* Gabriola Island, BC: New Society.

HHS (U.S. Department of Health and Human Services). 2010. *Health United States 2010.* Washington, DC: U.S. Government Printing Office.

Hochschild, Arlie. 1989. *The Second Shift.* New York: Viking.

Hochschild, Arlie. 2002. The Commodity Frontier. Working Paper, 1. Center for Working Family, University of California, Berkeley.

Hopkins, Terence, and Immanuel Wallerstein. 1987. Capitalism and the Incorporation of New Zones into the World-Economy. *Review,* 10(5/6): 763–780.

Jacks, David. 2013. From Boom to Bust? *Vox,* August 16. URL: http://www.voxeu.org/article/boom-bust (accessed November 20, 2013).

Kabeer, Naila. 2007. *Marriage, Motherhood and Masculinity in the Global Economy.* IDS Working Paper, 290. Institute for Development Studies, University of Sussex.

Keats, Sharada, and Steve Wiggins. 2010. *Non-staple Foods & Micro-nutrient Status.* London: Overseas Development Institute.

Kjellstrom, Tord, R. Sari Kovats, Simon J. Lloyd, Tom Holt, and Richard S. Tol. 2009. The Direct Impact of Climate Change on Regional Labor Productivity. *Archives of Environmental & Occupational Health,* 64(4): 217–227.

Klein, Naomi. 2007. *The Shock Doctrine.* New York: Metropolitan.

Kloppenburg, Jack. 1988. *First the Seed.* Cambridge: Cambridge University Press.

Landes, David. 1969. *Prometheus Unbound.* Cambridge: Cambridge University Press.

Langley, Paul. 2002. *World Financial Orders.* New York: Routledge.

Lefebvre, Henri. 1991. *The Production of Space.* Oxford: Blackwell.

Leonardi, Emmanuele. 2012. Biopolitics of Climate Change. PhD dissertation. University of Western Ontario, Canada.

Levins, Richard, and Richard Lewontin. 1985. *The Dialectical Biologist.* Cambridge: Harvard University Press.

Lewontin, R.C. 1998. The Maturing of Capitalist Agriculture. *Monthly Review,* 50(3): 72–84.

Leyshon, Andrew, and Nigel Thrift. 2007. The Capitalization of Almost Everything. *Theory, Culture & Society,* 24(7–8): 97–115.

Livingston, Gretchen, and D'Vera Cohn. 2010. The New Demography of American Motherhood. Pew Research center. URL: http://www.pewsocialtrends.org/2010/05/06/the-new-demography-of-american-motherhood/ (accessed November 10, 2013).

Lohmann, Larry. 2009. When Markets are Poison. Corner House Briefing Paper, 40. The Corner House, Dorsey, UK.

Luke, Timothy. 2009. Developing Planetarian Accountancy. *Current Perspectives in Social Theory,* 26: 129–159.

Mahnkopf, Birgit. 2013. Peak Everything – Peak Capitalism? Working Paper, 02/2013. DFG-KollegforscherInnengruppe Postwachstumsgesellschaften, Jena, Germany.

Mansfield, Becky (ed.). 2009. *Privatization.* New York: Routledge.

Marx, Karl. 1967. *Capital.* Volume I–III. New York: International.

Marx, Karl. 1973. *Grundrisse.* New York: Vintage.

Marx, Karl. 1977. *Capital.* Volume I. New York: Vintage.

Marx, Karl. 1978. "Contribution to the Critique of Hegel's Philosophy of Right." In Richard Tucker (ed.), *Marx-Engels Reader.* New York: W.W. Norton.

McAfee, Kathleen. 1999. Selling Nature to Save It? *Society and Space*, 17(2): 133–154.

McAfee, Kathleen. 2003. Neoliberalism on the Molecular Scale. *Geoforum*, 34(2): 203–219.

McMichael, Philip. 1991. Slavery in Capitalism. *Theory and Society*, 20(3): 321–349.

McMichael, Philip. 2005. Global Development and the Corporate Food Regime. *Research in Rural Sociology and Development*, 11: 269–303.

McMichael, Philip. 2012. *Development and Social Change.* Fifth ed. Beverly Hills: Sage.

Meadows, Donella, Dennis Meadows, Jorgen Randers, and William Behrens III. 1972. *The Limits to Growth.* New York: Signet.

Merchant, Carolyn. 1980. *The Death of Nature.* San Francisco: Harper & Row.

Midnight Notes. 2009. Promissory Notes. From Crisis to Commons. URL: www.midnightnotes.org (accessed July 17, 2009).

Mies, Maria. 1986. *Patriarchy and Accumulation on a World Scale.* London: Zed.

Mintz, Sidney W. 1978. Was the Plantation Slave a Proletarian? *Review*, 2(1): 81–98.

Moody, Kim. 1988. *An Injury to All.* London: Verso.

Moore, Jason W. 2000. Sugar and the Expansion of the Early Modern World-Economy. *Review*, 23(3): 409–433.

Moore, Jason W. 2003. Nature and the Transition from Feudalism to Capitalism. *Review*, 26(2): 97–172.

Moore, Jason W. 2007. Ecology and the Rise of Capitalism. PhD dissertation. University of California, Berkeley.

Moore, Jason W. 2010a. "Amsterdam is Standing on Norway" Part I. *Journal of Agrarian Change*, 10(1): 35–71.

Moore, Jason W. 2010b. "Amsterdam is Standing on Norway" Part II. *Journal of Agrarian Change*, 10(2): 188–227.

Moore, Jason W. 2010c. The End of the Road? Agricultural Revolutions in the Capitalist World-Ecology, 1450–2010. *Journal of Agrarian Change*, 10(3): 389–413.

Moore, Jason W. 2011a. Transcending the Metabolic Rift. *Journal of Peasant Studies*, 38(1): 1–46.

Moore, Jason W. 2011b. Ecology, Capital, and the Nature of Our Times. *Journal of World-Systems Analysis*, 17(1): 108–147.

Moore, Jason W. 2012. Cheap Food & Bad Money. *Review*, 33(2–3): 125–161.

Moore, Jason W. 2013a. El Auge de la Ecologia-Mundo Capitalista, I. *Laberinto*, 38: 9–26.

Moore, Jason W. 2013b. El Auge de la Ecologia-Mundo Capitalista, II. *Laberinto*, 39: 6–14.

Mumford, Lewis. 1934. *Technics and Civilization.* London: Routledge and Kegan Paul.

Niblett, Michael. 2013. The "Impossible Quest for Wholeness." *Journal of Postcolonial Writing,* 49(2): 148–160.

O'Connor, James. 1998. *Natural Causes.* Beverly Hills: Sage.

Oloff, Kerstin. 2012. "Greening" the Zombie. *Green Letters,* 16(1): 31–45.

Ortiz, Roberto José. 2013. Latin American Agro-Industrialization, Petrodollar Recycling, and the Transformation of World Capitalism in the Long 1970s. Unpublished paper. Fernand Braudel Center, Binghamton University, USA.

Overton, Mark. 1996. *Agricultural Revolution in England.* Cambridge: Cambridge University Press.

Parenti, Christian. 2012. The Book That Launched a Movement. *The Nation,* December 24–31: 24–26.

Petram, Lodewijk O. 2011. The World's First Stock Exchange. PhD dissertation. University of Amsterdam, the Netherlands.

Pickles, John. 2004. *A History of Spaces.* New York: Routledge.

Postone, Moishe. 1993. *Time, Labor, and Social Domination.* Cambridge: Cambridge University Press.

Radetzki, Marian. 2006. The Anatomy of Three Commodity Booms. *Resources Policy,* 31: 56–64.

Rostow, Walt Whitman. 1978. *The World Economy: History & Prospect.* Austin: University of Texas Press.

Sacks, Michael. 1977. Unchanging Times. *Journal of Marriage and Family,* 39(4): 793–805.

Schor, Juliet. 1991. *The Overworked American.* New York: Basic Books.

Schor, Juliet. 2003. "The (Even More) Overworked American." In John de Graaf (ed.), *Take Back Your Time.* San Francisco: Berrett-Koehler.

Scott, James. 1998. *Seeing Like a State.* New Haven: Yale University Press.

Scott, John. 2011. Who Will Take Over China's Role as the World's Factory Floor? *Saturna Sextant Newsletter,* 5(7).

Seccombe, Wally. 1995. *Weathering the Storm.* London: Verso.

Steffen, Will, Jacques Grinevald, Paul Crutzen, and John McNeill. 2011. The Anthropocene: Conceptual and Historical Perspectives. *Philosophical Transactions of the Royal Society,* 369(1938): 842–867.

Tang, Ke, and Wei Xiong. 2012. Index Investment and Financialization of Commodities. *Financial Analysts Journal,* 68(6): 54–74.

The Economist. 2013. Women in South Korea: A Pram Too Far. *The Economist,* October 26. URL: http://www.economist.com/news/special-report/21588207-faced-overwhelming-pressures-south-korean-women-have-gone-baby-strike-pram-too (accessed March 10, 2014).

USDC (United States Department of Commerce). 2013. Assess Costs Everywhere. URL: http://acetool.commerce.gov/labor-costs (accessed April 24, 2013).

van der Mensbrugghe, Dominique, Israel Osorio-Rodarte, Andrew Burns, and John Baffes. 2011. "Macroeconomic Environment and Commodity Markets." In Piero Conforti (ed.), *Looking Ahead in World Food and Agriculture*. Rome: Food and Agriculture Organization.

Wallerstein, Immanuel. 1974. *The Modern World-System I*. New York: Academic Press.

Wallerstein, Immanuel. 1980. *The Modern World-System II*. New York: Academic Press.

Wallerstein, Immanuel. 2013. End of the Road for Runaway Factories? Commentary 351, April 15, 2013. URL: http://www2.binghamton.edu/fbc/commentaries/archive-2013/351en.htm (accessed 14 November, 2013).

Webber, Michael. 2012. The Dynamics of Primitive Accumulation. *Environment and Planning A*, 44(3): 560–579.

Williams, Raymond. 1980. *Problems in Materialism and Culture*. London: Verso.

Wood, Ellen Meiksins. 2002. *The Origin of Capitalism*. London: Verso.

World Bank. 2009. *Global Economic Prospects 2009*. Washington, DC: World Bank.

Worster, Donald. 1990. Transformations of the Earth. *Journal of American History*, 76(4): 1087–1106.

Wright, Justin, and Clive Jones. 2006. The Concept of Organisms as Ecosystem Engineers Ten Years On. *BioScience*, 56(3): 203–209.

Zivin Joshua, and Matthew Neidell. 2010. Temperature and the Allocation of Time. Working Paper, 15717. National Bureau of Economic Research, Washington, DC.

14

Preceding and Governing Measurements: An Emmanuelian Conceptualization of Ecological Unequal Exchange

Carl Nordlund

With the combination of world-system analysis and ecological economics, the concept of unequal exchange has been interpreted in biophysical terms. Typically depicted as non-compensated net transfers of biophysical resources, several scholars have engaged with ecological unequal exchange by linking uneven consumption of natural resources with the stratification of the contemporary world-system. Proposing an alternative conceptualization of ecological unequal exchange, this chapter addresses two drawbacks with existing approaches. First, rather than depicting ecological unequal exchange in the net transfer sense, this chapter proposes a conceptualization that builds on the original Emmanuelian idea of factor cost differentials. Secondly, instead of using national resource consumption indicators as proxies for ecological unequal exchange, the herein suggested approach looks at actually occurring trade flows. Exemplifying the approach, world trade in fuel commodities for the 1990–2010 period is analyzed.

Introduction

In a world where the biophysical walls are literally closing in on us, the recent combination of world-system analysis and ecological economics provides a novel way to address one of the most pressing contradictions of global capitalism: the uneven distribution of natural resources and environmental burdens. As two scholarly strands sharing several conceptual overlaps, the biophysical lens of ecological economics can shed new light on existing ideas, themes and questions within the world-system school, as well as formulating new ones.

This disciplinary combination is characterized by its ecological interpretations of unequal exchange. Typically depicted as monetarily non-compensated net transfers of biophysical resources, a cadre of scholars has spent the last two decades specifying, theorizing, and operationalizing the concept of ecological unequal exchange. Seemingly, these attempts make analytical sense: in contradiction to the presumed equalization effect of mainstream theories of international trade, the global distribution of resources and environmental risk seems to constantly favor the few haves over the many have-nots.

Offering new insight into the biophysical dimension of the modern world-system, there are nevertheless shortcomings with existing conceptualizations of ecological unequal exchange. First, although explicitly concerned with exchange, few studies look at actual exchange that occurs on the world market. Rather, contemporary operationalizations seem more focused on national indicators of resource usage and environmental burdens, thus assuming that these reflect international exchanges that, additionally, are assumed to be of an ecologically unequal kind. Secondly, contrary to how unequal exchange was originally described, the ecological variety typically signifies the actual phenomenon of net resource transfers per se, rather than representing a hypothesis of the mechanism causing this phenomenon. As such, existing analyses are somewhat detached from relevant theoretical foundations found in the heterodox development tradition. Related to this, thirdly: despite claims of building on the original formulation, *l'échange inégal biophysique* has very scant—if any—ties to how Arghiri Emmanuel specified unequal exchange in terms of factor-cost differentials.

Building on insights from global commodity chain studies, this chapter proposes an alternative Emmanuelian conceptualization of ecological unequal exchange. Similar to the original formulation, it is a theory about factor-cost differentials, but instead of looking at labor and how wages differ between nations, the proposed theory looks at the third, oft-forgotten Ricardian production factor of "land"/resources. Building on Jorgenson's structural theory, the hypothesis is that such factor-cost differentials are related to positionality in the world-system, but rather than operationalizing such structural properties using Jorgenson's index, which I argue to be unreliable in this context, network methods for role analysis and blockmodeling are used to determine structural positionality.

Analyzing trade flow data between 1990–2010 for three commodities—coal, crude oil, and liquefied natural gas—selected to represent the "land" production factor, combined with a more comprehensive role analysis of the world economy of 1999–2001, this chapter exemplifies how this novel conceptualization of ecological unequal exchange can be operationalized and measured. A general evaluation of ecological unequal exchange as factor-cost differentials concludes this chapter.

Ecological economics: Taking world-system analysis beyond the social sciences

Extending the postwar neo-Marxist and dependency traditions into the *longue durée* of the French Annales school of history, the world-system perspective offers a unique way to describe, analyze, and theorize about social change and global dynamics, past and present. Surpassing the ontogenetic assumptions of the "whole nation biases" as found in related disciplines (e.g., Snyder and Kick, 1979, 1097; Wellhofer, 1988, 282ff.), world-system analysis deems the only feasible unit of analysis in the modern world to be the world-system itself, where individuals, cities, nations and regions in various ways are tied together into a codependent and coevolutionary whole.

Despite a label that reflects its research area, it has been argued that world-system analysis is not primarily concerned with analyzing such singular historical world-systems:

> World-systems analysis is not a theory about the social world, or about part of it. It is a protest against the ways in which social scientific inquiry was structured for all of us at its inception in the middle of the nineteenth century. (Wallerstein, 1987, 309)

And indeed, the existing, and ongoing, partitioning of our knowledge about ourselves into distinct disciplines—anthropology, economics, political science, history, etc.—does obstruct our ability to ask questions about the social world that overlap these artificial domains, and it is this refusal to view the social, the economic, and the political as separate spheres of human existence that allows for social inquiry that surpasses the ontogenetic assumptions of each discipline.

But what about inquiries that, by their very nature, need to stretch into the natural sciences?

The world-system perspective has increasingly been combined with the strand of thinking known as ecological economics (e.g., Martinez-Alier, 1987; Costanza et al., 1997). Whereas mainstream economics begins with social entities—individuals, households, firms, institutions, etc.—and an assumed type of rationality among such agents, ecological economics typically starts off with the biophysical system which the economic system is seen as embedded in. Rather than describing economic processes and flows in terms of socially determined value schemes, ecological economics describes economic systems using the terminology of the underlying "base system"—such as flows of energy and materials, emission of hazardous chemicals, appropriated bioproductive hectares, and the like. This difference also separates ecological economics from environmental economics: whereas environmental economics "deal with the application of concepts of economics to the study of nature", such as reflected in its assignment of monetary values to biophysical resources and services, ecological economics represents "the ecological approach to the study of human society and economy" (Martinez-Alier, 1987, x).

World-system analysis and ecological economics have conceptual overlaps that make their combination particularly seamless. First, both schools are interested in the totality of systems, viewing such as something more than the sum of their parts. Instead of looking at individual sub-entities in Hobbesian isolation, both schools place greater emphasis on the structures that tie these parts into a grander whole. Through this, secondly, both schools recognize the finiteness of planetary systems, implying a greater emphasis on the distribution of resources and risks within single systems rather than modeling component parts as something detached from the evolution of others.

The usefulness of this scholarly combination is its provisioning of a biophysical dimension to the study of one of the most pressing and conflict-laden contradictions of global capitalism, i.e., the unequal sharing of planetary bounties and environmental burdens. Bridging the social and the material, this "new historical materialism" (Bunker and Ciccantell, 1999, 107) provides world-system analysis with the tools needed to situate studies of the contemporary world-economy into the grander biophysical system of which it has undeniably found itself to be a part.

Contemporary interpretations of ecological unequal exchange

The hallmark of this scholarly combination is the ecological approach to unequal exchange. Although interpreted in various ways—e.g., externalization of carbon dioxide emissions (Muradian et al., 2002; Roberts and Parks, 2007), distribution of organic water pollution (Shandra et al., 2009), transfers and appropriation of genetic resources (Fowler et al., 2001) etc.—ecological unequal exchange is typically used to signify monetarily non-compensated net transfers of biophysical resources (Bunker, 1984; 1985; Hornborg, 1998; 2001; 2003; 2006; 2009; Röpke, 2001; Martinez-Alier, 2004; Jorgenson, 2006; 2009; 2011; 2012; Rice, 2007a; 2007b; 2008; Jorgenson and Clark, 2009; Jorgenson et al., 2009; Hermele, 2012). This "net transfer" interpretation of ecological unequal exchange stipulates that even though the equality of a market exchange is defined by the mere occurrence of the exchange itself, the trading of goods of equal exchange value could very well imply an unequal exchange with regards to their biophysical properties, the resources that went into their production, or the environmental impact of their production and distribution. This is the underlying idea behind the works of Bunker, Hornborg, and Jorgenson, but variations in their respective analytical approaches and operationalizations motivate a closer look at these three scholars.

The idea of under-compensated net resource transfers is not a novel idea,[1] but the origin of the modern-day interpretation of ecological unequal exchange is typically attributed to Stephen Bunker (1984; 1985; see Martinez-Alier, 1987, 238; Rice, 2007a, 1371; Hornborg, 2009, 249). Proposing a functional distinction between extractive and productive economies, Bunker (1984, 1018, 1054) argued that "the unbalanced flows of energy and matter from extractive peripheries to the productive core provide better measures of unequal exchange in a world economic system than do flows of commodities measured in labor or prices," as "[t]he fundamental

---

1   In his impressive thesis on the history of unequal exchange, John Brolin (2006) finds a precursor to ecological unequal exchange in the mercantilist mind of Richard Cantillon, who combined labor values and income levels with trade in appropriated hectares: "When a State exchanges a small product of Land for a larger in Foreign Trade, it seems to have the advantage; and if current money is more abundant there than abroad it will always exchange a smaller product of land for a greater. When a State exchanges its Labour for the produce of foreign land it seems to have the advantage, since its inhabitants are fed at the Foreigner's expense." (Cantillon, 1931 [1755], 255; from Brolin, 2006, 28).

values in lumber, in minerals, oil, fish, and so forth, are predominantly in the good itself rather than in the labor incorporated in it." Without ruling out other possible manifestations of unequal exchange, Bunker (1985, 122) argued that a continued excessive concern with labor values, wages and profits sterilizes the development discourse by restricting it within its purely social domains.

Hornborg (e.g., 1992; 1998; 2001; 2003; 2006; 2009) has spent the last two decades refining his ideas on ecological unequal exchange. Although the biophysical metrics used by Hornborg have evolved during this time—from exergy/negentropy (Hornborg, 1992; 1998; 2001), to ecological footprints, space, and time (Hornborg, 2003; 2006; 2009)—a number of themes permeate all his studies. First, critical of how technology, economy and ecology are treated as separate fields of inquiry, Hornborg argues that an integrated perspective is necessary to understand the world-system and its societal distribution of planetary bounties and risks. A second recurrent theme is his critique towards "machine fetishism" where industrial technology, in liaison with neoclassical ideology, facilitates the unequal exchange of productive potential, labor time, and bioproductive space. Inspired by Georgescu-Roegen (1971) and Gudeman (1986), Hornborg takes a very thermodynamic perspective on international exchange, placing more emphasis on thermodynamically defined properties and less[2] on the social valuations that underpin such exchanges. Keeping the two realities analytically separated, Hornborg (2006) focuses on the intersection between socioeconomic valuations and objective material properties: as demonstrated in his study on nineteenth century English exports of manufactured textiles and imports of wool and cotton, it is the exchange ratio of such vertically traded commodities that, he argues, will reveal ecological unequal exchange.

From the macrosociological tradition, Andrew Jorgenson's writings on ecological unequal exchange are rich in empirical data and statistical methods. Contrasting how Hornborg envisions the combination of world-system analysis and ecological economics, Jorgenson treats the latter more as a supplement for understanding the effects of world-system dynamics. Seeing the biophysical dimension, such as ecological footprint indicators, as a missing piece of the puzzle (Jorgenson, 2003, 376), the puzzle in which this piece fits is nevertheless the macrosociological world-system perspective. In his articles, he argues that environmental outcomes, as reflected in national biophysical indicators on consumption, resource usage, and environmental burdens, are a function of world-system structural positionality. Modeling the latter as the independent variable and national environmental indicators as

---

2   "We can completely disregard the subjective 'utility' of the products, which is more or less arbitrary and ephemeral anyway—arbitrary because it is culturally defined (cf. Sahlins 1976), and ephemeral because it diminishes rapidly with use—and observe that if a finished product is priced higher than the resources required to produce it, this means that 'production' (i.e., the dissipation of resources) will continuously be rewarded with even more resources to dissipate" (Hornborg, 2001, 45).

dependent variables, as such underlining the above-mentioned conceptual difference with Hornborg, Jorgenson proposes, and thoroughly tests, a structural theory
of ecological unequal exchange. Nevertheless, Jorgenson indeed depicts ecological
unequal exchange as a net transfer of biophysical resources taking place through
the assumed "vertical trade" between low- and high-income countries, where the
former exchange their primary products for manufactures, but the implicit assumption in Jorgenson's work is thus that such unequal exchange is accurately reflected
in the biophysical national indices selected for analysis.

The different environmental indices used by Jorgenson range from per-capita
ecological footprints (Jorgenson, 2003, 2009; Jorgenson and Clark, 2009), deforestation (Jorgenson, 2006), both of these two (Jorgenson et al., 2009), and carbon emissions (Jorgenson, 2011). He also conceptualizes structural positionality in various
ways—from the composite Kentor-index of world-system positionality (Jorgenson,
2003; see Kentor, 2000) and percentages of exports sent to higher income countries
(Jorgenson, 2011) to his own weighted export index:

$$D_i = \sum_{j=1}^{N} p_{ij} a_j$$

where D_i is the weighted export index for country i, p_{ij} is the proportion of exports
from country i sent to country j, and a_j is the per-capita GDP of receiving country j.
The p_{ij} variables, summing up to unity for all values of j for each country i, is based
on total export flows in two articles (Jorgenson, 2006; Jorgenson and Clark, 2009),
whereas only primary goods exports are used in the latter (Jorgenson et al., 2009)
article.

Shortcomings with existing conceptualizations of ecological unequal exchange

Strictly economically, unequal economic exchange is an oxymoron: even though
markets may be imperfect and rational actors might find themselves rollercoast-
ing the demand curves, the actual exchange that occurs on a market defines the
exchange value equality of the goods, services, money, and credit changing hands. A
barrel of oil contains a given amount of oil, but it is the spatiotemporal variations in
supply, demand, and purchasing power that determine how much wheat this barrel
of oil can be traded for. Even though a hectare of arable land is always a hectare of,
hopefully, arable land, market exchange makes it possible, and likely very rational,
to let the market transform one hectare of cash crop into two hectares of food-
stuff—until saturated demand, changing preferences, and economies of scale (elsewhere) effectively could reduce that hectare to a fraction of its former capacity for

sustenance. Intersecting the social and the material, ecological unequal exchange is uniquely situated to address such questions.

Whereas "ecological unequal exchange" denotes the net flow phenomenon per se, both Hornborg and Jorgenson provide theories on its underlying mechanisms. According to Hornborg, it is prices per se, and mediums of exchange, that acts as ideological agents, making market exchanges to appear as reciprocal (e.g., Hornborg, 2009, 240, 242ff.). Accordingly, ecological unequal exchange is the result of how the neoclassical school of economics upholds a cultural (mis)understanding of value, making people believe that they need, and thus value, a car, a CPU and a refridgerator more than the raw materials and energy that went into their production.

As a contrast, Jorgenson's structural theory (e.g., Jorgenson, 2006) is more open for formal hypothesis testing. In addition, Jorgenson's concern with the structural properties of the international network of trade as reflected in his weighted export index is more in line with core issues of world-system and dependency studies, such as monopoly capitalism, asymmetric trade structures, and dendritic trade structures (e.g., Frank, 1966; Galtung, 1971). Although an interesting hypothesis, there are, I argue, a couple of shortcomings in its operationalization and, more generally, in how ecological unequal exchange has been conceptualized so far.

First, although the concept explicitly refers to exchange, the studies by Jorgenson look at national environmental indicators that are assumed to reflect international trade flows that, it is further assumed, are of an ecological unequal kind. National indicators of consumption are also assumed *only* to reflect such net resource transfers among nations, excluding would-be endowments and domestic sink capacity. As Jorgenson look at the contemporary world-economy, for which detailed commodity trade data exists, less assumptions would be necessary in the study of ecological unequal exchange that looks at actually occurring exchange. In Hornborg's (2006) study of the textile trade of England in the 1850s, Hornborg partly uses historical trade flow records when estimating the trade ratio between raw materials and manufactures. Aware of possible errors in such data, it is surprising that Hornborg has not yet attempted to verify his thesis using contemporary, readily available, trade flow data.

Second, Jorgenson's operationalization of world-system structural positionality is, I argue, somewhat flawed. Intended to capture a country's trade dependence,[3] this index can be criticized on two accounts. First, although the proportions of ex-

---

3   Possible alternatives to the weighted export index (and the measure used in Jorgenson 2011) that captures a similar notion of structural positionality are the share-of-trade index employed by Gidengil (1978, 56) and the relative acceptance index (Savage and Deutsch, 1960; see also Domínguez, 1971). Designed to capture partner concentration within core-periphery/hub-and-spoke structures, these indices are not only more established (and thus tested) than the weighted export index but they are also applicable identifying *both* core and periphery alike, i.e., not only a predetermined set of low-income countries.

ports to other countries (i.e., the p_{ij} variables) are calculated using relational data, their marginal-normalization *de facto* discards differences in significance of exports between countries.[4] Second, the multiplication of proportions with per-capita GDP of the receiving country (i.e., a_j) has a profound impact on results. Hypothetically, if all export vectors were perfectly balanced (i.e., where the shares of exports from each country are perfectly distributed across potential receivers), the rank order of the weighted export index and GDP per capita would be identical. As high-income countries mostly trade with each other, their weighted export indices would thus be very high.

Third, the existing conceptualizations of ecological unequal exchange have scant, if any, ties to how Arghiri Emmanuel defined unequal exchange as based on factor-cost differentials. Emmanuel (1969; 1972) built his theory of unequal exchange on assumptions of free international trade and perfect competition, void of market irregularities, where the difference between labor and capital was the (partial) mobility of the latter. His model contained no monopoly capitalism or asymmetrical trade in the dependency tradition (e.g., Frank, 1966), nor was it technological rent, capital-intensity differentials,[5] product-specific properties, or Singerish demand elasticities that caused unequal exchange. Rather, a wage differential between developed and developing countries was the exogenous independent variable that led to unequal exchange (Emmanuel, 1975a, 39; Brolin, 2006, 179, 215; see also Emmanuel, 1972, 126ff.). Thus, although Hornborg, Jorgenson, and Rice dutifully refer to Emmanuel, placed alongside dependency and world-system scholars, claiming that their respective conceptualization builds on Emmanuel (e.g., Jorgenson et al., 2009, 264), they are not concerned with production factors and their cost differentials that characterized unequal exchange according to its founder. Even though Hornborg's (2006) study on the English textile trade is only a paragraph away from Emmanuel's factor-cost-oriented specification of unequal exchange, no such connection is made; instead, Hornborg proposes a continued mapping of "total" ecological unequal exchange, encompassing *all* traded commodities.

As global resources are channeled through the global market, the differences in the magnitude of one's consumption and, particularly, the geographic range from which resources are obtained are by themselves, I argue, adequate indicators for the

---

4   For instance, a country whose relatively insignificant exports go to a singular high-income country would get a higher scoring than another country whose relatively significant exports go to another high-income country with a slightly lower GDP.

5   Emmanuel (1962) began his theoretical exposition by describing the exchange of products with unequal amounts of socially necessary labor time and based on different capital intensities, this being referred to by his tutor Bettelheim as unequal exchange in the broad sense. However, although many authors have referred to Emmanuel's *two* types of unequal exchange (e.g., Chase-Dunn, 1989, 231), the capital-intensity variety was not unequal exchange according to Emmanuel (1975b, 80), but only a demonstrational device to distinguish and compare with the wage-differential situation of unequal exchange proper (Brolin, 2006, 180).

existence of under-compensated net resource transfers. Describing such flows in minuscule quantitative detail could be worthwhile, but it does not necessarily help us understand their historical roots and underlying mechanisms. Additionally, as the social valuations that determine an economic exchange are disconnected from the biophysical properties of the goods and services changing hands—e.g., the decision to buy the *Plants vs. Zombies* smartphone game is based on perceived fun and purchasing power rather than its inherent productive potential (which I have found to be negative) or the resources that went into its production—we can safely assume that practically *all* exchanges are ecologically unequal as any linear relationship between social valuations and material properties would be nothing but coincidental.

Even though Jorgenson's structural theory is tied to world-system ideas on inter-national structures, contemporary conceptualizations of ecological unequal exchange do not utilize existing theory, insights, and lines of thought to their fullest extent. Rather, the world-system tradition and the heterodox strands of social and economic development thinking are more of a compatible backdrop to the ecological-econometrics on fairly obvious net transfers of biophysical resources, rather than providing the historical ideas and conceptions that should precede and govern such measurements. In what follows, an alternative conceptualization of ecological unequal exchange will be proposed that, I argue, is more in line with the original idea of unequal exchange as specified by Arghiri Emmanuel. Refining Jorgenson's structural theory through network-analytical methods, furthermore looking at actually occurring exchange rather than assumed proxies of such exchanges, the proposed conceptualization is nevertheless first and foremost a theory in the Emmanuelian mold, i.e., a theory about factor-cost differentials.

Towards an Emmanuelian interpretation of ecological unequal exchange: Learning from global commodity chains

Proposed by Hopkins and Wallerstein (1982; Wallerstein and Hopkins, 2000 [1986]), the global commodity chain (GCC) approach was conjured up to address a particular historical question: whether a world-economy, characterized by fragmented production and an international division of labor, existed between the sixteenth and eighteenth century. The study of internationally segmented chains of commodity production and the local and global causes and effects of such—the origins, costs, and provisioning of inputs, organic compositions, regulations and institutions, social and environmental impacts, the local share (and distribution among factors) of total value-added etc.—has crystallized into a distinct speciality (e.g., Gereffi, 1994; Applebaum et al., 1994; Heintz, 2006; see particularly Bair, 2005, 2009). Whether the Age of Reason had its GCCs or not, their contemporary counterparts are definitely more than hypothetical constructs—the Ford Escort I had in Sweden was apparently produced in 15 different countries, spanning three continents (Gereffi and Korzeniewicz, 1994, 1)—and the constant reconfigurations of chain segments reflect a rational search for cost minimization and profit maximization. The study of such chains poses a new, upgraded approach for understanding distributional aspects of the world-economy (see also Heintz, 2003, 2006):

> If one thinks of the entire chain as having a total amount of surplus value that has been appropriated, what is the division of this surplus value among the boxes of the chain? This is the kind of issue that lay behind the debate on unequal exchange. (Hopkins et al., 1994, 49)

This chapter draws on two somewhat more rudimentary insights from the GCC school. The first insight is that the traditional perception of an industrial core and a non-industrial periphery is too simplistic:

> What the commodity chain construct makes evident is that the Colin Clark trinity of primary, secondary, and tertiary sectors is descriptive and not terrible helpful. Each box in the chain transforms something and is therefore "industrial." . . . In any case, there is no long-term fixed priority for the "secondary" sector as a motor of capitalist development. (Hopkins et al., 1994, 50)

This contemporary logic of dislocation makes it somewhat straggling to ground debates on unequal exchange on assumptions of vertical trade. If machines and industrial technology constitute the engines for core dominance and if the exports of manufactures characterize the beneficiary of ecological unequal exchange, can the relative (secondary sector) deindustrialization of the core fit into such a theory? Global commodity chains do not end ecological unequal exchange as we know it, but they do change the inbound parameters and assumptions—little has changed since 2006 and much has changed since the 1850s (cf. Hornborg, 2006).

Secondly, global commodity chains tell us something about international factor mobility that differs from neoclassical assumptions of immobility (e.g., Ohlin, 1933; Samuelson, 1948). Similar to most assumptions of mainstream trade theory, the factor immobility postulate was inherited from the classics:

> Experience . . . shows that the fancied or real insecurity of capital, which not under the immediate control of its owner, together with the natural disinclination which every man has to quit the country of his birth and connections, and intrust himself, with all his habits fixed, to a strange government and new laws, check the emigration of capital. (Ricardo, 1996 [1817], 95)

Ricardo's family history tells another story about factor mobility. Abraham and Abigail Ricardo, a Dutch banking family originally from Portugal, were apparently okay with a strange government and new laws when, prior to David's birth, moving from Amsterdam to London. Salvaging Ricardo's theory on comparative cost advantages, John Stuart Mill (1849 [1848], 113) redefined international trade as trade between regions separated by factor immobility (Condliffe, 1950, 187), a definition that implies that international trade today is pretty much nonexistent.

Although a prerequisite for global commodity chains, the mobility of a production factor depends on its type. Indeed, foreign guest workers constitute 94 percent of Qatar's economically active population and the Swedish company Norrskensbär employs seasonal Thai workers to pick lingonberries, but the mobility of labor is not at par with the seemingly frictionless global movement of capital. Reflecting most strands of development thinking, the focus remains on these two production factors—capital and labor—and specifically on how the mobility of the former combines with the overall immobile latter in different organic compositions of production at various locations, resulting in chains that, for instance, stretch over three continents and 15 countries.

Through ecological economics, the world-system perspective can access the full triad of production factors: labor, capital, and land. Representing physical raw materials, this third Ricardian production factor is typically ignored in the Marxist discourse on wages and profits, as well as neoclassical Cobb-Douglas production functions. The "production" of natural resources roughly follows their geographical endowment patterns, but once commodified, they are injected into the same global commodity trade networks as any other commodity, eventually combined with labor and capital around the world. As demonstrated by its significant share of total global trade (see Figure 1), the (Alfred) Weberian logic of industrial location between resources and markets hardly seems like a determining factor in chain

Figure 1: Trend in composition of global material flows, 1980–2010

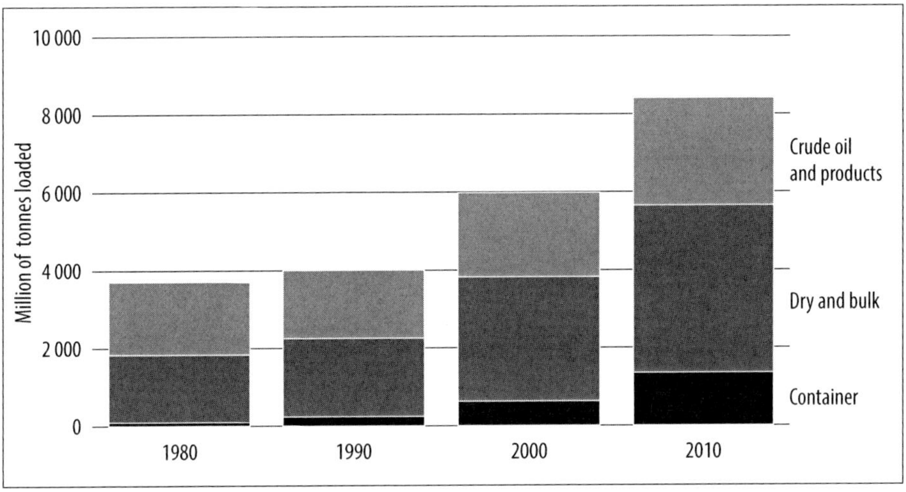

Source: UNCTAD (2011, 10).

configurations; rather, similar to capital, and possibly to an even greater degree, the third production factor made tangible through the biophysical lens of ecological economics traverses the network of international trade, feeding segments and chains with the material basis of production.

Ecological unequal exchange as factor-cost differentials

Following Emmanuel, the conceptualization of ecological unequal exchange proposed in this chapter is concerned with factor-cost differentials. Whereas Emmanuel examined national price differentials for labor, i.e., wages, this chapter looks at national price differentials for the land production factor. Emmanuelian ecological unequal exchange is thus not concerned with measuring total net resource flows between countries; instead, focusing explicitly on commodities representing this particular production factor, it is perceived as would-be differences in import costs (and export revenues) per unit of biophysical resource.

Similar to Emmanuel's theory of unequal exchange, the hypothesis here is that factor-cost differentials are related to the properties of social systems. However, whereas Emmanuel theorized that wage differentials between countries reflected national differences in the organization of labor, the hypothesis here is that cost differentials for "land" are related to structural positionality in the contemporary world-economy. Following Jorgenson, and the world-system and dependency traditions at large, the hypothesis is that advantageously positionalized actors in global exchange networks typically are at the "better end" of ecological unequal exchange, whereas those disadvantageously positionalized are relatively worse off in terms of relative factor costs.

In what follows, the proposed Emmanuelian conceptualization of ecological unequal exchange, including its structural theory, is exemplified using fossil fuel trade data for the period 1990–2010. The data and methods chosen for this analysis, and the structural theory per se, do not rule out other possible ways to measure would-be price differentials of the third Ricardian production factor across the world and to theorize about such occurrences.

Testing the factor-cost version of ecological unequal exchange

To test the structural theory of Emmanuelian ecological unequal exchange, i.e., whether cost and revenues of the third production factor are related to structural positionality in the world-economy, two data series are needed: an index that adequately captures the notion of structural positionality in world-systems, and national data on import costs (and export revenues) per traded unit of natural resource.

Production factors of the third kind: Fuel commodities

Selected as adequate representations of the "land" production factor with a huge importance in global trade, the commodities chosen (and their respective SITC categories[6]) are (non-agglomerated) coal (SITC 3212), crude oil (SITC 3330), and liquefied natural gas (SITC 3431). Data on bilateral commodity flows between 96 countries, measured in exchange value (US$) as well as physical mass (metric tonnes), were prepared[7] for three time periods: 1990–1992, 1999–2001, and 2008–2010. Whereas original mass quantities were used in the commodity-specific analyses below, these were converted into total energy flows in the aggregate analyses.

Structural positionality: Network analysis and regular blockmodeling

The use of blockmodeling and role analysis in world-system analysis have a relatively long and, seemingly successful, track record (e.g., Snyder and Kick, 1979; Nemeth and Smith, 1985; Smith and White, 1992; Mahutga, 2006), and a sequence of studies traces the growing confidence in the "natural wedding" (Snyder and Kick, 1979, 1123; see also Breiger, 1981, 354; Nemeth and Smith, 1985, 521; Smith and White, 1992, 858). Contrary to categorizations into core, semiperiphery and periphery based on country attributes (e.g., Kentor, 2000), measures that "do not represent such positions any more than an individual's income or education measures his or her (discrete) class position" (Snyder and Kick, 1979, 1102), network-analytical studies engage with the structural tenets of the world-system school in a "referential context," where "the focus of the analysis is no longer on characteristics of individual countries, but on the relationships between countries" (Nemeth and Smith, 1985, 522).

Similar to these studies, this chapter uses regular blockmodeling to determine world-system structural positionality. As a general network-analytical procedure, blockmodeling groups social entities (actors) into role-equivalent sets based on

---

6   Explicitly recommended for comparative analyses by United Nations Statistics Division, the Standard International Trade Classification (SITC) nomenclature (3rd revision) was chosen for this study.

7   Extracting data from the Comtrade database (UNCTAD, n.d.) for a total of nine years, three-year averages were calculated for each period. Bilateral data with missing quantity units were excluded from the dataset. Whereas excluded flows were insignificant for coal (<0.05 percent), 17.5 percent of the value of crude oil flows in 1992 had missing quantity units, thus only 1990 and 1991 were used to calculate mean annual trade in crude oil for the 1990–1992 period. Whereas the original data covered 118 countries, those with total imports below one million U.S. dollars were excluded from the analysis, resulting in a set of 96 countries.

similarities in their interaction patterns.[8] Even though it is plausible that the structure of the world-economy changed, possibly considerably, between 1990 and 2010, this chapter establishes structural positionality for the 1999–2001 period only.

The multilayer data for the role analysis consists of trade flow values for six broad commodity categories,[9] measured in exchange value, among the 96 countries in the fuel commodity data (see above), with the assumption that such commodity flow patterns reflect the structure of the contemporary world-economy. Using five iterations of the REGE algorithm[10] (White and Reitz, 1983, 1985) in a simultaneous analysis of these six flow matrices, a subsequent single-link hierarchical clustering determined the various sets of role-equivalent sets at different cutpoints. Anova density tests[11] guided the number of partitions to choose: the highest absolute R^2 value occurred at eight partitions, where the largest relative increases occurred when going from two to three, and from four to five partitions. As we are only looking at one aspect of the world-economy, we are not theoretically bound to the assumed trimodality of the world-system; to increase resolution, a partition with eight positions[12] was chosen. These positions and their aggregate net value and energy flows for the selected commodities are given in Table 1.

The United States separates itself from the countries in position D forming a singleton position at the 7-positional partition. Whereas most high-income European countries are found in position D, this position also contains the Southeast Asian countries (including Japan) as well as Mexico and Canada, both deeply connected to the United States. The Scandinavian countries are found in position C, which they share with the Central and East European countries, India, South Africa, and a few

---

8   Role analysis and blockmodeling is a well-established approach within social network analysis, see, e.g., Wasserman and Faust (1994) and Scott (2000).

9   Included commodities were Food, Live animals (SITC 0), Mineral fuels, etc. (SITC 3), Chemicals, related (SITC 5), Manufactured goods (SITC 6), Machinery etc. (SITC 7), Miscellaneous Manufactures (SITC 8). Together, the commodities in these six SITC divisions correspond to 92 percent of total trade in the 1999–2001 period. Note that this data used to determine structural positionality is at a higher aggregate level than the 4-digit SITC categories used to determine factor-cost differentials.

10   Even though used previously in world-system contexts (Smith and White, 1992; Mahutga, 2006), the REGE algorithm is not the only way to partition a network according to regular equivalence (cf. Doreian et al., 2005; Reichardt and White, 2007; Ziberna, 2008). Despite its popularity, the REGE algorithm has been criticized for its point-scoring procedure and its ability to identify regular role-equivalence, particularly in valued datasets (see Borgatti and Everett, 1991; 1993). For simplicity in this example study, I assume that the REGE-derived partitions reflect subsets of nations sharing similar structural positionality.

11   See Luczkovich et al. (2003) for an example on how Anova density tests are used to identify suitable partitions.

12   In network-analytical terminology, a "position" is a subset of actors that are considered role-equivalent and/or part of a blockmodel.

Table 1: The 8-positional partition of international trade 1999–2001 (with positional net flows of value and energy content)

Position	Countries	Positional net flows (selected commodities)	
		Millions of U.S. dollars	Terajoules
A	Pakistan, Sri Lanka	1 324	588 849
B	Costa Rica, Ecuador, El Salvador, Guatemala, Honduras, Nicaragua, Panama, Peru, Trinidad and Tobago	−704	−191 407
C	Argentina, Belarus, Chile, Czech Republic, Denmark, Egypt, Finland, Greece, Hungary, India, Israel, Luxembourg, New Zealand, Norway, Poland, Portugal, Romania, Russian Federation, Slovakia, Slovenia, South Africa, Sweden, Tunisia, Turkey, Ukraine	−15 582	−4 993 119
D	Australia, Austria, Belgium, Brazil, Canada, China, Hong Kong, France, Germany, Indonesia, Ireland, Italy, Japan, Malaysia, Mexico, Netherlands, Philippines, Republic of Korea, Singapore, Spain, Switzerland, Thailand, United Kingdom	103 911	30 689 393
E	Albania, Bolivia, Croatia, Cyprus, Estonia, Ghana, Iceland, Jordan, Kenya, Latvia, Lebanon, Lithuania, Madagascar, Malta, Mauritius, Paraguay, Senegal, Serbia and Montenegro, Macedonia FYR, Uruguay	2 882	1 057 555
USA	United States	59 199	18 027 776
F	Algeria, Colombia, Iran, Iraq, Kuwait, Nigeria, Oman, Qatar, Saudi Arabia, United Arab Emirates, Venezuela	−151 086	−45 192 434
G	Mozambique, Nepal, Uganda, Tanzania, Zimbabwe	56	13 387

Source: Comtrade (UNCTAD, n.d.) (see footnote 7).

geographically dispersed countries in North Africa, the Middle East, and southern Latin America. The northern Latin American countries, however, have their own position (B). Even though fuel commodities only constituted one (out of six) major commodity categories, these flows are apparently sufficiently distinct (and apparently substantial—see Figure 1) to result in the distinct role-similar position F. Apart from position F and A, the other (non-singleton) positions contain a mix of net-importing and -exporting countries.

Complementing the blockmodel, a regular image graph was created,[13] see Figure 2. Mapping the functional anatomy of the network, the regular ties between and within each position were identified using a heuristic explicitly designed to handle datasets with huge value spans (Nordlund, 2007), where the different shades reflect criteria-fulfillment for regular ties. Compared with what a regular block image for

---

13 The criteria-fulfillment percentage was calculated using formula 3 in Nordlund (2007, 63). The 2-dimensional coordinates were established using a force-directed layout algorithm using the criteria-fulfillment percentages as relational data. Visualized using Ceunet (cnslabs.ceu.hu).

Figure 2: Regular image graph of world trade, 1999–2001

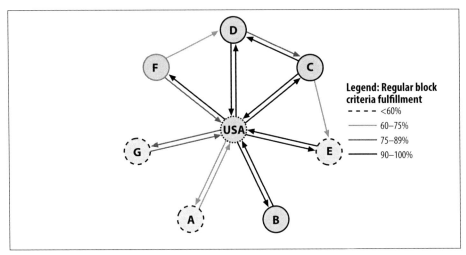

Notes: Cf. Table 1 for more details on positions A–G.
Source: Comtrade (UNCTAD, n.d.) (see footnote 9).

Galtung's (1971) structural topology looks like,[14] we are indeed looking at a core-periphery topological structure, especially as the United States and the countries in position D merge at partitions below seven positions.

Ecological unequal exchange as monetarily under-compensated net energy flows

Converting the quantity flow matrices for each fuel commodity type into corresponding energy flow matrices, subsequently calculating aggregate matrices containing total value and energy flows, we can assess occurrences of ecological unequal exchange in the net transfer sense for these three commodities. The scatterplot in Figure 3 depicts national net flows of value and energy for the 1999–2001 period.

Evidently, the trend is strongly linear: a net inflow (outflow) of energy implies a net import (export) of commodity value, and the ratio between energy and value appears to be relatively similar. Still, the scatterplot above obfuscates an exception: even though Guatemala had a (mean) annual net import of fuel commodities in the 1999–2001 period, valued at US$47.5 million, its external trade in these three

---

14 A regular block image of Galtung's (1971, 89) classical feudal interaction structure as a typological core-periphery structure results in two role-equivalent positions—a core and a periphery—where the core has a regular self-tie, the periphery lacks such, and there is a regular tie between core and periphery.

Figure 3: National net flows (energy and value), 1999–2001

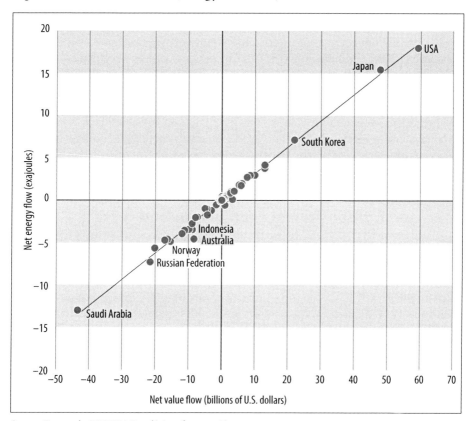

Source: Comtrade (UNCTAD, n.d.) (see footnote 7).

fuel commodities implied a net energy *outflow* of 2.9 petajoules. A closer inspection reveals that almost all of Guatemala's imports of fuel commodities came from Venezuela, carrying a relatively high price tag of US$3.98 per gigajoule, whereas Guatemala's subsequent export of fuel commodities, overwhelmingly to the United States, only gave US$2.33 per gigajoule in revenue. Even though the Venezuelan data could be unreliable,[15] the low cost of U.S. energy imports from Guatemala is

---

15 With obvious anomalies removed from the datasets, the export price data from Venezuela was consistently higher than the world average. However, as import data rather than export data was used in this analysis, would-be error sources should be found among importers rather than exporters such as Venezuela, thus making it difficult to motivate a removal of the Venezuelan export vectors in the flow matrices.

nevertheless approximately a dollar cheaper than what it on average pays its energy suppliers.

As we are only looking at three fuel commodities in this analysis, the observed proportionality between energy and value is not very surprising. As indicated by Hornborg (2006), a complete mapping of this net flow variety of ecological unequal exchange must by necessity cover virtually all commodities traded on the global market, and by including more commodities of different types, it is more feasible that we would find countries placed in the "unequal" quadrants as well. What the above trend line does show us, albeit slightly, is that there are indeed slight variations in the cost and revenues from energy trade. Russia, placed slightly below the trend line, earns less per exported joule than Saudi Arabia and Norway, placed above the trend line. Similarly, the United States gets fewer joules per dollar than South Korea and Japan do.

Inter- and intrapositional energy flows and costs

Continuing with the total energy flow data for 1999–2001, Table 2 contains energy flows (in terajoules; 10^{12} J) within and between the eight role-equivalent positions. By far the largest positional energy flow goes from the energy exporters in position F to the mostly high-income countries of position D. Corresponding to about a third of all energy flows in the dataset, these 27.3 exajoules are more than double the energy flow from position F to the United States. However, the second largest value represents *intra*positional flows within position D, i.e., energy flows between these 23 "developed" countries, thus by far outranking the cohesiveness of the other positions (see Table 2).

Expressed as petajoules (10^{15} J) and excluding positional flows below one petajoule, the topological features of inter- and intrapositional flows are highlighted better in Figure 4. The contrast between the significant cohesiveness of position D and the low intrapositional density of position F is per se a definition of a core-pe-

Table 2: Inter- and intra-positional energy flows (terajoule), 1999–2001

	A	B	C	D	E	USA	F	G
A			2340	24214				
B		186621		155304	1	497419	45	
C	2971	8828	5219949	10296598	567495	940891	11059	103
D	56922	75540	1637011	15832736	21233	6686728	247456	
E		23	82675	110673	3523	3964	1	69
USA		3976	106066	1516341	1788		8541	
F	555511	372995	5005571	27306821	663601	11535487	9674	19554
G			1254	4240	842		2	101

Notes: Cf. Table 1 for more details on positions A–G.
Source: Comtrade (UNCTAD, n.d.) (see footnote 7).

riphery topology (Borgatti and Everett, 1999), especially since the criterion of connectivity is fulfilled by the flow of 27 exajoules (10^{18} J) between F and D.

As already noted (Table 1), position C acts as an alternative net energy exporter in the system. Contrary to the main fuel-exporting position (F), position C is quite cohesive, having the second-largest intrapositional flow. However, even though C is an aggregate net energy exporter, only seven of its 25 countries are net energy exporters—including Norway and Russia with net energy exports[16] at 5.6 and 7.3 exajoules respectively.

Providing position D with an alternative source for its energy needs, it is noteworthy that very little energy flows from position C to the United States. Instead, it is position D that is the second largest source of U.S. imports of energy: even though position D is the largest net energy importer in the structure, the 6.7 exajoules from D to the United States are quite significant.

By dividing the aggregate value flow matrix with its energy counterpart, the cost-per-joule for each bilateral flow for the period 1999–2001 is calculated. Mapping this price matrix on the blockmodel and its partition, we arrive at the cost-per-energy prices given in Figure 5. Several interesting observations can be made here, par-

Figure 4: Inter- and intra-positional energy flows (petajoule), 1999–2001

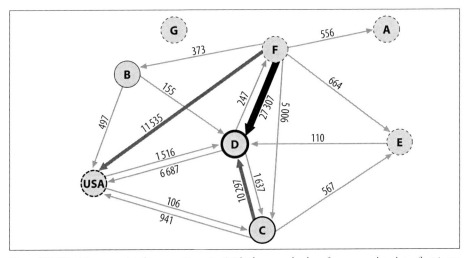

Notes: Cf. Table 1 for more details on positions A–G. Thickness and color of arrows and nodes reflect inter- and intra-positional flow magnitudes. Dashed lines for nodes reflect intra-positional energy flows below 1 petajoule.
Source: Comtrade (UNCTAD, n.d.) (see footnote 7).

16 The net energy export figures for Norway and Russia include exports to other countries within position C.

Figure 5: Inter- and intra-positional energy prices (U.S. dollars per gigajoules), 1999–2001

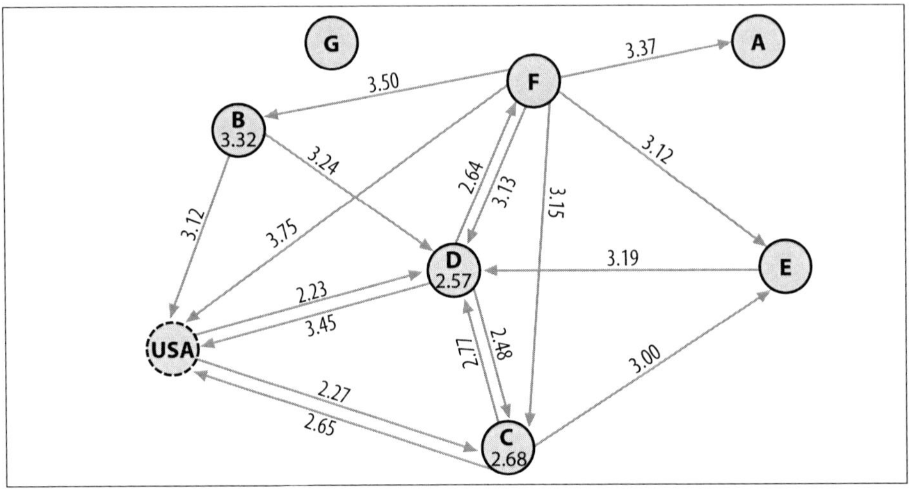

Notes: Cf. Table 1 for more details on positions A–G.
Source: Comtrade (UNCTAD, n.d.) (see footnote 7).

ticularly with regards to position D. First, regarding imports from position F, it can be noted that position D pays less per joule than the United States pays (3.13 vs. 3.75 US$/GJ). Also, it can be noted that the energy flows from C to D are even lower[17] at 2.77 US$/GJ. But even if these energy costs are relatively low, the intrapositional energy cost within position D is significantly lower than that for its extrapositional trade.

Apart from paying relatively little for its energy inflows, position D is also the second largest source for the United States. Although slightly cheaper than U.S. imports from position F, position D earns US$3.45 for each gigajoule flowing to the United States. Together, this points to the peculiar situation of the United States: highly dependent on a singular positional energy source (F), supplemented by imports *from* the largest net-importing position (D), and paying relatively a lot for each imported joule, the United States actually seems to be on the disadvantageous side in Emmanuelian ecological unequal exchange of these commodities.

17 The relative insignificance of energy flows from C to the United States makes their price tag equally insignificant.

Price trends and positional differences: Individual fuel commodities

Although total energy flows are interesting from a purely thermodynamic perspective, it is doubtful whether different dollar-per-energy measurements are readily comparable with each other. Obviously, the price of a particular fuel commodity does not only reflect its energy density: even though an exchange of one tonne of crude oil for 1.67 tonnes of coal might be thermodynamically equal, it is doubtful that trading partners would consider this an equal exchange. The missing component is of course utility: not only is coal 67 percent heavier than energy-equivalent crude oil, but solid coal is also less versatile than liquid oil. Few large-scale power plants run on crude oil and even less cars run on coal: just as with labor and capital, there are different kinds of "land," and this empirical analysis is rounded off by looking at cost differentials for the respective fuel commodity.

Based on total flows of exchange value and quantities of coal and crude oil, Figure 6 illustrates how fuel commodity prices increased during the 1991–2009 period. Whereas prices remained relatively stable between 1991 and 2000, there was a sharp price increase for the two commodities during 2000–2009.

Whereas the import costs and export revenues for the respective fuel commodity were relatively similar among positions in the first two periods, the sharp post-2000 increase corresponds to positional differences with regards to import costs and/or export revenues. Exemplifying this, Figure 7 depicts the import cost of coal

Figure 6: Price trends for coal and crude oil, 1991–2009

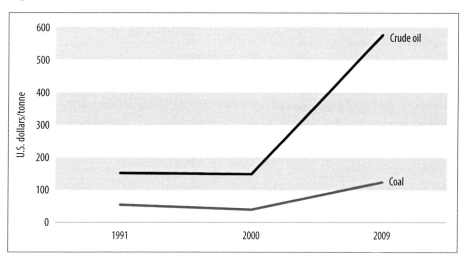

Notes: These price trends were calculated using the extracted trade flow data alone.
Source: Comtrade (UNCTAD, n.d.) (see footnote 7).

Figure 7: Coal: mean positional import prices

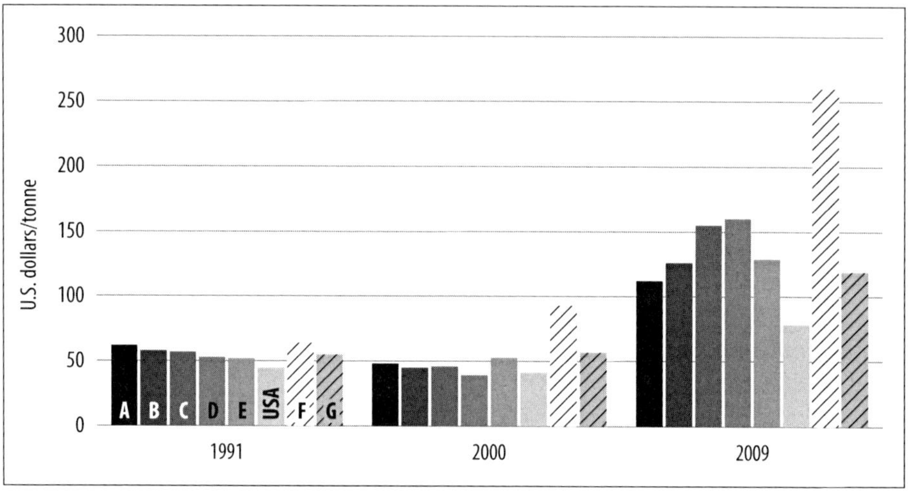

Notes: Cf. Table 1 for more details on positions A–G.
Source: Comtrade (UNCTAD, n.d.) (see footnote 7).

for each position and time period. Of particular interest is the price of U.S. coal imports: although increasing from US$45 to US$79 per tonne over the whole period, this increase remains relatively modest in comparison to the doubling, tripling, and, in the case of position F,[18] quadrupling of import costs for coal from 1991 to 2009.

Combining import costs with export revenues for 2009, Figure 8 depicts cost-revenue differentials of coal for respective position. With a significantly lower import cost relative to other positions, the United States seems to accumulate US$70 for each exported tonne of coal that is matched to a corresponding import. Contrasting with this, the "throughput" ratio of coal imports and exports for position F is, despite relatively high revenue for its exports, seemingly very detrimental.

Corresponding comparisons of costs and revenues for the other two commodities in 2009 are given in Figure 9 (crude oil) and Figure 10 (liquefied natural gas). Whereas the high cost of crude oil imports to position F should be interpreted with care (being based on five relatively minor flows), the findings for position D could point to a more interesting situation. Obtaining US$788 per exported tonne, most of it exported to the United States, position D seemingly "earns" US$193 for each tonne of crude oil that passes through. For liquefied natural gas (Figure 10), it is instead position C that has a significant differential between import costs and export

---

18 Although position F is a net exporter in coal, particularly due to Colombia being the fourth largest coal exporter, gross coal imports for position F rose from 837 million to 1.2 billion tonnes over the period studied.

Figure 8: Coal: comparing positional import costs with export revenues, 2009

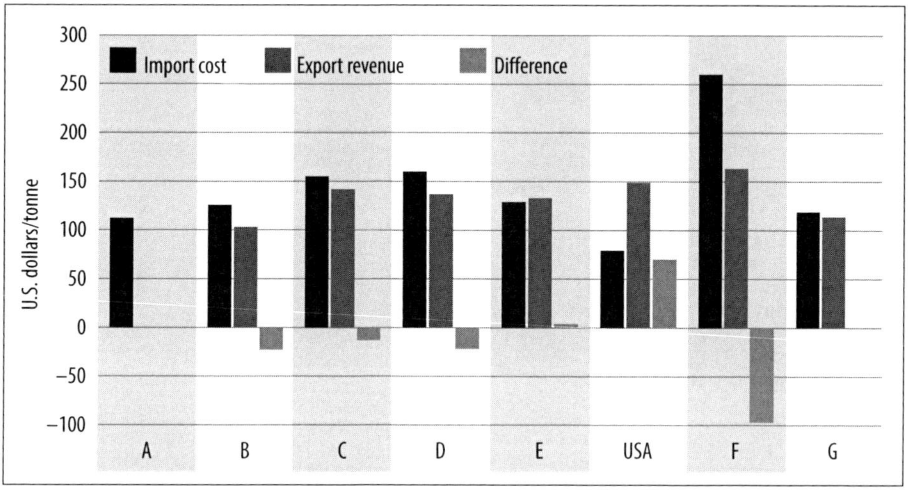

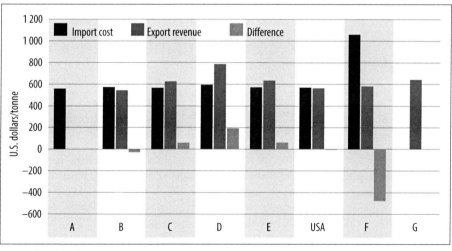

Notes: Cf. Table 1 for more details on positions A–G.
Source: Comtrade (UNCTAD, n.d.) (see footnote 7).

Figure 9: Crude oil: comparing positional import costs with export revenues, 2009

Notes: Cf. Table 1 for more details on positions A–G.
Source: Comtrade (UNCTAD, n.d.) (see footnote 7).

Figure 10:   Liquefied natural gas: comparing positional import costs with export revenues, 2009

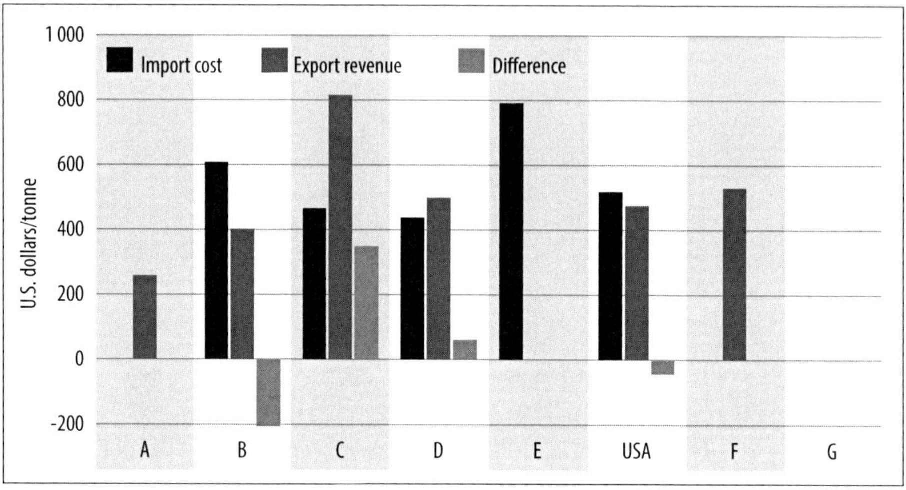

Notes: Cf. Table 1 for more details on positions A–G. In contrast to coal and crude oil, the number of available data points for liquefied natural gas is somewhat lower, only allowing for interpreting cost-revenue differences for positions C, D, USA, and possibly also B. The number of data points for import prices for these positions (in brackets) are 4 (B), 47 (C), 107 (D) and 9 (USA). Corresponding data coverage for exports are 23 (B), 36 (C), 44 (D), and 7 (USA).
Source: Comtrade (UNCTAD, n.d.) (see footnote 7).

revenues (US$349), seemingly categorizing its trade in liquefied natural gas on the beneficial side of ecological unequal exchange as interpreted in terms of factor-cost differentials.

The dissolving of significant distinctions

To aggregate coal, crude oil and natural gas into a common biophysical unit seems like a straight-forward exercise: as the utility of these commodities is obtained through incineration, the energy content is a suitable unit for the biophysical accounting. Still, even for these very similar commodities, it is apparent that their values not only reflect energy content, but other properties as well. That is: ecological equal exchange is likely only equal in the thermodynamic sense.

When aggregating *different types* of raw materials, finding a common biophysical unit complicates matters further: how to convert lumber, fuel, rubber, metal ore, water and other production factors of the third Ricardian kind into a common unit that makes sense in the context of ecological unequal exchange, whether net-flow or Emmanuelian? Seemingly imperative for measuring "total" (net flow) ecological unequal exchange, efforts striving towards common monodimensional units, such as ecological footprints, should indeed be questioned. It is true that "[t]he alchemy of money, with its power of commensuration, lies in its ability to dissolve distinctions between value schemes or measuring rods, and to create the fiction that a flattened, comparable world exists" (Gudeman, 2001, 15), but this does not imply that a similar simplification can be made with respect to the outer, biophysical system. Thus, even though the aggregate energy flow matrices tell us something thermodynamically, we are in effect mixing apples and oranges in a way that is not necessarily required.

As a snapshot of the 1999–2001 period, the mapping of energy flows and their prices onto the blockmodel does nevertheless give us some interesting insights. With significant internal trade and relatively low import costs from multiple sources, the role analysis did identify position D as a core in the network-topological sense. Even though the United States joins the countries of position D at a lower partition cutoff level, its role is evidently different, with a singular and relatively expensive source for most of its energy imports, only supplemented with equally expensive imports from position D. Another interesting phenomenon is position C: as an alternative energy source to position F, it is more cohesive but earns slightly less per exported gigajoule than position F.

Thus, even though a net-flow analysis depicts the United States at the receiving end of ecological unequal exchange in the net-flow sense, the Emmanuelian conceptualization of ecological unequal exchange, where the focus is on factor costs rather than net flows, points to a less advantageous situation for the United States and a significantly better one for position D.

The analysis of individual fuel commodities reveals a more nuanced picture of Emmanuelian ecological unequal exchange. In the case of coal, a consistently low price tag on U.S. imports over the period results in an advantageous throughput ratio. Position F suffers from a disadvantageous situation, where the cost of an imported tonne of coal overshadows the revenues from an exported tonne. For crude oil, position D is the clear beneficiary. As a partial gateway between position F and the United States, position D accumulates almost $200 for each tonne of crude oil that passes through its positional borders. Position F is also interesting in this regard: even though rich in natural endowments of crude oil, this does not translate into an exceptionally high price tag on oil exports: the price tag of oil exports from D exceeds those from position F by approximately $200 per tonne. Finally, although the data flows for liquefied natural gas are somewhat sparse, the 2008–2010 data allows some interpretation: it can be noted that position C is a beneficiary of Emmanuelian ecological unequal exchange, earning significantly more per exported tonne than positions D, E, F, and the United States.

The commodity-specific analysis indicates that position C, D and the United States each have their own commodities that they are benefiting from—liquefied natural gas in the case of C, crude oil for position D, and coal in the case of the United States.

Concluding remarks

Critical of existing conceptualizations of ecological unequal exchange, this chapter proposes an alternative approach that is, it is argued, more in line with the original formulation of Arghiri Emmanuel. Rather than mapping total net transfers of biophysical resources, the emphasis here is, similar to the original formulation of Emmanuel, on factor-cost differentials among nations. Whereas Emmanuel looked at labor and wage differential, the herein proposed conceptualization of unequal exchange looks at the third Ricardian production factor, i.e., land/natural resources, and cost differentials of such. The suggested hypothesis, building on Jorgenson's structural theory of ecological unequal exchange, is that such factor-cost differentials are related to structural positionality within the world-system.

To test the proposed conceptualization, three fuel commodity categories were chosen to represent the land production factor. Looking at bilateral trade data for 96 countries in the last three decades, factor-cost differentials were compared with structural positionality determined through a blockmodel analysis for the 1999–2001 period. Aggregated as total energy flows, as well as for individual commodities, the analyses yielded novel findings for both of these approaches.

The chosen raw material commodities could be different, and structural positionality could be operationalized differently, but it seems evident that the proposed Emmanuelian conceptualization of ecological unequal exchange yields interesting insights worthy of further research, both methodologically and substantively.

However, despite its ties to the foundational ideas of unequal exchange, a conceptual orthodoxy might not necessarily serve us well. As underlined by Wallerstein (2000, 153), concepts relate to, and are best defined through, particular historical systems and timespace context, and it is indeed possible that an Emmanuelian, factor-cost-based conceptualization of ecological unequal exchange is more orthodox than useful for understanding contemporary global dynamics. Still, as a historically oriented field of study, we are nevertheless obliged to connect past and present thoughts, something that I hope this chapter has succeeded in doing.

Acknowledgments

This research was sponsored by Budapesti Közép-Európai Egyetem Alapítvány (CEU BPF). The views expressed in this chapter are those of the author and do not necessarily reflect the views of CEU BPF. I would like to thank participants, including the organizing committe and staff, at the PEWS/WSF conference at UC Riverside, April 2013, for providing me with valuable feedback on a previous version of this manuscript. I would also like to thank colleagues and students at the

Center for Network Science as well as the Department of Political Science, particularly fellow researchers in the Political Economy Research Group (PERG), at Central European University, for valuable feedback and comments. I am also grateful to my former colleagues at the Human Ecology Division, Lund university—Pernille, Alf, John et al.—for helping me sharpen my arguments and ideas on ecological unequal exchange.

References

Applebaum, Richard P., David Smith, and Brad Christerson. 1994. "Commodity Chains and Industrial Restructuring in the Pacific Rim: Garment Trade and Manufacturing." In Gary Gereffi and Miguel Korzeniewicz (eds.), *Commodity Chains and Global Capitalism*. Westport, CT: Praeger Publishers.

Bair, Jennifer. 2005. Global Capitalism and Commodity Chains: Looking Back, Going Forward. *Competition and Change*, 9(2): 153–180.

Bair, Jennifer (ed.). 2009. *Frontiers of Commodity Chain Research*. Stanford: Stanford University Press.

Borgatti, Steve P., and Martin G. Everett. 1991. "Regular Equivalence: Algebraic Structure and Computation." In *Proceedings of the Networks and Management Conference*. Irvine: University of California.

Borgatti, Steve P., and Martin G. Everett. 1993. Two Algorithms for Computing Regular Equivalence. *Social Networks*, 15(4): 361–376.

Borgatti, Steve P., and Martin G. Everett. 1999. Models of Core/Periphery Structures. *Social Networks*, 21: 375–395.

Breiger, Ron L. 1981. "Structures of Economic Interdependence among Nations." In Peter M. Blau and Robert K. Merton (eds.), *Continuities in Structural Inquiry*. London and Beverly Hills: Sage.

Brolin, John. 2006. *The Bias of the World: Theories of Unequal Exchange in History*. Lund: Studentlitteratur.

Bunker, Stephen G. 1984. Modes of Extraction, Unequal Exchange, and the Progressive Underdevelopment of an Extreme Periphery: The Brazilian Amazon, 1600–1980. *The American Journal of Sociology*, 89(5): 1017–1064.

Bunker, Stephen G. 1985. *Underdeveloping the Amazon: Extraction, Unequal Exchange, and the Failure of the Modern State*. Chicago, IL: University of Chicago Press.

Bunker, Stephen G., and Paul S. Ciccantell. 1999. "Economic Ascent and the Global Environment: World-Systems Theory and the New Historical Materialism." In Walter L. Goldfrank, David Goodman, and Andrew Szasz (eds.), *Ecology and the World-System*. Westport: Greenwood Press.

Cantillon, Richard. 1931 [1755]. *Essai sur la nature du commerce en général*. English translation by H. Higgs. London: Macmillan & Co.

Chase-Dunn, Christopher. 1989. *Global Formation: Structures of the World-Economy*. Oxford: Basil Blackwell Ltd.

Condliffe, John B. 1950. *The Commerce of Nations*. New York: Norton.

Costanza, Robert, John Cumberland, Herman Daly, Robert Goodland, and Richard Norgaard. 1997. *An Introduction to Ecological Economics*. Boca Raton, FL: St. Lucie Press.

Domínguez, Jorge I. 1971. Mice That Do Not Roar: Some Aspects of International Politics in the World's Peripheries. *International Organization*, 25(2): 175–208.

Doreian, Patrick, Vladimir Batagelj, and Anuška Ferligoj. 2005. *Generalized Blockmodeling*. Cambridge: Cambridge University Press.

Emmanuel, «Arghiri. 1962. "Échange inégal." In Arghiri Emmanuel and Charles Bettelheim, *Échange inégal et politique de développement*. Problèmes de planification, No. 2. Sorbonne: Centre d'Étude de Planification Socialiste.

Emmanuel, Arghiri. 1969. *L'échange inégal: Essais sur les antagonismes dans les rapports économiques internationaux*. Paris: François Maspero.

Emmanuel, Arghiri. 1972. *Unequal Exchange: A Study of the Imperialism of Trade*. New York and London: Monthly Review Press.

Emmanuel, Arghiri. 1975a. Unequal Exchange Revisited. IDS Discussion Paper, 77, Institute of Development Studies, University of Sussex, Brighton.

Emmanuel, Arghiri. 1975b. "Réponse à Eugenio Somaini." In Arghiri Emmanuel, Eugenio Somaini, Luciano Boggio, and Michele Salvati (eds.), *Un débat sur l'échange inégal: Salaires, sous-développement, impérialisme*. Paris: François Maspero.

Fowler, Cary, Melinda Smale, and Samy Gaiji. 2001. Unequal Exchange? Recent Transfers of Agricultural Resources and Their Implications for Developing Countries. *Development Policy Review*, 19(2): 181–204.

Frank, Andre G. 1966. The Development of Underdevelopment. *Monthly Review Press*, 18(4): 17–31.

Galtung, Johan. 1971. A Structural Theory of Imperialism. *Journal of Peace Research*, 8(2): 81–117.

Georgescu-Roegen, Nocjpöas. 1971. *The Entropy Law and the Economic Process*. Cambridge, MA: Harvard University Press.

Gereffi, Gary. 1994. "The Organisation of Buyer-Driven Global Commodity Chains: How U.S. Retailers Shape Overseas Production Networks." In Gary Gereffi and Miguel Korzeniewicz (eds.), *Commodity Chains and Global Capitalism*. Westport, CT: Praeger Publishers.

Gereffi, Gary, and Miguel Korzeniewicz (eds.). 1994. *Commodity Chains and Global Capitalism*. Westport, CT: Praeger Publishers.

Gidengil, Elisabeth. L. 1978. Centres and Peripheries: An Empirical Test of Galtung's Theory of Imperialism. *Journal of Peace Research*, 15(1): 51–66.

Gudeman, Stephen. 1986. *Economics as Culture: Models and Metaphors of Livelihood*. London: Routledge & Kegan Paul.

Gudeman, Stephen. 2001. *The Anthropology of Economy: Community, Market, and Culture*. Malden, MA: Blackwell.

Heintz, James. 2003. *The New Face of Unequal Exchange: Low-Wage Manufacturing, Commodity Chains, and Global Inequality.* Political Economy Research Institute working paper series, 59, University of Massachusetts Amherst.

Heintz, James. 2006. Low-Wage Manufacturing and Global Commodity Chains: A Model in the Unequal Exchange Tradition. *Cambridge Journal of Economics,* 30: 507–520.

Hermele, Kenneth. 2012. *Land Matters. Agrofuels, Unequal Exchange, and Appropriation of Ecological Space.* Lund: Lund University.

Hopkins, Terence, and Immanuel Wallerstein. 1982. *World-Systems Analysis: Theory and Methodology.* Beverly Hills: Sage.

Hopkins, Terence, Immanuel Wallerstein, Eyüp Özveren, and Sheila Pelizzon. 1994. "Commodity Chains in the Capitalist World-Economy Prior to 1800." In Gary Gereffi and Miguel Korzeniewicz (eds.), *Commodity Chains and Global Capitalism.* Westport, CT: Praeger Publishers.

Hornborg, Alf. 1992. Machine Fetishism, Value, and the Image of Unlimited Good: Towards a Thermodynamics of Imperialism. *Man,* 27(1): 1–18.

Hornborg, Alf. 1998. Towards an Ecological Theory of Unequal Exchange: Articulating World System Theory and Ecological Economics. *Ecological Economics,* 25(1): 127–136.

Hornborg, Alf. 2001. *The Power of the Machine: Global Inequalities of Economy, Technology, and Environment.* Walnut Creek, CA: Altamira Press.

Hornborg, Alf. 2003. The Unequal Exchange of Time and Space: Towards a Non-Normative Ecological Theory of Exploitation. *Journal of Ecological Anthropology,* 7: 4–10.

Hornborg, Alf. 2006. Footprints in the Cotton Fields: The Industrial Revolution as Time-Space Appropriation and Environmental Load Displacement. *Ecological Economics,* 59(1): 74–81.

Hornborg, Alf. 2009. Zero-Sum World: Challenges in Conceptualizing Environmental Load Displacement and Ecologically Unequal Exchange in the World-System. *International Journal of Comparative Sociology,* 50(3–4): 237–262.

Jorgenson, Andrew. 2003. Consumption and Environmental Degradation: A Cross-National Analysis of the Ecological Footprint. *Social Problems,* 50(3): 374–394.

Jorgenson, Andrew. 2006. Unequal Ecological Exchange and Environmental Degradation: A Theoretical Proposition and Cross-National Study of Deforestation, 1990–2000. *Rural Sociology,* 71(4): 685–712.

Jorgenson, Andrew. 2009. The Sociology of Unequal Exchange in Ecological Context: A Panel Study of Lower-Income Countries, 1975–2000. *Sociological Forum,* 24(1): 22–46.

Jorgenson, Andrew. 2011. Carbon Dioxide Emissions in Central and Eastern European Nations, 1992–2005: A Test of Ecologically Unequal Exchange Theory. *Human Ecology Review,* 18(2): 105–114.

Jorgenson, Andrew. 2012. The Sociology of Ecologically Unequal Exchange and Carbon Dioxide Emissions, 1960–2005. *Social Science Research,* 41: 242–252.

Jorgenson, Andrew, Kelly Austin, and Christopher Dick. 2009. Ecologically Unequal Exchange and the Resource Consumption/Environmental Degradation Paradox: A Panel Study of Less-Developed Countries, 1970–2000. *International Journal of Comparative Sociology*, 50(3–4): 263–284.

Jorgenson, Andrew, and Brett Clark. 2009. The Economy, Military, and Ecologically Unequal Exchange Relationships in Comparative Perspective: A Panel Study of Ecological Footprints of Nations, 1975–2000. *Social Problems*, 56(4): 621–646.

Kentor, Jeffrey. 2000. *Capital and Coercion: The Economic and Military Processes That Have Shaped the World-Economy, 1800–1990*. New York: Garland Press.

Luczkovich, Joseph J., Stephen P. Borgatti, Jeffrey C. Johnson, and Martin Everett. 2003. Defining and Measuring Trophic Role Similarity in Food Webs Using Regular Equivalence. *Journal of Theoretical Biology*, 220: 303–321.

Mahutga, Matthew C. 2006. The Persistence of Structural Inequality? A Network Analysis of International Trade, 1965–2000. *Social Forces*, 84(4): 1863–1889.

Martinez-Alier, Juan. 1987. *Ecological Economics: Energy, Environment and Society*. Oxford: Blackwell.

Martinez-Alier, Juan. 2004. Marxism, Social Metabolism, and Ecologically Unequal Exchange. Working paper, Unitat d'Història Econòmica, Universitat Autònoma de Barcelona.

Mill, John S. 1849 [1848]. *Principles of Political Economy, with Some of Their Applications to Social Philosophy*. Volume II. 2nd edition. London: Longmans, Green, and Co.

Muradian, Roldan, Martin O'Connor, and Juan Martinez-Alier. 2002. Embodied Pollution in Trade: Estimating the "Environmental Load Displacement" of Industrial Countries. *Ecological Economics*, 41: 51–67.

Nemeth, Roger J., and David A. Smith. 1985. International Trade and World-System Structure: A Multiple Network Analysis. *Review* (Binghamton), 8(4): 517–560.

Nordlund, Carl. 2007. Identifying Regular Blocks in Valued Networks: A Heuristic Applied to the St. Marks Carbon Flow Data, and International Trade in Cereal Products. *Social Networks*, 29(1): 59–69.

Ohlin, Bertil. 1933. *Interregional and International Trade*. Harvard Economic Studies 39. Cambridge, MA: Harvard University Press.

Reichardt, Jörg, and Douglas R. White. 2007. Role Models for Complex Networks. *The European Physical Journal B*, 60: 217–224.

Ricardo, David. 1996 [1817]. *Principles of Political Economy and Taxation*. 1st edition. Amherst, NY: Prometheus Books.

Rice, James. 2007a. Ecological Unequal Exchange: International Trade and Uneven Utilization of Environmental Space in the World System. *Social Forces*, 85(3): 1369–1392.

Rice, James. 2007b. Ecological Unequal Exchange: Consumption, Equity, and Unsustainable Structural Relationships within the Global Economy. *International Journal of Comparative Sociology*, 48(1): 43–72.

Rice, James. 2008. Material Consumption and Social Well-Being within the Periphery of the World Economy: An Ecological Analysis of Maternal Mortality. *Social Science Research,* 37: 1292–1309.

Roberts, J. Timmons, and Bradley C. Parks. 2007. Fueling Injustice: Globalization, Ecologically Unequal Exchange and Climate Change. *Globalizations,* 4(2): 193–210.

Röpke, Inge. 2001. "Ecological Unequal Exchange." In Veena Bhasin, Vinay K. Srivastava, and M. K. Bhasin (eds.), *Human Ecology in the New Millennium.* Journal of Human Ecology Special Issue 10. Delhi: Kre Publishers.

Samuelson, Paul A. 1948. International Trade and the Equalisation of Factor Prices. *The Economic Journal,* 58(230): 163–184.

Savage, I. Richard, and Karl W. Deutsch. 1960. A Statistical Model of the Gross Analysis of Transaction Flows. *Econometrica,* 28(3): 551–572.

Scott, John P. 2000. *Social Network Analysis: A Handbook.* 2nd edition. London: Sage.

Shandra, John M., Eran Shor, and Bruce London. 2009. World Polity, Unequal Ecological Exchange, and Organic Water Pollution: A Cross-National Analysis of Developing Nations. *Human Ecology Review,* 16(1): 53–63.

Smith, David A., and Douglas R. White. 1992. Structure and Dynamics of the Global Economy: Network Analysis of International Trade 1965–1980. *Social Forces,* 70(4): 857–893.

Snyder, David, and Edward L. Kick. 1979. Structural Position in the World System and Economic Growth, 1955–1970: A Multiple-Network Analysis of Transnational Interactions. *American Journal of Sociology,* 84(5): 1096–1126.

UNCTAD. n.d. United Nation Comtrade Trade Database. URL: http://comtrade.un.org (accessed November 10, 2012).

UNCTAD. 2011. *Review of Maritime Transport 2011.* New York and Geneva: United Nations.

Wallerstein, Immanuel. 1987. "World-Systems Analysis." In Anthony Giddens and Jonathan H. Turner (eds.), *Social Theory Today.* Cambridge: Polity Press.

Wallerstein, Immanuel. 2000. *The Essential Wallerstein.* New York: New Press.

Wallerstein, Immanuel, and Terence Hopkins. 2000 [1986]. "Commodity Chains in the World prior to 1800." In Wallerstein, Immanuel. *The Essential Wallerstein.* New York: New Press. [Orig. publ. in *Review,* 1986, 10: 157–170].

Wasserman, Stanley, and Katherine Faust. 1994. *Social Network Analysis: Methods and Applications.* Cambridge: Cambridge University Press.

Wellhofer, E. Spencer. 1988. Models of Core and Periphery Dynamics. *Comparative Political Studies,* 21(2): 281–307.

White, Douglas R., and Karl P. Reitz. 1983. Graph and Semigroup Homomorphisms on Networks of Relations. *Social Networks,* 5(2): 193–224.

White, Douglas R., and Karl P. Reitz. 1985. Measuring Role Distance: Structural, Regular and Relational Equivalence. Unpublished manuscript. University of California, Irvine.

Ziberna, Ales. 2008. Direct and Indirect Approaches to Blockmodeling of Valued Networks in Terms of Regular Equivalence. *The Journal of Mathematical Sociology*, 32(1): 57–84.

Contributors

Scott Albrecht, M.S., is a graduate student at the University of Maryland, College Park. His dissertation, The Global in the Local: The Spatial Configuration of US Economic Inequality, explores in historical perspective the impact of global competition and crisis on economic inequality within the United States. E-mail: stalbrecht@gmail.com.

Salvatore J. Babones is Associate Professor of Sociology & Social Policy at the University of Sydney. His current empirical research focuses on the structure of the contemporary world-economy and the prospects for growth in middle-income countries. He also publishes broadly on quantitative methodologies for the social sciences. E-mail: sbabones@sydney.edu.au.

Albert J. Bergesen is Professor and Director of the School of Sociology at the University of Arizona. His research focuses upon contemporary geopolitics, great power war, and international security. E-mail: albert@email.arizona.edu.

Antonio José Escobar Brussi is Professor at the Universidade de Brasília Political Science Institute. His research focuses on development studies, social stratification and political change with special reference on the Brazilian politics and economy. E-mail: ajbrussi@gmail.com.

Christopher Chase-Dunn is Distinguished Professor of Sociology and Director of the Institute for Research on World-Systems, University of California, Riverside, USA. E-mail: christopher.chase-dunn@ucr.edu.

Jenny Chesters is a Post-Doctoral Research fellow at the ESTeM Faculty of the University of Canberra, Australia. Her research focusses on social inequality and the global distribution of wealth. E-mail: jenny.chesters@canberra.edu.au.

Rakkoo Chung is a PhD candidate in Sociology at the University at Albany, SUNY in the United States. Research interests include political sociology, organizations/economy/work, globalization, democracy, and race/class/gender. Area studies include South Korea and Nigeria. Methodologies include quantitative methods, comparative historical analysis, and a mixed-methods approach. E-mail: rakkoo.chung@gmail.com.

Wilma A. Dunaway is Professor in the School of Public and International Affairs at Virginia Tech. Her research focuses on gender inequality, households, slavery, indigenous peoples, Appalachian, and Asian food insecurity in the modern world-system E-mail: wdunaway@vt.edu.

Tamer ElGindi is a Ph.D. candidate in the Department of Planning, Policy and Design at the University of California, Irvine. His research interests focus on income inequality, neoliberal globalization, natural resources, and sustainable development. E-mail: telgindi@uci.edu.

Bruno Hendler is Professor at the Department of International Relations of the Centro Universitário Curitiba. His research focuses on power transitions in the modern world-system, United States-China relations, International Security Studies and Regional Security Complex Theory. E-mail: bruno_hendler@hotmail.com.

Roberto Patricio Korzeniewicz, Ph.D., is Professor and Chair of Sociology at the University of Maryland, College Park (USA). His current research focuses on global patterns of income inequality, social stratification and mobility, and on historical and current patterns of political change in Latin America. E-mail: korzen@umd.edu.

Robert MacPherson is a PhD candidate at the Department of Sociology of the University of California, Irvine. His research focuses on social movements, commodity chains, and Post-Keynesian and Marxian political economy. E-mail: rmacpher@uci.edu.

Jason W. Moore teaches world history and world-ecology in the Department of Sociology at Binghamton University. He has published widely on the history of capitalism, environmental history, and the capitalist world-ecology. He is presently completing Ecology and the Accumulation of Capital (Verso) and Ecology and the Rise of Capitalism (University of California Press). E-mail: jasonwsmoore@gmail.com.

Carl Nordlund holds a PhD in human ecology from Lund university, Sweden, and is currently a postdoctoral research fellow at Central European University, Budapest, Hungary, with a joint position at the Center for Network Science and the Department of Political Science. Focusing primarily on network-analytical methods for valued networks, his substantive research interests are world-system analysis, ecological economics, economic sociology, political and economic geography, and algorithms and data structures. E-mail: nordlundc@ceu.hu.

Tom Reifer is Associate Professor of Sociology at the University of San Diego, and an Associate Fellow at the Amsterdam based Transnational Institute. He has published widely on social change, human rights and social movements in global perspective, and is currently completing two books, Lawyers, Guns & Money: Wall Street & the American Century, and Earth, Wind & Fire. E-mail: reifer@sandiego.edu.

Anthony Roberts is a Ph.D. candidate in the Department of Sociology at the University of California-Riverside and a research associate at the Institute for World-Systems Research. His research focuses on income inequality, labor market institutions, globalization, development, and macro-comparative research methods. E-mail: anthony.roberts@email.ucr.edu.

William I. Robinson is professor of sociology, global and international studies, and Latin American studies, at the University of California-Santa Barbara. His most recent books are Latin America and Global Capitalism (2008) and Global Capitalism and the Crisis of Humanity (2014). E-mail: w.i.robinson1@gmail.com.

Christian Suter is Professor of Sociology at the University of Neuchâtel and President of the World Society Foundation, Zurich, Switzerland. He has published on global debt crises, economic and social inequalities, and political transformation in Latin America. E-mail: christian.suter@unine.ch.

World Society Studies
A series edited by the World Society Foundation, Zurich

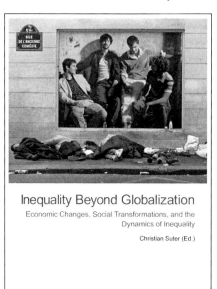

Inequality Beyond Globalization
Economic Changes, Social Transformations, and the Dynamics of Inequality

Christian Suter (Ed.)

LIT

World Society in the Global Economic Crisis
Christian Suter, Mark Herkenrath (Eds.)

LIT

Christian Suter (Ed.)
Inequality Beyond Globalization
Economic Changes, Social Transformations, and the Dynamics of Inequality
This volume debates the complex nature of the relationships between globalization, social and economic transformations and growing inequalities. Employing a global, world-historical and comparative perspective, the 16 articles brought together in this volume deal with three central questions: Firstly, the question of the spatio-temporal evolution and variations of growing inequalities, secondly, the relative importance of globalization as compared to other factors explaining growing inequalities and, thirdly, institutional variations of inequality dynamics and globalization impacts.
vol. 3, 2010, 400 pp., 29,90 €, br.,
ISBN-CH 978-3-643-80072-5

Christian Suter; Mark Herkenrath (Eds.)
World Society in the Global Economic Crisis
The global financial and economic crisis started in 2008 with the collapse of Lehman Brothers. Four years later, despite massive national and international countermeasures, it is still not over. This volume examines the considerable economic, social and political consequences of the present global crisis for world society. In particular, the 16 contributions focus on three central issues: Firstly, crisis impacts on world society structures and evolutionary dynamics, secondly, crisis perceptions and public discourses with their social and political consequences and, thirdly, experience of the global crisis at local and regional levels, as well as the responses to it.
Bd. 4, 2012, 352 S., 29,90 €, br., ISBN 978-3-643-80073-2

LIT Verlag Berlin – Münster – Wien – Zürich – London
Auslieferung Deutschland / Österreich / Schweiz: siehe Impressumsseite